Beyond Turk and Hindu

Florida A&M University, Tallahassee
Florida Atlantic University, Boca Raton
Florida Gulf Coast University, Ft. Myers
Florida International University, Miami
Florida State University, Tallahassee
University of Central Florida, Orlando
University of Florida, Gainesville
University of North Florida, Jacksonville
University of South Florida, Tampa
University of West Florida, Pensacola

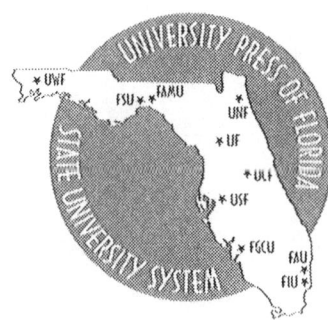

Beyond Turk and Hindu

Rethinking Religious Identities in Islamicate South Asia

Edited by David Gilmartin and Bruce B. Lawrence

University Press of Florida
Gainesville · Tallahassee · Tampa · Boca Raton
Pensacola · Orlando · Miami · Jacksonville · Ft. Myers

Printed in the United States of America on acid-free paper

05 04 03 02 01 00 6 5 4 3 2 1

Library of Congress Cataloging-in-Publication Data
Beyond Turk and Hindu: rethinking religious identities in Islamicate
South India / edited by David Gilmartin and Bruce Lawrence.
p. cm.
Includes bibliographical references and index.
ISBN 0-8130-1781-5 (cloth: alk. paper) 0-8130-2487-0 (pbk)
1. Islam—Relations—Hinduism. 2. Hinduism—Relations—Islam.
3. India—Ethnic relations. 4. Ethnicity—India. 5. India—Religion.
I. Gilmartin, David. II. Lawrence, Bruce.
BP173.H5 B47 2000
297.2'845'0954—dc21 00-055977

The University Press of Florida is the scholarly publishing agency for the State University System of Florida, comprising Florida A&M University, Florida Atlantic University, Florida Gulf Coast University, Florida International University, Florida State University, University of Central Florida, University of Florida, University of North Florida, University of South Florida, and University of West Florida.

University Press of Florida
15 Northwest 15th Street
Gainesville, FL 32611–2079
http://www.upf.com

Contents

List of Figures, Maps, and Tables vii
Acknowledgments ix
Introduction 1
David Gilmartin and Bruce B. Lawrence

Section 1: Literary Genres, Architectural Forms, and Identities

1. Alternate Structures of Authority: Satya Pīr on the Frontiers of Bengal 21
Tony K. Stewart

2. Beyond Turk and Hindu: Crossing the Boundaries in Indo-Muslim Romance 55
Christopher Shackle

3. Religious Vocabulary and Regional Identity: A Study of the Tamil *Cirappuranam* 74
Vasudha Narayanan

4. Admiring the Works of the Ancients: The Ellora Temples as Viewed by Indo-Muslim Authors 98
Carl W. Ernst

5. Mapping Hindu-Muslim Identities through the Architecture of Shahjahanabad and Jaipur 121
Catherine B. Asher

Section 2: Sufism, Biographics, and Religious Dissent

6. Indo-Persian Tazkiras as Memorative Communications 149
Marcia K. Hermansen and Bruce B. Lawrence

7. The "Naqshbandī Reaction" Reconsidered 176
David W. Damrel

8. Real Men and False Men at the Court of Akbar: The *Majalis* of Shaykh Mustafa Gujarati 199
Derryl N. MacLean

Section 3: The State, Patronage, and Political Order

9. *Shari'a* and Governance in the Indo-Islamic Context 216
Muzaffar Alam

10. Temple Desecration and Indo-Muslim States 246
Richard M. Eaton

11. The Story of Prataparudra: Hindu Historiography on the Deccan Frontier 282
Cynthia Talbot

12. Harihara, Bukka, and the Sultan: The Delhi Sultanate in the Political Imagination of Vijayanagara 300
Phillip B. Wagoner

13. Maratha Patronage of Muslim Institutions in Burhanpur and Khandesh 327
Stewart Gordon

Glossary 339
List of Contributors 345
Index 347

Figures, Maps, and Tables

Figures

5.1 Jami Mosque, Amber 124
5.2 Fakhr al-Masajid from street, Shahjahanabad, Delhi 125
5.3 Shivalaya of Dhumi Mal Khanna, Katra Nil, Shahjahanabad, Delhi 128
5.4 Chandnee Chauk, Delhi 130
5.5 Entrance to the Sri Brijnandji Temple, Jaipur 131
5.6 Mosque of Maulana Zia al-Din Sahib, Jaipur 133
5.7 Interior, mosque at Dargah Zia al-Din Sahib, Jaipur 134
5.8 Interior courtyard of the haveli-style Ladliji temple, Katra Nil, Shahjahanabad, Delhi 137

Maps

10.1 Temple desecrations, 1192–1394 272
10.2 Temple desecrations, 1394–1600 273
10.3 Temple desecrations, 1600–1760 274

Tables

10.1 Instances of temple desecration, 1192–1760 274a
12.1 Narrative structure of Vijayanagara's founding 310a

Acknowledgments

This volume originated with a conference held under the auspices of the Rockefeller Foundation. Without the encouragement and support of Lynn Szwaja of the Arts and Humanities Division, we would not have pursued our application to the foundation. It was a grant to the Triangle South Asia Consortium that made possible a three-year Rockefeller Residency Institute on South Asian Islam and the Greater Muslim World. The conference was held at Duke University in April 1995, and most of the papers included in this volume were originally presented on that occasion, although some have been significantly revised to suit the scope and theme of the current volume. Other scholars presented papers or made comments at the conference that could not be included in this volume. We would like to give special thanks to the following conference participants: Simon Digby, Eleanor Zelliott, James Laine, Sanjay Subrahmanyam, Anisuzzaman, Philip Lutgendorf, Daniel Ehnbom, Carol Salomon, Gregory Kozlowski, and Tazim Kassam.

John Richards of Duke University played a central role in conceptualizing and organizing the 1995 conference. From 1994 to 1998, he served with Bruce Lawrence as codirector of the Rockefeller Residency Institute, and he was instrumental in the early stages of this volume's preparation. We would also like to thank both Katherine Ewing and Munis Faruqui, who not only participated in the conference but also helped to ensure its success. Among those who gave time and energy to planning the conference, Constance Blackmore of the Comparative Area Studies Program at Duke University deserves special mention.

In preparing these papers for publication, we are indebted to the outside reviewers from University Press of Florida. They read and commented on the initial draft in painstaking detail. It was due to their insight that we reorganized the essays and also reduced their number.

Nor could we have produced a readable volume without the skill of John Caldwell in the initial scanning and editing of these essays and the labor of Rob Rozehnal in formatting the final version of essays to conform to University Press of Florida guidelines. Patient in all aspects of drafting, copying, and preparing the manuscript for publication was Lillian Spiller, administrative assistant to the Department of Religion at Duke University. We acknowledge their collective assistance, even while absolving them of responsibility for the content of this manuscript. The editors are the sole custodians of blame, while all the above are to be thanked for making possible a volume that is at once unique in content and challenging to received wisdom about South Asia.

Note on Transliteration

A volume including papers drawn from such a wide variety of linguistic sources as this one presents unusual problems of transliteration. Since many words of Islamicate origin appear in variant forms in Indic languages, we decided that it would violate the spirit of the volume to attempt to impose any standardized system of transliteration. We have thus left it to individual authors to use whatever system suited them. Some have employed a full range of diacritics while others have not. We have attempted to note in the glossary some of the more common variant spellings that appear in the volume.

Introduction

David Gilmartin and Bruce B. Lawrence

Muslims have been an integral part of South Asia for over a thousand years. Why then is it so hard to define them as "indigenous"? Why are they not as seamlessly Indian as Sikhs, who have been there for less time, or as Jains, who have been there longer but in fewer numbers?

Part of the difficulty lies with the stress on Islam and Hinduism as religious worldviews. Not only are Islam and Hinduism seen as alternative belief systems but they are deemed competitive and irreconcilable in their differences. Here is how a prominent Egyptian jurist, Judge Muhammad al-Ashmawy, whose major life's work has been both to chart Islamic humanism and to demonstrate how compatible Islam is with Judaism and Christianity, describes Muslim-Hindu interaction: "On the Indian subcontinent the relationship between the Hindu (the majority population) and the Muslim (the minority population) forms a dark and disturbed chapter in the history of interreligious relationships. This is partially due to the great differences between Islam and Hinduism." He then goes on to enumerate in terms of belief, whether it is belief in a deity (Muslims do, Hindus do not) or belief in the next life (Muslims think it is judgment at the end of each life, while Hindus opt for reincarnation).[1]

Judge Muhammad al-Ashmawy is not wrong to cite differences between Islam and Hinduism, whether as worldviews or as belief systems. The differences he cites do exist, and they are not unimportant, especially if one thinks of religion as, above all, belief or ritual. Yet religion also includes everyday life and social exchange; it elides with what is sometimes called "culture," and from the viewpoint of religion as culture Judge al-Ashmawy has overweighted differences in belief as determinative of all other patterns of exchange between Muslims and Hindus.

Still more serious is his presumption that Muslims and Hindus have always and everywhere been fixed as oppositional groups, each pitted irreconcilably against the other. The actual history of religious exchange suggests that there have never been clearly fixed groups, one labeled "Hindu," the other—both its opposite and its rival—labeled "Muslim."

To open up the space between reductive religious orientations and mobile collective identities, one needs a new vocabulary that is not restricted to modern connotations of words such as *Muslim* and *Hindu*. It was to remedy the inadequacy of English popular usage that historian Marshall G. S. Hodgson coined the term *Islamicate*. For Hodgson, the neologism *Islamicate* allowed students of civilizational change to refer to the broad expanse of Africa and Asia that was influenced by Muslim rulers but not restricted to the practice of Islam as a religion.[2] It is for the same reason, to suggest the breadth of premodern South Asian norms beyond Hindu doctrine or practice, that we employ the term *Indic* in the essays that follow. Both *Islamicate* and *Indic* suggest a repertoire of language and behavior, knowledge and power, that define broad cosmologies of human existence. Neither denotes simply bounded groups self-defined as Muslim or Hindu.

The goal of the contributors to this volume is thus contrarian: they do not accept popular notions, even those espoused by major and influential world figures, that invoke identity as set, unchanging, and exclusive. Instead, the contributors have tried to understand within the frames of Indic and Islamicate norms those discrete processes of identity formation that shaped religious identities in precolonial South Asia. The aim is to move beyond a fixation with bounded categories, whether religious or ethnic, Hindu or Turk, in order to pluralize the ways that these categories operated in varying historical contexts.

While our goal is contrarian, we do not ignore common sense: both editors and authors recognize the pervasive importance attached to religious systems that can be defined, pursued, and separated as Islamic and Hindu. Yet we vigorously contend that there is a larger point to make, namely, that the constant interplay and overlap between Islamicate and Indic worldviews may be at least as pervasive as the Muslim-Hindu conflicts that Judge al-Ashmawy and others take to be symptomatic of all life in the subcontinent.

It is because the distinction between Islamicate and Muslim, Indic and Hindu, has been repeatedly obscured that not only South Asians but also scholarship on South Asians have been mired in controversy. If all history is present-minded, as Croce long ago asserted, then the histories of India and Pakistan are excessively so. South Asians of varying political persuasions have long searched for genealogies of modern identity that could be authenticated by being extended back to the precolonial era. The founder of Pakistan, Muhammad ʿAli Jinnah, thought that there had always been two nations in the subcontinent. He saw them separated primarily by cultural practices, which he took to be fixed markers between two distinct groups. In Jinnah's view, these markers justified the creation of a bounded nation: Pakistan. More recently, visionaries of India as a Hindu state have followed a line of reasoning similar to Jinnah's. They have seen every instance of Muslim political rule or military victory or architectural creation as evidence of a long struggle between fixed Muslim and Hindu groups. Not local Indian rulers but Hindu norms were defeated in the period from the Ghaznavids to the Mughals, and they were defeated not by certain Muslim rulers but by Islam itself.

Some historians of religion have noted the degree to which practitioners of their own craft have been implicated in popular quests for genealogies of religious identity. Some have suggested that nineteenth-century British categorization of major religions as global or world religions played a formative role in facilitating the imagination in South Asia of fixed religious communities extending backward in time, each universal in scope and exclusive in loyalty. Tony Stewart, for example, describes in this volume how even many fair-minded historians have often read fixed religious categories back into history laden with modern valences. Even when the categories palpably do not fit the evidence, scholars are often reluctant to jettison them, opting instead to suggest the existence of hybrid or syncretic forms, defined by the mixing of "irreconcilable" religions, or by the lack of those attributes that are thought to be essential to a given world religion.

This is not to suggest, of course, that there is any unbridgeable divide between the operation of religious identities in modern and precolonial settings. While terms such as *religion* and *nation* are, in their common contemporary usage, laden with modern assumptions, the processes of identity formation described in this volume are ones that could be found in all historical periods. Terms of identity are inevitably shaped by the larger frames of knowledge in which they are embedded. While these frames of meaning differed in precolonial South Asia from those provided by modern science, capitalism, and colonialism, the processes by which identities were forged were nevertheless strikingly similar.

It is thus in the interaction between the particular and the general that we must embed the analysis of identity. While most contributors simply presume that identities are constructed in particular historical circumstances, it is, above all, the particular meanings attached to the categories Hindu and Muslim that must be understood in relation to the historical circumstances in which they existed. Such circumstances are both local and universal. They include the full range of other context-specific interests with which particular identities interacted as well as the larger Islamicate and Indic contexts that framed all categories of identity.

Section 1: Literary Genres, Architectural Forms, and Identities

In the first section of this book, literary genres and architectural forms are the topic of investigation. Contributors examine the texts and constructed remains that scholars have used to determine the nature and scope of religious identities. We are confronted not only with texts but also with relationships between texts, and the recurrent desideratum is to understand the link behind a specific text and its multiple contexts.

The initial three essays focus on the rhetorical strategies by which identities were created. The analysis of texts exposes processes of identity construction that were at once complex and nuanced, for texts were not simply windows on identities but keys to the process by which identities were generated. Most critically, an analysis of rhetoric suggests the critical interplay of difference and sameness in the construction of all identities. The construction of difference inevitably involved the simultaneous construction of sameness, for difference could only be asserted in opposition to an "other" of like category. One thus finds categories of comparison closely allied to categories of opposition, with both being shaped by the forms and structures of textual presentation. As these essays show, the manipulation of genre was often as critical to processes of identity formation as were the precise labels of identity that authors used.

Indeed, the interplay of genre and language is critical to the analysis of identity as it emerges in these essays. Those scholars who have studied the vocabulary of religious identity in Indian texts have often found complex invocations of oppositional categories and meanings. As Carl Ernst has shown elsewhere,[3] Arabic and Persian use of the term *Hindu* had a range of meanings that changed over time, sometimes denoting an ethnic or geographic referent without religious content. By the same token, Indic texts referring to the invaders from the northwest used a variety of terms in different contexts, including *yavanas, mleccchas, farangis, musalmans,* and *Turks.* Such terms sometimes carried a strong negative connotation, but they rarely denoted a distinct religious community conceived in opposition to Hindus.

In and of themselves, however, such terms tell us little. To understand the usage of these terms, one must move beyond the terminology itself—beyond *Turk* and *Hindu*—to analyze the framing categories and generic contexts within which these terms are used. While genre itself is often elusive, it is this which links processes of identity formation in their local contexts to the wider worlds of knowledge that framed them and gave them meaning. Genre expectations are embedded in universalist frames of knowledge, yet they also provide a vehicle for expressing the most particularistic identities.

Uncovering the ambivalent, bidirectional force of genre in shaping identities is, in fact, one of the most significant contributions of this collection. The importance of linking the global to the local, and the local to the global, has been widely observed in the modern world but less developed in the analysis of identities in precolonial South Asia. Consider the case of modern national identities. As many scholars have observed, national identity rests at once on an assertion of the irreducible differences among nations and also on a recognition of the common participation of all nations in an international system of order and knowledge. Nationalism could not function without a simultaneous expression of sameness and difference, at once powerful and ineffable. Even the most chauvinistic expressions of national distinctiveness imply—indeed, rely on—the commonality inherent in the generic category "nation."

While this global framework of internationalism did not operate in the same way in precolonial South Asia, it was nevertheless the case that identities in Islamicate India were also constructed in relation both to particularistic categories and to larger framing systems of knowledge and order. Frames were at once Indic and Islamicate, defining the parameters of the world of genres in which identities emerged. Essays in this section focus on elements of both these frames and on the interplay between genre and meaning, in both texts and architecture.

The power of genre in exploring, and exploding, identity is evident in Tony Stewart's inquiry into Bengali literature in chapter 1. Stewart focuses on the stories of Satya Pīr, a mythical holy man of Bengal with both Hindu and Muslim identity markers. Some scholars have tried to make of Satya Pīr a syncretic figure, since he was appealed to by Hindus and Muslims alike. But Stewart rejects the explanatory value of syncretism, since it reads modern definitions of religious identity into the past. Instead, Stewart moves beyond the terminology of identity in order to call attention to ways that the narratives of Satya Pīr themselves revealed distinctive identities. Identities, in Stewart's view, arise here not from distinct traits associated with differing groups but rather from the different "orientations to power" that mark the narrative structures of different types of stories.

Stewart analyzes two distinct groups of stories. Each group illustrates a distinctive orientation to power, embodied in a distinctive "narrative code." Indeed, Stewart's approach suggests how identity is rooted in the simultaneous play of commonality and difference linking these groups of stories. The stories are alike in that they evoke Satya Pīr as a figure of power capable of assisting the search for wealth and prosperity. All the stories are a product of the social and political pressures that redefined Bengal as a frontier society in the centuries following Mughal expansion eastward. And yet within this common frame, the two groups of stories are structurally quite distinct. One group drew on Vaisnava terminology and appropriated Satya Pīr as an avatar of Visnu. The other group drew on Sufi terminology and offered Satya Pīr as a figure demanding recognition from the common people. On one level, these structural differences can be read as defining contrasting orientations toward power, orientations that can perhaps be linked loosely to terms such as *Hindu* and *Muslim* or, more narrowly, *Vaisnava* and *Sufi*. But such identities were inescapably framed by commonalities as well as differences. Both were products of a frontier society. As Stewart demonstrates, it is the interplay between narrative structure, on the one hand, invoking different notions about the operation of divine power, and common coping with the everyday world of Mughal Bengal, on the other, that empowered the Satya Pīr narratives.

The importance of genre as a framing context for a nuanced understanding of terms and their relationship to identities is also highlighted by Christopher Shackle in chapter 2. He explores the *qiṣṣa*, or romance, among the most popular genres in the Punjab. Punjabi qiṣṣas drew heavily on both Islamicate and Indic images. Yet the major significance of this genre derived from its ability to tap into the tension between localized boundary markers and civilizational frames. Indeed, Shackle's analysis suggests the ways that the terminology of local social boundaries—although critical to the qiṣṣa—was given a distinctive meaning through the framing structure of the qiṣṣa as a literary genre.

Shackle quotes a verse from the Sufi poet, Bullhe Shah (1680–1758):

Neither Arab am I nor man of Lahore
Nor Indian from the town of Nagaur
Neither Hindu am I nor Turk of Peshawar.

The language here depicts a world where fixed identities mattered. Yet, as Shackle suggests, the very structure of the qiṣṣa, as Bullhe Shah's lines indicate, involved transcending such divisions. The best-known Persianate romances, in fact, commended the transgression of "almost every conceivable kind of social as well as psychic boundary," including those of tribe and status, "social and religious, sexual and spiritual standing." External boundary markers, such as Turk and Hindu, are not only invoked but are also necessary to the structure of these texts—but only to suggest that the *real* business of identity involves moving beyond them.

The main vehicle for boundary transgression in the qiṣṣa, of course, was love, which drew its power—and its symbolic meaning—from its links to the universal values of larger civilizational traditions. This was indicated by the lovers' inventories, which often opened such romances, inventories linking each romance to the larger Islamicate civilizational canon. But each qiṣṣa's appeal rested also on the localization of its setting, its creation of an imminent world replete with local actors and constraints, hopes and fears, dalliance and delight. What we find here is the palpable juxtaposition of an idealized world of love, which knows no bounds, and the inescapable, multiply bounded everyday world of Punjabi society. Without the tension between these two poles, the qiṣṣa loses its bivalent appeal, but through the constant reiteration of this tension it suggests the limited scope of either a purely universal or a narrowly local identity. To be real, to experience love, an individual's identity must always be open to transgression. Viewed in its generic context, the language of identity thus takes on meanings in the Punjabi romance that are far more fluid than those implied by the fixed language of group definition, although this itself was critical to the genre.

Similar processes are at work in the text described by Vasudha Narayanan in chapter 3. Her regional focus is Tamil Nadu, in South India. Her text, the *Cirappuranam,* is a seventeenth- century poem in praise of Muhammad, composed by a Tamil Muslim. Since the Prophet is its subject, it belongs to an explicitly Muslim devotional genre, the *sira,* or life of the Prophet. But it is also firmly embedded in an Indic devotional genre, the *purana.* In the *Cirappuranam,* we thus confront a poem that manipulates genre to position the Prophet simultaneously within two worlds.

Far more directly than in the texts analyzed by Stewart and Shackle, the *Cirappuranam* uses genre to undercut any notion of clear Hindu and Muslim boundaries. As in Stewart's analysis, it is not syncretism at work here but rather a bivalent process. The generic, elite literary conventions analyzed by Narayanan are at once resilient and adaptable; although Indic in origin, they translate the sira, a life of Muhammad, into a familiar Tamil cultural world. Here Tamil literary convention transcends any attempt to define clearly bounded Hindu and Muslim identities.

Processes of identity formation can be traced, of course, not only in literary texts but also in material production. Indeed, few identity markers have maintained a stronger hold on the imaginations of historians than the religious buildings—mosques, temples, shrines—that dot India's landscape. It was the destruction of the Baburi Masjid in 1992 that perversely revealed the multiple symbolic meanings attached to religious buildings in contemporary India. Yet the multivalent meaning of such structures must also be historically traced, through accounts of their construction and destruction, if we are to move beyond Turk and Hindu in looking at processes of identity formation in premodern South Asia.

Carl Ernst reminds us at the outset of chapter 4 that such buildings are defined not just by their ritual use or iconic content but also by their historical location and political deployment. Ernst's essay focuses on Rafi ad-din Shirazi, an official of the Bijapur Sultanate. A prolific author, Shirazi included in his 1612 Persian history of Bijapur a description of the temples at Ellora. As Ernst notes, modern analysts of Ellora have often used the frame of religious identities to define Ellora's distinctive Hindu, Buddhist, and Jain features, seeing them as constitutive of the monument's significance.

Yet Shirazi argues that the proper cultural frame for understanding structures like those at Ellora was not the frame of distinctive religious art forms, much less competing truth claims at the core of juxtaposed religions. Rather, in his view, the proper frame for understanding the Ellora complex was the competition for glory between kings, whether Persian or Indian. Ernst's essay shows how a Muslim official could attribute to Ellora a cultural meaning shaped by his view of dynastic rivalry. Difference here was not primarily defined by opposing religions but by opposing polities, in this case the polities of royal monarchs competing for a greater historical legacy. As Ernst notes, Shirazi saw Indian and Persian monarchs as kindred spirits in their common quest for "recognition through monumental art." Shirazi's interpretation thus underscores both the role of the larger Islamicate framework in shaping generic understandings of identity and also the contextual demands placed on Shirazi by his own position as a Muslim official in a state whose major edifice is an Indic temple complex. It suggests that in matters of material culture, as in the interpretation of literary texts, the determination of cultural identity is a fluid process, depending on both point of view and generic context.

To understand the ground level, operative relationship between religious structures and group identity in premodern North India requires, of course, a different sort of approach to material evidence. Catherine Asher provides just such an approach in her analysis of the role of religious buildings within the context of urban space in North Indian cities. Asher argues that in North Indian cities, whether built under Muslim patronage (Shahjahanabad) or Hindu patronage (Jaipur), mosques and temples tended to occupy very different types of spaces. Mosques were visible public structures, while temples tended to be deliberately hidden and obscured.

As Asher speculates, placement within urban space may well have defined the distinctive meanings associated with mosques and temples as foci for religious identity. Mosques and temples, although sharing a generic commonality as religious buildings, reflected in their placement and structure differing "orientations to power," just as did the contrasting narratives of Satya Pīr analyzed by Tony Stewart. Mosques proclaimed identity through their public presence in India's urban spaces, while temples offered a place to nurture the gods—and also maintain "one's identity among one's own community members"—in a space set off from the public realm. They thus occupied distinct, though not necessarily commensurate, places within a common urban framework. As Asher notes, historians need to do far more research into the Islamicate urban context, especially into the nature of urban patronage, if they are to understand how to interpret such religious structures as definers of collective identities.

Section 2: Sufism, Biographies, and Religious Dissent

The essays in section 2 move beyond texts and contexts to explore in more detail the operation of the Islamicate frame of social and intellectual ordering in India. However critical specific texts and contexts are to the understanding of the production of identities, it is critical also to understand the ways that broad civilizational traditions operated in India, not as the foundation for generic identities but rather as frames shaping the articulation of, and the meanings attached to, more particular identities. It has been one of the outcomes of modern structures of knowledge that civilizations have often been seen as fixed sources of bounded identity and culture. Yet the dynamic of identity construction that emerges from our analysis is one in which civilizations should probably be seen more as frames shaping the language and meanings within which more particularized identities operate while allowing enormous flexibility to local actors, conditions, and contexts.

As we noted earlier, it was Hodgson who first coined the term *Islamicate.* He coined it over thirty years ago in order to suggest a structure or frame of moral reference that characterized the span of the Afro-Eurasian world in which Muslims were major agents of exchange and control. *Islamicate* denoted the moral values and cultural forms that spread through the world system of Muslim trade and power in the centuries following the rise of Islamic polities. Hodgson distinguished Islamicate from that which was strictly Islamic or Muslim, relating to the practice of Islam as a religion, whether through creedal, ritual, or juridical loyalty. Although Muslims did not make this distinction—they had no need to—the distinction between Islamicate and Islamic/Muslim is extremely useful for us—moderns, or perhaps postmoderns, that we be. It is the term *Islamicate* which captures the civilizational dynamic for the framing of religious identities in India, including those of Muslims, that the authors in these sections attempt to capture.

Particularly powerful in Islamicate India were the normative concepts of authority drawn from the larger Perso-Islamic tradition, analysis of which is at the heart of the essays in this section. But the Perso-Islamic tradition did not operate independently of more local and particular forms of identity. For most people, neither particularistic identities nor civilizational ones could be fully conceptualized without the other. As Christopher Shackle's essay suggested, the tension between civilizational ideals and the realities of everyday divisions was often encapsulated in the structuring of regional Islamicate literary genres, such as the Punjabi qiṣṣa. But here the tension between these becomes the focus for a larger discussion of the rhetoric of religious identity. As the essays in this section suggest, it was the interplay between the universal and the everyday—and the tensions it generated—

that produced in Islamicate India the image both of civilizational identities and of a world in which competitive particularities were central.

Perhaps the most telling model for understanding this embrace of tensions within the Islamicate framework emerges from institutional Sufism. In chapter 6, Marcia Hermansen and Bruce Lawrence deal with the particular role of *tazkiras,* biographical literature on Sufi shaikhs, written by Indo-Persian elites. They project a model that helps us to understand the larger world in which Islamicate identities operated. Central to Indo-Persian culture, Sufism embraced many of the tensions that helped to define the structuring of Indo-Muslim identities more broadly.

For Hermansen and Lawrence, two elements are especially determinative: the relationship between personal authority and place in the structuring of identities, and the relationship between the distinctly Indian and transregional Islamic frameworks. As Hermansen and Lawrence show, whatever its metaphysical foundations, Mughal Sufism was rooted in devotion to specific persons and tied to concrete places. Tazkiras were written to glorify and to legitimize distinctive spiritual genealogies. The ties of Sufi authors to particular places and regions informed the way in which they invoked larger frameworks of legitimation. The tazkira, as an Islamicate genre, laid claim to Muslim space in South Asia by inscribing on the subcontinent new spiritual and intellectual centers, largely through memorializing Sufis.

Sufism, in this sense, provided a model for larger processes of Islamicate ordering and identity formation. Sufism defined a language of identity and authority linked to hierarchy, charismatic genealogy, and the distribution of *baraka* (blessing), a language that, by extension, served, as Richard Eaton argues in chapter 10, to justify political authority as well. Yet there was no consensus on the precise contours of a global Sufi model of authority. Tazkira writers appealed to Sufism as an overarching Islamicate model for the operation of charisma and the legitimation of authority, yet their aim in doing so was to establish competitively the particular precedence and distinctiveness of their own orders, genealogies, and places. Such was the aim of dynastic political leaders as well. What Hermansen and Lawrence thus suggest is a critical but seldom noted paradox intrinsic to the Islamicate context itself. Participation in local status competition, entailing the assertion of narrow, parochial identities, was inextricably intertwined with participation in the larger structures of Islamicate ordering.

This paradox can also give us insight into the possible meanings of the category "Indian" within the framework of Islamicate organization. As David Damrel indicates in chapter 7, scholars have often made sense of the reformist rhetoric of Indo-Persian elites, such as the Sufi mystic Shaykh Ahmad Sirhindi, by positing a fundamental opposition between Islamic and Indian as civilizational categories. The reformism of Sirhindi's so-called Naqshbandi reaction is thus seen as a product of the unsustainable cultural tensions created by the attempts of rulers such as Akbar, or by Chishti Sufi masters, to "reconcile" Islam to the Indian environment. But as Damrel argues, such an approach to Sirhindi's "reformism" hardly fits with the evidence. The attempts by previous scholars to create an opposition between "syncretic" Sufi orders (such as the Chishti) and "purifying" Sufi orders (such as Sirhindi's suborder of the Naqshbandiya) were predicated on the problematic notion that Hinduism and Islam actually existed as pure civilizational essences. Tony Stewart challenges that assumption, and Damrel shows that Sirhindi's project was far from essentialist. The master bridge builder of a new suborder, Sirhindi was influenced by both Chishtis and Naqshbandis. However much he may have made use of "purifying" reformist rhetoric, he produced in the end a distinctively "Indian" Sufi position. Sirhindi's concerns—about Sufi *dhikr,* prophetology, government employment of non-Muslims, and many other issues—all were framed by major normative debates within the larger Islamicate world. And yet Sirhindi's particular position was also informed by a set of affiliations—at once distinctive and oppositional—that shaped competition internal to Indian Sufism. His efforts thus dramatized the extent to which particularizing and universalizing identities fed off the other, creating tension and debate, to be sure, but also ensuring an expanded form of Islamicate-Indic identity that would have been unimaginable without such competition.

The crucial role of the rhetoric of corruption, purity, and reform in shaping identities is further explored, in a non-Sufi context, by Derryl MacLean. In chapter 8, MacLean analyzes the discourse of the debates at the Mughal court involving a prominent member of the millenarian Mahdavi movement in the late sixteenth century. Shaykh Mustafa Gujarati accused the Mughal *ulama* of moral impotence: they had failed to be "real men" by their pursuit of worldly advantage. Here, as in many of the later debates pursued by Sirhindi, competition for legitimacy was framed by an appeal to larger civilizational ideals, which were rhetorically configured in stark opposition to the corrupting influence of local and worldly interests.

Yet the Mahdavi shaykh avoided making this appeal in terms of oppositions between Islam and Hinduism or even between Arab and Indian. He did not want to compete with the ulama on their own turf. Instead, he deployed a rhetorical strategy at once bold and unexpected in its universalistic reach: He invoked gender norms. Accusing the ulama of lacking a "masculine" commitment to truth (evident in their slavish adherence not only to the political influence of the Mughal emperor but also to the opinions of the ulama of the Hijaz), Shaykh Mustafa claimed a universalist cachet for his own Mahdavi identity, which was uncontaminated by such worldly connections. Only he and his followers, by inference, could be considered "true men." In using such a rhetorical ploy, he was able to claim a pure identity, closely aligned with an Islamicate language, without denying the distinctively "Indian" roots of his identity. Once again, what is critical to Shaykh Mustafa, as to Sirhindi in a later generation, is the dynamic between the universal and the particular: Muslim protagonists asserted their own competitive identities and sought to undermine the identities of others, but always within the framing assumptions of Islamicate discourse.

In sum, the chapters of this section indicate ways that conflicts for local status and influence often generated powerful images of civilizational identity. This is not to suggest, of course, that the meanings attached to the universal were stable in Islamicate India. Islamicate rhetorics of identity were multiple. Nor did such frames operate independent of framing Indic idioms of identity. But at the heart of the analysis here is the way that the rhetoric of purity and reform, and of local competition for status, shaped an image of overarching civilizational identity. This was an image whose meaning and immediacy were inseparable from the reality of local particularized conflict and competition.

Section 3: The State, Patronage, and Political Order

A central arena for this conflict and competition was provided by the institutions of the Islamicate state. One reason for this, of course, is that states were vital sources of the cultural patronage so critical to the generation of identities. Equally important, however, the state stood at the nexus between the universal and the particular, between the legitimizing language of civilizational allegiance and local structures of power and social ordering.

The critical tensions shaping the operation of Muslim-ruled states in the Indian Islamicate context are suggested in essays by Muzaffar Alam and Richard Eaton. Alam focuses on the role of *shari'a*, or Islamic law, and its theoretical role in Islamicate political order in India. Symbolic deference to shariʿa was among the most powerful markers of a Muslim ruler's claim to standing within the larger Islamic world. But, as Alam argues, in pragmatic terms, the concept of shariʿa took on varying political meanings in India. Using evidence from Ziya ud-din Barani in the thirteenth century, he shows how, for some Muslim political theorists, shariʿa took on a narrow juristic meaning, rooting the stability of Muslim community in the narrow adherence to Islamic law as interpreted by the ulama. But he contrasts this with another interpretation of the shariʿa, strongly influenced by Persian *akhlaq* literature (and through it by Greco-Hellenic ideas and, perhaps, by Mongol political practice), which saw as the aim of shariʿa the maintenance of proper order in the community at large by balancing the interests of differing groups and communities, including religious communities (and allowing, in this context, for considerable freedom of worship). This second vision exerted a powerful influence on the structure of the Mughal empire, he argues, shaping shariʿa as a symbol linking the state to an international Islamic order and yet defining a structure of rule built on a recognition of the complex structures of division and difference that ordered Indian society.

These visions are evident also in Eaton's analysis of the role of Muslim states in that centerpiece of modern identity polemics: the Muslim destruction of Hindu temples. For modern polemicists, past destruction of religious structures has provided grist for invoking abstracted religious identities in order to wage modern-day warfare against "infidel" others. Yet as Eaton shows in chapter 10, Muslim temple destruction reveals patterns that are defiantly complex. His analysis operates on two levels. First, he draws the critical distinction between the rhetoric of temple destruction and its actual practice. For some Muslim sultans (as for some modern-day Hindu nationalists), an image of Muslim rulers as iconoclasts served legitimizing purposes, even when pragmatism dictated quite different policies. Stories of temple destruction, whether in Hindu sources or Muslim, thus require careful questioning. Second, and more fundamental to the argument, Eaton insists that even documented acts of temple desecration must be firmly grounded not in a narrative of religious competition but in the political history of Muslim state building. Attacks on religious structures, he argues, gained significance in a world where the construction and maintenance of religious edifices were central to political legitimacy, for Muslim and Hindu rulers alike. Those Hindu temples that were attacked were thus attacked almost invariably not as generic cultic sites but as symbols of Hindu royal authority. Desecration thus represented a critical symbolic act in delegitimating a rival sovereign in order to incorporate his territory into one's own realm.

Eaton's essay underscores, once again, the pragmatic nature of Islamicate rule in India. Both Hindu and Muslim places of worship shared a common value and vulnerability as focal points of spiritual devotion and political rule. Eaton's interpretation harks back to Ernst's essay on Shirazi's reading of the Ellora temple complex as above all a tribute to kingly ambition. Given this framework, however, Eaton must also explain why Muslim rulers did not destroy in the same way the mosques and shrines patronized by their defeated Muslim rivals. Here he turns to a more essentialist argument, namely, that royal Hindu temples and Muslim mosques and shrines did embody in their different forms distinct visions of the relationship between the divine and the political. Eaton's contention is thus not that differences between Hindu and Muslim are meaningless, even in matters of political legitimation. The prominence of symbolic religious acts in the rhetoric of dynastic legitimation makes this clear. Rather, his argument is that an examination of the norms and practices of Islamicate kingship provides a critical framework for the historical interpretation of these acts.

The importance of this framework is evident also in the analysis of the final three chapters, which examine practices relating to Indic kingship in the era following the spread of Muslim power in India. If temple destruction was, in certain circumstances, an important act of kingly legitimation for Hindu and Muslim kings alike, so was the patronage of historical chronicles legitimating dynastic authority as Talbot and Wagoner show. In chapter 11, Cynthia Talbot focuses on a sixteenth-century South Indian chronicle, the *Prataparudra Caritramu,* which deals with the last of the Kakatiya kings of Warangal. Written long after the end of the Kakatiya dynasty, the text is one intended, as Talbot sees it, to legitimate Telugu warrior influence within the framework of the new political order of the Vijayanagara kingdom in the early sixteenth century.

Strikingly, the symbolic evocation of opposition between Hindu and Muslim plays little role in this text. As in Eaton's argument, this is not because the mobilization of this dichotomy was of no potential legitimizing importance but because, in the particular historical circumstances in which the *Prataparudra Caritramu* was produced, the mobilization of such rhetoric served little purpose. Since the period was one in which alliances among Hindu and Muslim states in South India were as important as their oppositions, such religious oppositions held little appeal in legitimizing authority. This was hardly the case in all warrior chronicles of the period, as Talbot clearly notes. In some contexts, the language of resistance to Muslim "demons" could serve powerful legitimizing purposes, as it did, for example, among the warriors of Rajasthan whose epics of resistance to Muslim domination were analyzed decades ago by Aziz Ahmad as part of a cycle of challenge and response, "epic and counter-epic." By comparing this text with others in its genre, Talbot underscores the critical role of context in framing language of identity-creation. As in Eaton's argument, the pragmatic needs of power defined the way that identity was constructed. The *Prataparudra Caritramu* used a past Telugu (and Hindu) "golden age" to try to create a usable Telugu warrior identity within the increasingly Islamicate framework of the Vijayanagara state.

The meaning of the broader Islamicate context for the Vijayanagara state is explored more fully by Phillip Wagoner in chapter 12. Like the Maratha state (which is the subject of the final chapter, by Stewart Gordon), the Vijayanagara state has sometimes been presented in the literature as a "champion" of Hindu identity—the reviver and protector of "Hindu kingship" in the face of Muslim domination. However, as Wagoner shows, Vijayanagara narratives of legitimation cannot be understood without also understanding the state's Islamicate context. Wagoner examines sixteenth- and seventeenth-century narratives of the heroic fourteenth-century founders of the kingdom, Harihara and Bukka, and their relationship to the Delhi Sultanate. While standard modern narratives have seen Harihara and Bukka as apostates, converting to Islam to serve the Delhi Sultanate before apostatizing to create a Hindu kingdom, Wagoner discerns in these Sanskrit narratives of Vijayanagara's founding a very different story. Certainly, competition with Muslim states plays a significant role in the story of the founding of Vijayanagara. But critical to the story of Harihara and Bukka is their portrayal also as successors to the authority of the Delhi Sultanate, thus defining the Sultanate itself as one of the foundational, legitimizing sources of Vijayanagara's dynastic power. This was no accident, Wagoner argues, since by the time these narratives were written, Vijayanagara's competitive claims to regional power were rooted in its participation in an Islamicate state system, which was reflected in myriad ways in the structure of the state itself. Its claims to power were thus critically framed by the need of the Vijayanagara kings to legitimate themselves both within an Islamicate order of states and with reference to an Indic system of legitimation. Nowhere was this captured more dramatically than in the appellation sometimes applied to the Vijayanagara king himself, the "sultan among Hindu kings."

Stewart Gordon's essay provides further analysis of such simultaneous frames of legitimation through an examination of the Maratha state that arose during the declining years of Mughal power. Gordon, however, provides a different perspective on this phenomenon—a perspective drawn not primarily from chronicles but from local eighteenth-century Maratha revenue documents that provide a window on the local flow of patronage within the Maratha system. While Maratha chronicles sometimes portrayed Shivaji as an inveterate foe of the Muslims and a champion of Hindu *dharma,* Gordon finds powerful Islamicate structures of governance embedded in the most local operations of the Maratha state. Like the Mughals and the Deccan Sultanates before them, the Marathas' power depended heavily on their relations with local warrior elites, and like the Mughals and the Deccan sultans, they structured these relations around the reciprocal exchange of local, bureaucratically recorded revenue rights in return for state service. This structure of exchange provided the framework within which Maratha warrior families had long competed for honor under earlier Islamicate states, and it had now come to provide a critical frame for the validation of their local power, competition, and identity under the Marathas as well. It also provided the frame within which the Marathas, like Islamicate states before them, patronized both Hindu and Muslim holy men, embedding into local society the institutions that supported their authority and power. Here, then, we have evidence of the power of an Islamicate framework both in shaping state legitimacy and in framing a more particularized structure of local identities in an Indic state.

Most important in linking Indic and Islamicate framework was an ideology of "universal kingship," which stressed the importance of the maintenance of order and prosperity both as a dharmic duty and as the central legitimating function of kingship. This was a framework rooted in the pragmatic ability to maintain order and prosperity by balancing the interests of all groups, whatever their particular identities. Such a vision of kingship could, of course, be couched in either Indic or Islamicate terms—and Gordon suggests how the competing frames of legitimation for the state sometimes framed the struggle for influence and power among competing elites deploying different sets of legitimizing terminology. But it nevertheless provided an integrating vision of state legitimacy that focused authority on the person of the ruler.

Indeed, as all the chapters in this final section suggest, a focus on the integrating authority of the ruler is important for understanding the structuring of identities more generally. Individual religious differences between Muslims and Hindus (as between other generic religious categories, like Saiva and Vaisnava, Sunni and Shiʿa) were framed by their operation within a pervasive structure of personalized religious authority—a structure that, along with its bureaucratic technologies, defined the Islamicate state itself. This is not to say that marks of generic Hindu or Muslim identity were insignificant. But since religious virtue and spiritual power were embodied preeminently in holy individuals, religious identity was defined primarily in relation to individual teachers, masters, or Sufi exemplars. The structure of Sufism (and of Hindu religious and devotional lineages) represented, in some respects, an integrative cultural reflection of the assumptions about power ordering the larger Islamicate system. As markers of group identity or allegiance, the categories Hindu and Muslim were thus largely subsumed in more particularistic structures of devotion. And yet networks of individual loyalty and devotion were rarely constituted without at least some reference to the legitimizing language of authority provided by these larger framing categories.

Conclusion

Two large conclusions thus emerge from these essays—conclusions which take us back to the problems in the academic study of religious identities in South Asia with which we began.

First, focusing on the contexts that produced articulations of identity is critical to historicizing the vocabulary of religious identity and understanding how it may have changed over time. As the essays in the last section have suggested, the meanings of identities can best be understood in relation to the operation of power. Seeing how identities relate to the structure of the state and to its networks of patronage is critical to understanding how identities gained meaning. But as several of the essays have suggested, the authority of Islamicate states was itself embedded in larger frameworks of knowledge, and these frameworks defined the nature of power and its relationship to divine authority.

In short, we need to historicize Islamicate identities and to see how they changed in response to India's changing position in larger cultural and economic worlds. We can then see these changes in relation to the changes that marked the succeeding colonial period as well. As many scholars have argued, British colonial rule was itself linked to a distinctive structure of knowledge, tied to science and capitalism. This framed identities in new ways, introducing into South Asian parlance, for example, the language of enumeration, of ethnic groups as territorially mapped entities, and of religions as fixed communities, susceptible to counting under the census. This in turn was linked to a new language of "majorities" and "minorities," which were then presumed to be the constitutive units of South Asian politics. All of this, of course, helped to define and to legitimize—even as it was in turn shaped by—the political practice of the colonial state. But if much of this was new, it nevertheless grew out of a structural relationship between state political practice, structures of knowledge, and the framing of identities that had marked the operation of identities in premodern Islamicate South Asia. Focusing on structural frameworks for identity thus helps us to escape a dichotomous view of the "modern" and the "premodern," and instead to see how structures of identity had long shifted in response to the shifting place of South Asia—and of forms of state authority—within a larger world.

Second, and perhaps even more important, is the need to retain a vigilant eye on process, above all, the process of identity formation, for it is only through this process that we can see how identities were constructed not simply through the opposition and juxtaposition of fixed categories but also through the tensions generated by the simultaneous deployment of framing categories of commonality and the assertion of particularities of difference. Many of the essays in the volume have highlighted this process of identity formation, both through an analysis of political structures and through the analysis of texts. The structuring tensions of many texts—tensions between generic identity and particularity, between commonality and difference—mirrored in critical ways the tensions shaping the larger political order.

Critical to the structuring of the Islamicate world, then, has been attention to religion, but religion with movable parts and multiple forms. Hindus and Muslims alike experienced tension between universal ideals and the modeling of the way the world actually worked. More often than not, they perceived such tension as a welcome venue for addressing more complex ways of being both Indian and transregional in outlook. To grasp this process is to move beyond fixed identities such as "Turk" and "Hindu" in looking at premodern societies, and also their successors, in the subcontinent.

Notes

1. Muhammad al-Ashmawy, *Against Islamic Extremism* (Gainesville: University Press of Florida, 1998), 82.

2. Marshall G. S. Hodgson, *The Venture of Islam: Conscience and History in a World Civilization* (Chicago: University of Chicago Press, 1974), 57–60.

3. Carl Ernst, *Eternal Garden: Mysticism, History, and Sufism in a South Asian Center* (Albany: State University of New York Press, 1992), 22–37.

1

Alternate Structures of Authority

Satya Pīr on the Frontiers of Bengal

Tony K. Stewart

Interpreting Satya Pīr

Problems of Categorizing

Inhabitants of the northeastern section of the subcontinent (the territories of contemporary West Bengal, Orissa, and Bangladesh) have turned to the religious figure of Satya Pīr to protect against the vagaries of extended travel, to ensure the general weal of one's family, and perhaps most frequently, simply to get rich. The prominence of this latter feature led one public performer in the 1920s to satirize Satya Pīr as "Lord of the Bazaar," the purveyor of dime-store religion.[1] Yet Satya Pīr, whose rubric embraces all forms of the somewhat older figure of Satya Nārāyaṇa, numbers among his followers the populations of nearly all of the ethnic and religious communities of the region. Today he is most prominent among the middle and lower classes of both Hindus and Muslims. He has more Bengali texts dedicated to the telling of his stories than any other premodern mythic or historical figure, save the Vaiṣṇava leader Kṛṣṇa Caitanya (1486–1533). Even though he has been the subject of cycles of popularity similar to other religious figures and to gods and goddesses in Bengal, his overall popularity seems to have grown steadily, perhaps peaking in the mid-nineteenth century and early twentieth century, but still finding new adherents today.

Yet Satya Pīr has attracted little scholarly attention.[2] Part of the reason for this lies precisely in the fact that he is a figure who blurs the lines between Hindu and Muslim as religious categories. His historical appeal to both religious traditions is embodied in his name: *satya* is the Sanskrit and Bengali word for the "true" or "truth," while *pīr* derives from the Persian, designating the Muslim spiritual guide who is renowned for wisdom and the ability to translate spiritual achievement into a practical power to aid supplicants. When scholars do address Satya Pīr, he and the worship he engenders are generally damned to bear the label of "syncretism."[3] Syncretism seldom deals directly with its object. It relies on metaphor to make its point, comparing the thing in question to some other entity that is impermanent, the most popular metaphors being organic (such as a hybrid or half-breed), alchemical (such as mixture or solution), or construction (bricoleur). The metaphoric structure of that concept inevitably implies that no syncretistic entity is viable in its own right, for it combines elements that retain their identifier as discrete and mutually exclusive—in this case the categories of Hindu and Muslim—and because of that unholy alliance, it is artificially created and destined not to endure. Yet for about five centuries endure is precisely what Satya Pīr has done, even though he has certainly been subject to cycles of popularity similar to other religious figures and to gods and goddesses in Bengal. If anything, his overall popularity seems to have grown steadily, perhaps peaking in the mid-nineteenth century and early twentieth century, but still finding new adherents today. The proliferation of manuscripts and printed books, the widespread familiarity with his image and tales, and the development recently and for the first time of permanent places of commemoration, including the establishment of his *dargāh*—all the empirical evidence of his success—point to a scholarly failure to find an adequate explanation for him and what he means to his followers.

It has become a truism of our contemporary scholarship to recognize that what we consider important is shaped, if not driven, by complex ideological concerns. The constructions of South Asian religious history and literature of the last century or so have frequently sought to read modern religious identities back into the histories of the subcontinent to generate seamless ideal histories.[4] Ironically, in these many and complex and often subtly nuanced constructions, Hindu and Muslim all too frequently become monolithic in conception, and in this imposed uniformity they are assumed to be antithetical by nature. Satya Pīr, however, violates that purity of conception and thus falls outside the structure of this idealized religious history. Further, with his appeal concentrated largely in the lower social strata, and with his activities frequently focused on the pragmatic generation of wealth (especially as a prerequisite for morality), his study has been viewed by many as having little connection to the "higher aims" of the religious "Great Traditions" in Bengal. This has further marginalized the study of Satya Pīr, consigning him to the label "folk deity" and thus not legitimately part of the "proper" or high traditions.

His study, however, may help us to gain new perspectives on the problems we face in constructing our religious categories. Rather than assume that Satya Pīr represents a composite and therefore "unnatural" entity made from bits and pieces of two separate traditions—the syncretistic approach—perhaps we might more fruitfully ask how it is that people, whom we as scholars routinely designate by the terms *Hindu* and *Muslim*, can claim this religious figure without the overt conflict that one might predict based on contemporary political rhetoric. How is it possible that these individuals, no matter their label, can perform Satya Pīr's vows and take refuge in his protection without running afoul of the theological positions and ritual injunctions internal to each of the Great Traditions designated by those very labels of Muslim and Hindu? To start, I would like to propose that the purveyors and consumers of the Satya Pīr literature are not initially acting as members of either group. The common concerns framing the invocation of Satya Pīr were not those defined by membership in a religious group of any sort but rather those defined by the context of life in early modern Bengal. If we are to understand the stories of Satya Pīr, we must begin not with timeless religious categories but with context. What is important about Satya Pīr, religiously and culturally (those obviously are not exclusive either), is that he deals with pragmatic concerns of survival—not overt ideology, theology, or ritual; people accept that he wields a power to make their lives better and that is good no matter how it is labeled. Put another way, the questions of pragmatic power cross whatever imaginary divide we construct between Hindu and Muslim. To enjoy the benefits of this general weal does not require group participation to be valid; most of Satya Pīr's worship is, in fact, individual and ad hoc. To turn to Satya Pīr is a matter of opportunity and convenience, not one that requires constant reminders of commitment (so even being a member of an imagined group of Satya Pīr devotees seems to be limited to the time of actual invocation). If we can resist comparing the action described in the narratives of Satya Pīr—and the accompanying ritual, which is generally simple and unmediated—to the ideal standards of an Islam or Hinduism imagined in their pristine monologic purity and ideal praxis, we have then an opportunity to circumvent the tyranny of group inclusion as the dominant organizer of experience and the primary marker of identity.

Yet, at the same time, the stories of Satya Pīr do not suggest the complete irrelevancy of received religious categories. Rather, interpreting the stories requires that we carefully rethink their usage. Despite certain similarities, stories of Satya Pīr fall into clearly differentiated groups, reflecting differing vocabularies, narrative styles, and orientations toward divine and worldly power. As we shall see, some stories (which we might loosely label as "Hindu") see Satya Pīr as yet another incarnation of Viṣṇu, especially suited to the disintegrating times of the Kali Age wherein *dharma* is at extreme risk. Another group (which we might loosely label "Muslim") portray him as but a pīr, albeit a special one who resides in an ethereal Mecca and who can be conjured with a heartfelt call of his name; sometimes he is vaguely associated with the historical pīr Ḥusayn ibn Manṣūr al-Ḥallāj (d. 922) as the "True" Pīr,[5] but more often simply as a figure of local power, one pīr among a group, including Gāji Pīr, Mānik Pīr, Pīr Badār, and Khizr Pīr. Different genres of stories thus define in their narrative styles different orientations to power—orientations to power with links to the vocabularies of broader religious traditions. Yet the figure of Satya Pīr himself provides the common focus that frames these differing orientations, and the different genres of stories suggest not so much identification with different groups as they suggest differing visions of hierarchies of power within a common world. The stories illustrate how the same pragmatic (worldly) power can be mediated through different hierarchies of authority, and the precise role of Satya Pīr will vary depending on how the structure of authority is conceptualized and presented. Far from suggesting the existence of clearly distinct Hindu and Muslim groups, whose elements are combined in a "syncretic" cult, an analysis of the stories of Satya Pīr thus suggests how the interplay of vocabulary and genre define the common concerns linking all the followers of Satya Pīr, as a single figure, in the struggle to deal with worldly power, even as such an analysis shows, simultaneously, how narrative structure reveals the different orientations to power characterizing the stories' diverse audiences.

Frontier Narratives: Religious and Literary Typologies

Satya Pīr cannot be fixed historically in any temporal or geographic locale—and in this sense he is mythic, so his "history" is not so much his but that of his followers' acceptance of him. For nearly five centuries, perhaps longer, he has rated as one of the most popular pīrs of Bengal, and his legacy is captured in a corpus that is geographically dispersed throughout the region. His literature begins to emerge with regularity in the late sixteenth century, following the first known works by Phakīr Rāma, Ghanarāma Cakravartī, Rāmeśvara, and Ayodhyārāma Kavi.[6] A number of seventeenth- and eighteenth-century texts relate new exploits, but it is in the period of easy access to inexpensive printing and the concomitant creation of great entrepreneurial fortunes, the mid-nineteenth to early twentieth centuries, that his literature burgeons into one of the most prolific in Bengali. It is then that he moves into the rapidly expanding metropolitan areas of Calcutta and Dhaka. With the political realignments of the twentieth century, his popularity has shifted and today clings to the metropolitan fringe, while resurging in more rural areas that one might characterize as the new frontier of development, especially where population densities are still very much constrained by geophysical barriers, such as the mangrove swamps of the Sunderband and the mountain fringes ringing Bangladesh from Chittagong in the southeast to Rangpur in the north.

In these shifts, Satya Pīr has retained on the surface his apparent dual character, which is reflected in his physical appearance. Kṛṣṇahari Dāsa describes it:

He wears the dress of a *fakīr,*
the hair on his head the color of mud,
 the Prophet's patched scarf cinched at his neck.
His lotus body shimmers brilliantly,
Four times greater than a full moon
 perched above clouds thick with rain.
The sacred thread drapes his shoulder,
a chain belt hangs at his waist,
 in his hands tremble one's aspirations.
A short string of anklets jingle
in time with his dagger's clink
 to each clopping step of his wooden sandals.[7]

The appearance of this pīr becomes an explicit visual metaphor in the way he combines key marks of a public Muslim and Hindu allegiance. It is not unusual for Satya Pīr to approach significant religious figures in either community while quoting from the Qur'ān and *Bhāgavata Purāṇa*. Deliberately conflating signs that would ordinarily be disjunctive endlessly amuses or annoys characters in the narratives—a clear indication that the authors deliberately count on the effect and play on these symbolic currencies. This play has a very serious side, for the narrative strategy of conflation serves to create momentary confusions among the characters that predictably elicit spontaneous, unreflective responses of ridicule and invective. These outbreaks create an opening for Satya Pīr to instruct the naive in a way that is all the more compelling by virtue of the extreme situation he manipulates by playing on their prejudices, hubris, and ignorance to demonstrate their inappropriateness to the business of living. And to the delight of the listener or reader, he is not above resorting to more brutal magical persuasions to make his point. The content of these biting homilies varies dramatically, depending on the author's proclivity, for the narratives are anything but uniform in this regard. But apart from these occasional and short opportunities to lecture or preach, most of Satya Pīr's message emerges through the resolution of predictable dramatic situations, and these stories account for nearly all of the written material that exists; there is no formal theology.

The textual materials for glorifying Satya Pīr are, then, almost exclusively literary narratives, ranging from the sophisticated poetic productions of the royal courts of the eighteenth century to more rustic oral performances designed to be improvised and delivered by itinerant bards. While the authors limit overt and explicit theological speculation to occasional summary statements inserted extradiegetically into the narrative frame, they limit the inclusion of ritual materials even more. What ritual instructions we do have emerge most extensively during the frenzy of printing in the late nineteenth and early twentieth centuries, usually appended to the narrative as a result of deliberate attempts by certain individuals to Sanskritize the tradition by turning the simple offering of *śirṇi* (or *śinni*) into a more elaborate *pūjā*.[8] In spite of these efforts to incorporate the tradition into the mainstream of the daily pūjās, the ritual literature still accounts for less than 1 percent of all compositions. The handwritten *punthis* or manuscripts are nearly devoid of such ritual instructions, with most taking the form of the orally delivered *pālā gāna*, *pāñcālī*, and the increasingly popular *vrata kathā*.[9] While the vrata kathā has become ossified in its thematic structure, the other two forms yield an impressive diversity, and when all types are enumerated, they are as prolific as they are diverse. In the repositories of West Bengal and Bangladesh, I have located approximately 750 manuscripts composed by more than 150 authors stretching over the last five centuries,[10] some of which disappeared in the aftermath of the unfortunate confrontation at the Babri Masjid in December 1992.[11] Printed texts are numerous, with the collections and markets in London, Calcutta, and Dhaka yielding more than 160 titles by more than 100 authors. But even though authorship is diverse, the narratives do show a strong thematic unity and, perhaps more significantly, a predictable set of narrative plots that yield equally predictable results.

The situations described in the literature of Satya Pīr constitute a fairly limited narrative domain, using small numbers of fixed character types, in a limited set of possible fictional predicaments, whose primary complications are generally permutations of a much smaller set of underlying or controlling themes, e.g., worship Satya Pīr to get rich or to be rescued from trouble. These underlying themes, however, are not always approached the same way, so to describe the strategies for negotiating these situations we will borrow the narratological term *narrative codes*.[12] But in the case of Satya Pīr, and in much of the popular religious literature of South Asia, the narrative codes are not simply shaping literary fictions. They have a much more immediate connection to issues of everyday life, that is, they have a relevance to the way people live and come to understand how they should conduct themselves, how they might survive, in a world that does not always cooperate. In this, the narrative codes are different from their purely literary counterparts (if we can be allowed such a potentially artificial distinction for a "pure" vs. "practical" literature), and they reflect in every case the way actors marshal competing structures of authority to modulate the power of survival represented by the protagonist, Satya Pīr. This is a vital function because classification of these narrative codes will reveal something of the logic by which different people can and do think differently about the same contingent existence, interacting with the same figures in the same settings. Classification of these narrative codes, as indexes to the actors' "orientations toward authority," allows us to recognize other systems of signification, most obviously through intertextual references, both overt and implied (e.g., *Skānda Purāṇa*), or to other cultural institutions (e.g., dargāh), that are used to reinforce the orientation. Finally, because these individual items or subsets of alternate signification often stand in metonymic relation to the basic narrative code in the context of the narrative itself—they are often freely mixed and matched as elements in the story—their differences will ultimately reveal that the structures of authority are considerably more complex and subtly nuanced than the basic categories of Hindu and Muslim could ever recognize, and they often actively imbricate what are traditionally thought of as either exclusively Hindu or Muslim attitudes and acts.

In short, the narrative structures adopted by individuals or groups serve as a basis for categorizing action and orientation—different ways of thinking about and negotiating the way power is wielded in this world—far more dynamically than the assignment of monolithic labels of static theological and ritual ideals; they reveal part of the decision-making process, the factors that are weighed in determining proper courses of action, and how individuals with different backgrounds can use the same situation in interaction with the same figures for different ends or can arrive at the same ends by different means. This is not to say that individuals who preserve and propagate these tales of Satya Pīr would not recognize the content of the categories Hindu and Muslim, but those categories operate on a different level of experience most often associated with the symbolic posturing appropriate to the larger public sphere, and in that sphere they maintain a kind of consistency of image that everyone recognizes (e.g., the rules of public propriety, severely delimited ritual and symbolic action and dress, etc.). But in the narratives of Satya Pīr, those kinds of distinctions do not play in the negotiation of the private vicissitudes of daily experience on the frontiers of Bengal, and they can be easily ignored or, as will become apparent, when invoked—as in the description of Satya Pīr's garb noted above—they can be used as a foil to expose the ignorance of their improper application.

In order to produce a workable sample, more than a third of the manuscripts and nearly all of the printed literature available have been analyzed.[13] The narratives can be organized into three general types, sets that are determined by combination of the manifest identity of Satya Pīr and his direct role (or absence) in the plot; the social standing and vocation of the protagonists other than Satya Pīr; the nature and direction of instruction and subsequent conversion, if any; the occasional overt religious point or more general moral of the story; and the audience for which the stories were apparently intended and which can be determined only partially. Each set of characteristics contributes to the strategy that is adopted by the narrative, its narrative code, which ultimately defines its type. In characterizing these strategies, however, we will revert momentarily to the use of the general adjectives of *Hindu* and *Muslim,* but with the proviso that those be read as orientations (that are coherently conceived, but not at all consistent) as the result of individuals responding to the pragmatic results of the orientation, rather than choosing to be included in a group that goes by that name.

- *Satya Pīr as "Hindu" Vaiṣṇava God:* those tales that emphasize the Vaiṣṇava identity of Satya Pīr as the incarnation (*avatāra*) of Viṣṇu or Nārāyaṇa, who has descended to right the dharma for the Kali Age. The narrative code operates according to strategies of "domestication" and "appropriation."
- *Satya Pīr as a "Muslim" Moral Exemplar:* those tales that feature Satya Pīr as a pīr or fakīr, who challenges the hubris and exclusivity of a conservative brahmanical authority and the conniving ways of dishonest and irresponsible individuals, regardless of religious persuasion. These tales promote an Islamic perspective on ritual, theology (when noted), and conversion, even though Satya Pīr's persona often seems to invoke more the features of a Hindu deity. The narrative code dictates strategies of "recognition" and "accommodation."
- *Satya Pīr as Personal Spiritual Guide:* those tales that, at least on the surface, seem not to address any obvious religious issue, but focus instead on fundamental moral quandaries that ultimately lead to pragmatic resolutions of everyday problems, often through personal tests and unexpected alliances. Among these stories is a large subset of tales that focus on the acts of women who must survive compromising situations where there are no clear guidelines for propriety. The narrative strategy is for "moral improvisation" and "alliance."

What binds together all three of these narrative types is the common improvisation necessary to negotiate an often hostile or compromising environment using locally available sources of power, most notably the pīr, but also committed or converted kings, and especially their entrepreneurial merchants. The environment of their setting is always some kind of frontier, so these are generally read as narratives of survival, and as Richard Eaton has clearly shown, the land of Bengal where these stories proliferate has for centuries been conceived in just such terms.[14] The frontier, however, is plural and shifting, for it is geographic, political, economic, and religious—and the stories of Satya Pīr address them all. In these narratives, the frontier is an arena of human action that lies beyond the circumscribed limits of what is familiar and what constitutes the predictably settled world of "tradition." Therein lies much of the stories' interest and mystery, if not reason sufficient in itself to question the use of the larger categories of Hindu and Muslim which so often blur in these socially ill defined areas. These tales are a journey into the unknown, where dangers are manifold, not so much because they are inherently threatening, although the tales are littered with episodes of real danger to the protagonists, but often simply because the modes of action that are considered normal do not always hold true in a land that is unfamiliar. Yet, for many of the people who listen to the tales of Satya Pīr, that shifting frame of reference describes their Bengal precisely; it is a land of constantly renegotiated values, of improvisation, of attempts to impose stability. As a frontier it is a place where the social, political, and economic stakes are often high, with commensurate rewards for success or failure. In this formulation we discover part of the secret of Satya Pīr's social mobility and appeal. Meeting the needs of the frontier has allowed Satya Pīr to endure, for his pragmatic approach to the problems of the world is one that favors innovation and compromise in the pursuit of basic human needs, especially the elimination of penury and the quest for social dignity. His are the tales of survival in a world that does not always cooperate, and for many in Bengal, that is the commonplace of experience.

Satya Pīr as God: Vaiṣṇava Tales

Strategies of Domestication and Appropriation

Those tales that we are inclined to read as unmistakably "Hindu" are better described as exclusively Vaiṣṇava; and they place Satya Pīr into the framework of a generic purāṇic avatāra theory, part of its supplemental signification. Although the nature of that avatāra will vary, he is generally accorded the status of the *yugāvatāra,* Nārāyaṇa's incarnational descent for the Kali Age. The logic of this characterization is quite understandable, for as is so well known and frequently cited, Nārāyaṇa promises to descend whenever the dharma has languished (*Bhagavad Gītā* 4.7–8) and in whatever form meets the needs of the people of that age (4.11). Sizable numbers of these texts frame the descent in classical terms by opening the narrative in the heavens where Nārāyaṇa sleeps. Nārada—that celestial gadfly who is as responsible for stirring up problems as for coming to everyone's aid—journeys to Nārāyaṇa's court to alert him to the malaise that threatens to engulf civilization.[15] After an exchange of traditional greetings, Nārada invites Nārāyaṇa to survey the situation and determine an appropriate response. As Nārāyaṇa wakes up to the full extent of dharma's demise (those texts that begin *in medias res* generally begin here), Nārada prods him to descend in a form people will understand, and because foreigners alien to the traditional brahmanical homeland (*madhyadeśa*) are everywhere in power, the form of this particular descent, he reasons, should play on that familiarity. The prologue closes when Nārāyaṇa takes the advice to heart and descends in the form of Satya Pīr, overtly a pīr, but in reality none other than the celestial Viṣṇu. Even for those narratives that do not explicitly provide this narrative frame to justify the descent, some form of it is implied, for it everywhere replicates the purāṇic premise of the avatāra.

Where the justification does frame the story, it makes explicit several key features of the narratives that lend Satya Pīr his broad appeal and certainly contribute to his endurance and adaptability. The texts unambiguously identify the controllers of the land as "foreigners" (*yavana*); no other term is used until very late, well into the colonial age.[16] While *yavana* is often translated as "Muslim," its derivation is a word indicating "Ionian" or "Greek," with the implication that a yavana is someone who comes overland from the west (about the only direction from which new peoples entered Bengal in numbers until the colonial period). That they were almost always Muslim in this premodern age is only secondarily remarked, for usually the designations were more ethnically specific (e.g., Pathan or Turk). The implication of the nonspecific term *yavana* operates on the controlling premise that someone whose ways are not of the traditional "Hindu" (the term is occasionally used adjectivally, but never nominally) has taken control of the countryside, and that in itself poses a threat to the stability of a common brahmanical culture, especially in the unsettled reaches of Bengal. It is easy to see how the yavana category as a generic "other" becomes associated with its alternative *"phiriṅgī,"* applied specifically to the Portuguese (and French), but coming to designate all Europeans, many of whom arrived by ship through the Bay of Bengal. The land is controlled by yavanas (foreigners who look like us, but act differently) or by phiriṅgīs (foreigners who do not look like us and are even stranger and more unpredictable and less trustworthy in their actions).[17] Because of their generic nature and lack of historical specificity, Satya Pīr's narratives easily function with both connotations. When the texts do adopt these designations, they follow a sequence that begins with the earliest stories recognizing an initial opposition that establishes a brahmanical, specifically Vaiṣṇava, cultural norm (the term *Hindu* is never used here) against yavana (the term *Muslim* or any equivalent is likewise never used). By the end of the Vaiṣṇava cycle of narratives—and often other tales as well—the stories articulate a pragmatic alliance of Vaiṣṇava and yavana (both of whom are now considered indigenous) vying for power with an implied phiriṅgī or other oppositional category, such as Śaiva or Śākta. This somewhat unexpected alliance of Vaiṣṇava and yavana is possible because the Vaiṣṇavas domesticate the yavana through their theological constructs, their religious institutions, and their developing rituals.

Domestication is precisely Nārāyaṇa's strategy in these narratives, but to domesticate, one must first appropriate. With the decision to use the familiar form of the yavana in order to reveal a new dharma that will unite the yavana with the Vaiṣṇava, Nārāyaṇa follows Nārada's prompting by choosing to appropriate the form of the wandering mendicant. The *saṃnyāsī*, of course, was a familiar figure to the countryside, and there were a number of them who routinely found their way through Bengal during the period. They were homeless, and they had abandoned personal possessions in pursuit of a religious ideal, which was often attained through *yoga*. These saṃnyāsīs were figures of considerable power, much of it magical, thanks largely to those arcane yogic practices. (In fact, the *yogī*, who is strongly associated with the Nāthas, is perhaps a more ubiquitous and ambivalent figure during this period.) The saṃnyāsī (or yogī) is the first obvious analog to the image adopted by Satya Pīr; this analog is all the more compelling when he is designated a fakīr, for the fakīr is a homeless itinerant who has taken a vow of poverty for religious ends. Here the saṃnyāsī and fakīr serve as general institutional equivalents, utilizing in the narrative the expectations invoked by their different externally grounded signification systems. But Satya Pīr is actually often understood to be permanently attached to a place—one of his most popular homes is Mecca, although other candidates in and around Bengal and Orissa qualify—and he is called upon to guide his followers in a stable environment over time, a function much more consistent with established sheikhs or pīrs who tend not to be wandering mendicants. In this persona, his image bears all the marks of the god he ostensibly incarnates (now drawing on a conflation of signifying systems), with his personal abode in Mecca serving as an ersatz heaven in these Vaiṣṇava versions. But his historical equivalent may be more aptly found in the *vairāgī*, who is the Vaiṣṇava alternative to the saṃnyāsī, frequently married, and only infrequently itinerant if at all, but who in his rustic form often develops the kinds of powers associated with the yogī. This Vaiṣṇava image of piety provides a much closer analog to the pīr, although the associations are as much implied as explicit. Yet either association of saṃnyāsī, yogī, or vairāgī makes the external form of the pīr already familiar, and when taken together they make it intimate. The familiarity is made comfortable because both such sets of individuals were reliable institutions of local power in their ability to advise and guide, to help their followers negotiate the trials and tribulations of this world, and when truly necessary, to use their considerable extraordinary powers for mundane as well as spiritual ends. This seems to be key, for Satya Pīr exhibits traits common to all of these figures by his constant concern to meet the immediate needs of his constituency. The religious practices he proposes and the demands he makes are very much of this world. They do not promise futures in heaven, union with or annihilation in God, or escape from the cycle of life. They only promise basic prosperity, safety, and weal in this uneasy land.

The authors of these narratives oriented toward a Vaiṣṇava sensibility feel compelled to justify the decision made by Nārāyaṇa to appropriate the image of the pīr to Vaiṣṇava ends, for it is clear that the pīr's form represents something other than what is traditionally acceptable to brahmanical culture. Obviously, in public image any pīr is Muslim and not Vaiṣṇava. It is not enough that the purāṇic frame of the tale explains Nārāyaṇa's motivation. More is needed to convince the Vaiṣṇava audience, so these narratives almost always appear in a trilogy designed to persuade the audience in a step-by-step fashion of the necessity and efficacy of the act. Before total domestication is possible, the form of this pīr must not only be recognized as comfortably familiar but must also be made legitimate. Legitimation is the linchpin to the process of appropriation, for if the new form is to endure as a viable and appealing future alternative, it must be grounded in an unassailable logic of possibility; that is, it must be made to conform to expectations in a way that is undeniably appropriate to the Vaiṣṇava conception of, or at least orientation to, the world—and that is precisely where the narratives begin. The process of legitimation starts by having an experienced *brāhmaṇa*—the representative of traditional society, but a society that has failed to support him—recognize the form of Satya Pīr by affirming his "true" identity as Nārāyaṇa. From this simple beginning the pīr's form is gradually valorized throughout the whole of brahmanical society, which is "documented" in the set of three stories—and that set is the overwhelming favorite form for practicing Vaiṣṇavas. They tell of the conversion of (a) the old brāhmaṇa and his wife, (b) the local woodcutters, and (c) the merchant and his family, directly or indirectly ending with the local king himself.[18] While the final tale is occasionally the subject of an entire work,[19] nearly three-quarters of all manuscripts and printed texts are devoted to this complete three-part strategy precisely because its effectiveness lies in its progression; the two versions among them attributed to the Bengali poets Śaṅkarācārya and Rāmeśvara prove most popular.[20] Not surprisingly, it is this trilogy which is read directly into the purāṇic material in the *Skanda Purāṇa* (5.233–36) and *Bhaviṣya Purāṇa* (3.2.24–29), and which forms the basis for incorporation into the monthly *vrata* cycle of the wider Hindu households of Bengal,[21] another result of the Sanskritizing effort.[22] The tales can be summarized as follows.

The brāhmaṇa's tale

The tales begin with the saga of the old brāhmaṇa who is reduced to utter penury. He resides in Varanasi, that center of traditional piety, but cannot even beg a day's worth of alms to feed his wife and himself. He is distraught over his prospects because the downward spiral conspires to keep him from being productive as a priest, for the poorer he becomes, the less likely his employment. When his prospects dim to the point where he can no longer offer a viable service to the competitive world of that metropolis, he finds himself in the unthinkable horror of being pushed to the very edges of civilization, east into the wilds of Bengal.[23] In this pitiful state, he is approached by Satya Pīr, who holds out one last alternative. "Offer śirṇi to me," he commands, "and your wishes will be fulfilled." Ever polite and sorely tempted, the brāhmaṇa resists the cry of his stomach and refuses to jettison the last remnants of his dignity as a brāhmaṇa, demurring on the grounds that Satya Pīr is yavana and such worship would be improper. Satya Pīr acknowledges the brāhmaṇa's piety and instructs him to pay close attention. He gently suggests to that good but poor brāhmaṇa that he must never be fooled by outward appearance, for Satya Pīr is really none other than Nārāyaṇa-incarnate. The brāhmaṇa is skeptical and asks for proof, which Satya Pīr provides by displaying his six-armed form as Viṣṇu, the Satya Nārāyaṇa. Satya Pīr, he explains, is but an avatāra. Having witnessed with his own eyes, the brāhmaṇa happily acknowledges the revelation, proffers the śirṇi precisely as instructed, and in an instant grows wealthy, all to the extreme pleasure and benefit of him, his wife, and others around him. In every version of the story he does, in fact, live quite happily ever after.

The woodcutters' tale

Numerous woodcutters reside in the same area as the brāhmaṇa, and it falls to them to clear land for cultivation and provide wood for fuel in this expanding economy.[24] They have grown accustomed to passing the old brāhmaṇa beside the road as they make their daily trips deep into the forests. When the brāhmaṇa's fortunes abruptly change, they are astounded, for the transformation is both miraculous and nearly instantaneous; overnight he becomes successful and highly esteemed. Naturally, they want to know the source of his good fortune, and when they inquire, the brāhmaṇa proves himself worthy of Satya Pīr's trust. Being ever grateful to that mysterious pīr who has so dramatically secured his future, he does just as he has been instructed and shares the secret. He is blunt: "Sincerely worship Satya Pīr with śirṇi, and you too will become rich." Not slow to recognize the opportunity, the woodcutters follow the injunction and within a very short time they become controllers of fabulous wealth. So successful are they that they can build large fortresses on the tracts of land they clear, their estates expanding rapidly, while the frontier they are taming extends further eastward. Inevitably, their success brings more land under cultivation and makes it fit for habitation by traditional brahmanical society, for not only is it cleared but it is filled with moral people, including law-abiding kings to rule and brāhmaṇas, like the one who shared his secret, to ensure propriety.[25]

The merchant's tale

As the settlements develop, local rulers require certain royal items, both luxury and symbolic, to assert their status and claim to power, that is, simply to be kings of these new lands. To bring the requisite and rare goods to court, each king finds himself in need of reliable merchants, who, if they are successful, become fabulously wealthy and powerful in the process. Procuring these unusual items, however, entails great risks, for their source invariably lies beyond the seas, and any venture onto the ocean is risky. Through their own devices or with the financial backing of the king, the merchants set off to adventures only imagined by ordinary people. Their ships glide effortlessly through the familiar waters of Bengal, out into the Bay of Bengal and the Indian Ocean. When they dare to venture away from land, they cannot but encounter threats found only deep at sea, for instance, the report of Dayāla, who records "a tomb of marble floating on the sea with girls dancing around it to the musical accompaniment of celestial *kiṃnaras*, and deerskins spread like carpets on the surface of the waters, with four fakīrs saying their *namāz* facing West."[26] Because of such reports and with a practical estimate of their own limitations, they more often prefer to hug the coast as they work their way south. They stop periodically at cities and lands of decreasing familiarity until they reach the furthest outposts of civilization, Kalinga, then the Dravida region, and even the isle of Sri Lanka, which is always populated by demons and monsters, who just as predictably protect great wealth. To offset the dangers, the merchants turn to Satya Pīr, for the creator of instant wealth can likewise be counted on to watch over its acquisition. Thus Satya Pīr comes to be the protector of merchants and travelers in general. To ensure this success, the merchants promise to worship Satya Pīr to a degree commensurate with their acquired wealth. But if wealth and good fortune can be created at a stroke, so too can it be removed and destroyed; failure to maintain that promise to worship Satya Pīr will only result in disaster. Sometimes it is the merchant or his accompanying sons whose greed causes one of them to withhold the worship, which in turn precipitates the ship's foundering or which lands one of them in jail. In those vile dungeons they may languish for years with no hope of escape until they belatedly remember Satya Pīr. Equally disastrous is the negligent action of the merchant's wife who has remained at home, or more frequently it is the action of the selfish daughter-in-law, who offends Satya Pīr so that success is denied even as the ships sail back into view after years abroad, sinking in the estuary as they come to dock. The variations are many, but the theme is monotonous: if you fail to make good on your contractual promise to worship Satya Pīr in exchange for his protection, you are doomed. But here, when the worship is properly discharged, or the mistakes are acknowledged and corrected with appropriate humility, the merchant is successful: the king receives those goods he requires to maintain his status as rightful and just ruler of the land, the merchant accrues wealth and status for his reliable delivery, his wife and daughters-in-law receive appropriate protection of their fidelity in the merchant's absence, and the society as a whole confirms the validity of its attempt to maintain stability and order—all because Satya Pīr is widely worshiped. In short, dharma prevails, everyone prospers, and, say the stories, if you have paid attention, you can prosper, too.[27]

Seeking Equivalence: Pragmatic Implications of Vaiṣṇava and Sufi Theology

It is no surprise that of all the Hindu communities enjoying a substantial following in Bengal during the last several centuries—many different forms of Śaiva, Śākta, Nātha, Sahajiyā, and Kartā Bhajā, to mention only primary groups—it is the Vaiṣṇavas (and later Bāuls) who attempt to appropriate a figure who is clearly Muslim, for they alone can easily justify the action through their ever-expanding avatāra theory, which claims virtually any popular figure as its own. As becomes apparent through the other narrative types, the Vaiṣṇava model of God's descent, the avatāra, and the Islamic institution of the pīr, can be allied not only because the respective images of the holy man—pīr (and fakīr) and vairāgī (and saṃnyāsī)[28]—coincide so conveniently as metaphors of the embodiment of power, but because there is a basic theological compatibility that undergirds both conceptions of divinity to which they refer, and this consonance will generate apposite orientations toward authority that will prove their coherence in the narratives of Satya Pīr.

Like the vairāgī, the pīr does not prescribe the esoteric practices reserved for adepts like himself, but simpler and more popular forms of piety appropriate to the average follower; much of his guidance falls into the adjudication of everyday problems, marital issues, arbitration of disputes, and so forth. The image of divinity associated with these simpler prescriptive rituals and instructions will run the full gamut of experiences, just as they do in the Vaiṣṇava order. Not only are the institutional structures of the pīr and vairāgī, then, analogous in a general way, but their operational and theological underpinnings are closely equivalent, and this is borne out in comparisons of both general and historically specific dimensions of theology, such as the nature of the godhead and the injunctions to ritual practices. While it is easy to speculate in purely intellectual or theological terms why these two traditions may be inclined to find a mutual alliance, it is their operational dimension that bears out the practicality of it—and that allows the Vaiṣṇavas to appropriate the image of Satya Pīr with virtual impunity—in fact, one might even argue, with a very unsurprising anticipation if not expectation of its inevitability.

Given the similarity of the functions of the Vaiṣṇava and Sufi spiritual guides and the theological parallel, it is ultimately the fact that Satya Pīr is a mythic figure that effectively eliminates any possible challenge to the narratives' veracity, for no historical documentation of the pīr's life and teachings aligns him with any particular sectarian group.[29] This independence of the narrative from historical verification dramatically aids the process of appropriation by enabling the Vaiṣṇava to sanitize it. In this, Satya Pīr's image is plastic and malleable in the manner of a purāṇic figure and, indeed, he quietly slips into the *purāṇas* as just another form of Nārāyaṇa. This same kind of plasticity likewise extends to the use of the narratives, for it enables them to be applied to a wide range of generic situations, again quite apart from any explicit historical event. Each of the Vaiṣṇava episodes deals tacitly, if not explicitly, with generalized processes of reclamation—geographical and cultural—making habitable a land that had been off-limits to brāhmaṇas and therefore problematic for establishing a proper brahmanical society.[30] Because of its lack of specificity, the nature of that rehabilitation can be adjusted to the user's immediate circumstance. The progress documented in the trilogy of Vaiṣṇava tales parallels the historical events of the settling of Bengal. As the Gaṅgā shifted steadily to the east, the limits of what defined the traditional heartland or madhyadeśa of brahmanical culture could be extended, but only if brought under proper control. Making good use of the available powers, one agent of that Hindu domestication became the pīr, for the pīr could actually do what brāhmaṇas themselves could not: inhabit a wild land to tame it. Ironically, the pīr is often the very same agent for the analogous processes of Islamization, for the Sufi guide as pīr or fakīr is often the first into new countries and the first to convert the local population so that land may be brought into the line of traditional Islamic culture—and here Bengal was no exception. The same figure of the pīr serves two religious orientations in nearly exactly the same capacity.

Herein may lie the most important reason for Vaiṣṇavas to appropriate the pīr's image, for by doing so they not only unquestionably acknowledge the presence of Islam as a legitimate social organization and religious option in the region, but they also acknowledge that the pīr works as an effective source of local power. It is an act of a pragmatic "Realpolitik" in that the Vaiṣṇavas adopt a stance toward their rulers' culture and religion that does not try to wish away the reality of that rule but attempts to adapt to its presence and co-opt its power by appropriating it: they take one of the most effective tools of conversion and revalorize its image to their own ends. It comes as no surprise, however, that even though Satya Pīr is embraced, the embrace is not unmitigated or unconditional, because the Vaiṣṇavas do not elevate him to the level of their adored Kṛṣṇa, but ultimately absorb him into the lower strata of the brahmanical hierarchy, placing him squarely in the women's ritual cycle of the vrata, which is dominated nearly exclusively by lesser images of divinity, especially the benign household goddesses, such as Ṣaṣṭhī, Lakṣmī, et al., who are petitioned to make life easier and more fruitful. Satya Pīr proves his worth by doing much of the "dirty work" of making the land habitable and ensuring the wealth and weal of the family—the mundane role of lesser celestials—and in that proves his expediency. But in spite of the "official" recognition, he must remain a marginal figure at the lower end of the Vaiṣṇava and brahmanical world.[31]

Satya Pīr as Islamic Exemplar: Seeking Accommodation and Demanding a Place

The tales of Satya Pīr that are Islamic in their provenance and orientation take a decidedly different tack to the power of the pīr and the dynamics of interacting with the local populace. For obvious reasons, no time need be spent justifying Satya Pīr's existence, as was necessary for the Vaiṣṇavas, for pīrs are part of the everyday world. Nor is there any attempt to equate Satya Pīr with a saṃnyāsī or vairāgī or yogī, even though the authors routinely refer to these figures in ways commensurate with the analogs of fakīr and pīr, and in so doing draw upon the associations of their underlying signification systems. Because the form of the pīr functions in Bengal's culture as a source of local power and moral fortitude, any pīr would be an obvious choice for literary interest. But documenting Satya Pīr's triumphs as a way of celebrating his superiority is clearly subsumed to the larger interest of proving or confirming that he is worthy of a following in the first place. These triumphs are not always narratively sequenced as they are in the Vaiṣṇava trilogy, nor are they ordered for consumption in any way similar to the incorporation of his tales into the *vrata* cycle. Most are independent or only loosely related to others, but the liveliest coordinated group can be found in one expansive collection, *Baḍa satya pīra o sandhyāvatī kaṇyāra punthi* of Kṛṣṇahari Dāsa,[32] which is structured in the form of an anecdotal hagiography of the hero.

This lengthy book opens by invoking the glory of Allāh and the Prophet and describing the wonders of Behest (paradise). Because a certain Hindu (but not Vaiṣṇava) king named Maidānava had been persecuting pīrs and fakīrs indiscriminately, God ordered the goddess Cāndbibi to descend to earth to initiate a plan that would reestablish a just society. When Cāndbibi accepted that order, she began to fulfill a longheld prophecy that Satya Pīr would be born in the Kali Age to save humanity (note the Hindu cosmology), and so she was born to Priyāvatī, the wife of the evil king, as his daughter Sandhyāvatī. When she was bathing in the river one day, she picked up and smelled a flower petal that had been floating downstream, and with that inhalation the just prepubescent girl immaculately conceived Satya Pīr. Her mother was distraught and tried to force an abortion, but to no avail. When she was about to give birth, her mother banished her to the forest, where she was taken and left to die. Her cries alerted Allāh, who sent an angel to protect her, while from the womb, Satya Pīr called on Lokamāna Hākim[33] to build her a suitable abode. When she gave birth, there was no child but a clot of blood, which she sadly consigned to the river. But a sin-filled tortoise swallowed that blood and was instantly transformed. The tortoise gave birth to Satya Pīr and retired directly to Paradise. Satya Pīr returned to his mother after five years of extended study with various famous *murshids.* She was still alone in her palace in the woods, so he used his persuasive powers to relocate an entire population into the Jhārikhaṇḍa Forest,[34] clearing massive areas of land and establishing a community. Here he came into conflict with local kings, whose inhabitants he stole, beginning the long saga of righting the wrongs that had been perpetrated against good and pious pīrs and fakīrs.

The tale then traces Satya Pīr's exploits through his youth and adult life, each tale adding to the strength and depth of his miraculous powers and his ever-expanding circle of influence. The book is of special interest because it attempts to create a "life" for Satya Pīr on the order of the hagiographies devoted to historical figures of the premodern period; in fact, this would appear to be the only hagiography devoted to a "mythic" pīr among the dozen or so who are popular throughout Bengal. But being anecdotal, it is only loosely organized with no ending and is, therefore, infinitely expandable. The range of exploits is considerably greater than its more tightly controlled and limited Vaiṣṇava counter narratives, whose protagonists are other than the pīr, for in those tales, as we saw above, the pīr primarily serves as a catalyst for action and the object of worship, but he is never the direct protagonist of the story. The function of Satya Pīr in the Vaiṣṇava tales is similar to his function in the third type of apparently nonsectarian tale where his role is to initiate action, complicate the plot, or provide the raison d'être for the protagonists' adventures. In contrast, the Muslim-oriented tales focus on Satya Pīr as the hero, but it is perhaps significant that the opening gambit is precisely the same impulse that operates in the Vaiṣṇava stories, for Satya Pīr begins the process of reclaiming the forests of Bengal while he is still gestating in the womb. Furthering the contrast with the timelessness of the purāṇic-style Vaiṣṇava trilogy (previously analyzed) or with the nonsectarian type (not analyzed here),[35] the Muslim tales appear to be somewhat more historically fixed in the immediately precolonial and early colonial world. There are, for instance, references to historical figures, such as Satya Pīr's encounter with Mān Siṅgh late in the opening book, *Mālañca pāla*.[36] Satya Pīr encounters individuals who wield European rifles and cannons. It is reported that he is strapped to a cannon and blown to bits, only to miraculously rematerialize before the eyes of the miscreants, who then receive their much deserved punishment. Other tales bear witness to a phiriṅgī presence, whereas the Vaiṣṇava tales never finger the phiriṅgī directly, but leave it to be supplied by the auditor as appropriate to an immediate crisis. Some of the more moralizing tales, however, do exhibit some ambiguity of historical location, and that allows their messages to be transferred and adapted more easily to immediate or generalized exigencies regardless of time or place. A good example is Satya Pīr's instruction to the greedy and selfish Dhanañjaya, a prosperous milkman,[37] summarized as follows.

Dhanañjaya's tale

As Satya Pīr wandered through the delta, he approached the expansive home of Dhanañjaya the milkman. He sat down and recited the names of God and the Prophet, then called out for food, but Dhanañjaya, being a mean and selfish man, was ungracious and ordered him to wait for some leftovers. Satya Pīr was annoyed at the affront and quickly cursed him: "You are doomed, for you have no faith in fakīrs or *saṃnāysīs*. From this day your house will be abandoned by Lakṣmī, the goddess of wealth and prosperity." Dhanañjaya scoffed at his anger and called him a raving (*pāgala*) fakīr, which he attributed to starvation from fasting. He announced defiantly that no matter how much Satya Pīr tried to make him suffer, he would never beg. "That wealth was given by God, and none other can take it away. If God protects me, who can hurt me?"

Satya Pīr restrained himself long enough to offer Dhanañjaya the opportunity to repent by lecturing him on the sins of hubris and greed and on the sin of serving polluted garbage, especially to good Musalmāns: "Anyone who offers contaminated garbage to any living being plunges into the bottomless pit of hell! You, like a haughty brāhmaṇa, greet the Musalmān's *salām* with the raised hand of false sincerity and then to that same Musalmān you have dished out rancid, polluted garbage. He who gives the Musalmān such garbage must, in the final accounting, stand before the Prophet. You have ground your dharma into dust. In your next life you will be born as a jackal or a dog and will eat the garbage you have distributed in this. Your sin can be expiated only after you yourself have consumed the leftover garbage from twelve different social groups (*jāti*)."

The milkman was indifferent and mocked him as a crazy fakīr made daft from starvation. But his final mistake was to punctuate this contempt by turning his back on the pīr as he was speaking. The pīr grew furious. He commanded a high-flying kite to snatch the plate from Dhanañjaya's hand. Because the command of a pīr must be obeyed, the kite instantly dove from the sky, plucked the plate in his beak, and soared back to the heavens whereupon he dropped the plate on the milkman. The plate hit its mark, smashing into his head like a bolt of lightning. The spurts of blood and cries of agony only intensified Satya Pīr's anger. The moment the pīr set foot in the milkman's home, Lakṣmī fled in fear. The milkman's pots of money were soon ground into shards, and his pots of milk were spilled onto the ground. His rice granary crackled into a fiery conflagration that resembled hell itself. The fructifying cows that packed his sheds were soon transmogrified into deer, who fled deep into the forest, terrified of the raging fires. As the milkman lay comatose and bleeding, Satya Pīr took his leave, and soon bands of thieves looted whatever was left. Dhanañjaya, along with his four sons, was reduced to utter penury, to the very begging he swore he would never do.

It took nearly six months for Satya Pīr's anger to subside, but being an ocean of mercy, he eventually felt a twinge of compassion for Dhanañjaya. The fakīr proceeded to Dhanañjaya's house, ready to forgive. He chanted the customary *dhikr* as he approached. The milkman was terrified, for it was precisely that sound which had preceded his downfall. Dhanañjaya did not recognize Satya Pīr, but was quick to acknowledge the power of all such pīrs. He fell at the pīr's feet, rubbing his face in the dust, and with all humility implored him to be merciful. He related the sad tale of his previous stupidity and ugly behavior toward some anonymous pīr. He observed that even though he was now a worthless beggar, he had learned hard the lesson of his pride and promised to make an offering a hundred times over anything the pīr might be pleased to ask.

Satya Pīr questioned the integrity and sincerity of the milkman, for, as he noted, as far as he could see, God had already been very kind to him, gracing him with large herds of cattle. Dhanañjaya was nonplussed, but sensing perhaps an opportunity to regain his wealth, he promised Satya Pīr that he would offer śirṇi made from the milk of a hundred cows, should that former wealth be restored. Because it was clear that the milkman meant what he said, Satya Pīr restored everything as it had been with the simple wave of his left hand. With his sons in tow, Dhanañjaya hustled to herd the cows, for they were in sore need of milking, as Satya

Pīr smiled and slipped quietly away. The author concludes: "I have come to the end of this tale, meditating on Rādhākānta the Tolerant. Muslims call him Allāh, while Hindus call him Hari."

The author's assertion that Allāh and Kṛṣṇa are but two names of the same God introduces a new level of ambiguity by failing to designate a clear sectarian orientation; the adjectives are likewise derived from both traditions—Rādhākānta, "the beloved of Rādhā," and *kṣānta,* "the tolerant," a standard attribute of Allāh. The frame created by the author's signature line (*bhaṇitā*) at the close of the narrative—a common technique in Bengali poetry from the period—creates the illusion that the two traditions are somehow not different. The effect, however, is to invite the reader to insert his or her own god as the one to whom the other god has been assimilated, so Vaiṣṇavas will read it as a confirmation of the truth of the already established trilogy that makes Satya Pīr an avatāra of Nārāyaṇa (even though Satya Pīr is not mentioned by name in the bhaṇitā). Conversely, Muslims can read the text to interpret Satya Pīr as the pīr he is, while acknowledging that Vaiṣṇavas are sincerely religious, even though they do not recognize the full truth of God. Given the ambiguity of this double reading, it is easy to see why this tradition is given the label of syncretic, but that is not at all what the author proposes. Consistently through the more than two hundred pages of this text describing scores of adventures, Satya Pīr demonstrates an Islamic orientation toward divinity and worldly power, and just as the opening frame story suggests, he is intent on establishing that in the world. When he actually converts the wayward (as opposed to simply making them recognize his power and give respect to pīrs), it is always a conversion to Islam, usually initiated by the recitation of the *kalima*. The author seems to be equally comfortable articulating a cosmology that encompasses Lakṣmī, the Hindu goddess of wealth, and the Prophet, as a celestial figure; so, too, an Islamic judgment day side-by-side with references to transmigration. The author makes no attempt to rectify these and other apparently contradictory references because they are not being used to construct a consistent syncretic cosmology. They function to demonstrate certain equivalences, acting as metaphoric alternatives or simply different ways that people have of describing the same reality, while still acknowledging differences among the religious perspectives, not trying to fuse them. But these, too, lend themselves to the same convenient double reading as the bhaṇitā, which disguise the thrust of the narrative. Even the author's own name gives one pause, for Kṛṣṇahari Dāsa is a Vaiṣṇava epithet.[38]

What exactly the author intended by this dual strategy of obfuscation and metaphoric equivalence we can only speculate, but the effect of this strategy we can certainly gauge. Disguising the Muslim orientation of the narrative by suggesting that the Muslim God and the Vaiṣṇava God are not different, but simply approached differently, functions as a plea for *recognition*. The stories confirm it by having Satya Pīr routinely humiliate his opponents into recognizing his right to be honored, and this humiliation is effected by an awesome display of magical prowess. Demonstrating unchecked power guarantees attention, and this is how Satya Pīr ensures that he will be taken seriously. Satya Pīr projects this power in two ways: to convince the skeptic and to assure the already convinced, who in turn mirror the two audiences. His *karāmāt* or miracle working (which is often described as a kind of *śakti*) enables him to twist nature to his own ends in a way that is possible only by the most accomplished of spiritual adepts—and this power is generally marshaled for the sake of the noncommitted, the skeptic, or the utter *kāfir* (infidel). The demonstrations, as Dhanañjaya attests, can be extremely violent, but may just as easily be used to counter someone else's ill will, as will be the case in the story of King Kāśīkānta below. When he has gained their undivided attention, he achieves the recognition of his power and the truth of the Islamic cosmology that makes it so, but that acknowledgment does not necessarily require conversion. Recognition is, however, a necessary prerequisite for an ultimate goal of accommodation, to find a place in the shared cosmology of Bengal. Satya Pīr seeks to maintain a permanent position in this world by extending his power to protect those who recognize him. The texts will generally use the term *baraka* (benevolent blessing) to describe the power that blankets the right-minded and morally pure in a general weal that is measurable in terms of increased wealth or rule in a kingdom of peace. The stories abound with the results of this protection, but to be literarily effective, that is, to make the causal relationship of acknowledgment and benefit unequivocal, they must be more dramatic and entertaining. Like all such hagiographical tales designed to glorify the hero, the authors exaggerate the blindness and stupidity of the antagonists in the face of Satya Pīr's obvious superiority. This narrative strategy provides the opportunity for Satya Pīr to enact a decisively dramatic conversion of the antagonist to drive home the point. The summary of the conversion of King Kāśīkānta is illustrative.[39]

The Tale of King Kāśīkānta

One day Satya Pīr wandered into a brāhmaṇa village dressed half as a Vaiṣṇava brāhmaṇa and half as a Muslim fakīr, carrying a string of *tulasī* beads, a chain around his waist, ash smeared on his forehead, and sandal paste on his feet. In this garb he headed for the Sanskrit school. Although students at the school taunted and insulted him, Satya Pīr was undaunted as he asked for food, specifically requesting unboiled milk, banana, honey, and rice flour.[40] He also requested a parasol, so that he could be seated with them, and a fresh sacred thread, all of which prompted a fusillade of imprecations. Enduring the invectives, Satya Pīr eloquently rejoined, cursing to illiteracy for seven generations one particularly dull and arrogant young brāhmaṇa, who had dared to insult him in pidgin-Sanskrit. Somewhat mollified at the spectacle, he then retired to meditate under a tree he conjured.

As he sat deep in meditation, Satya Pīr summoned the sacred threads of those arrogant brāhmaṇas. One after the other, the threads snaked down the road to join their master.[41] Trailing behind was an equally long line of dejected and obsequious brāhmaṇas who by then had had their pride curbed and their curiosities piqued. They plaintively inquired just who he was and why he tormented them so. Satya Pīr responded,

"You may be brāhmaṇas
but you are no different from the rest,
  for the serpent of Time and Death bites equally.
Be respectful of all saṃnyāsīs and fakirs,
treat them with kindness, lest they show you
    to be nothing but students of Sayatān."

He then revealed his true identity as a pīr favored by God, and the brāhmaṇas not only submitted to his authority but made restitution by offering the śirṇi they had previously denied him.

When their king, Kāśīkānta, heard of this strange behavior, he raised the cry of blasphemy and summoned the brāhmaṇas to account for themselves by bringing Satya Pīr to demonstrate his power. Because he had no faith, he stupidly challenged the pīr to do something extraordinary, something which could demonstrate that he was more powerful than the king himself. Satya Pīr quietly replied that that should be easy, for a king who could not even control his own wives could not wield too much might. The king's ire was sparked, and he demanded an instant apology, but Satya Pīr demurred, preferring to offer proof of his contention. He transformed himself into a white fly to wing his way unmolested into the queens' quarters. There he began to incite them, gently at first, but with increasing pressure, to dance. The queens in turn were struck suddenly with mysterious and outrageous sexual urges, causing them to writhe in uncontrollable lust. Like a contagion, the undulations swept through the *zenāna*, and these queens began to dance, giving vent to their true natures, base and lascivious. In a frenzy, the women broke out of their quarters and violated the public hall, where they enraptured the audience but enraged and humiliated the king with their salacious advance. Unable to stop her, King Kāśīkānta looked on in absolute horror as his beloved chief queen disgraced herself by performing a striptease in front of the throne. Finally Satya Pīr sent them scurrying to recover their modesty.

The completeness of the king's humiliation made him all the more obdurate, and he refused to capitulate. Instead of acknowledging Satya Pīr's power, he ordered him hurled into the deepest well in the palace. Satya Pīr pulled the king down with him, his sacred thread having snaked around the king's neck. Try as he might, the king could not break the thread to stop his descent. Finally, recognizing his defeat, he allowed Satya Pīr to climb the thread and drag them both to safety.[42] In spite of the outcome, the king's submission was initially grudging. Satya Pīr accepted it nonetheless, lecturing his now captive audience on the nature of royal propriety and the modes of dharma and proper action. He initiated the king into the recitation of the kalima, transforming Kāśīkānta into a God-fearing, law-upholding Muslim king. As the benefits became clear, the king enthusiastically honored Satya Pīr, who turned away and headed home.

In the narratives, Satya Pīr demands that people publicly acknowledge his legitimacy as an effective source of moral power, and from that the legitimacy of his worship. For those who do so, numerous benefits accrue. His relentless insistence and the concomitantly harsh forms of persuasion suggest that this acceptance was hard won, that coercion was in fact on occasion necessary. These struggles and their inevitable confrontations complicate the plots, and their consistently antibrahmanical tenor is often undisguised. But in spite of that, the condemnation is selectively, not universally, applied. It is not that brāhmaṇas are inherently bad but that brāhmaṇas are too frequently blinded by their own hubris, which results from an overvaluation of their social standing; that is, they confuse the privileges of their rank with an inalienable birthright, rather than seeing it as a fragile commodity that must be maintained through virtuous conduct. Significantly, the brāhmaṇas in Kāśīkānta's tale are not forced or even asked to convert. They are asked simply to honor and respect Satya Pīr, for which they will be restored to their position of respectability. Brāhmaṇas are just another social group in a Muslim cosmology, but as the top of a Hindu hierarchy they metonymically represent the whole of society, just as we saw in the opening episode of the Hindu trilogy. Kings who support such brāhmaṇas are a more serious target because they perpetuate this arrogance and misuse of status, ensuring it as the norm for society. The need to convert King Kāśīkānta in no way challenges his right to rule by replacing him with another individual chosen by Satya Pīr, who in this and other narratives could easily do so. The conflict is adjudicated on a moral battleground, so Satya Pīr proves that the king has but a frail hold on dharma by effortlessly undermining the moral integrity of his own palace and family. Since, in the traditional constructions of dharma, propriety traditionally flows from the king into his realm, the corruption of his personal life will inevitably be manifest in the society at large. Because the Hindu model has been shown deficient here, its dharma unstable and easily subverted, Kāśīkānta must be converted to a just and moral order of kingship in an Islamic mode. Then goodness and mercy will undoubtedly reign—and pīrs and fakīrs can practice their *Kraft* unmolested.

There is no way to determine just how closely any of these tales may approximate historical circumstances, for fictions at best can only allude, but we can see in them the imagination that presents an idealized perspective geared to a pragmatic survival. In these stories, Hindus of any type who acknowledge Satya Pīr can and do retain their Hindu status and prosper. The stories teach that everyone must recognize and demonstrate a sincere respect for Satya Pīr, if not all pīrs, and that deference will invariably result in worldly success. But its moral is also clear, for status and wealth once gained carry special responsibilities and must redound to the greater good of society. The proper conduct common to both the Vaiṣṇava and Islamic God, as articulated by the Muslim portrayal of Satya Pīr, hinges on humility and benevolence, not exclusion, persecution, or greed.[43] It is no coincidence, then, that the Vaiṣṇava tales of Satya Pīr assume a correlative position to the Muslim tales by arguing that a condition of utter penury obviates any chance for an individual to act in a morally responsible way, hence Satya Pīr's concern to provide wealth. And here we have a strong indication that even though the Vaiṣṇava and Islamic narratives target different audiences, they manage somehow to articulate a very closely related set of religious, or perhaps more basic existential, concerns.

The world of Satya Pīr's narratives is one where pragmatism takes precedence over idealism in matters of social organization and religion. This literature makes clear that in the minds of its authors, the encounter of people we might tend automatically to label as Hindus and Muslims in premodern Bengal does not automatically produce conflict, nor does it require differences among people to be effaced. In this world, the "other" is clearly recognized and often easily tolerated, if not embraced. The narratives typical to our sample depict similar dramatic acts viewed from religiously opposing positions in a way that acknowledges the legitimacy of both religious traditions without threatening either, which suggests that it is not the Great Traditions that are at stake here but lower-order symbolic concerns. The reason is simple: everyone needs a place for a figure who, in the all-important task of generating wealth for survival, comes to the aid of everyone regardless of social status and religious orientation. But this place is very pointedly low in the cosmological hierarchies of both communities. For Hindus, he fits into the women's world of household concerns and is petitioned for what he can give for success in this life, not distantly future gains. For Muslims, he ironically idealizes the acquisition of wealth, the very thing that is often seen to hinder spiritual development among Sufis, but epitomizes the survival techniques valued by traders and rulers. It is perhaps here that the narratives have given us a clue regarding his insatiable desire for śirṇi, for even though Sufis have historically vacillated between fasting and satiety, poets have for centuries referred in derogatory terms to the *halvah*-sucking mendicant, "the Sufi with milk-white hair who has made the recollection (dhikr) of sugar, rice, and milk his special litany"[44]—the very ingredients of śirṇi. In these stories, filling this pīr's stomach equates indirectly with being moral, for those are the two things he rewards with wealth. He instructs in morality, but does not give explicit religious instruction to a following of spiritual adepts, disciples (*murīd* or *śiṣya*), as we might expect. In this he is unlike his historical counterparts. His vanity and thirst for recognition prompt him to keep his magical powers on prominent display, and these are directed toward issues of pride and place, consistent with the desires of his lay following for miraculous intervention in life's demands. His niche has become secure at the bottom of both religious hierarchies as a metaphor for getting by in a tough world—and in this, while valuing Satya Pīr's acts differently, these two orientations to authority appear so closely related as to be but complementary dimensions of one Bengali world.

Notes

I would like to thank Richard J. Cohen, Margaret Mills, Robin C. Rinehart, Carl W. Ernst, and Edward C. Dimock Jr. for their close reading and suggestions. But a special thanks goes to David Gilmartin, with whom many of the ideas contained herein were fleshed out over months of sustained discussion.

1. Sañjīvakumāra Bāgachi, *Satyanārāyaṇa: nāṭya kāvya* (Dinājapura: Kālīpada Bāgachi and Raṇajit Kumāra Bāgachi, 1334 B.S. [1926–27]), preface.

2. Compared with other figures in premodern and contemporary Bengal, the amount of scholarship is grossly disproportionate to the manuscript and printed material devoted to him. When I first began this research in the mid-1980s, fewer than two hundred pages in all languages of academic writing had been focused on him, and nearly all of that was a simple recounting of his tales. Several new works have started to remedy the situation, however. The most complete accounting is in Girīndranātha Dāsa, *Bāṅglā pīra sāhityera kathā* (Kājīpāḍā, Bārāsāta, 24 Paragaṇās: Śehid Lāibrerī, 1383 B.S. [1975–76 C.E.]). The first extended set of translations has been published, all attributed to the Oriya poet Kavikarṇa; see Bishnupada Panda, ed. and trans., *Pālās of Śrī Kavi Karṇa*, Kalāmūlaśāstra Series, vols. 4–7 (New Delhi: Indira Gandhi National Centre for the Arts and Motilal Banarsidass, 1991). Some of the tales are in Bengali or in a mixed Oriya and Bengali idiom in manuscripts that are written in Bengali script, while many of the Oriya tales overlap with Bengali counterparts in plot and theme. Cashin has also included a translation of Vallabha's *Satyanārāyaṇera punthi* in his chapter on "The Cult of the Pīr," in David Cashin, *The Ocean of Love: Middle Bengali Sufi Literature and the Fakirs of Bengal*, Skrifter utgivna av Föreningen för Orientaliska Studier no. 27 (Stockholm: Association of Oriental Studies, Stockholm University, 1995), 251–82.

3. See, e.g., Asim Roy, *The Islamic Syncretistic Traditions of Bengal* (Princeton: Princeton University Press, 1983), esp. 214–18, and his earlier article, "The Pīr-Tradition: A Case Study in Islamic Syncretism in Traditional Bengal," in *Images of Man: Religion and Historical Process in South Asia*, ed. Fred W. Clothey (Madras: New Era, 1982), 112–34, esp. 129–32. See also the recent article by Kānāi Lāla Rāya, "Satyapīr," *Bāṅlā Ekāḍemī Patrikā* 36, no. 2 (Śrāvaṇa-Āśvina 1399 B.S. [1991–92 C.E.]): 71–82. For a critique of the concept of syncretism, see Tony K. Stewart and Carl W. Ernst, "Syncretism," in *South Asian Folklore: An Encyclopaedia*, ed. Margaret A. Mills and Peter J. Claus (New York: Garland, forthcoming).

4. For the litany of the scholarly constructions of India, see Ronald B. Inden, *Imagining India* (Oxford: Basil Blackwell, 1990).

5. This popular story is asserted by the editor in Kavivallabha, *Satyanārāyaṇa punthi*, ed. Munsī Abdul Karim, Sāhitya Pariṣad Granthāvalī no. 49 (Calcutta: Baṅgīya Sāhitya Pariṣat by Rāmakamala Siṃha, 1322 B.S. [1914–15 C.E.]), 7, and then repeated frequently in the secondary literature as "hearsay." The most explicit connection is proposed by Louis Massignon, *La Passion de Husayn Ibn*

Mansûr Hallâj, new ed., 2 vols. (Paris: Gallimard, 1975), 2:299–302. I have not seen any primary documentation of this association. The same goes for Satya Pīr's identity as the son of the daughter of the famous ruler of Bengal, Husain Shāh (r. 1493–1519), which is frequently repeated; for the earliest citation, see Dineshcandra Sen, *The Folk Literature of Bengal* (Calcutta: Calcutta University Press, 1920), 100, who credits manuscripts of Kavi Aripha and Śaṅkarācārya. I have been unable to confirm the passage in any version of either text.

6. Sukumāra Sena, *Bāṅālār sāhityera itihāsa*, 4 vols. in 6 pts. (Calcutta: Eastern, 1963), vol. 1, pt. 2: 471.

7. Kṛṣṇahari Dāsa, *Baḍa satya pīra o sandhyāvatī kaṇyāra punthi* (Calcutta: Nurūddin Āhmād at Gāosiya Lāibreri, n.d.), 214.

8. Worship is an aniconic form that involves the heartfelt offering of śirṇi in a simple mixture of rice (or rice flour), sugar, milk, banana, and spices. During the first decade of the twentieth century, the *Satyanārāyaṇa o śubhacanīra kathā*, 2d ed., ed. Śyāmācaraṇa Kaviratna (Calcutta: by the editor through Gurudāsa Caṭṭopādhyāya at Bengal Medical Library, 1315 B.S. [1907–8 C.E.]), gave seven detailed pages of instruction just for making the offering of śirṇi, which now includes twenty-eight ingredients. In the same year, the *Satyanārāyaṇa vratakathā*, edited with Bengali translation by Rāsavihārisāṃkhyatīrtha (Murshidabad: Rāmadeva Miśra for Haribhaktipradyinīsabhā of Baharamapura at Rādhāramaṇa Press, 1315 B.S. [1907–8 C.E.]) gives twelve pages of the same. A decade later, Rāmagopāla Rāya's version, *Satyamaṅgala bā satyanārāyaṇa devera vratakathā o pūjāpaddhati* (Calcutta: Jayakṛṣṇa Caudhurī, 1835 Śaka), contains twenty-two detailed pages for performing the offering. In a book that was probably published during the 1970s, fifteen pages are devoted to the offering of the pūjā, including illustrations of thirteen hand *mūdras;* see Ratneśvara Tantrajyotiṣaśāstrī, ed., *Śrīśrīsatyanārāyaṇa o śubhacunī pūjāpaddhati* (Calcutta: Puṣpa, n.d.).

9. The pāñcālī and pālā gāna are set to music for public performance, while the vrata kathā is a story told at the time of women's household ritual vows, into which cycle Satya Pīr has been incorporated.

10. For the most complete listing of these manuscripts, see Jatindra Mohan Bhattacharjee, *Catalogus Catalogorum of Bengali Manuscripts*, pt. 1 (Calcutta: Asiatic Society, 1978). There are many other manuscripts in private hands and in collections whose catalogs had not been compiled when Jatindra Mohan compiled his monumental catalog.

11. The Śrīhaṭṭa Sāhitya Pariṣat in Bangladesh was razed in retaliation for the toppling of the Babri Masjid; there have been other unconfirmed reports of manuscripts being destroyed.

12. Gerard Genette, *Narrative Discourse: An Essay in Method*, trans. Jane Lewin (Ithaca: Cornell University Press, 1980).

13. In order to maximize the use of manuscripts, I generally read only complete versions of texts and no more than three versions by any one author (there were only minimal variations), and I surveyed as many authors as possible, starting with the oldest texts available, but I tried to maintain a balance of names

that appeared to represent the general distribution of "Hindu" and "Muslim" names. The latter proved to be misleading, for the names do not necessarily reflect the author's religious preference, confirming secondarily the inappropriate assumption of "naming" and "belonging" noted earlier.

14. Richard Eaton, *The Rise of Islam and the Bengal Frontier, 1204–1760* (Berkeley: University of California Press, 1993).

15. Occasionally the interlocutor will be Yudhiṣṭhira or some other celestial figure, e.g., the prominently titled work by Dvārakanātha Pāla, *Satynārāyaṇera pācālī: kṛṣṇa yudhiṣṭhirera saṃbāda o kalāvatīra upākhyāna* (Ḍhākā: Lachamana Basāka at Ḍhākā Bāṅglā Press, n.d. [1285 B.S., or 1877–78 C.E.]).

16. As far as my survey can determine, the texts do not use the Bengali term *Musalmān* until very late in the nineteenth century. And that term is itself not entirely unambiguous, but seems generally to refer to Muslims who are not of Arabian origin but who follow a culture rooted in Perso-Arabic ideals. A "muslim" is one who "submits" (*aslama*) to the will of God (Allāh), and in the Indian context historically it refers to those who can trace their direct ancestry to the tribes of Arabia at the time of Muhammad in the seventh century. The word *Musalmān*, while often confused with *Muslim*, more connotatively refers to those whose lineages originate in South Asia or outside of Arabia but who converted to Islam. For more on the term, see the authoritative Persian dictionary, *Laghut nāma* by ʿAlī Akbar Dikhudā, 15 vols. (Tehran: Muʾassasah-ʾi Intishārāt va shāp-e dānishgāh-i, 1993–95), s.v. *"musalmān"* (fasc. 211, pp. 428–29, microfiche 113:1). I am indebted to Carl W. Ernst for first pointing out the potentially pejorative reading of Musalmān and for the reference to Dikhudā.

17. For a very useful and pointed analysis of the nature of such comparisons, especially as they apply to religious situations, see Jonathan Z. Smith, "Adde Parvum Parvo Magnus Acervus Erit," *History of Religions* 11, no. 1 (August 1971): 67–90. Starting with the basic division of "we" vs. "they," he extends the formulation by (apparently) running it through the transformations dictated by the semiotic square.

18. Occasionally a fourth tale will be appended making the connection with the king explicit; it is the story of a king who loses his sons after failing to join the worship of Satya Pīr by a group of cowherds he meets in the wilderness. See the previously noted work edited by Rāsavihārisāṃkhyatīrtha (supra n. 8), who refers to it as the *Tuṅgadhvaja gopa saṃvāda;* and *Satyanārāyaṇa vratakathā*, compiled by Meghanātha Bhaṭṭācārya (Calcutta: Saṃskṛta Press Depository, 1306 B.S. [1898–99 C.E.]), who calls it the *Vaṃśadhvaja gopa saṃvāda*.

19. See, e.g., the elegant tale of Vikrampura poet Lālā Jayakṛṣṇa Sena, *Harilīlā*, ed. Dīneśacandra Sena and Basantarañjana Rāya (Calcutta: Calcutta University, 1928), who finished the text in 1772 (p. 7), and the powerful narrative of Kavivallabha in his aforementioned *Satyanārāyaṇa punthi* (supra n. 5), which was composed earlier in the eighteenth century (p. 15). Both of these texts are substantially larger than the standard Hindu trilogy taken as a whole.

20. These two texts are available in multiple Baṭṭalā editions and have been

printed together as many times as they have been issued separately. I have personally examined more than fifty such publications. Typical among them are Śaṅkarācārya and Rāmeśvara, *Śrīśrīsatyanārāyaṇera pācālī: līlāvatī kalāvatī daridra brāhmaṇera upākhyāna* (Calcutta: Tārācānda Dāsa and Sons, n.d.); Śaṅkarācārya and Rāmeśvara, *Śrīśrīsatyanārāyaṇera pācālī: līlāvatī kalāvatī daridra brāhmaṇera upākhyāna (pūjādravya pūjāvidhi, dhyāna o praṇāma sambalita)*, 3d ed., comp. and ed. Avināśacandra Mukhopādhyāya, rev. Surendranātha Bhaṭṭācārya (Calcutta: Calcutta Town Library by Kārttika Candra Dhara, 1360 B.S. [1952–53 C.E.]); and Śaṅkarācārya and Rāmeśvara, *Śrīśrīsatyanārāyaṇera pācālī: līlāvatī kalāvatī daridra brāhmaṇera kāhinī (pūjādravādi o pūjāvidhi sambalita)*, ed. Gaurāṅgasundara Bhaṭṭācārya (Calcutta: Rajendra Library, n.d.).

21. For translations of different versions of these three tales from the Vaiṣṇava *vrata kathās*, see Tony K. Stewart, "Satya Pīr: Muslim Holy Man and Hindu God," in *Religions of India in Practice*, ed. Donald S. Lopez Jr. (Princeton: Princeton University Press, 1995), 578–97; selections come from Śaṅkarācārya, Dvija Rāmabhadra, Bhāratacandra Rāya, and Ayodhyārāma Kavicandra Rāya. For the Sanskrit versions and an analysis of their pūjā, see Gudrun Bühnemann, "Examples of Occasional *Pūjās: Satyanārāyaṇavrata*," in *Pūjā: A Study in Smarta Ritual*, De Nobili Research Library Publications, vol. 15 (Vienna: Institute for Indology, University of Vienna, 1988), 200–213. For a contemporary version of the story and an account of the pūjā, see Anoop Chandola, *The Way to True Worship: A Popular Story of Hinduism* (Lanham, Md.: University Press of America, 1991).

22. The prefaces and introductions to a number of editions at the turn of the century document the widespread desire to Sanskritize the tradition. For example, in 1904, Priyanātha Ghoṣala complained bitterly about the sorry state of the textual materials and pūjā instruction. He attempted to remedy the situation by producing a clear and properly edited Sanskrit text and *paddhati* after consulting numerous printed texts and unpublished manuscripts; Priyanātha Ghoṣala, *Satyanārāyaṇa vratavyavasthā, pūjāpaddhati o pañcavidha māhātmyakathā* (Calcutta: Patrick Press, 1310 B.S. [1902–3 C.E.]). The previously noted edition by Śyāmācaraṇa Kaviratna (supra n. 8), with its twenty-eight *śirṇi* ingredients, was written with the express intention of eliminating the use of popular and misleading *pāñcālī* texts in a very self-conscious effort to clean up (Sanskritize) the tradition. In a different type of foliation, one author notes the injunction in the *Skanda Purāṇa* to make music and dance (*nṛtyagītādikaṇcaret*) while offering the pūjā has prompted him to adapt the offering of śirṇi to a musical mode, including extensive musical notation, in the text. By his own admission, he also takes the opportunity to "correct" common mistakes in theology in an effort to universalize the message; see Suranātha Bhaṭṭācārya, *Śrīśrīsatyanārāyaṇa vratakathā*, with the basic text, pūjā instruction, Bengali verse translation, and songs for accompaniment (Calcutta: B.P.M.'s Press, n.d. [132? B.S.]).

23. It is interesting that the eastern reaches of the delta region have always provided last-ditch money-making opportunities for poor brāhmaṇas, for the

dearth of brāhmaṇas in the region puts their services at a premium; even Kṛṣṇa Caitanya made the journey when his family was in financial straits. Being momentarily itinerant in the region does not seem to overly affect the status of the brāhmaṇa, but residence in the region during this period does seem to compromise status, for most of Bengal sits outside the boundaries of madhyadeśa, the traditional brahmanical homeland, and therefore lies beyond the reaches of civilization, a barbaric frontier; it is, then, the ideal place for a pīr to exercise his power.

24. It should be noted that the woodcutters' tale is always the shortest of the set, often reduced to a few lines, yet never eliminated completely, apparently because it is necessary to complete the progressive appropriation of Satya Pīr following the logic of the need to domesticate the land in stages. The extension of habitable land, then, includes social, economic, agricultural, and, with the concern for kings and righteous rule demonstrated in the final tale and other non-Vaiṣṇava versions, political dimensions.

25. This eastward push parallels the eastward shift of the Gaṅgā River. But it contrasts with the next category of "Muslim" tales, which articulate a different frontier, and one where they are already present when the Vaiṣṇavas arrive, which affects their narrative strategy or code.

26. Sukumāra Sena, *Bāṅālār sāhityera itihāsa*, vol. 1, pt. 2: 474–75.

27. Sukumāra Sena completely ignores the woodcutters' tale, while declaring the merchant's tale to be an unimaginative recapitulation of the *Dhanapatī khullana* in the *Caṇḍī maṅgala;* ibid., 471. The merchant's tale is indeed sufficiently close to be called a variant, but the question of historical priority—that is, whether Satya Pīr's story or Caṇḍī's story is earliest—is never considered.

28. And we can easily add the Nātha *yogī* and popular (but in Bengal, not necessarily Sufi) *dervish* to this set.

29. I have been unable to locate a single instance of a historical pīr or other Muslim figure being appropriated by the Bengali Hindu traditions; all other adoptions have been mythic or legendary figures. For a summary of some of these important figures, see Girīndranātha Dāsa, *Bāṅglā pīra sāhityera kathā*, which gives stories of thirty-three historical pīrs and nine legendary pīrs in Bengal during the nineteenth and early twentieth centuries.

30. Ronald B. Inden has argued that in previous centuries the genealogical histories include several mythic episodes for the royal importation of brāhmaṇas with a proper Vedic knowledge to people the land and make it properly habitable; the last of these kings fades into the historical figure of Vallāla Sena. See Inden, *Marriage and Rank in Bengali Culture* (Berkeley: University of California Press, 1976), 49–82. It should be noted that Hindu Bengal has been, including in the myths, a two-*varṇa* society, composed of brāhmaṇas and *śūdras*.

31. Ironically, but not at all surprisingly, the scholarship from Hindu nationalists treats Satya Pīr essentially the same way, perhaps taking its cue from the obvious use to which he is put in the society.

32. Kṛṣṇahari Dāsa, *Baḍa satya pīra o sandhyāvatī kaṇyāra punthi*, 214.

33. Lokamāna Hākim can be identified as Luqmān Ḥakīm, the legendary Arab sage who is mentioned in the Qur'ān (31:11–19).

34. The Jhārikhaṇḍa Forest traditionally extends through the wild regions of southwest Bengal, south of Viṣṇupura, and runs into the Midnapur districts and the northern reaches of Orissa and southeastern Bihar on part of the Chotanagpur plateau. Much of it remains a frontier today.

35. See Tony K. Stewart, "Surprising Bedfellows: Vaiṣṇava and Shi'a Alliance in Kavi Āriph's 'Tale of Lālmon,'" *International Journal of Hindu Studies* (forthcoming).

36. Dinesh Candra Sen sees this as corroborative evidence to the report of Satya Pīr being the son of the daughter of Husain Shāh; see his *Folk Literature of Bengal*, 102–3.

37. Kṛṣṇahari Dāsa, *Baḍa satya pīr*, 214–16.

38. Dinesh Candra Sen pronounces Kṛṣṇahari Dāsa unequivocally to be a Muslim, in spite of his name (*Folk Literature of Bengal*, 101 ff.); based on the content of the narrative and the direction of the action, I am inclined to agree with the general orientation (with the proviso previously stated regarding inclusion in a group). Girīndranātha Dāsa refers to him as a Bāul-Daraveśa [=Dervish] (*Bāṇglā pīra sāhityera kathā*, 470), which is, of course, simply another form of syncretism. It is perhaps significant that the woodcuts in the printed version show the image of Satya Pīr very much in the mode of a Bāul, but given the mixing of sectarian emblems of hair, clothing, bag, and so forth, it might well be that Satya Pīr proves to be more the prototype for the Bāul than the other way around, i.e., he is a generic "holy man" with associations of saṃnyāsī, vairāgī, dervish, pīr, fakīr, etc.

39. Kṛṣṇahari Dāsa, *Baḍa satya pīr*, 206–14.

40. This is śirṇi, although he does not call it that in this passage, for then it might well be interpreted by the antagonists as an offering, and that would be premature for its place in the plot. But the refusal to give him such food is a direct refusal to offer worship to Satya Pīr, and that is an offense that requires punishment.

41. This is a variant of the old rope trick.

42. This is the rope trick.

43. It is perhaps ironic that it is the exclusive intolerance of the brāhmaṇa that is brought into question, rather than that of the Muslim, who is all too frequently characterized in scholarship and the contemporary press by that charge.

44. Schimmel, *Mystical Dimensions of Islam*, 117, quoting 'Abūl-Majd Majdūd Sanā'i's *Ḥadīqat al-ḥaqīqat wa sharī't aṭ-tarīqat*.

2

Beyond Turk and Hindu

Crossing the Boundaries in Indo-Muslim Romance

Christopher Shackle

If there is a discrete South Asian context shaped by geography as well as by history, then the Panjab resembles other parts of the subcontinent while also projecting the cultural influence of its own topographical features. Above all, we are concerned with cultural geography, and it is our argument that the topographical features of the Panjab provide a backdrop that fosters a strategic tension, otherwise seen as a fluidity of metaphor, that characterizes the literature of this region at the same time that it influences Indo-Muslim identity.

Dichotomies and Unions

What are those features of Indo-Muslim identity within the premodern world of Islam that have been shaped by cultural geography? At one level, they embrace physical setting and material culture, yet they also include that great range of nonmaterial phenomena which, whether as customs and attitudes or as languages and legends, form everyday culture, and it is the interplay of physical setting with its connotative, everyday expression that helps make Indo-Muslim identity at once different from, but allied with, its counterpart: Indic identity.[1]

Above all, identity is shaped by what Tony Stewart has called "pragmatic concerns of survival," and while these concerns, in his apt words, "cross whatever imaginary divide we construct between Hindu and Muslim," they, in turn, are shaped by class markers and expectations. In India, and especially in the Panjab, the cultural disjunctions between elite and native, *sharīf* and *desī*, are too marked to be ignored. Nowhere are they more apparent than in the area of language, with its exceptionally marked cultural diglossia between Persian as a widely used elite standard language, both imported and pan-Indian, and localized Indo-Aryan or Dravidian languages.

Immediately associated with this contrast is the presence of two types of creative literature. The cultivation of Persian poetry was always a central marker of the cultural identity of the elite,[2] whose efforts to distance themselves from Indic cultural associations led to the formation of an elaborately self-contained symbolic system underlying the interlinked genres of *qasida*, *ghazal*, and *maṣnavī*. Such purism was not limited to Muslim elites; it also extended to the practice of Hindu poets from the Persianizing classes.[3] Increasingly from the late premodern period, we find more popular types of lyric and narrative poetry being cultivated by Muslim as well as non-Muslim authors in indigenous languages. Such verse proliferates in styles sometimes entirely indigenous and at other times a blend of these with elements from the Persian tradition.

In other words, the wide-ranging and profoundly differentiated views of the premodern period are not associated with the Hindu-Muslim divide itself; they are marked more by class than by creedal separations.[4] And among the genres of poetry that attempt to cross class boundaries we also find crucial examples of the interplay between Muslim and Hindu sensibilities. None is more intensive than Panjabi love lyrics. It is in these lyrics that we find the theme of love between Muslim and Hindu (or between Turk and Hindu). Such love is at once transgressive and assimilative, for at the same point that Panjabi poets highlight it as illicit love, they also undermine the very categories Muslim and Hindu as oppositional or incommensurate.

The Transcendence of the Lyrical Setting

Annemarie Schimmel has explored the opposition of Turk and Hindu in classical Persian poetry,[5] but it takes a different turn in South Asia precisely because of the cross-class and cross-creedal intensity of flowering regional verse, such as the Panjabi love lyrics that are our principal subject.

Consider the lyrics of the Qādirī poet Bullhe Shāh (1680–1758). In the famous *kāfī* whose refrain asks, "*Bullhā kīh jānāṅ maiṅ kaun?*" (Bullhā, how should I know who I am?) the poet answers his own question in one verse. Its rhymes tumble, in English as also in the original Panjabi:

Neither Arab am I nor man of Lahore
Nor Indian from the town of Nagaur
Neither Hindu am I nor Turk of Peshawar.[6]

With a complementary appropriateness, the same simple idea recurs in Bullhe Shāh's poems composed in a "Hindi" style reflecting Hindu religious vocabulary,[7] as in the kāfī whose refrain opens, "Hindu, no! nor Musalman," with the final verse:

Bullhā, once God filled my thoughts,
Hindus, Turks, I quit both sorts.

Through their continually vivid repetition of such fundamentals,[8] Bullhe Shāh and the other great local Sufi lyricists of the later Mughal period, like their *nirgun bhakti* and Sikh predecessors and contemporaries from the other side of the Muslim-Hindu divide, have continued as mother tongue literary classics, but they have also molded in the Panjab a diffuse conception of South Asian religious identity that is as immensely influential as it is dimly understood.

A major difficulty is translation, not just from Panjabi to English but from the idiom of the aorist tense, which denotes past continuous action, without limits in either time or space, to the unmarked past tense in English. In the original Panjabi, both the above quotations from Bullhe Shāh confirm that the simplest of truths are aorist in their expression. Once the inner meaninglessness of outward religious and social distinctions is grasped, it can be grasped forever, and the preferred practice is to internalize such insights repetitively and permanently through song.[9] The message and its form reinforce each other: Just as the lyric naturally elides with the aorist tense, so the primary status of the lyric in the provincial as well as the Persianate literatures of South Asia derives from this intrinsic timelessness of the genre.[10] It is particularly suitable for singing, which makes its rhyming verses even easier to memorize.

Ironically, it is just this universalizing quality of timelessness which makes the Sufi lyric an ideal justification for academic generalizations about Islam, generalizations that dwell on the eternal constancy of its irenic strands.[11] What is important to note, however, is its originary impulse: not that it is eternal but that it evokes the eternal or the timeless by its ability to move between different registers of verse and connotation.

Without actually doing so, it seems to cross *all* dividing lines—time and place, creed and class.

It is this boundary crossing that gives Sufi poetry its power in shaping a distinctive language of identity. The existence of worldly identities, rooted in the realities of everyday life, is essential for its structure and message. These identities—whether of religion, ethnicity, occupation, or class—provide the critical backdrop that creates the literary form. The evocation of these identities is in many respects central to the evocation of place, to the distinctive cultural geography that shapes an image of the Panjab. And yet it is central to the genre—and to the *qiṣṣa*, the Panjabi love lyrics of which we will have more to say—that such identities are repeatedly transgressed by love. Indeed, it is the constant tension between these that defines a framework for understanding identities, a framework whose contours can only be understood with the generic contours of this literary production.

The interplay of these elements in defining a distinctive regional ethos was suggested in Persian verse by the *Nairang-e ʿIshq* (1683) by Ġhanīmat of Kunjah near Gujrat, which became the most popular masnavi to have been produced by a provincial Persian poet from the Panjab.[12] Why? ʿAzīz (Noble), son of the local governor, falls in love with Shāhid (Beauty), the orphaned child of poor parents who has been trained by a troupe of traveling entertainers (*ṭavā'if*). ʿAzīz confounds all expectations of class and custom by installing Shāhid as his live-in partner. Shāhid is even described in such tantalizingly gender-neutral fashion that her feminine identity only becomes apparent to the reader after she has finally left ʿAzīz. Their separation occurs on a hunting trip, where Shāhid meets and falls instantly in love with the handsome country lad Vafa (Fidelity). After a succession of events perhaps too swift not to have been drawn from life, Beauty marries Fidelity. Deftly the poet downplays this crossing of the urban-rural divide, even though it would have been evident to all listeners. Instead, he focuses on the affair between the noble born (*sharifzada*) and the dancing girl (*ṭā'ifa*).

Yet the verse itself makes clear the extent to which Ġhanīmat's world becomes very much one of town rather than country, nearer to the Hira Mandi than to Hīr, in the grace of its opening invocation of the Panjab as "land of love":

No land so irresistible I've seen
None matches fair Panjab's delightful scene . . .

To glimpse Panjab its only aim—
Kashmir at heart is turned to shame . . .
In all its cities beauties throng the mart
In eagerness to buy a lover's heart.[13]

This prologue undoubtedly had a special resonance for the poem's original local audience,[14] but by the mid-nineteenth century, when *Nairang-e 'Ishq*, along with so much Persian poetry, was translated into Urdu, it added no more than an exotic touch to the opening pages of the version, less graceful both in its meter and in its enforced preservation of the masculine gender for Beauty, which was produced far to the east in Avadh by Bhagvant Rā'e "Rāḥat" of Kakori as the *Nigāristān-e Ulfat* (1852):

The land of Panjab is so fair—
Canals with water flow there.
A country so cool and so clear
Whose breezes chill even Kashmir.
Its beauties wait ready to take
The goods of both Brahmin and Shaikh.[15]

There is a somewhat pallid exoticism here, perhaps to be expected in a fairly faithful adaptation. But in its exhibition of this quality, Rāḥat's "Gallery of Intimacy" typifies the story of the Urdu masnavi in northern India. Apart from copies and translation, it is dominated by the religiously neutral fairy-tale mode of its only acknowledged masterpieces, the *Siḥr ul Bayān* of Mīr Ḥasan (d. 1786) and the *Gulzār-e Nasīm* (1833) of Pandit Dayā Shankar Nasīm (d. 1843).[16]

The Lovers' Inventory

I draw attention to the fate of one lyric in later Urdu rendition, in contrast to its original Persian/Panjabi composition, in order to demonstrate how place, though no more than a seeming backdrop, is nonetheless crucial to the everyday expectations of poet and listeners alike. Few genres show a more powerful attachment to the specificities of place than the Panjabi verse romance called the qiṣṣa (plural qiṣṣe),[17] which was largely the creation of Panjabi Muslim poets.[18] Here the attachment to place supersedes not only class and creed but also gender markings. Sometimes the Panjabi kāfīs revolve around key aspects of individual stories, giving ample scope for the poet to make affecting use of the well-known Indic preference for the feminine persona as the voice of the lyric. Elsewhere, use is made of the favorite topos of the "lovers' inventory," in which whole lists of lovers are lined up as collective testimony to the power of love. Like most such topoi, this has its classic Persian exemplars, but it brings to the fore one obvious criterion for distinguishing Indo-Muslim literatures from those of other parts of the Islamic world—their use of local stories. Whereas the Urdu *ghazal* relies for its characters on the old stories that were given their definitive narrative shape in the Persian masnavis of Niẓāmī (d. 1199), Khusrau (d. 1325), and Jāmī (d. 1494), the Panjabi kāfī is characterized by an abundance of references to local romantic legends. The lovers' inventory, while grounding Panjabi stories in a literary genealogy suggesting the power of love as a defining civilizational frame, underscored as well each story's specific place and context.

As always, Bullhe Shāh provides a particularly long and fine example, embracing both Islamic and Indic mythology, as well as some of the most famous local lovers, in Kāfī no. 65.

First love the mighty came on Hīr
And then her Rāṅjhā pierced his ear
To wed his Ṣāḥibāṅ so dear
Was Mirzā sacrificed.
Losing Sassī in the desert hot
Drowning Sohnī on her unbaked pot
Love for Roḍā did destruction plot—
It had him chopped and sliced.

Such lovers' inventories, moved from the international sets found in the Persian masnavi to include local tales, are found in the Panjabi qiṣṣa; as I have suggested elsewhere, these came by the later Mughal period to be a more or less consciously articulated part of a region's "vernacular literature capable of re-articulating the Muslim identity of its inhabitants in local terms by drawing on the deepest range of their cultural roots."[19] Although they could become a rather mechanical device in the qiṣṣe of inferior later poets, they continued to be used to powerful effect in the works of the best poets, even into the nineteenth century. A good example is provided by that last master of the qiṣṣa genre, the great Panjabi poet and Qādirī saint Miyāṅ Muḥammad Bakhsh (1830–1907) of Khari in the Mirpur district of Jammu, now in Azad Kashmir.[20]

With a fine symbolic appropriateness, the completion of his first masterpiece almost exactly coincided with the British defeat of the rebels outside Delhi at Badli ki Sarai on 8 June 1857, which won them the Ridge whence their catastrophic assault on the old capital of the Indo-Muslim world was soon to be launched. This was Miyāṅ Muḥammad's qiṣṣa on the story of *Sohnī Mahīṅvāl,* finished on the afternoon of Wednesday, 12 Shavvāl A.H. 1273. The section of its prologue devoted to description of the havoc-wreaking workings of love contains the following finely planned inventory:

> Love caused the sight of Lailā's face to be the cause of Majnūn's pain
> It used Shīrīn's sweet lips to steal Parvez's heart and kill Farhād
> From Yūsuf's coat too it displayed a dream to snatch Zulaikhā's heart
> Jalāli's fire made Roḍā burn, love dazzled Rāṅjhā with Hīr's flash
> Beneath bright Chandarbadan's sun, Ma'yār's green garden turned to ash
> By Sohnī's spark from this same fire was Mahīṅvāl reduced to ash
> Encamped within illusion dwells the essence of the Absolute.[21]

Here, as often in such inventories, the primary reference is to the universal romances of the Persianate world, whose three most famous representatives are continually exploited core elements of the poetic language of all genres. Collectively they embrace the three symbolic worlds of Arabia with the Lailā-Majnūn story, of Iran with Shīrīn's rival lovers Parvez and Farhād, and of the Qur'an with the tale of Yūsuf and Zulaikhā, as mediated through Jāmī's version.[22] Yet these three great romances—even disregarding all their subsidiary characters and subplots—embrace almost every conceivable kind of social as well as psychic boundary crossing, and it is this suspension of the everyday which evokes their unusual force. It also mirrors the madness of love, which may be exacerbated by tribal rivalry, as in the case of Lailā and Majnūn, or abetted by the disparities of status between technician and prince, as happened for Farhād in his rivalry over Shīrīn with Khusrau Parvez, or challenged by social and religious, sexual and spiritual hierarchies, which must have separated a passionate pagan lady and chastely enslaved prophet in the tale of Zulaikhā and Yūsuf.

If it is this supreme transregional trinity which provides the archetypal frame for the modeling of the local romances, the latter—in all but the feeblest adaptations—also preserve an independent vitality by virtue of their separate local origin, and while one must stress both continuity and change, it is important to note how pragmatic concerns for everyday vitality constitute the heart of the literary "matter of Panjab." Like most things Indo-Islamic, these local romances participate profoundly in both the Islamic and the Indic worlds but also emerge as entities sui generis independent of either precisely because the everyday world is not lost but heightened in their nimble narratives.

At the same time, of course, the lovers' inventory also sets up a tension between the universal claims of the great romances of the Islamicate world and the more localized significance of the settings tied to the Panjab. Many poets of the first order of creativity ignored local stories in their lists in favor of the international romances of the Persianate world. The very embeddedness of Panjabi stories in the local and everyday life made them not only less desirable for some elites but also less accessible to neat categorization in such lovers' inventories. That these lists were far from being fully standardized is suggested by the differences between Bullhe Shāh's list and Miyāṅ Muḥammad's. But it is significant that both these inventories did include several stories with Panjabi settings along with those of more universal Islamicate provenance, including the story of Sohnī and Mahīṅvāl; the tale of Mirzā and Ṣāḥibāṅ, typologically important for its bridging of the romantic and the heroic;[23] and the story of Sassī and Punnūṅ, the only one of these four with a non-Panjabi setting.[24] Perhaps most prominent generally in such inventories was the story of Hīr and Rāṅjhā. Lying at the very heart of the local romantic canon, this story furnishes much of Bullhe Shāh's symbolism.

Crossing the Boundaries

First, let us consider the hero of these romances. All have a Muslim youth as their hero, the Ego of their psychic universe. The hero is defined through his adventures, inspired by a love that must involve suffering even if it does not end in tragedy. Both the object of the hero's love and the secondary characters with whom his adventures bring him into contact collectively include many varieties of Other, different from the hero in sex, status, age, origin, or belief (or in various combinations of these). The hero's quest for his beloved and his encounters with secondary characters accordingly involves him in the crossing of boundaries, leading to at least partial loss of his initial identity—typically through his becoming a *faqīr* or *yogi*—and his partial assimilation of a different identity. This new identity at least prepares him for his destined union with the Other, which is as likely as not to be finally achieved only after the further loss of identity consequent upon physical death of both Ego and Other. This shift in register to underscore the value of *fana*, or annihilation of Ego, is especially crucial for explicitly Sufi poets like Miyāṅ Muḥammad, but Sufi categories also appear in other qiṣṣe, even those by non-Muslim poets.

What are the typical implications of these changes for the hero's identity as a Muslim? While an additional poignancy may be conveyed to a romance by a religious incompatibility between the lovers, Muslim-Hindu relationships are no more central to most of the Panjabi romances than is the contrast between Turk and Hindu to most Indo-Persian poetry, or indeed than romantic connections with Muslims would appear to be in the largely Hindu-inspired narrative poetry of classical Hindi literature.[25] Differences of status or origin within Indo-Muslim society are of greater concern, and the recurring dynamism of the poetry is its ability to reflect the tension within sharp class divisions without violating their actual boundaries. Fixed identities are underscored even as they are transcended by the structure of the genre.

Consider the most popular story of the premodern Panjabi Muslim romance, Hīr and Rāṅjhā, which reaches its climax in the great qiṣṣa by Vāriṣ Shāh.[26] When the halfway point of the story is reached with Hīr's marriage to Saidā the Kheṛā, Rāṅjhā has to undergo the usual hero's transformation into an ascetic before he will be able to win her back. A Muslim *pīr* may have played this role, but the Muslims of premodern India had an even more striking model of asceticism across the religious frontier in the yogis of Hinduism,[27] and it is into a yogi that Rāṅjhā is regularly described as having been transformed. Already in the earliest extant Panjabi version, supposedly composed before 1650 by Damodar Gulāṭī, Rāṅjhā follows Hīr's written instructions and seeks initiation from the spiritual chief of the great center of the Gorakhnāthī Kānphaṭ ("split-eared") yogis on the lofty summit of the Tilla Jogian in District Jhelum.[28] In the description of their straightforward encounter,[29] ample employment is made of that useful stylistic device always so readily available to writers in chronically multilingual India. The Hindified expressions put into Rāṅjhā's mouth demonstrate his readiness for yogic initiation:

Then Rāṅjhā made entreaties with humility:

From you, whose favor is salvation's guarantee,
For yoga I ask like Gopīchand and Bhartharī.[30]

In Vāriṣ Shāh, of course, the implications of all this are magnificently teased out,[31] and along with a dalliance across religious boundaries he introduces a sexual undercurrent to this supposedly ascetic episode. It is given expression by Bālnāth's jealous disciples: shocked to see the favorable impression Rāṅjhā has made, they exclaim: "A taste for boys affects those yogis, whose wits God has confounded!"

Whatever else its multiple implications, Rāṅjhā's yogic transformation is not about actual conversion, any more than the pretended hostilities of his subsequent courtship of Hīr are literally about interfaith relations, although they may be taken as such metaphorically. At least for the period from 1650 to 1850, when the Panjabi qiṣṣa tradition was at its most creative, the literary evidence would not suggest that relations of this kind were of such profoundly overriding concern to Muslims of the Panjab that they needed to be explored through creative writing. There is only one well-known Panjabi qiṣṣa from the period that does explore this theme explicitly, the exception that perhaps proves the rule.

This is the tale of Chandarbadan and Ma'yār, frequently cited in the inventories of other qiṣṣe. It is exceptional not only in its theme but also, tellingly, in that its origin is Indian but not Panjabi; its provenance is the Deccan. The story was first treated as the report of an incident that actually occurred in the time of Ibrāhīm ʻĀdilshāh (1580–1626) in the artless Dakani Urdu masnavi by Muqīmī (d. c. 1665), where the lover is called Mahyār.[32] Its contents may be conveniently recalled in an adaptation of Schimmel's deft summary: A Muslim merchant, Mahyār, fell in love with Chandarbadan, the daughter of a Hindu raja. When she undertook a pilgrimage to Kadrikot he confessed his love to her. Being rejected, he spent a whole year as a hermit in the jungle. The following year, when Chandarbadan visited the temple again, he cast himself at her feet; but she turned away, amazed that he was still alive. Dismayed, he committed suicide. Ibrāhīm ordered that Mahyār should be given an honorable burial. The funeral procession with the bier stopped at the princess's mansion and could not move farther. Deeply moved by Mahyār's love which lasted even beyond the grave, Chandarbadan embraced Islam, clad herself in pure white garments, and placed herself beside him on the bier. The two lovers were buried together.[33] "By no means an outstanding work of art," as Schimmel charitably remarks, Muqīmī's poem is chiefly remarkable for its naiveté. Only occasionally does this perhaps bestow a certain pathos, as on Chandarbadan's tentative first steps to Islam:

> She said: "How should I purify myself?
> I know not how to purify myself."[34]

Transmitted to the northwest by one of those routes which always look as if they should be far easier to document than in fact turns out to be the case,[35] the Chandarbadan story resurfaced in Panjabi, perhaps receiving its first full-length treatment in the qiṣṣa by the prolific Aḥmad Yār (d. 1848).[36] The most popular published version, however, was that by Imām Bakhsh (d. 1863).[37] Chandarbadan is firmly located in Hindu India as the daughter of Rangāpatī, *raja* of Patna! Ma'yār, still a wealthy merchant's son in spite of the slight change to his name, first sees her in a picture painted by an artist friend who glimpsed her on a visit to a temple. It takes him a year to come before her. By now a faqir who rejects her offers of money, he entreats her as a humble Farhād to her royal Shīrīn. She, however, will have none of him on religious grounds: "I am a Hindu, you a Muslim—we have no ties of faith." To which he retorts: "Love cares not for attributes, nor lovers for creeds and faith, O queen!"[38]

There are many more exchanges of this type, whose frequency in most types of premodern Indian literature is actually far less than the predilections of many modern historians sometimes lead them to suggest. The story follows a somewhat tangled course, partly because of well-meaning interventions by the Muslim king who adopts Ma'yār as his pet madman; it involves various yearlong journeys from one distant city to another. Finally, on the insistent prompting of Ma'yār's stationary bier, Chandarbadan is granted the doubly joyous fate prescribed for Hindu lovers in the Muslim romance: conversion and burial with her beloved. As the poet observes:

> The whole world knows that it will never do,
> O king, to couple Muslim with Hindu.[39]

From Mughal to Mahīṅvāl

The Chandarbadan story expands the spectrum of Panjabi romantic verse, but in the premodern period its subject matter was nowhere near as compelling as that of the principal romances of the Panjab. Why? Because the geographical universe of these core romances is symbolically established by the river glades where Hīr first comes to Rāṅjhā and the Tilla where he becomes a yogi, and then almost equally important, by the desert sands in which Sassī dies in search of Punnūṅ, and by the rivers that give the Panjab its name. In this context, the greatest of these is the Chenab, the Panjab's great "river of love," and the love story to which it is most central, the legend of Sohnī and Mahīṅvāl.

Although this romance furnishes significant symbolical material to earlier lyric poetry, notably to Bullhe Shāh,[40] full-length versions do not seem to predate 1800.[41] Of the pre-1850 versions, Aḥmad Yār is said to have composed a qiṣṣa on this theme, as did Hāshim Shāh and Qādir Yār. All these, however, were completely overtaken in popularity by the inflated version produced in 1849 by Fażal Shāh (1828–90).[42] Besides being a gifted wordsmith adept at the flashy verbal effects so favored by Panjabi audiences, Fażal Shāh was fortunate in his close association with Lahore at a period when the rise of the publishing industry in that city was to reduce most other centers of Panjabi literary creation to relative insignificance. His version of Sohnī Mahīṅvāl thus came to enjoy an immense reputation in the late nineteenth century.

The classic story line common to all these versions tells how ʿIzzat Beg (Sir Noble), the son of a wealthy merchant in Bukhara, comes to Delhi with a caravan of goods to trade. On its return trip, the caravan halts at Gujrat by the Chenab. There ʿIzzat Beg falls in love with Sohnī (Beautiful), the lovely daughter of Tullā the potter. Bidding his companions farewell, he spends all his money buying pots so as to have a pretext to keep on seeing her, until he is forced by poverty into looking after Tullā's buffaloes as Mahīṅvāl (Herdsman). He becomes a faqir, with a cell out in the wilderness. Sohnī slips out to see him there, using a pot as a float to get her across the river. Mahīṅvāl feeds her fish kebabs, for which once—when bad weather makes fishing impossible—he offers a piece of his own thigh. Eventually Sohnī's sister-in-law discovers her secret and substitutes an unbaked pot. Unwittingly using this to cross on the following wild and stormy winter's night, Sohnī is drowned. As soon as he hears this dreadful news, Mahīṅvāl plunges in to join her in death.

Such climactic episodes act as the focus of attention for most of the qiṣṣa writers, along with the lyricists and the artists who produced visual representations of the story. In that qiṣṣa of 1857 by Miyāṅ Muḥammad, however, with which all this exploration of an inventory began, other emphases are also notably at work. Like all Miyāṅ Muḥammad's work, his Sohnī Mahīṅvāl has a meditative quality entirely in keeping with its profoundly Sufi focus. Along with this overtly mystical dimension, there also emerges one that appears to address one of the essential issues of Indo-Muslim identity: the relation between the majesty of an authority that has come from abroad and the realities of indigenous existence. This relation between foreigner and native is typically visualized as one between male and female, which may of course have its own overtones for modern Indian critics,[43] but equally crucial is the way in which the theme can be updated and criss-crossed from one historical context to another.

Although this theme was certainly available to earlier Indo-Muslim romance, the Chandarbadan story chose instead to become stuck with Ma'yār's bier. Only when Indo-Muslim political authority was definitively lost, as it had been in the Panjab and Kashmir, first to the Sikhs and Dogras, then to the British, did it perhaps become possible to begin undertaking a fuller imaginative exploration of how the actual history of Muslims in the Panjab reflected, or deflected, their present and future identity. It may be therefore plausibly argued that the Sohnī Mahīṅvāl story emerged into full popularity at just that time in the mid-nineteenth century because its shift in register suited the crisis of declining Mughal elites.

Although Miyāṅ Muḥammad's version is too rich a poem to be properly analyzed here, some impression of its scope may be conveyed through sketching the hero's progress from Mirzā ʿIzzat Beg the wealthy Mughal to the humble Mahīṅvāl. Along with frequent prophetic glimpses of what is to come and retrospective glances at what has occurred earlier in the story, besides a continual swirl of lovers' inventories around its every point, one of the features that helps to make Miyāṅ Muḥammad's poem a far more substantial creation than might be indicated by its relatively brief physical length is the solidity of its geographical setting. After ʿIzzat Beg has left Delhi, city of royal palaces and site of the holy tomb of Khwāja Niẓām ud Dīn (the Chishti pīr and paragon of Indo-Muslim piety), he comes to Lahore, where he visits the tomb of Jahāngīr and enjoys its splendid gardens. He then approaches the Chenab (24–25):

The Mirzā passed the Beas and Ravi,
brought to the Chenab by fate
Whose magic waters steal all sense,
and love's delirium instate.

This is where his fate is to be decided (25):

> The waters of the Chenab-crossing
> made the noble Mughal ponder.

For it is here that Sohnī's chastity has been preserved for him (27):

> Who'd touch the Mughal's trust?
> What God had kept fault-free and pure?

When he meets Sohnī in Gujrat, he abandons his home outside India forever (34):

> The Mughal, slain by love,
> cast off his Balkh-Bukhara for Gujrat.

The cost of loving her is the sacrifice of all his former status and wealth (36):

> The Mughal now was Mahīṅvāl,
> once rich, impoverished by love.

Even his name and title are lost in this fated demotion from the ranks of the foreign-born *ashraf* (38):

> Once Mirzā 'Izzat Beg, now victim of her eyes, her Mahīṅvāl.

There is, of course, much more to this complex narrative, which abounds with subtleties of detail.[44] Overall, however, it might be said that Miyāṅ Muḥammad's achievement in his richly reflective picture of the changes undergone by Mahīṅvāl is to have shown how Grandeur is fated to be lost through the pull of the Other, leading to Disempowerment, even to Annihilation (fana). In its own way, this is a spectacular attempt to wrestle with the ambiguities and perplexities of premodern Indo-Muslim identity, and it is in the multifaceted appeal of this as a story both local and universal that the Panjabi romantic verse can be said to lie enduringly at the heart of the "matter of Panjab."

Notes

1. The use of *everyday* here is suggestive of an approach counter to Freudian and Marxist analyses alike. It elides more closely with the reflections of Bakhtin, or at least the early Bakhtin, who argued that time and the world become historical not just in the festival but in the tension between the anticipation of the festival and the commonplace expectations of the everyday; in premodern India, as in premodern Europe, poetry bridges the register of the carnival and the ha-

bitual. For a general discussion of some of these issues, but from an entirely Eurocentric viewpoint, see Peter Osborne, *The Politics of Time: Modernity and Avant-Garde* (London: Verso, 1995), esp. chap. 5.

2. See Francis Robinson, "Perso-Islamic Culture in India from the Seventeenth to the Early Twentieth Century," in Robert L. Canfield, ed., *Turko-Persia in Historical Perspective* (Cambridge: Cambridge University Press), esp. 106–7.

3. Most recently surveyed in Saʿīd ʿAbdullāh, *Adabiyāt-e fārsī dar miyān-e hinduvān*, trans. from Urdu into Persian by Muḥammad Aslam Khān (Tehran, 1992).

4. See Carl W. Ernst, *Eternal Garden: Mysticism, History, and Politics at a South Asian Sufi Center* (Albany: State University of New York Press, 1992), 22–37.

5. Annemarie Schimmel, "Turk and Hindu: A Poetical Image and Its Application to Historical Fact," in Speros Vryonis, ed., *Islam and Cultural Change in the Middle Ages* (Wiesbaden: Otto Harrassowitz, 1975), 107–26.

6. *Kulliyyāt-e Bullhe Shāh*, ed. Faqīr Muḥammad Faqīr (Lahore: Panjabi Adabi Academy, 1960), kāfī no. 27. Due to the limits of space, and in order to project the broader points of this theme, I have not included the original Panjabi verse. For those who seek the text, either consult the just cited edition or contact me at the School of Oriental and African Studies.

7. For further examples, see Denis Matringe, "Kṛṣṇaite and Nāth Elements in the Poetry of the Eighteenth-Century Panjabi Sūfī Bullhe Śāh," in R. S. McGregor, ed., *Devotional Literature in South Asia: Current Research, 1985–1988* (Cambridge: Cambridge University Press, 1992), 190–206.

8. It may, however, be observed that secondary sources reflecting twentieth-century enthusiasms for earlier statements of communal harmony (see note 21 below) make it easy to overestimate the actual frequency of such repetitions. In Bullhe Shāh, for instance, other notable instances of "neither Turk nor Hindu" are substantially confined to isolated verses in kāfī nos. 21, 22, 48, 90, 95, 118, and 120.

9. Here, as Annemarie Schimmel's many wide-ranging surveys have so well demonstrated, it must be remembered that negations of formal religious differences have always been characteristic of Sufi poetry throughout the Islamic world, so that the negation of the Turk-Hindu distinction is no more than an expansion—albeit one with a particular local relevance—of such already well established denials of difference as the equations between Kaʿba and idol-temple. See the Urdu Sufi verses cited in Christopher Shackle, "Urdu as a Side-line: The Poetry of Khwāja Ghulām Farīd," in Shackle, ed., *Urdu and Muslim South Asia: Studies in Honour of Ralph Russell* (London: School of Oriental and African Studies, 1989), 82–83.

10. For the general dominance of the lyric in Asian poetic systems, see Earl Miner, *Comparative Poetics: An Intercultural Essay on Theories of Literature* (Princeton: Princeton University Press, 1990), esp. 9, 82.

11. This does little justice to the Sufi lyricists' emphasis, in full conformity

with universal human experience, that the transcendence of otherness is inherently fraught with pain. A particular role here is played by the interpretations of Hindu writers, especially by Lajwanti Rama Krishna, *Pañjābī Sūfī Poets, A.D. 1460–1900* (Calcutta: Oxford University Press, 1938), a doctoral thesis long overdue for replacement as a standard work of reference in English, although not by S. R. Sharda, *Sufi Thought: Its Development in Panjab and Its Impact on Panjabi Literature* (New Delhi: Munshiram Manoharlal, 1972). The necessary corrective is provided by the best Pakistani critics, but unfortunately it is not available in English; see, e.g., ʿAlī ʿAbbās Jalālpūrī, *Vaḥdat ul Vujūd te Panjābī Shāʿirī* (Lahore: Pakistan Panjabi Adabi Board, 1977).

12. See Christopher Shackle, "Persian Poetry and Qadiri Sufism in Late Mughal India: Ghanimat Kunjahi and His *Mathnawi, Nayrang-i ʿIshq*," in L. Lewisohn and D. Morgan, eds., *Late Classical Persianate Sufism* (Oxford: Oneworld, 1999).

13. *Nairang-e ʿIshq* (Lahore: Panjabi Adabi Academy, 1962), 8–9.

14. Yet it does not convey the nationalist sentiments doubtless intended to be evoked by the later inclusion of the passage in a Pakistani anthology, Muhammad Ikrām, ed., *Armaghān-e Pāk*, 2d ed. (Karachi: Idāra-e Maṭbū'āt-e Pākistan, 1953), 249–50.

15. *Nigāristān-e Ulfat* (Lucknow: Gulzār-e Avadh Press, 1899), 5–6.

16. The traditional comparison between the two is presented in supercilious summary by Muhammad Sadiq, *A History of Urdu Literature* (London: Oxford University Press, 1964), 138–42. Besides the Urdu critical studies cited in the preceding note, see D. J. Matthews, C. Shackle, and Shāhrukh Ḥusain, *Urdu Literature* (London: Urdu Markaz, 1985), esp. 28 ff., 66–69, for a brief account of the Urdu masnavi in English.

17. Described with many further references to the secondary bibliography in Christopher Shackle, "Transition and Transformation in Vāriṣ Shāh's Hīr," in C. Shackle and R. Snell, eds., *The Indian Narrative: Perspective and Patterns* (Wiesbaden: Otto Harrassowitz, 1992), 241–63, esp. 243–48, 263.

18. For reasons yet to be investigated in that comparative framework of Indo-Muslim literary studies which has still to be properly established, the romance also appears to be a genre of relatively much greater importance in Panjabi than in such typologically similar Indo-Muslim literatures as those produced in Sindhi or Kashmiri, as described, for example, in Annemarie Schimmel, *Sindhi Literature* (Wiesbaden: Otto Harrassowitz, 1974), and Braj B. Kachru, *Kashmiri Literature* (Wiesbaden: Otto Harrassowitz, 1981).

19. "Early Vernacular Poetry," 288.

20. I am engaged in a fuller study of Miyāṅ Muḥammad, whose pivotal position for generic studies of masnavi and qiṣṣa may be indicated here only in passing by a bare mention of his unique Panjabi version of the *Nairang-e ʿIshq*. Lack of space, unfortunately, prevents a fuller discussion of this most suggestive poem.

21. Muḥammad Bakhsh, *Sohnī Mahīṅvāl* (Jhelum: Malik Ġhulām Nūr, 1964), 11–12.

22. The poem is known to have been a particular favorite of Miyāṅ Muḥammad's. See the abridged English prose translation by David Pendlebury (London: Octagon Press, 1980). For Niẓāmī's versions of the other two romances, which were probably a good deal less familiar to most qiṣṣa poets, it would be sufficient to cite here the English summaries in Peter J. Chelkowski, *Mirror of the Invisible World: Tales from the Khamseh of Nizami* (New York: Metropolitan Museum of Art, 1975), 21–67.

23. The most famous version is attributed to Pīlū (c. 1600) and is recorded in R. C. Temple, *The Legends of the Panjab*, 3 vols. (Bombay: Education Society's Press, 1884–1900), 3:1–23.

24. The classic version of this story, set in the river and deserts of Sind, is the short qiṣṣa (c. 1800) by Hashim Shāh, translated by Christopher Shackle (Lahore: Vanguard Books, 1985), and given in an incomplete bardic version in Temple, *Legends*, 3:24–37. The differences in the structuring of Panjabi and Sindhi identity might be partly mapped in terms of the inventory of such narratives and the frames of their transmission. Even a superficial comparison will show quite marked differences in Sindhi, for example, in the stories drawn on for the encyclopedic lyrical treatment (which is quite without real parallel in Panjabi) of the classic *Risālo* of Shāh ʿAbd ul Laṭīf (d. 1753), most recently treated in English in Durreshahwar Sayed, *The Poetry of Shāh Abd al-Latif* (Jamshoro/Hyderabad: Sindhi Adabi Board, 1988).

25. Little evidence to the contrary, at least, is forthcoming from R. S. McGregor, *Hindi Literature from Its Beginnings to the Nineteenth Century* (Wiesbaden: Otto Harrassowitz, 1984). The Sufi romance in Avadhi is, of course, an important case apart but one which cannot be properly addressed here.

26. See further Shackle, "Transition and Transformation."

27. This is shown by Simon Digby in a series of chronologically and geographically wide-ranging studies.

28. The qiṣṣa of Pūran Bhagat is more closely concerned with yogis than the Hīr story and perhaps for this very reason is popular across the communal boundary in the Panjab, even though by far the best-known version is by the Muslim Qādir Yār (1802–91). See especially M. Athar Tahir, *Qādir Yār: A Critical Introduction* (Lahore: Pakistan Panjabi Adabi Board, 1988), 97–99, plates IX–XIII.

29. Gurdit Singh Premi, ed., *Damodar Rachnavali* (Patiala: Bhasha Vibhag, 1974), 192–96, whence the following quotation from *pauri* 673.

30. See Temple's introductory note to the "Legend of Raja Gopal Chand" (in the dramatic format of a Hariyanvi *svang*) in *Legends*, 2:1–77. The Gopichand story is an "anti-romance" quite as important for the understanding of premodern Hindu cultural identity of the Panjab as the romances considered in this essay are for its Muslim counterpart.

31. See my "Transition and Transformation," 255–59.

32. Muḥammad Akbar ud Dīn Siddīqī, ed., *Maṣnavī Chandarbadan-o Ma'yār* (Hyderabad: Majlis-e Isha'at-e Dakani Makhtutat and Dakhini Sahitya Prakashan Samiti, 1956).

33. Annemarie Schimmel, *Classical Urdu Literature from the Beginning to Iqbal* (Wiesbaden: Otto Harrassowitz, 1975), 138.

34. Muqīmī, 116.

35. Neither the literary histories nor the British Library catalogs appear to provide evidence of North Indian Urdu versions of the Chandarbadan story. Gyan Chand Jain, *Urdu Masnavi Shimali Hind men* (Aligarh: Anjuman-e Taraqqi-e Urdu [Hind], 1969), 128, is much taken with its Liebestod motif of "union in death," repeated as the conspicuously similar climax of Mir Taqi Mir's well-known *Darya-e 'Ishq*, which is summarized in Khurshidul Islam and Ralph Russell, *Three Mughal Poets* (1969; Delhi: Oxford University Press, 1991), 101–3, but his discussion has nothing to say about the difference of the lovers' religions.

36. The earlier literary histories (see, e.g., Kushta, *Tazkira*, 144–49) provide intriguing notices of Aḥmad Yār, clearly a major literary figure of his time and one who was associated with the court of Ranjit Singh. Earlier accounts have been superseded by the extended doctoral study of the poet published as Shāhbaz Malik, *Maulavi Aḥmad Yār: fikar te fan* (Lahore: Meri La'ibreri, 1984), which suggests (89 ff.) that Aḥmad Yār's *Chandarbadan* may be no longer extant, like his *Sohnī Mahīṅvāl* and quite a number of other qiṣṣe.

37. See Kushta, *Tazkira*, 150–51. His poem is available in a number of good Gurmukhi editions, including Dīvān Singh and Roshan Lāl Āhūjā, eds., *Sohṇī Mahīṅvāl Fażal Shāh*, rev. ed. (Jalandhar: New Book Company, 1976).

38. Imām Bakhsh, *Chandarbadan ba-zabān-e Panjābī* (Lahore: Matba'-e Sulṭāni, 1876), 8.

39. Ibid., 16.

40. Especially kāfī no. 42, with the refrain *Tangh mahī dī jaliyāṅ* (I burn with love, my dear herdsman).

41. See the detailed account of the many available Panjabi versions in M. S. Amrit, *Panjābī Sohṇī-kāvī dā Ālochnātmak Adhiain* (Amritsar: Guru Nanak Dev University Press, 1989). Amrit's introduction disposes of the connection supposed to exist between this story and the legend of Chandarbadan and Ma'yār, on the confusing basis of the similarity between the latter's name and that of Mahīṅvāl's Sindhi counterpart, Mehār, on which see Nabī Bakhsh Baloch, ed., *Mashhūr Sindhī Qiṣṣa: 'Ishqiya Dāstān 2, Suhṇī-Mehār aiṅ Nūrī Jām Tamāchī* (Hyderabad: Sindhi Adabi Board, 1972). Neither of these works explains the puzzling discrepancy between an apparent lack of Urdu or Persian treatments of the romance and its great popularity in the Avadh area from the eighteenth century as a subject for paintings, as described in Stephen Markel, "Drowning in Love's Passion: Illustration of the Romance of Sohnī and Mahinwal," in P. Pal, ed., *A Pot-Pourri of Indian Art* (Bombay: 1988), 99–114. The earliest Persian masnavi mentioned in Bāqir, *Panjābī Qiṣṣe*, 193 ff., is that by Ṣāliḥ, which dates only from 1841.

42. On whom see Kushta, *Taẓkira*, 191–96.

43. Particularly notable in this regard is Sudhir Kakar and John Munder Ross, *Tales of Love, Sex, and Danger* (London: Unwin Paperbacks, 1987), whose discussion of the Hīr and Sohnī stories is much colored by its vision of Islamic patriarchalism and its neurotic need to control female sexuality (see esp. 60, 67). More straightforward modern English retellings of the romances show how much is lost by just sticking to the story line, whether this is done by Pakistani authors, as in Zainab Ghulam Abbas, *Folk Tales of Pakistan* (Karachi: Pakistan Publications, 1957), or Masud-ul-Hasan, *Famous Folk Tales of Pakistan* (Karachi: Ferozsons, n.d.), or by Indians, as in Laxman Komal, *Folk Tales of Pakistan* (New Delhi: Sterling, 1976), which is Sindhi-based, given the companion volume by Mulk Raj Anand, *Folk Tales of Panjab* (New Delhi: Sterling, 1974), although the latter tellingly omits the romances in favor of more socially meaningful animal fables. Similar considerations apply to modern retellings in Panjabi prose, e.g., Haribhajan Singh, ed., *Kissā Panjāb* (New Delhi: National Book Trust, 1972).

44. Like Tullā's use of the money 'Izzat Beg paid for his pots to provide a dowry for Sohnī to be married to another (45).

3

Religious Vocabulary and Regional Identity

A Study of the Tamil *Cirappuranam*

Vasudha Narayanan

India is our motherland.
Islam is our way of life.
Only Tamil is our language.
Song from a Tamil cassette, "*Makka nagar Manapi*"

We emphatically say that we who live in the south are the oldest Muslims in India. We take pride in that.
K. P. S. Hamid, 1973

Muslims from South India pride themselves on being descendants of people who converted to Islam while the Prophet was alive and in thus being the oldest among the Muslim communities of India. Of the 2.5 million Muslims in Tamilnadu, about 1.7 million are said to speak Tamil.[1] Their spoken and written Tamil contains many Arabic and Persian loan words, yet it is closely aligned with Standard Tamil and borrows from Sanskrit as well.

Most Tamil Muslims see themselves as participating in Tamil literary history. There is a long tradition of Muslim scholarship on both secular and sacred forms of Tamil literature, Islamic and non-Islamic. Muslim men and women have been among the most eminent scholars, for example, in interpreting the ninth-century Tamil Ramayana composed by Kampan (known as *Iramavataram* or the *Kampa Ramayanam*). M. M. Ismail, the former chief justice of the Madras High Court and noted scholar of the Tamil Ramayana, who has written almost forty books on the subject, remarked with justifiable pride that in every generation there is at least one Muslim who is an authority on the Tamil Ramayana.[2] Muslims also participate in the Festival of Kampan (Kampan Vila), an annual celebration devoted to the scholarship on this poet.[3]

Generally speaking, Tamil Hindus have not paid the same scholarly attention to Islamic literature in Tamil. Instead, their encounter with the Islamic tradition has been more on the level of myth and ritual. The Hindus of this region incorporated some Muslim saints and teachers into their pantheon, made pilgrimages to their tombs, and wove stories of Muslim devotees into the legends of Hindu gods. For instance, Lord Ranganatha, the manifestation of Vishnu in Srirangam, has a Muslim consort, and there is a special shrine for her in the temple complex. This pattern is repeated in several other Vaishnava shrines. Performers of classical South Indian "Carnatic" music also incorporated what were perceived to be Muslim melodies into the traditional *raga* structure of classical South Indian music, which itself shows significant Persian influence.[4]

But the interactions that have shaped the distinctive character of Tamil Muslim identities have only just begun to be studied.[5] Muslim authors have expressed their understanding of Islam through a variety of literary genres that have defined their Islamic identity and their "Tamilness" as well. This essay will begin to address this complex process of identity construction among Tamil Muslims by examining one important seventeenth-century text, the *Cirappuranam* (Life of the Prophet). It will highlight the importance of literary vocabulary, literary images, and literary conventions in shaping cultural values and expectations shared by Muslims and Hindus, even in a work whose purpose was to underscore the distinctive claims of Muslims to participate in a religion of foreign origins.

The Origins of Muslims in Tamilnadu

Many Tamil Muslims understand that they are descendants of seafarers who encountered Islam and converted to the new religion.[6] Muslims in some areas of Tamilnadu have the last name Marakkayar. This name derives from the Tamil word *marakkalam* (ship) and means "shipmen." Although the Tamil lexicon states that the origin of the word may possibly go back to the Arabic *markab*, the name Marakkayar (shipmen) attests to the Muslims' belief that their ancestors were sailors. There is also a legend of a king in the present state of Kerala who witnessed a miracle and who, after learning that the prophet Muhammad was responsible for it, converted to Islam.[7] It is important to note that the Marakkayars believe that their ancestors either came directly from Arabia or were Tamil natives who accepted Islam after direct contact with Arab traders within a few years of the Prophet's death (and by some accounts during his lifetime), not after the conquest by Muslims from northern India. In other words, they believe that they are descendants of early Tamil converts or of Arab traders who settled down in the Tamil-speaking areas in the seventh and eighth centuries C.E. Command of Tamil literature and language are thus marks of their claims to an "early" origin that brings them close to the time of the Prophet.

K. P. S. Hamid argues that the Tamil Muslims are the oldest Muslims in India. He relates an incident at the Second World Tamil Conference on Tamil in 1968. His friend, Dr. K. K. Pillai, professor of history, apparently said in a panel called "Milestones in South India" that while some Muslims in North Arcot, Thanjavur, Tirunelveli, and Kanyakumari Districts were of Arab descent, many of them were descendants of those who converted to Islam after the time of Tippu Sultan (c. 1749–99). "We live with such ignorance of our ancient history," Hamid laments, "that we think that Muslims came to South India just a century ago, just after the time of Tippu Sultan. A society which forgets the pride of its ancient history is a society that has forgotten itself."[8]

Hamid goes on to quote Colonel Wilks's *History of Mysore* to say that Islam came to the southern tip of India during the reign of one Hajjaj ibn Yusuf of the Hashim clan (*kulam*). Muslims escaped his persecution and settled in Kanyakumari district in the seventh century C.E. These earliest Muslims called themselves Lappai, Marakkayar, Malumikal, and Nayinar. For Hamid, the arrival of Islam in India was thus only one part in the larger narrative of the merchants who, "with the companionship of the south-east winds and the north-west winds," took the religion to Lanka, Malaysia, Indonesia, and China. As proof, he refers to a small mosque in Tirucchirapalli. This city (then called Uraiyur) was the capital of the ancient Chola empire. Hamid says that the small mosque is similar to Jain and Buddhist places of worship and has an Arabic inscription dating it to 738 C.E. (Hijri 116). Hamid reminds us of the Muslims' pride in their ancestry and the antiquity of their residence in Tamilnadu.[9]

Tamil Works on Islam and Tamil Works by Muslims

Muslims in the state of Tamilnadu have composed hundreds of works in the last thousand years, and participation in the larger world of Tamil literature has represented an important marker of their identity. Not all these works deal with Islam. The earliest work is a partial preservation of a poem written between the twelfth and fourteenth centuries. Eight verses from the canta *Palcantamalai* (Garland of many metric verses) are preserved in a longer commentary.[10] This work seems to focus on inner love (*akam*) in the style of the classical Tamil genre of akam poetry.

The *Palcantamalai* is only the first poem in a long line of works on Islam in Tamil. Over the centuries, Muslims in Tamilnadu have studied both secular works and Hindu religious poetry and utilized many of the traditional Tamil literary conventions with great skill in their religious writings. Religious works in Tamil written by Muslims include the following:

(a) Several *kappiyam* (Sanskrit: *kavya*, epic poems) of which the *Cirappuranam*, a seventeenth-century biography of the prophet Muhammad, is the best known.

(b) Hundreds of devotional Tamil poems about many Muslim leaders, including the Prophet, the early caliphs, the prophets, the Prophet's grandsons, and many Muslim *walis* or saints. Some are addressed to a goddess and written in a mystical Sufi genre. Some of the Tamil literary genres adopted by Muslims in writing about Islam include *kirtana* and *sintu* (different kinds of songs in South India), *kummi* (folksong for a dance by girls, sung to the clapping of hands), *ammanai* (sung by girls while playing certain games, throwing stones or balls in the air and then catching them), *ecal* (songs that insult another person), *temmanku* (rural songs), and *tiruppukal* (sacred praise).

(c) Miscellaneous works, including folklore that portrays a shared world of metaphors between Tamil literature and Arab stories.[11]

(d) Descriptions of holy places like Nagore in South India.

(e) Arabic genres adapted to the Tamil language. These include *kissa* (the most famous works being one on Joseph and one on Ali and Zaytun), *pataippor* (leading an army into battle), *nama*, and *masala*.

Umaru Pulavar

The most famous work on Islam in Tamil is the *Cirappuranam* of Umaru Pulavar (Omar the Poet), who lived in Kilkarai, the site of many recent Tamil Islamic conferences.[12] Umaru's date of birth, 1665, as with other dates in premodern and early modern India, is disputed, and some scholars say he was born in Hijri 1052, on the ninth day of the waning moon in the month of Shabban, and they calculate this to be November 2, 1642. There is no disagreement about his death, which is said to have occurred on July 28, 1703.[13] His composition made its debut around that time but was first printed only in 1842 by Ceykku Aptul Katir Neynar (Sheikh Abdul Khader Nayanar).

There is no written evidence of Umaru Pulavar's life, and almost all that we know about him is from oral tradition. His name is not mentioned in his epic work. He was apparently born in Ettayapuram.[14] His father, Ceku (Sheikh) Mutali, was a dealer in spices and perfumes. His ancestors were apparently Arab merchants who settled down in Tamilnadu.[15] Umaru is thus said to be of the Conakar (foreign, especially Greek or Arab) community. He married and lived in Kilkarai; in honor of his residence there, whenever a Muslim marriage takes place there, the families donate money to charity known as "the poet's share."

Umaru's brilliance impressed Citakkati (1650–1715), a Muslim philanthropist who was a patron of Hindu and Muslim scholars. Citakkati's real name was Sheikh Abdul Qadir, and he was the financial adviser of Vijaya Raghunatha Cetupati, the ruler of Ramnad.[16] Citakkati apparently asked Umaru to compose a work on the life of the Prophet. Umaru then went to Lappai Ali Hajjiyar to learn about the Prophet's life from Arabic and Persian sources. The teacher did not accept Umaru initially because Umaru was dressed like a Hindu.[17] The Prophet then appeared in the dreams of both Umaru and Lappai, and Umaru was directed to Lappai's brother in Parankipettai (meaning "town of foreigners").[18]

The first public reading of the *Cirappuranam,* according to some versions, took place under the patronage of Apul Kacim Marakkayar (Abdul Kasim Marakkayar), after the death of Citakkati (although the traditional dates ascribed to Umaru and Citakkati cast doubt on this story). Umaru mentions Apul Kacim Marakkayar as his patron in the *Cirappuranam* and praises him twenty-two times. It is said that Umaru lived in Apul Kacim's house while he composed the *Cirappuranam*. Since the patron's name is not mentioned in the last third of the poem, some scholars speculate that either the patron withdrew his support (rather unlikely) or Umaru did not believe in exaggerated praise of the patron. It is also possible that his patron died.[19]

There are other stories that are part of oral tradition, which scholars agree need extensive research if their accuracy is to be validated. For example, one story is that the patron's wife was so entranced by the poem when she heard the section on the birth (*avatara*) of the Prophet that she did not direct the milk properly to her nursing child, and the child died (possibly of choking). Not wanting to interrupt the flow of the recitation, the mother kept quiet, holding a dead child in her arms until the poem was recited in full.[20] Umaru also composed two small works. One was a *kovai*,[21] a poem dealing with various aspects of love in honor of his earlier patron, Citakkati, and the other was *Mutumolimalai* (Garland in the old/mature language), eighty-eight stanzas modeled on earlier *bhakti* poems on the prophet Muhammad.

The *Cirappuranam*

The Tamil title of Umaru Pulavar's *Cirappuranam* is indicative of the blending of genres in its text. *Cira* is the Tamil form of the Arabic *sirah*, a word used for hagiography, specifically the biography of the Prophet. *Purana* (Tamil *Puranam*) is a genre in Hindu literature, a Sanskrit term that occurs in Tamil and other Indian vernaculars. *Puranas* include pious accounts of the salvific deeds of a divine being, sometimes seen as an incarnation of the supreme deity, and they contain long poetic accounts of this person's wondrous qualities. Thus, there are puranas addressed to the Hindu gods Vishnu and Shiva, to the goddess Durga, and so on; the *purana* addressed to Vishnu speaks of his various incarnations to save human beings. Tamil *puranams* generally deal with deities, saints, or the sanctity of a sacred place. Unlike the Tamil epics like *Civika Cintamani*, the *Ramayanam*, or the *Cilappatikkaram*, Tamil puranams usually do not focus on one character but are narrative accounts of gods or saints. Sanskrit puranas deal with the creation of the world, evolution of this creation, genealogy of the gods or divine beings, world "history," and history of royal families. Famous biographical puranas in Tamil focus on Skanda (Murukan) as well as on Saiva saints. Calling the life of the prophet Muhammad a purana, therefore, predisposes one to have certain expectations of the central figure in the text. The combination of a foreign (here Arabic) word with a Sanskrit one in the title gives us a hint of what is to follow: the presentation of a "foreign" religion in a genre predominantly used by Hindus—a genre shaping a vocabulary of praise and devotion shared with Muslims. The *Cirappuranam* thus incorporates Tamil literary conventions and customs and the Tamil landscape into the description of the lives of the Prophet and members of his family. The author shows exquisite knowledge of earlier Hindu devotional literature in Tamil and seems to be acquainted with the ninth-century

Tamil version of the Hindu epic *Ramayana* (Story of Rama) composed by Kampan as well as the tenth-century *Civika Cintamani*. The *Civika Cintamani* (Jivaka, the wish-fulfilling gem) was composed by Tirutakkatevar (Sri Daksa Deva), a Jain monk, and deals with the love life and conquests of Jivakan.

The 5,028 verses of the *Cirappuranam* are presented as three cantos:

> "Vilatattuk Kantam" (24 chapters; 1,240 verses)
> "Nupuvat Kantam" (21 chapters; 1,105 verses)
> "Kicurattu Kantam" (92 chapters, 2,683 verses)

The names of the cantos derive from Arabic words. *Viladattu* means birth, *nupuvat* is from *nubuvat* (prophethood), and *kicurattu* is the Tamil form of *hijrat*.

Cirappuranam's Opening Chapter: "Praising the Lord"

The *Cirappuranam* begins with salutations to God and the prophet Muhammad. The first verse describes God as *tiruvinnun tiruvai* (being the *tiru* of *Tiru*). The Tamil word *Tiru* is the equivalent of *Sri*. One way in which the word *Sri* is used is as a name for the goddess Lakshmi. In more general terms it means "auspicious," "fortune," "wealth," or "sacred." Thus, the names of many of the Tamil sacred compositions begin with the word *Sri* or *tiru* (wealth). In Vaishnava literature, both in Sanskrit and Tamil, one finds words strikingly similar to Umaru Pulavar's beginning words, *tiruvinin tiruvai*. In the ninth century, Tirumankai Alvar referred to Vishnu in the town of Terazhundur[22] as "becoming the *tiru* of even *Tiru*" (*tiruvukkum tiruvakiya*). Vishnu was called the wealth of the goddess who personifies all fortune.

The *Cirappuranam* thus begins with auspicious words in the Tamil language. Umaru then venerates Muhammad:

> He, the Handsome One, appeared
> as the light of the *four Vedas*
> which showed the path in the world.
> Those who keep the words of this leader
> ever in the center of their mouths
> will be celebrated by poets
> and praised by all.
> They will know the Truth
> so doubts are slashed
> and their ears are appeased.

Thoughts that give rise to evil deeds
will go away.[23]

The verse itself is important in many ways. It speaks of the four Vedas and the words of the Prophet. The commentator expounds on the four Vedas: the *Taurat* (*Torah*) given to Musa (Moses), the *Capur* (*Zabur*) given to Tavoot (David), the *Injil* (Gospel) given to Isa (Jesus), and the *Purukan* (*Furqan* or the Qur'an) given to Muhammad.[24] The words that one is supposed to keep constantly on one's tongue are called the *mula mantra* (primary mantra). This mula mantra, he says, is the *shahada*, or "*La illah illallah . . .*" In these and other verses, the framing vocabulary is shaped by Hindu tradition—witness the commentator's explanations of the four Vedas and the mula mantra—but the exegesis is clearly Islamic in character.

In the opening chapter of the *Cirappuranam*, after eight verses praising the Lord and Muhammad, the poet pays his respects to the first four Caliphs, the *wali* Mukiteen (Muhiyudin Abd al- Qadir al-Jilani, 1078–1166) of Baghdad, and then his teacher Capatullah Appa. He reverentially places their feet on himself. The verse addressed to Uthman is a typical example:

Uthman decreed that one form of
the Sacred (*tiru*) Veda
    which came from the tongue
    of the Prophet
    whose effulgent body
    makes the moon cringe
sweep through this world.
Uthman holds as his life
those who know the *four great Vedas*
the elders, and the young ones.
Not ever forgetting him
let us place his twin feet
firmly within us.[25]

The chapter concludes with a sense of humility, and the poet expresses his unworthiness to compose this work. Beginning a work with praise of gurus and a confession of unworthiness is typical of the *stotra* (panegyric) genre in South Indian Vaishnava works in Sanskrit; the works of Yamuna and Kurattalvan in the eleventh century and of Vedanta Desika in the thirteenth century bear testimony to this style. Umaru writes:

Like a little ant, grown weak from hunger
exhaling its breath
In front of the squalls and gales that churn
the seven seas and storm the mountains
as though their very nature were to change
I compose my poem
in front of the exalted Tamil poets.

Line by line,
I see nothing but fault
in all that I compose.
Step by step,
the exalted poets of yore
have obtained knowledge.
To compose in front of them
is to measure the noise that comes
when I snap my fingers
with the sound of rolling thunder.[26]

In earlier stotra literature in Sanskrit, we see verses like the following:

> Though I know of my ignorance, I am shameless enough to wish to string together these words of love for the feet of our Lord; for even when the river Ganga which is naturally pure is licked by a dog, it is still known as "holy water."[27]

Although the sentiments are similar, we see how Umaru gets our attention with simple and unpretentious similes. In other verses of the first chapter, Umaru Pulavar pays reverence to or refers to the twin feet of the exalted teachers, and one can easily recognize that these references are typical of Hindu devotional literature where a poet reveres the sacred feet of the teacher or the deity.

The Tamil Landscape in Arabia: The Use of Literary Conventions from Cankam Poetry

As did the Tamil epic poets Kampan and Tirutakkatevar, Umaru Pulavar gives extensive descriptions of the country and the city where the Prophet is to "descend" (*avatara*). This is followed by a list of the ancestors of Muhammad. Umaru apparently never traveled to Arabia, and his description of the country is a description of Tamilnadu. In the utilization of this method, too, he has a predecessor. Kampan, the author of the

Tamil *Ramayana*, transposes the Tamil landscape to Ayodhya in northern India. Descriptions of the river Kaveri are transferred to the river Sarayu. Umaru Pulavar also transfers the Tamil landscape to Arabia.

A typical feature of Tamil classical poetry, especially the *puram* verses (typically dealing with chivalry, kings, and war), was description of the wonders of a king's land. In the Tamil verses of classical (Cankam) poetry, we find roaring cascades (the presence of water indicated prosperity in South India where drought was all too common), fertile fields that are well irrigated, lush fields of paddy and cane sugar, blossoming lotuses, and bees sucking nectar from flowers redolent with honey. The waterfalls and rivers carry precious gems fallen from the jewelry worn by people who bathe in them—obviously indicating that the king's land is filled with rich people. This is also seen in a description of Lord Murukan's domain in the fifth-century (?) poem *Tirumurukarruppatai:*

> The cataracts of the mountains look like varied, waving flags of glory . . . they spill . . . sweet-smelling, huge honeycombs built upon lofty hills that kiss the sky. . . . The cascades gush along . . . the falling waters bear in their bosom the pearl-bearing white tusks of huge elephants; the torrents leap along with fine gold and gems shining on their surface, washing aside glittering dusts of gold . . . the hills abound in groves with ripening fruits. God Muruga is lord of such hills.[28]

The cities are also described in considerable detail in Cankam literature: prosperous seaports, terraces looming like mountains, palaces stretching to the sky. They are centers of culture where bards and courtesans flourish.

The wealth of a nation rests on its ability to produce food, and this depends on rainfall. Poets describe the prosperity of a land by the abundant rain it receives. Umaru Pulavar talks of the white clouds drinking up the seawater, becoming dark and heading for land (Arabia). The clouds cover the mountains, and storms rage. The storms abate, but the heavy rains continue, flooding the place, and it becomes chilly. Elephants, lions, and other animals feel the cold and, forgetting the enmity between them, go to one place. Elephants, deer, squirrels, tigers, bisons, giant lizards, monkeys, lions, spotted deer, anteaters, lemurs, bears, wild dogs, buffalos, porcupines, humped bulls, and other animals huddle in the cold, shivering. Because of the high winds, trees on the mountains fall. Flocks of birds fly, frightened, and floods of water come down the emerald slopes of the mountains onto the plains. The flooding streams approach the houses of the gypsy women (with wide eyes and red lips) who live on the foothills. The streams drop as water falls over the emerald mountains knocking down the banana trees and wood-apple trees. The floods sweep away gems from the mountains just as a courtesan embraces a king and sweeps away his gold, gems, and priceless pearls.[29] Kampan, the author of the *Ramayana,* also uses this analogy:

Like a courtesan embracing her lover
his head, his body, his feet, as if in desire
all for a minute [and fleeing with his ornaments]
the floods embrace the peak, the slopes, the foothills
and sweep away everything.[30]

Compare this with the following verses from the *Cirappuranam:*

Like a courtesan embracing the mountain-like king
giving him pleasure, and sweeping away
gold which gives us prosperity,
precious gems, pearls, and all splendid things,
and flees the frontiers, the floods flow
carrying with them all riches.[31]

A waterfall carrying gems is also a traditional image in Tamil literature. Nammalvar, a ninth-century poet, speaks of the waterfalls of Tirupati hills:

Lord of Venkata hill
where clear waterfalls crash
spilling gems, gold, and pearls.[32]

This is, of course, part of the wealthy, fortune-filled land that is being described. The waters rush like an elephant. The streams, when they slow down, look like lovely girls. Their white froth looks like white garments worn by maidens; the dark silt resembles dark hair; the fish look like the eyes of a girl; the water bubbles seem to be like breasts, and the whirlpools circle like the navel. These descriptions and analogies are generally necessary in Tamil poetry to prove one's mettle as a poet. Like a Vaisya merchant, the streams carry sandalwood, ivory, pearls, and gems.[33] Here, too, Umaru Pulavar follows Kampan:

Carrying the pearls, gold, peacock feathers,
beautiful white ivory from an elephant, aromatic *akil* wood,

sandalwood, matchless in fragrance,
the floods looked like the *vaniya* merchants.[34]

In the *Cirappuranam* we find the following:

Carrying the fallen sandalwood, branches from the dark *akil* tree,
pearls from the broken elephant's horn, white ivory,
more precious than these, red rubies, radiant in three ways,
carrying these all towards the sea,
the stream laden rich bamboo, looked like a *vaniya* merchant.[35]

The river flows through the Kurinci (mountainous) land, presumably of Arabia, through the desert (a recognized category in the landscapes of Tamil poems), and into the forests. Reaching *marutam* (cultivated land), it fills the lakes, ponds, and tanks. The streams break through the lakes and approach farmlands. They sweep through the sugarcane plantations and slush up the ponds where the fragrant lotus flowers bloom. The water is then contained and used for irrigation. The single body of water held in many tanks, ponds, lakes, and areas where lotus bloom is compared by Umaru to life (Tamil: *uyir*), which appears in hundreds of millions (Tamil: *cata koti* from Sanskrit *Satha koti*) of beings. This idea reminds one of the Advaitin notion that a single soul (*atman*) appears in many forms and bodies and seems to be many. While Umaru does not elaborate on his analogy, it is striking that he seems at home with these Vedantic ideas.[36]

Where did all these descriptions come from? The earliest Tamil literature composed in the earliest centuries of the Common Era recognizes five landscapes. The Cankam poems (also known as the poems of the classical age or the "bardic corpus"), dealing with romantic or heroic themes, refer to five basic situations. These situations correspond in poetry to five landscape settings (*tinai*), birds, flowers, times, gods, etc. The five basic psychological situations for akam poems are lovemaking, waiting anxiously for a beloved, separation, patient waiting of a wife, and anger at a lover's real or imagined infidelity. These correspond to the mountainous (*kurinci*), seaside (*neytal*), arid (*palai*), pastoral (*mullai*), and agricultural (*marutam*) landscapes.[37] More specifically, Umaru's descriptions closely resemble the descriptions of Kampan in the first two chapters of his version of the *Ramayanam*. However, even though the details are exquisitely similar in spirit and in concept, each poet has his own inimitable style. Reading both descriptions is similar to listening to the same raga played by two maestros.

After describing the mountainous regions, Umaru Pulavar speaks of the wealth of the cultivated land and the beauty of its women. He projects the practices of the (presumably Hindu) farmers from Tamilnadu onto the fertile rice fields of Arabia. In a striking verse, he talks about the farmers' worship of the sun and the earth before they sow the seeds in the field, and then he waxes eloquent about the beauty of the women:

Wearing jewels, quaffing toddy,
Worshiping the Sun with their hands, and then
Worshiping the god of their clan,
Milling in crowds, those who labor in the fields
gather and praise Earth.
Their right hands shake the sprouting seeds
and scatter them thick on the ground.
They fall like golden rain on earth.[38]

Modern Muslim commentators interpret this verse in two ways. Justice M. M. Ismail merely says that the poet is conversant with the farming practices of South India and then projects them on to Arabia. However, in his detailed exegesis of the *Cirappuranam,* Kavi (poet) Sherip (Sherif) says that these practices may have existed in Arabia before the time of the Prophet.[39] Sherip also takes a more literal view of Umaru Pulavar's description of the mountains and streams of Arabia and says that this kind of landscape can be found in Yemen.

Descriptions of women are found soon after these verses; in Tamil poetry, a flourishing land is filled with voluptuous women wearing dazzling jewelry. These women have participated in the sowing of the seeds and are walking through the well-tilled, fertile fields, which are prosperously slushy with life-giving waters:

With twin eyes made red by drinking palm-toddy,
with slender bamboo-like shoulders heaving,
the women walk with drunken steps,
swaying softly like a swan.
Their feet tread the well-tilled land,
Mud splashes on their breasts
that soar like the tusks
of a lusty elephant.
Their breasts speckled with slush

look like the tender buds of lotus flowers
swarming with tiny bees.[40]

There are half a dozen verses like this describing their teeth, coral lips, victorious demeanor, etc. While these descriptions may seem somewhat startling in a work that purports to be the life of the Prophet, the phrases and general tone of the verses are almost standard fare in any self-respecting Tamil poem and not at all unusual in Tamil literature.

Umaru Pulavar also follows the conventions of Tamil poetry in describing the city of Mecca (Tamil: Makka). Takkatevar, the author of the Jain epic poem *Civika Cintamani,* and Kampan described the towns and urban culture in considerable detail. The city of Mithila, hometown of Sita, is described with great poetic skill by Kampan. Following the description of the countryside, Umaru Pulavar describes Mecca, beginning with a number of Tamil/Hindu cosmological details. The verses are strikingly "Hindu" in origin but again a part of the common lore to which Umaru Pulavar had access:

I shall now expound in brief
on the great city of Mecca.

The expansive lakes
filled with radiant conches
brimming with pearls
seem like a moat with waves.
Many kinds of lotus blossoms
filled with lustrous gems
ring the town.
The prosperous fort appears like
a lotus flower with golden petals.
Wealth and luxurious fortune
ever increase in this prosperous town.

The seven isles invite the northern mountains
to surround them on one side
and install them there.
A tall mountain they establish
as the crest of the crown
and surround it on all four sides
with fortresses.

The sea surrounds the land
on three other sides like a moat.
The city of Mecca appears
like the gem on the sacred head
of the King of Serpents [Adi Sesa].[41]

This city resounds with the noises of busy life, horses running swiftly, chariots, elephants trumpeting like thunder, such that even the sea is afraid of making noise. This is the standard city of Tamil poetry: fortresses, lakes, lotuses, horses, chariots, elephants, and so on. Almost every literary convention in the description of the prosperous city is included in Umaru Pulavar's portrait of Mecca. Umaru also refers to Hindu deities occasionally. Abu Talib, he says, is brave, knowledgeable about the arts, and ever triumphant. Lakshmi, the goddess of good fortune, reigns victorious at the portals of his house.[42] But apart from a few allusions like this (such as references to the path of Manu, the generosity of Surabhi, the wish-fulfilling cow, and so on), there is no attempt made to incorporate Hindu deities within the worldview of Islam in either a positive or a negative fashion. The appropriation of the Prophet into a Tamil world shared by Muslims and Hindus alike is accomplished through the generic use of convention and language.[43]

The Chapter on Fatima's Wedding

Other Tamil literary conventions are used with equal skill by Umaru Pular. The long chapter on Fatima's wedding (Pattima Tirumanappatalam) contains a beautiful description of Ali's procession through the city of Medina that parallels Rama's procession through Mithila in Kampan's *Ramayanam*. Let us consider the swarming of women in Mithila rushing to get a glimpse of Rama:

Like a herd of deer closing in
Like a flock of peacocks wandering
Like a shower of brilliant meteors [or "a galaxy of splendrous stars"]
Like flashes of lightning coming close
With bees that flutter around their garlands humming in tune
With bands of anklets and rings tinkling,
Women, their hair adorned
with flowers soaked [with honey]
swiftly thronged around.

Not attending to their hair that loosened and cascaded down
Not heeding their waist belts that broke loose
Not pulling up the flower-soft clothes that slip away
Not pausing to rest their tired waists
they closed in [on Rama].
Coming close they cried, "Make way, make way!"
Women who lend splendor to the city
swarmed around him like bees tasting honey.[44]

Women in Medina overflow from the balconies trying to catch a glimpse of this handsome bridegroom, and when they see him, they are filled with longing and wonder: Is all this charm and beauty to be monopolized by just one woman? Describing the women of Medina, the poet adopts a strategy common to Sanskrit and Tamil literature known either as *padadi kesa varna* (description from the feet to the hair) or *kesadi pada varna* (description from the hair to the feet). Umaru thus describes the women of Medina:

The anklets swirled on the feet,
the golden belts around their hips tinkled.
The ornaments on their radiant breasts—
  breasts as sharp as the tusks
  of a lusty elephant—
flashed.
Their hair, adorned by flowers
fragrant and fresh, dripping honey
spilled out from their constraints.
Like many moons flowering on the ocean,
young maidens, thronged around.[45]

The women in Medina, watching Ali's procession, are seen to be wearing jewels (anklets, *mekalai*, or waist belt) like Tamil women, and traditional descriptions of their breasts and hair follow. Their breasts are pointed and sharp, their hair is long and collected together in swirls of fragrant flowers filled with honey. Their hair, which is to be demurely gathered together, loosens in their mood of abandon. The words suggest an erotic mood, appropriate for the wedding. They are filled with longing at the sight of Ali. According to Tamil literary conventions, a woman's body becomes pale when she is parted from her lover or husband. This special lovesickness signified by a pallor is seen in the young women of Medina. They swarm around like an ocean, says Umaru, and then he uses metaphors connected with the sea to describe them:

Eyes like darting fish,
necks, exulting like conches;
teeth like white pearls, smile
through parted lips,
which flash like corals.
With golden skins growing pale with longing
flowers loosened like shining foam,
A sea of women, swarm thick
without any gap between them.[46]

The poet uses the sea as the primary metaphor and says the women splash forth like the ocean. The poet comes from and lives on the seashore and is lavish in his use of metaphors from the sea. Fish, conches, corals, pearls, and sea foam are all used as elements of comparison in describing these women. A poet's skill was frequently seen in the use of metaphor and similes, and descriptions of the human body—for both men and women—were particularly relished by the audience. Umaru certainly excels according to all Tamil standards in these areas.

Apart from literary convention, the poem utilizes words extensively found in other forms of religious literature in Tamil. Many are Sanskrit loan words. We have already noted the use of the word *Veda*. The Qur'an is called Veda and frequently spoken of as the *marai* ("mystery," Tamil synonym for *Veda*).[47] The word *marai* means "hidden, that which is a secret, a mystery." The Vedas and the Upanishads were called *marai* in the Tamil texts written in the first five centuries of the Common Era. We find this word in the *Tolkappiyam*, the *Paripatal*, and other Cankam works. The word *marai* functioned as a literal translation of *Vedas;* thus the village of Vedaranyam (Forest of Vedas) in Tanjore District was called Maraikkatu in the Tevaram. The Upanishads were called *marai cirai* (the head of the Vedas). The Lord who reveals the Qur'an to Muhammad is called "Srutiyon." *Sruti* is Sanskrit for "that which is heard" and another synonym for the Veda. We can certainly see how apt the use of the word *Sruti* is to the Qur'an, which was heard by Muhammad. The deity who reveals this is called *srutiyon* (he of the *Sruti*).

What did these words mean for the Hindus writing in Tamil? Several philosophers, especially those from the Nyaya (Logic) and Mimamsaka schools, had already discussed the term *Veda* in some detail, and the Vedanta teachers including Ramanuja, the most important Srivaisnava teacher, had clearly discussed the trans-human nature of the Sanskrit Vedas in commentaries on the *Vedanta Sutras*. All schools of thought agreed on the transcendental aspect of the Vedas and their authoritative nature, but differed on what was meant by the trans-human (*apauruseya*) nature of their composition. The followers of the Nyaya school believed that God was their author, and since God was perfect, the Vedas were infallible. The Mimamsakas, on the other hand, starting from at least the second century B.C.E., said that the Vedas were eternal and authorless.[48] The Vedic seers (*rsi*) saw the *mantras* and transmitted them; they did not compose or author them. Calling the Qur'an a Veda, therefore, includes at least some of these meanings as understood in Hindu writings.

Other theologically loaded words are used. For instance, the birth of the Prophet is referred to as *avatara* ("Vilattattu Kantam, Napi Avatara Patalam"). *Avatara* (descent) is used in Hindu theology to refer to the incarnations of Vishnu, who descended into this world "to save the good and destroy evil" (*Bhagavad Gita* 4:9). The use of this term for Muhammad, therefore, exalts him as more than human. This word is generally not used for the birth of human beings in Tamil literature. He is also called the *tiru tutar* (sacred messenger). *Tutar* is the Tamil form of the Sanskrit *dhuta,* which means "messenger." While the word is used in secular and sacred language, in Hindu religious literature it is Krishna who is associated with the word *dhuta* and is frequently called "Pandava dhuta" or "the messenger of the Pandavas" during the Mahabharata war. Muhammad's mother is called the abode of *dharma,* and this word is used frequently in the biography. Abucakal is said to follow "the path of Manu" (*manu neri*) ("Nupuvattuk Kantam, Matiyai Alaitta Patalam," v. 152). The use of this religious vocabulary thus helped to shape a distinctive Tamil appreciation of Islamic theology. While not implying any sort of self-conscious accommodation to Hindu ideas, this vocabulary provided the conceptual framework in which much of the Prophet's life was explained and understood.

Modern Implications: The Testimony of Tamil Songs Written by Muslims

None of this implied, of course, that such writings provided a charter for Muslim and Hindu participation in common ritual practices. To the contrary, at least on the level of popular practice, it was more common for Hindus, in spite of their general lack of interest in Islamic literature, to incorporate Muslim holy men into their devotional exercises than the reverse. As Susan Bayly has demonstrated, Muslim saints and their shrines came to be important sites in the Tamil sacred landscape, frequented by Hindus and Muslims alike.[49]

The significance of a work such as the *Cirappuranam,* however, lies in a different direction; it illustrates how the generic conventions of Tamil literary production have defined a framework for Muslim participation in the Tamil religious world. This was the case even though the focus of devotion was a figure who lived in a foreign land, the prophet Muhammad. On the one hand, as a *sirah,* or life of the Prophet, the *Cirappuranam* linked Tamil devotees of the Prophet generically to a wider Islamic world; the text defined clearly the connections of Tamil Muslims to a world of devotion to the Prophet whose boundaries were far wider than either Tamil vocabulary or Tamilnadu. On the other hand, the poet Umaru's claims to recognition depended on his skill in manipulating a Tamil devotional idiom defined by the text's generic claim to be a puranam. The conventions and vocabulary of the text thus rooted devotion to the Prophet in a Tamil conceptual world—a world shared by both Hindus and Muslims. It was generic conventions that helped to construct a framework for identity that was *simultaneously* Muslim and Tamil.

The tensions in the process by which such identities are formed also have their modern sequel in Tamilnadu. Analysis of the *Cirappuranam* provides historical perspective on the more recent claims by many Tamil Muslims to superior status *as Muslims* because of the antiquity of their connections to Tamilnadu. Familiarity with Tamil literary conventions, like early links to Arabia, does provide evidence of their comparative antiquity as an Indian Muslim community. But how did Tamil Muslims relate to other South Asian Muslims who were not as ancient as themselves? Tamil Muslims had, of course, long adapted Arabic and Persian forms of literature to Tamil genres, and they showed reverence to Muslim saints from other parts of India and the Middle East. At the same time, they did not identify strongly with Muslims in the rest of India, whether in Kerala, Hyderabad, or the north, nor did the trauma of partition seem to affect the deep south.

Yet the logic of remaining connected with, but aloof from, other Muslims of the subcontinent has recently been challenged with the rise of Hindu nationalism. The belligerent stance of some Hindu nationalists in the 1980s and 1990s has prompted a growing sense of insecurity among Tamil Muslims. Their anger, sorrow, and bewilderment have now surfaced in public through new Tamil Muslim songs sold in prerecorded audiocassettes. Packaged along with standard songs on the glory of Muhammad and Mecca are songs that are very patriotic, some filled with distress, others filled with rage. These cassettes go under titles such as "Makkanakar Manapi" (Great Prophet of Mecca), "Makkavai Nokki" (Looking toward Mecca), or "Pallivacalil kutuvom" (Let us gather at the gates of the mosque). The lyrics of two songs from "Makkanakar Manapi" suggest new frameworks for identity:

Song 1

India is our motherland
Islam is our way of life
Tamil is our language . . .
Who is it who said we are enemies?
Our forefathers worked and fought for freedom
Muslims fought to get rid of the nation's sorrow.

They have forgotten gratitude.
Is this betrayal? Are these the sins we have done?
The blood spilled by the Mappillas in Kerala is not yet dry
The wounds we got in Bengal are not yet healed
Mysore's lion Tipu's bravery will not change
Your heart cannot bear the grief of Bahadur Shah
Do you know we have ruled India for eight hundred years?
The Taj Mahal and the Kutb Minar are witnesses, have you forgotten?
You cannot deny it, You cannot conceal truth.

Song 2

I swear on the earth
I swear on the heavens
I swear on the mother who bore me
I swear on God who created [all].
We will not lose our faith as long as we are alive
We will not weaken in resolve as long as we are alive
Leaving the Land of India, forgetting its glory
We will not flee in fear
We will not flee in fear of anyone.

This is the land where Muslim Kings ruled for eight hundred years.
Say, does anyone have this pride [of rulership] other than us?
We have never betrayed this country.
Muslims have served this land without end.

Our crowd rose first to seek freedom.
That is why blood began to flow in Kerala.
Will my heart forget the sacrifice of the Mappilas?
We will do countless sacrifice again, for the country.
Think of the sacrifice of Bahadur Shah who ruled Delhi
when enemies gave him his son's head on a platter. . . .
There is no one equal to us in devotion (bhakti) to the country.
He was born as the brave son of Haidar, Mysore's king. . . .
Tipu gave his life in war.
He tried hard to free his mother-country.
He bore endless grief in the British prisons.
Maulana Muhammad Ali Saukat died pining for freedom.

Two strategies are immediately visible from these verses. First, the composers are now aligning themselves with Muslims from all over India and not just the south (although a southern emphasis is evident in the references to the Mappilas and Tipu). Second, the verses remind the listeners of the sacrifices made by Muslims all over India during the independence movement. Since the simplistic war cry of the aggressive Hindu is to tell the Muslim to go to Pakistan, the Tamil Muslim songs emphasize that India is their home. This patriotism is woven with songs on the Islamic faith.

The songs suggest a new aggressiveness and hardening of religious boundaries, as Hindus and Muslims compete for the right to speak for the nation. Yet they also suggest the ways in which popular literary or musical genres continue to define commonalities and a common identification with Tamil language, even as they shape new conceptions of difference. Although far removed from the shared generic literary conventions that defined the *Cirappuranam,* the language of these songs projects another type of shared generic convention—a devotionalism, now linked to country, that is rooted in a long generic heritage of devotional poetry shared by both Hindus and Muslims. Indeed, many of the audiocassettes on which these songs appear continue to be simply categorized by the stores that sell them, along with songs in praise of the Prophet, as "Muslim Devotional (*bhakti*) songs."

Notes

1. *Statistical Abstract: India 1990* (Central Statistical Organisation, Ministry of Planning, Government of India), 33; see also *Muslim India* (January 1984), 18, quoted by Syed Shahabuddin and Theodore P. Wright Jr., "India: Muslim Minority Politics and Society," in John L. Esposito, ed., *Islam in Asia* (New York: Oxford University Press, 1987), 167. According to Shahabuddin and Wright, the total number of Muslims in Tamilnadu in 1981 was 2.5 million.

2. Interview with Justice M. M. Ismail, July 1993.

3. Looking through the programs on the debates and discussions in the Festival of Kampan held between 1991 and 1993, one finds names like Parveen Sultana, Abdul Khader, and Abdul Karim.

4. In music, the categories of Muslim and Hindu ragas are misnomers; we may more accurately speak of Indian and Persian forms of music. Because geographic origin was often associated with religious affiliation (the word for Muslim in Tamil is *tulukka* from *turka* or Turkish), music from Persia was characterized as Islamic. It has also been claimed that Sufi writings in Tamil affected Tamil Siddha poetry. This is probably true, but it has not yet been demonstrated.

5. Paula Richman discusses possible reasons for the neglect of Islamic Tamil literature in the appendix of "Veneration of the Prophet Muhammad in an Islamic *Pillaitamil*," *Journal of the American Oriental Society* 113.1 (1993): 57–74. The encounter between Hindus, Christians, and Muslims in Tamilnadu and Kerala has been discussed in Susan Bayly, *Saints, Goddesses, and Kings* (Cambridge: Cambridge University Press, 1989). See also David Shulman, "Muslim Popular Literature in Tamil: The Tamimancari Malai," in Yohanan Friedmann, ed., *Islam in Asia*, vol. 1, *South Asia* (Boulder, Colo.: Westview Press, 1980).

6. Interview with Justice M. M. Ismail, July 1993. See also Mattison Mines, *The Warrior Merchants: Textiles, Trade, and Territory in South India* (Cambridge: Cambridge University Press, 1984), and Susan Bayly, *Saints, Goddesses, and Kings.*

7. Annemarie Schimmel, *And Muhammad Is His Prophet* (Chapel Hill: University of North Carolina Press, 1985), 70.

8. K. P. S. Hamitu (Hamid), "Tennakattil Islattin tonmai," *Islamiyat Tamil Araycci Manatu*-1 (Research Conference on Islamic Tamil) (Tiruccirapalli: Islamiyat tamil ilakkiyat kalakam, 1973), 51.

9. Ibid., 52–53. On the existence of this small mosque, see Bayly, *Saints, Goddesses, and Kings*, 87.

10. Ma. Mu. Uvais (Uwise), *Islam Valartta Tamil*, 16–17, quoting Vaiyapuri Pillai, *Tamil Ilakkiya Varalaru-14an nurrantu* (Cennai [Madras]: Ulakat Tamilaraycci niruvanam, 1984), 335.

11. See Shulman, "Muslim Popular Literature in Tamil."

12. On the maritime importance of Kilkarai and the fact that it is home to many prominent Muslims, see Susan Bayly, *Saints, Goddesses, and Kings*, 81–85.

13. Uvais, "Cirapuranamum Umaruppulavarum," in *Cirappuranam*, ed. M. Ceyyitu Muhammatu "Hasan" (Cennai [Madras]: Maraikkayar Patipakkam, 1987).

14. K. Zvelebil, *Lexicon of Tamil Literature* (Leiden: E. J. Brill, 1995), 721.

15. Uvais, "Cirapuranamum Umaruppulavarum," v. His father's name was probably Sheikh Muhammad Ali, which was changed to Ceku (Sheikh) Mutali. Mutali is a respectful suffix added to the names of Hindu devotees, and it is noteworthy that Umaru's father's name was transformed in this way. Others say his name was Mappilai Mukammmatu Nayinar.

16. For a discussion of 'Abd al-Qadir as Citakkati, see V. Narayana Rao, David Shulman, and Sanjay Subrahmanyam, "On the Periphery: State Formation and Deformation," in *Symbols of Substance: Court and State in Nayaka Period Tamilnadu* (New Delhi: Oxford University Press, 1992), 292–304.

17. K. Zvelebil, *Lexicon of Tamil Literature*, 721. Uvais, "Cirapuranamum Umaruppulavarum," viii, gives the teacher's name as Catakkatulla Appa, as does Umaru himself.

18. Uvais, "Cirapuranamum Umaruppulavarum," viii. Either Lappai Ali Hajjiyar or his brother was the teacher, according to this account. Yet another version, again received by oral tradition, says that Umaru, through the grace of Nakur Cakul Amitu Antavar (Shahul Hamid, a saint buried in Nagore), received the ability to sing.

19. Ibid., xii.

20. K. Zvelebil, *Lexicon of Tamil Literature*, 722.

21. A *kovai* poem may be composed on God, a chieftain, or a king. The word literally means "string" or "arrangement." A kovai poem frequently has four hundred verses, each dealing with an aspect of love. The most famous is the *Tirukkovaiyar* of Manikkavacakar.

22. This town was the birthplace of Kampan, who wrote the Tamil Ramayana. Umaru Pulavar, of course, is very knowledgeable in the Tamil Ramayana, and it is a striking coincidence that he begins his poem with the very words used to describe the deity of the place where Kampan was born.

23. *Cirappuranam*, "Vilatattuk Kantam, Katavul Valttu Patalam" (The chapter on praising the Lord), 6.

24. *Cirappuranam*, "Vilatattuk Kantam," pt. 1, ed. with commentary by Kalaimamani Kavi Ka. Mu. Sherip (Sharif), commentary on v. 6, p. 17.

25. *Cirappuranam*, "Vilatattuk Kantam, Katavul Valttu Patalam," 11.

26. Ibid., 19.

27. Kurattalvan (twelfth century), *Vaikuntha Stava*, 8.

28. Translated by R. Balakrishna Mudaliyar, *The Golden Anthology of Ancient Tamil Literature*, 3 vols. (Tirunelveli and Madras: South Indian Saiva Siddhanta Works Publishing Society, Tinnevelly, 1959–60), 2:20.

29. *Cirappuranam*, "Vilattatuk Kantam, Nattu Patalam" (The chapter on the countryside), 2–9.

30. *Kampa Ramayanam*, "Bala Kantam, Arruppatalam," 6.

31. *Cirappuranam*, "Vilatattuk Kantam, Nattu Patalam," 9.

32. Nammalvar, *Tiruvaymoli*, 6.10.3.

33. *Cirappuranam*, "Vilatattuk Kantam, Nattu Patalam," 10–11.

34. *Kampa Ramayanam,* "Bala Kantam, Arruppatalam," 7.

35. *Cirappuranam,* "Vilatattuk Kantam, Nattu Patalam," 12.

36. Ibid., 12–17.

37. To these five situations of love two more are added: *peruntinai* and *kaikkilai,* which have no corresponding landscape. *Peruntinai* indicates mismatched love, and *kaikkilai* unrequited love. For discussions of the landscapes, see A. K. Ramanujan, trans., *The Interior Landscape: Love Poems from a Classical Tamil Anthology* (Bloomington: Indiana University Press, 1967), 104–12; K. Zvelebil, *Tamil Literature,* 98–99; K. Zvelebil, *Smile of Murugan* (Leiden: Brill, 1973), 85–110.

38. *Cirappuranam,* "Vilatattuk Kantam, Nattu Patalam," 26.

39. *Cirappuranam,* "Vilatattuk Kantam," pt. 1, p. 80.

40. Literally, "covered with six-legged beetles." *Cirappuranam,* "Vilatattuk Kantam, Nattu Patalam," 30.

41. *Cirappuranam,* "Vilatattuk Kantam, Nakara Patalam" (The chapter on the city), 1–3.

42. *Cirappuranam,* "Vilattattu Kantam, Pukaira Kanta Patalam," 2.

43. The pattern is quite different here from the incorporation of Krishna in Bengali Muslim literature described by Asim Roy, *The Islamic Syncretistic Tradition in Bengal* (Princeton: Princeton University Press, 1983).

44. Kampan's *Ramayanam,* "Bala Kantam, Ulaviyar Patalam," 1–2.

45. *Cirappuranam,* "Kicurattu Kantam, Pattima Tirumanappatalam" (The chapter on Fatima's wedding), 132.

46. Ibid., 134.

47. *Marai* is frequently used by the alvars and in the classical Cankam poetry to refer to the Vedas. It literally means "mystery."

48. Jaimini composed the sutras in the second century B.C.E. and Sabara commented upon them around the second century C.E. On the views of Jaimini, see Francis X. Clooney, *Retrieving the Purva Mimamsa of Jaimini.*

49. For a discussion of dargas in Tamilnadu, see Bayly, *Saints, Goddesses, and Kings,* chaps. 3 and 4. Among the most important dargas was that at Nagore, which I have in "The Zam Zam in Nagore, Tamilnadu: Shahul Hamid in the Tamil Landscape," paper presented at the national meeting of the American Academy of Religion, New Orleans, November 1996.

All translations in this paper are mine, except where other sources are cited. Tamil words are transliterated according to the style accepted by the Tamil lexicon. This is not very helpful in pronouncing the words. Tamil has one letter to denote *ka, kha, ga* and *gha,* one for *ca, cha, ja,* and *jha,* one for *ta, tha, da,* and *dha,* one for *ta, tha, da,* and *dha,* one for *pa, pha, ba,* and *bha.* A native speaker would know how to pronounce the words, which may also vary by community and by region. Centamil or pure Tamil also lacks the letters *sa, sha,* and *ha;* these letters are borrowed from Sanskrit. Thus Sirah is written as Cira but pronounced as Sira. Tamil does not have an equivalent for the English *f* sound and substitutes the letter *p.* Thus, Fatima is written as Patima in Tamil.

4

Admiring the Works of the Ancients

The Ellora Temples as Viewed by Indo-Muslim Authors

Carl W. Ernst

One of the recurrent problems in the interpretation of Indo-Muslim identity is the attempt to ascribe a consistently Muslim attitude toward Hindu temples. This problem arises initially with the incorporation of building materials from Hindu temples in the construction of mosques or other buildings commissioned by Muslim patrons. Although the evidence for the significance of this kind of recycling is sometimes later and retrospective, it is hard to avoid the conclusion that this phenomenon involves the triumphal political use of trophies. Perhaps the most notable example is the Quwwat al-Islam (or Qubbat al-Islam) mosque near the Qutb Minar in Delhi, which contains numerous columns with partially effaced Hindu caryatids and Jain (or Buddhist?) figures, as well as the famous Iron Pillar.[1] This kind of triumphal reuse of temple materials and ancient royal monuments has been seen since British times as evidence of the insatiable propensity of Muslims to destroy idols at every opportunity. Today it affords ammunition to the Hindu extremists who led the attack on the "Baburi" mosque at Ayodhya; the supposition is that the mosque not only rests on the site of the birthplace of Rama but also took the place of a preexisting temple.

There are, of course, competing theories of the exact relationship between the Ayodhya mosque and any preceding temple. Some believe that the mosque was built of the remains of the temple and that the construction of a mosque thus required the demolition of a temple; the reverse of this zero-sum game is that the erection of a temple on that spot would require the destruction of the mosque, as indeed took place in

December 1992. Others like P. N. Oak assume that Muslim buildings are only partially defaced Hindu structures, so that in theory only a slight amount of restoration would presumably be required to return them to their original functions, rather than full-scale destruction and reconstruction; this has the appearance at least of a less costly program. The problem arises, however, when these modern interpretations of Muslim iconoclasm deduce Muslim attitudes from an essential definition of Islam rather than from historical documentation of the significance that particular Muslims attached to Hindu temples. Attempts to describe Muslims as essentially prone to idol-smashing are confounded by the historical record, which indicates that Muslims who wrote about "idol temples" had complex reactions based as much on aesthetic and political considerations as on religion. The concept of unchanging and monolithic Muslim identity accordingly needs to undergo serious revision.

This article is an attempt to fill out the historical dossier, by presenting a translation and analysis of a brief text in which a Muslim author, Rafiʿ al-Dīn Shīrāzī, has set forth a striking interpretation of one of the jewels of Indian architecture, the Ellora cave temples. Shīrāzī viewed Ellora not as religious architecture but as a primarily political monument, which fit best into the category of the wonders of the world. When Shīrāzī's reaction to Ellora is compared with other accounts of it by Muslim authors, with Muslim accounts of other "pagan" monuments in Egypt, and with descriptions of Ellora by early European travelers, his aesthetic and political reaction does not seem very unusual. This account is another reminder that, for premodern Muslims, the monolithic Islam defined by twentieth-century discourse was far from being the only or even the primary category of judgment.

The text in question is *Tadhkirat al-mulūk* (Memorial of kings), a Persian history of Bijapur written by Rafiʿ al-Dīn Shīrāzī in 1612.[2] The author (born in Shiraz in 1540) had a long career in Bijapur government service, from the age of thirty serving Sultan ʿAlī ʿĀdil Shāh as a steward and scribe. In 1596, Sultan Ibrāhīm ʿĀdil Shāh appointed him ambassador to Ahmadnagar, and he also held posts as governor of the Bijapur fort and treasurer. Shīrāzī witnessed many important events over more than half a century in the Deccan, and he was also steeped in the tradition of Persian historical writing, having written abridgements of standard court chronicles such as Mīr Khwānd's *Rawḍat al-ṣafāʿ* and Khwānd Amīr's *Ḥabīb al-siyar*. His history is an important independent historical source comparable to the chronicle of Firishta.

In the handwritten edition of Khālidī, the outline of the text is as follows, divided into an introduction, ten parts, and an appendix:

Introduction (1–15)
I. The Bahmanī dynasty (15–35)
II–V. The ʿĀdil Shāhi dynasty (36–83)
VI. Dynasties of Gujarat, Ahmadnagar, and Golconda (84–156)
VII. Various events in the Deccan (157–96)
VIII. Ibrāhīm ʿĀdil Shāh, the author's patron (197–269)
IX. The Mughals (270–93)
X. The Mughals and Safavids (294–496; in some MSS this lengthy section is divided in three parts to make twelve parts in all)
Appendix. On Wonders and Rarities (497–566)

The section under discussion occurs toward the end (476–83) of the tenth part, and although its title includes the phrase "wonders and rarities," it does not fall into the appendix proper; instead, it is sandwiched between accounts of military campaigns of the Safavids and the Mughals. The appendix consists of a series of accounts of *mirabilia* of the *ʿajāʾib* genre of wonders long established in Arabic and Persian literature.[3] Some of these wonders are related by others, although a few were seen by the author himself. These include narratives based on the Persian *Book of Kings* by Firdawsī (497–517), travelers' tales of strange islands (517–32), and accounts of the rivers and geography of India (532–43), followed by brief reports of natural wonders (544–66).

Shīrāzī's location of his account of Ellora in the dynastic history proper, and not in the appendix on wonders, suggests that he wished to treat it as a serious political concern, framed around a legendary Indian monarch named Parchand Rāō. It thus remains separate from the superficially similar stories about fabulous islands and idol temples that occur in the appendix. Those remain comfortably in the realm of two-headed calves and other marvels, but the serious point that Shīrāzī wanted to make about art and royal monuments required that he situate the story of Ellora amidst similar political and military narratives. In this kind of arrangement Shīrāzī resembles the Egyptian chronicler of the pyramids, al-Idrīsī, who kept his meticulous measurements and historical accounts of the pyramids in one chapter and saved the bizarre and the miraculous for the last chapter of his book.[4] Shīrāzī's chapter has, however, been circulated separately as a "Treatise on Wonders and Rarities," and in this form it would not have taken on the political coloring afforded by its contextual position in the larger history.[5] Here follows a translation of the extract:

Description of the Wonders and Rarities of the Building of Ellora in Daulatabad, Which Parchand Rāō, the Emperor of India, Built Nearly 4,000 Years Ago

1. Parchand Rāō was an emperor. With great majesty, he had brought under his control all the land from the border of Sind, Gujarat, the Deccan, and Telingana to the limit of Malabar, and most of the neighboring kings were his subjects. He was noble, just, and upright, and he lived in harmony with the people. The peasant and the soldier in the days of his reign were in all ways happy and free from worry. They passed all their lives in happiness, joy, contentment, and pleasure.

2. In the springtime, when the climate was perfectly mild, Parchand Rāō would go on a tour of the kingdom, and he let the people partake of his magnificence. He made every effort to bring about justice and fairness. In every place that he saw abundant water, greenery, and good climate, he laid foundations for buildings, and he supplied the officials of the kingdom every resource for completing them. In this way, having traveled through the entire kingdom three times, he constructed and brought to completion lofty idol-houses (*but-khāna*) outside the buildings just mentioned throughout most of his kingdom.

3. Now as for the famous Daulatabad—fine and elegant fabrics were available there, and in the neighborhoods and environs merchants brought them as gifts and donations, and they still are active and do so; wealthy merchants full of tranquillity are always dwelling in that city, both Muslim and Hindu. Every year nearly a thousand ass-loads of different kinds of silken and gold-woven fabrics are brought to its neighborhoods and environs, and general welfare prevails. The same Parchand Rāō made Daulatabad his capital, and people from the four corners of the world headed in the direction of Daulatabad. Most of this multitude came to a place that was nearly five or six farsakhs away, and having built houses and gardens, they settled there; tall houses were set up with some difficulty.

4. One day in the assembly of Parchand Rāō there was a discussion of the construction of buildings and abodes, and the king said,

"During my reign, I have built and finished many buildings in my dominion, but these ordinary buildings do not have much permanency. I want a building that will be truly permanent, so that it will be spoken of for years afterward, and there should be wonders and rarities in it so that it will endure and remain lasting for long years and uncounted centuries, and its construction will be famed and well known throughout the world."

5. Some of the architects, engineers, and stoneworkers were dedicated to the emperor and spoke his language, because of the many buildings that they had made. They said, "In the region of this very city there is a mountain that is unlike any of the mountains of the world. This is because the mountains that we have seen and see today are mostly of this kind: part is bedrock, and part is soft and has cracks and fissures. In this city there is a great and lofty mountain that has absolutely no cracks, joints, fissures, or rubble. In this way, one can make a great and lofty house, which every great king can do, for lofty buildings have been repeatedly built. If one brings together all the eighteen workshops of the realm, which are famous and well known, so that the supervisor does not need to have any other building built, and he has the capacity and basis associated with that workshop, and the quantity of men and animals necessary for those workshops, then they will prepare everything from stone: the assembly of the king's realm, the private palaces, the soldiers in attendance on the king—all will be carved in stone, so that each will be established in the proper place. Until the dawn of the resurrection, that court, those workshops, and those people will all be preserved, each in the proper place. Such a court as this, this foundation, and this army will all be in five or six sections of stone, with the human and the other animals of proper proportions in the same form and size in which they were created, neither larger nor smaller."

6. The emperor said, "This account that you have given, if it is possible and can indeed take form, is a wonder. By all means, let them make a model from wax or chalk so that I can have a look." When the artisans, engineers, and stoneworkers heard that the emperor asked for a model, they had to come to agreement and make a completed model such as the emperor had asked for from brick, clay, and chalk. When they invited the emperor to their premises [to see the model], he became very happy, and he consented with delight.

7. Beginning from the middle of the mountain, they made a great open space in the palace, which they call the retreat (*khilwat-khāna*). On all four sides of the open space, they cut open spaces (*sar-sāya,* lit. "shades") in the stone, perfect in height, width, and length, with a polished and proportioned foundation. In most places these are carved in the fashion of great arches (*ṭāq*) needing no pillars. The carving is extremely even and polished, or rather, is even given a luster. In some of these open spaces there are alcoves (*bahl,* usually *bahla,* lit. "purse") with caves. Their ability reaches such subtlety that if the master artist wished to paint one with a brush made from a single hair, nowhere would it be easy for him [to match their skill]. In some of the arches there is a string of camels, and in some a stable of horses. Some are with saddle, and some with colored blankets. There is no need to mention the extraordinary workmanship and subtlety again. One should compare the alcove with the palace; in each one of these palaces there are some human forms in the attitude of servants, which are necessary in those palaces. One would say that all are standing ready to serve, while some appear in such a way that one would say they are in the act of being rejected. The remaining animals, wild beasts and birds . . . are everywhere in the manner of delivering an obligatory reply to a question. The forms of armed and equipped soldiers, to the number of one or two hundred, are as if ready for service, each one established in his own place. On the courtyard in front of the palace gate, here and there several large and small elephants are standing in order. Around each elephant a few attendants stand in their regalia.

Description of the Foundation of the Palace Fort and Its Capacity

8. Four arches (*ṭāq*) cut from stone are on one side of the courtyard, and within, two shorter ones are in the place of the gate. Symmetrical in height, breadth, and length, these four are linked by a single roof. Two great benches (*ṣuffa*) are built into the great arches, as a seat for servants, for the servants of the fort and the courtyard are within. Nearly five or six hundred people are sitting in their places, some standing fully armed. Outside of that, many weapons are carved in various places, such as swords, daggers, dirks (Hindi *kat-āra*), spears, bows, quivers, and arrows. One remains in astonishment at the subtle and painstaking work. In the

courtyard, inside the four arches, are benches, porticoes (*ayvān*), and rooms carved and hollowed out in the same style. On one side are the imperial workshops, such as the armory, stable, waterworks, kitchen, storehouse, and wine cellar. In every one of these palaces there are at least fifty or sixty human forms, each one of which appears to be in the act of performing something. The skill of each workshop is cut into rock to such a degree that the human mind cannot imagine it. Everyone who goes there says that the people [in the stone reliefs] are having a party. One should spend several days at the palace if one wishes to see them all, and to understand them fully a long lifetime would be needed. Many wild beasts and birds have also been added to these festivals to adorn the palace.

9. Proceeding behind this palace, there is a fort and some other palaces pertaining to the previously mentioned palace. Here too a multitude of figures is made in the form of servants, done with great workmanship, in a more prominent position, and the courtyard of this is greater than that in the previous palace. Some workshops are set up in this palace, and benches, arches, and porticoes have been raised up to heaven. By way of workshops, things such as the bachelor quarters (*dār al-ʿazab*), goldsmith shop, fountain shop, wardrobe, treasury, and the like [have been made] with such subtlety and workmanship that a hair of a single brush could not have rendered it. The attendants of the workshops, their trade, tools, and basis of each workshop have been made to the necessary extent, each one being made in the performance of [the appropriate] action, and each servant of these palaces has been made firm in the proper position.

A Hint of Conditions of the Court and the Arrangement of the Place of the Workmen and Attendants

10. Having made another palace with the arch and portico in perfect proportion, and having placed some smaller palaces to the sides with workmanship and beauty, and the imperial throne at the front of the portico, they fixed the portrait of the emperor upon it, depicting that amount of ornament on the limbs of the emperor that is customary among the people of India, some sculpted and some in relief. Its painstaking subtlety is beyond description. To the left and right of that throne, half-thrones have been prepared with solid foundations, and on each of these they have sat princes

and nobles of the realm. Behind the head and shoulders of the emperor are servants, friends, and relatives, each in the proper place. There are some watchmen holding swords with handkerchiefs in their hands, in the Deccan fashion. Waterbearers in their own manner and order hold vessels of water in their hands, and waiters (*shīra-chī*) hold a few flagons with cups in their hands. Winebearers, by which I mean betel-leaf servers, hold trays of betel leaf in their hands with suitable accompaniments, some trays having sweet-scented things, for in each tray are cups of musk, saffron, and other items. The saucers in those trays are made in the fashion of cups, with pounded ambergris, sandalwood, and aloes, and aromatic compounds are set forth, and trays full of roses. This portico, which is subtler in arrangement than a rose, is such that the description, beauty, workmanship, and subtlety of workmanship of that assembly do not fit into the vessel of explanation.

11. In front of that portico of the court, the chief musician (*sar-i nawbatān*) and the court prefect (*shiḥna-i dīvān*) stand in the proper arrangement and position in their places. On both sides, nearly 2,000 horsemen, extremely well executed, are in attendance in the proper fashion. In the courtyard of the court and the portico, across from the emperor, there are several groups of musicians, each standing with his own drum and lute; one would say that they are dancing. In the same courtyard, tumblers, jesters, wrestlers, athletes, and swordsmen exhibit their skill. One would say that each group in its particular area and assembly is right in the middle of its activity. Several famous and large elephants, which were always the apple of the emperor's alchemical eye, are in his presence, and several head of elite imperial horses, which were always present with the court drum, are present in the customary fashion.

12. So many beautiful and well wrought things are in those buildings and courtyards that, if one wished to explain them all, he would fail to reach the goal. The listener should prepare for fatigue of the brain!

13. Outside this assembly, several other small banquet assemblies have been made and constructed, which tongue and pen are unable to explain. Three or four private palaces have been built, and in each palace are the private inhabitants, who are the women and eunuchs—more than one or two hundred. Each one is in a distinct style and position, and a detailed account of the motions

and postures of those palaces would not be inappropriate; it can be generally summarized in a few words. In each of these palaces some obscene activities—none repeated—are taking place.

14. In general, of that which is actually in existence at Ellora, not one part in a thousand has been mentioned. Few people have reached the limit of its buildings, and those who have [come] simply take in the generality of it with a glance. What is presently observable and displayed takes up nearly two farsakhs. Even further, there are places with buildings and hunting lodges, but a wall of chalk and stone has been firmly set up, so no one goes past that place. It is famous.

15. There is a smaller building like this in a village at least fifty farsakhs from Ellora. It is said that in every place palaces, buildings, and hunting lodges have been built in the same fashion, and it is still in existence. But God knows best as to the realities of the situation.

Description of Various Matters on the Same Subject

16. There are several constructions of similar form in the neighborhood of Shiraz, and that region is called Naqsh-i Rustam and The Forty Towers (Chihil Sutun, i.e., Persepolis). In *The History of Persia* it is well known that there were four such towers that Jamshid had made, and on top of all the towers he had made a single tall building, so that these towers were pillars for that building. He spent most of his time in that building sitting on the seat of lordship and holding public audience. The people from below bowed to him and worshiped him. In that building of Ellora, most places are roofed and dark. Some places are made with illumination from windows, and most rooms have no roof and are perfectly illuminated. Since this was three or four thousand years ago, and in that time lifetimes were long, and humans were mighty of frame and full of power and strength, such places as have been written of [above], which they made—if anyone of this age wished to make them, and had a thousand people and a period of a thousand years, it is not known whether it could be carried out to completion. In fact, the intellect is astonished at that construction.

17. There was always a joke about that building which was shared between the former Burhān Niẓām Shāh and Shāh Ṭāhir. The Niẓām Shāh used to say that sodomy was brought to the Deccan during the present time by foreigners [i.e., Persians]. Shāh

Ṭāhir objected that this practice is immemorial in this kingdom. Once when they went to visit the buildings of Ellora, Shāh Ṭāhir saw a depiction of two men embracing each other. He took the hand of the Niẓām Shāh and brought him near that depiction, saying, "Have foreigners brought this also?" By this example, he removed the Niẓām Shāh's displeasure with foreigners.

Description of the Idol Temple of the Town of Lakmīr

18. In the neighborhood of Bankapur is a town called Lakmīr. In ancient times, it was the capital of one of the great emperors of unbelief. With the greatest architectural skill, the emperors, princes, and pillars of the realm built many idol temples in imitation of one another, extremely large and well built. Years passed, and most of the buildings fell into ruin, and only a few were still inhabited. But four hundred idol temples remained perfectly sound, having been constructed with the utmost of painstaking and elegant workmanship. At the time when we saw it, we saw many wonders and rarities, and astonishment increased upon astonishment. Out of all those, we saw one idol temple with dimensions of seventy cubits by fifty cubits. Both inside and outside of it a trough (*taghārī*) had been cut in relief. Its subtlety was to the degree that in the space of a hand, in natural proportions, the forms of ten men had been made, along with the forms of ten or fifteen animals, both beasts and birds, in such a way that the eyelashes and fingernails were visible. On the border were roses, tulips, and trees of the locality, about the size of one hand. This degree of artistry has been forgotten.

19. Imagine how much work has been done on the inside and outside of all the idol temples, and how many days and how much time it took to complete them. May God the exalted and transcendent forgive the World-Protector [i.e., ʿAlī ʿĀdil Shāh, d. 988/1580] with the light of his compassion, for after the conquest of Vijayanagar, he with his own blessed hand destroyed five or six thousand adored idols of unbelief, and ruined most of the idol temples [at the battle of Talikota or Bannihatti, January 1565]. But the limited number [of buildings] on which the welfare of the time and the kingdom depended, which we know as the art of Ellora in Daulatabad, this kind of idol temple and art we have forgotten.

There are several striking aspects to this text. First of all, Shīrāzī makes hardly any reference to Indian religions in his description of

Ellora. Second, he appreciates the monument on an aesthetic level, and he explains its origin in political terms. For him, Ellora is a royal monument that depicts the court life of an ancient king of India, making it comparable to pre-Islamic Persian monuments such as Persepolis.[6] The statue of Shiva in the Kailas temple is explained as a royal portrait. Third, and most unexpectedly, he only makes a strong bow to religion when he calls upon God to forgive his former patron, Sultan ʿAlī ʿĀdil Shāh, for destroying the temples of Vijayanagar. This last gesture turns the stereotype of Muslim iconoclasm on its head. Shīrāzī acknowledges that temple destruction has taken place in military and political contexts of conquest, but he deplores it as a violation of beauty and, ultimately, as an offense against God. Although he does not mention it, the temple at Bankapur, which he also admires, was evidently the "superb temple" that ʿAlī ʿĀdil Shāh destroyed and replaced with a mosque when he took the city in 1575.[7] Shīrāzī's strong emotional and religious reaction against the destruction of temples is all the more noteworthy in view of his basically conservative Muslim attitude; his account of the religious innovations of the Mughal emperor Akbar is highly critical, closely resembling Badā'ūnī's negative view of Akbar rather than the universalist perspective of Abū al-Faḍl.[8]

Shīrāzī was not the first Muslim to appreciate the importance of Ellora. The Arab scholar Masʿūdī (d. 956) spent several years as ambassador to the powerful Rashtrakuta empire, under whose auspices some of the temples of Ellora were constructed; the Rashtrakutas had friendly relations with the Arabs, whom they viewed as allies against the Gurjaras of northern India.[9] In his *Meadows of Gold*, in the context of a lengthy disquisition on temples of the ancient world, Masʿūdī briefly describes the temple of Ellora in the following passage, noting that in another place (unfortunately, a lost work) he has more fully discussed "the temples (*hayākil*) in India dedicated to idols (*aṣnām*) in the form of Buddhas (*bidada*), which have appeared since ancient times in the land of India, and information about the great temple which is in India, known as Ellora; this is an object of pilgrimage (*yuqṣadu*) from far distances in India. It has a land endowment, and around it are a thousand cells, where monks supervise the worship (*taʿẓīm*) of this idol in India."[10]

It should be noted that in this account, Masʿūdī does not distinguish between Hindu, Buddhist, or Jain temples and images; the words for "idol" in Arabic (*bidada*) and Persian (*but*) were in fact derived from *Buddha* (he immediately follows this reference with a vague note about the temple to the sun in Multan).[11] Indian temples are viewed here in a continuum with Roman, Egyptian, and Ṣābian temples, a point to which we shall return. Later references to Ellora by Muslim authors belong to the period after the Turkish conquest of the Deccan, when the temples of Ellora had ceased to function as an active religious center. According to Firishta, it was during some unofficial sightseeing at Ellora in 1307 that some Turkish soldiers stumbled across the Hindu princess Dewal Rānī, whom they captured and brought to Delhi as a bride for Khīḍr Khān.[12] In 1318, Sultan Quṭb al-Dīn Mubārak Shāh Khaljī spent a month at Ellora awaiting the return of his general, Khusraw Khān, from campaigns in Warangal.[13] A tradition related in a current gazetteer maintains that ʿAlīʾ al-Dīn Ḥasan, founder of the Bahmanī dynasty of the Deccan, visited Ellora in 1352, "taking with him those who could read the inscriptions and understand the significance of the frescoes and statuary on the walls."[14] We have seen above how the ruler of Ahmadnagar, Burhān Niẓām Shāh, and his Persian minister, Shāh Ṭāhir, used to visit Ellora for pleasure.

The most surprising of all the admirers of Ellora is none other than the Mughal emperor Awrangzīb, who spent years in the Deccan, first as governor under Shāh Jahān, and later as emperor reducing the Deccan sultanates and quashing Maratha rebels. He was buried in 1707 in the Chishtī shrine complex at Khuldabad, just a few miles down the road from Ellora. In a letter, Awrangzīb recorded a visit to Khuldabad, Daulatabad, and Ellora, describing the latter as "one of the wonders of the work of the true transcendent Artisan (*az ʿajāʾibāt-i ṣunʿ-i ṣāniʿ-i ḥaqīqī subḥānahu*)," in other words, a creation of God.[15] The tourist visiting Ellora today is inevitably informed that half-ruined elephants, etc., are due to Awrangzīb's fanatical destruction of idols, but there is no historical evidence to indicate that the emperor engaged in any destruction there, or why he would have stopped with so much left undone. J. B. Seely, a British soldier who spent several weeks on furlough at Ellora in 1810, recorded many reports from local informants on idol smashing and cow slaughter by Awrangzīb at Ellora, but he viewed them with the same skepticism that he reserved for tales of Portuguese doing the same.[16] Catherine Asher has pointed out that the reports of Awrangzīb's iconoclasm in the Deccan are typically from late sources that may reflect nothing more than legends that were hung on Awrangzīb; his documented acts of temple destruction were almost all associated with putting down political rebellions.[17] Ironically, some of the examples of

Awrangzīb's temple destruction given by these late sources are failed attempts, frustrated by snakes, scorpions, or a deity. It seems that temple destruction is viewed as an essential characteristic of Awrangzīb, regardless of whether he succeeded in actually carrying it out.[18]

The reaction of Shīrāzī to the destruction of Vijayanagar's temples can be compared to that of certain Muslim writers in Egypt in the thirteenth century, who were enthusiastic admirers of the great pyramids at Giza. As Ulrich Haarmann put it, they were "deeply disturbed by the brutal demolition of intact pharaonic remains and the mutilation of pagan pictorial representations in the name of Islam, yet in reality all too often out of a very mundane greed for cheap and at the same time high-quality building materials."[19] Similarly one may quote the physician ʿAbd al-Laṭīf, who in 1207 made the following remarks about Egyptian temples: "It is useless to halt to describe their greatness, the excellence of their construction and the just proportion of their forms, this innumerable multitude of figures, of sculptures both recessed and in relief, and of inscriptions that they offer to the admiration of spectators, all joined to the solidity of their construction and the enormous size of the stones and materials in use."[20] The literature of Muslim travelers in fact contains much of this kind of admiration for ancient "pagan" monuments.

The non-Islamic origin of these temples does not seem to have been a particularly big stumbling block to Muslim tourists. Some, like Shīrāzī, simply found religion irrelevant to their appreciation. Others were able to assimilate the non-Islamic religious traditions to acceptable categories. A number of Muslim authors interpreted the religion of the ancient Egyptians as forming part of the Ṣābian religion, an obscure Qur'ānic term which permitted groups such as the Hellenistic pagans of Harran to function as "people of the book" for centuries.[21] Popular Coptic mythology combined with Hermetic lore permitted Muslims to identify the great pyramids as the tombs of Agathodaimon (Seth), Hermes (Idris), and Sab, founder of the Sabeans, or else as the constructions of the Arab ancestor Shaddād ibn ʿĀd.[22]

Further examples can be added to the dossier of Muslim tourists who wrote appreciatively of Indian temples. The Timurid ambassador ʿAbd al-Razzāq Samarqandī, who visited Vijayanagar at the order of Shāh Rukh in 1442, reported with delight on the functioning temples he visited en route near Mangalore and Belur. He compared these temples to the paradisal garden of Iram mentioned in the Qur'ān, and remarked that they were covered from top to bottom "with paintings, after the manner of the Franks and the people of Khata [Cathay]."[23] Another instance is the Afghan traveler Maḥmūd ibn Amīr Walī Balkhī, who wrote a Persian narrative of a journey from Balkh to India and Ceylon and back, completed after seven years' travel in 1631. He traveled for pleasure only, and on his return to Balkh he was appointed to a librarian's position. He has described at length, though with some disparagement, the rituals performed at the Krishna temple constructed by Rāja Mān Singh near Mathura. More entertainingly, he has related his own participation in the festival at the Jagannath temple in the city of Puri, where by his own admission he doffed his clothes and joined the throng of pilgrims, thus participating in the dramatic rituals firsthand.[24] There are undoubtedly other similar accounts.

Shīrāzī's aesthetic delight in Ellora places his reaction in a category separate from the moralizing reactions to vanished earthly glory, the theme of *ubi sunt qui ante nos in mundo fuere.* Shīrāzī would have been familiar with the great Persian poem of Khāqānī (d. 1199) on the ruins of the ancient Persian palace at Ctesiphon, the famous *Tuḥfat al-ʿirāqayn.* Unlike Khāqānī and the Egyptian al-Idrīsī, Shīrāzī does not draw an admonition (*ʿibrat*) from the fall of kingly power.[25] In his view, the destruction of the temples of Vijayanagar is a cause for meditation not on the vanity of human wishes but rather on the tragedy of the loss of beauty. Shīrāzī's perspective contrasts with that of figures such as the Naqshbandī Sufi leader Āḥmad Sirhindī, whose anti-Indian attitude led him to regard the ruins scattered over India as evidence of divine punishment for failure to pay heed to divinely inspired messengers.[26] Later Muslim tourists at Ellora would combine moralizing reflection on the decline of ancient pagans with enjoyment of the beautiful natural and artistic setting. Here is how this kind of reflection is presented in the *Maʾāthir-i ʿĀlamgīrī,* a history of Awrangzīb's reign, completed in 1711:

> A short distance from here [i.e., Khuldabad] is a place named Ellorā where in ages long past, sappers possessed of magical skill excavated in the defiles of the mountain spacious houses for a length of one *kos.* On all their ceilings and walls many kinds of images with lifelike forms have been carved. The top of the hill looks level, so much so that no sign of the buildings within it is apparent [from outside]. In ancient times when the sinful infidels had dominion over this country, certainly they and not demons (*jinn*) were the builders of these caves, although tradition differs on the point; it was a place of worship of the tribe of false believers. At present it is a desolation in spite of its strong foundations; it

> rouses the sense of warning [of doom] to those who contemplate the future [end of things]. In all seasons, and particularly in the monsoons, when this hill and the plain below resemble a garden in the luxuriance of its vegetation and the abundance of its water, people come to see the place. A waterfall a hundred yards in width tumbles down from the hill. It is a marvelous place for strolling, charming to the eye. Unless one sees it, no written description can correctly picture it. How then can my pen adorn the page of my narrative?[27]

In this passage the moralizing tone is almost a perfunctory note, inserted in what is for the most part an enthusiastic report.

To modern Muslim scholars, Ellora provides a very different sort of lesson. Now equipped with the religious analysis that separates Hinduism, Jainism, and Buddhism, the contemporary Iranian Indologist Jalālī Nā'īnī cites Ellora as one of a series of Indian monuments that form an outstanding ancient example of that modern religious virtue, religious tolerance. "Apparently, prior to the edict [of Ashoka] in the Indian subcontinent, as early as the Vedic age, there was a kind of tolerance and patience between followers of various religions in terms of differing beliefs. Support for this assumption includes the hymns of the Veda and the caves of Ajanta and Ellora. In these caves the temples of three religions—Hindu, Jain, and Buddhist—are located in the bosom, the very heart of the mountains and hills of the Vindhya mountain range, about 60 miles from Aurangabad, and they can be taken as a clear sign of religious freedom and the search for peace and tranquillity among the followers of the three indigenous religions of India."[28]

The vocabulary and conceptual apparatus of this remark derive from the European enlightenment rather than from medieval Islamicate culture. Nonetheless, one might characterize it as yet another Muslim reaction to Ellora, which puts the cave temples into a historical sequence constructed in terms of the relations between religions. It is also interesting to consider the estimate of Ellora by the former head of the archeological service of Hyderabad state, the well-known Muslim scholar Ghulam Yazdani: "At Ellora the religious fervor of the followers of the Brāhmanical faith has carved out in the living rock temples which might well have been considered to be the work of gods not only by the votaries of that religion but also by the most discerning critic of the period, because they are unique specimens of this kind of architecture in the world."[29] The British, in contrast, tended to be reassured by looking at these monuments, since they saw no one in India capable of building such grandeur who thus might prove an obstacle to their plans.[30] As Seely put it, "Surely these wonderful workmen must have been of a different race to the present degenerate Hindoos, or the country and government must have been widely different from what it is at the present day."[31] We would doubtless ascribe this reaction to the colonial mentality rather than to any internal imperative derived from Christianity.

Today every Indian schoolchild is taught the names of the ancient and medieval kings of India. Harsha and Candragupta Maurya are at least as well known as Alexander and Caesar are to western history texts. It is often forgotten that before the nineteenth century, and the prodigious antiquarian efforts of early orientalists and the Archeological Survey, these names had vanished from living memory. The rise and fall of multiple dynasties had erased the meaning of many monuments that dot the Indian landscape. Oral narratives were bound to replace lost traditions with plausible tales about the mighty men of old capable of building such wonders. We do not know what stories were told to Bijapur officials by local dwellers in the vicinity of Daulatabad about the impressive temples of Ellora, but they may well have been connected to images of the Daulatabad fort, which has notable stylistic similarities with the construction of Ellora.[32] Shīrāzī's political interpretation of the monument does not seem strange when compared with the explanations that were offered to Seely by his guides in 1810. Large guardian figures were still being identified with Persian terms from Indo-Muslim court life, such as *chūbdār* (mace-bearer) and *pahlavān* (wrestler).[33]

It is hard to recall that, before the age of modern tourism, travelers were not likely to see evidence of what we would call a foreign culture. The first European explorers of Asia and the New World went equipped with fantasies like *The Travels of Sir John Mandeville*, and they saw the cannibals, Amazons, and giants that they were prepared to see. Early European engravings of Indian idols have more than a passing resemblance to Roman deities. When the Portuguese explorer Vasco da Gama and his crew arrived in India in 1498, so great was their relief in seeing buildings that were evidently not "Moorish" mosques that they accepted the Hindu temples of Calicut as Christian churches, kneeling in prayer before goddesses that they described as images of the Virgin Mary and the saints (they were evidently unconcerned by the unusually large teeth and extra arms of these images).[34] Seely notes that the first Indian soldiers sent to Egypt, in British military expeditions to combat

Napoleon, announced in amazement that the ancient Egyptians clearly worshiped Hindu gods in their temples; this was probably the first Indian hermeneutic of pharaonic antiquities.[35] In a sense the response of the sepoys was a repetition of the reactions of early visitors from Herodotus onwards, who described the gods of Egypt in terms of their own theologies. When Shīrāzī saw Ellora as analogous to Persepolis, he was only making a natural comparison from his own experience of ancient monuments. Seely did much the same when he described what he saw as Sphinxes at Ellora.[36]

Muslims were not the only ones to reinvent Ellora's significance along new lines. When the Rashtrakutas conquered the Chalukyas and took over power in the Deccan in the seventh century, in addition to adding new Hindu monuments such as the Kailas temple, they converted Buddhist viharas into Hindu temples, chiseling out many Buddha images at Ellora and covering or replacing some with images of Vishnu.[37] Architectural guidebooks unfortunately do not indicate what essential characteristic of Hinduism caused this extreme form of renovation. The Yadavas of Deogir were not a direct extension of the Rashtrakutas, and they must have formed their own interpretations of the meaning of Ellora, a monument near the center of their empire. While we can only speculate about the way the Yadavas positioned themselves in relation to Ellora, their interpretation must have reflected their own self-interpretation as a successor-state to the Rashtrakutas. The founder of the Mahanabhuva sect, Cakradara, is said to have briefly established a new form of worship in Ellora that was completely unrelated to the Shaiva, Buddhist, and Jain traditions of earlier eras.[38] Ellora evidently took on a new significance among the elites of the Marathas, starting from the sixteenth century. As James Laine points out, Maloji, grandfather of the Maratha warrior Shivaji, is buried in an Islamicate tomb in the village of Ellora.[39] In the eighteenth century, Ellora evidently received further patronage from the ruling Maratha family of the Holkars, who must have interpreted the monuments in terms of their own political and religious position.[40]

European travelers such as Anquetil du Perron in 1760 and Seely in 1810 were informed by local brahmins that Buddha images in some of the caves actually represented Vishvakarma (a form of Vishnu), and Seely was given conflicting opinions about the meaning of Jain figures in a cave that the guides regarded as dedicated to Jagannath (another form of Vishnu).[41] These Hindu names for Buddhist and Jain temples are still used in current guidebooks. Anquetil was also told that a number of Ellora temples were the various tombs of Vishnu; his brahmin informants said that other cave temples near Bombay had been built by Alexander.[42] Goddess figures at Ellora were always identified for Seely as Bhavani, following her ascendancy in modern Maratha culture. Seely occasionally caught his guides changing their identifications of images, but this he attributed to the confusion inherent in Hindu mythology rather than to any other cause.[43] Col. Meadows Taylor, author of *Confessions of a Thug,* claimed that a Thug told him that the Ellora caves contained depictions of all the methods of murder employed by the Thugs.[44] All this goes to say that Ellora, like any ancient monument, has not had a single fixed meaning over time. The precincts were constructed over centuries, with multiple religious patterns that we today distinguish by the categories of Hindu, Buddhist, and Jain. Different generations of patrons contributed their own interpretations with their commissions and constructions. Just as the monuments themselves are subject to physical modification by later visitors and patrons, so their meaning has been adjusted to the symbolic parameters of new civilizational orders.

As far as the question of Muslim iconoclasm is concerned, the evidence of Muslim travelers who visited Hindu temples does not provide justification for assuming that idol-smashing activity is easily detectable, much less the visceral instinct that it is often assumed to be. The examples cited above are not random or selective, but constitute the results of a fairly extensive search for textual reactions by Muslims to Hindu temples. Why should we assume that Muslims are by nature and training iconoclastic, and when they do violence to idols or temples, why do we assume that this behavior is rooted in Islamic faith? Take the example of Babur, in an incident that took place near Gwalior in 1528. On that occasion, he recorded a bout of severe opium sickness with much vomiting. The next day, he saw some Jain statues, which he described as follows: "On the southern side is a large idol, approximately 20 yards tall. They are shown stark naked with all their private parts exposed. Around the two large reservoirs inside Urwahi have been dug twenty to twenty-five wells, from which water is drawn to irrigate the vegetation, flowers, and trees planted there. Urwahi is not a bad place. In fact, it is rather nice. Its one drawback was the idols, so I ordered them destroyed." The following day, he visited Gwalior fort. "Riding out from this garden we made a tour of Gwalior's temples, some of which are two and three stories but are squat and in the ancient style with dadoes entirely of figures sculpted in stone. Other temples are like madrasas, with porches and large, tall domes and chambers like those of a madrasa. Atop the lower chambers are stone-carved idols. Having examined the edifices, we went out."[45] At that point he enjoyed an outdoor feast.

What part of Babur's behavior during these three days was Islamic? On day one, he was hung over from drug intoxication, on day two, he destroyed two naked Jain idols, and on day three he enjoyed a pleasant excursion to Hindu temples with the governor of Gwalior fort and left the idols there intact. Why did he destroy idols on one day and enjoy them the next? His good mood on the third day may have had something to do with either his recovery from hangover or the embassy of submission he received that morning from a major Rajput ruler. Alternatively, he may have considered it ill-mannered to destroy part of a monument he was being shown, in a fort that one of his subordinates was in charge of. In any case it is clear that it is highly problematic to predict political behavior (such as destruction of temples) from the nominal religious identity that may be ascribed to an individual or group, without reference to personal, political, and historical factors.

Above all, it is noteworthy that the occasions when Muslim writers have invoked God and religion in relation to Hindu monuments have been when they have been awed by the creation of beauty. While Rafīʿ al-Dīn Shīrāzī in a sense reduced the significance of Ellora to the familiar terms of imperial monuments, he was also stirred to protest on religious grounds against the iconoclasm of his imperial patron. It does not seem accidental that at the moment of praising the extraordinary, even in what seems the stereotyped convention of the wonders of the world, the emotion of reverence should take control. It would be a shame if contemporary ideological conflicts blinded us to the perception of the profound admiration that Indian monuments like Ellora have evoked in Muslim visitors. More to the point, accounts like Shīrāzī's indicate that Muslims had complex reactions to non-Muslim religious sites. Their responses could be dictated by a variety of factors, including their education and temperament, the political situation, and whether the building fell into the category of ancient wonder or living temple (Muslims seem to have enjoyed both). The popular one-dimensional portrait of Muslim iconoclasm survives as a durable stereotype because it does not acknowledge its subjects as actors in historical contexts. The iconoclasm stereotype derives not from the actual attitudes of Muslims toward temples, but from a predetermined normative definition of Islam. The reasons for the appeal of such religious stereotypes, ironically, will need to be sought elsewhere.

Notes

1. To this category of the trophy belongs the transport of Ashokan columns and other ancient pillars, of which the Iron Pillar of Delhi is but one example. These trophies may be found in royal mosques of the Sultanate period at Hisar and Jaunpur as well as the Quwwat al-Islam mosque of Delhi, and possibly at Tughluqabad as well. Cf. Mehrdad Shokoohy and Natalie H. Shokoohy, "Tughluqubad, the Earliest Surviving Town of the Delhi Sultanate," *Bulletin of the School of Oriental and African Studies* 57 (1994): 548.

2. I am basing this analysis on the critical edition of the text established by the late Abū Naṣr Khālidī, which has been entrusted to me by his son, Omar Khālidī, to see through the press; it is to be published by the Islamic Research Foundation of the Asitan-i Quds-i Rizawi in Mashhad, Iran. For further information on this author, see my articles "Shīrāzī, Rafiʿ al-Dīn," in *The Encyclopaedia of Islam*, ed. H. A. R. Gibb et al., 2nd ed. (Leiden: E. J. Brill, 1960–), IX, 483 (cited henceforth as EI^2), and "Ebrāhīm Shīrāzī," in *Encyclopedia Iranica* (Costa Mesa, Calif.: Mazda Publishers, 1986–), VIII, 76.

3. C. E. Dubler, "ʿAdjāʾib," EI^2, I, 203–4.

4. Ulrich Haarmann, "In Quest of the Spectacular: Noble and Learned Visitors to the Pyramids around 1200 A.D.," in *Islamic Studies Presented to Charles J. Adams*, ed. Wael B. Hallaq and Donald P. Little (Leiden: E. J. Brill, 1991), 65–66.

5. Hājī Muḥammad Ashraf, *Catalogue of Persian Manuscripts in the Salar Jung Museum and Library*, vol. 2, *Biographies, Geography, and Travels* (Hyderabad: Salar Jung Museum and Library, 1966), 277, no. 643.

6. On Persepolis, see M. Streck [G. C. Miles], "Iṣṭakhr," EI^2, IV, pp. 219–22. It is worth noting that the author of this article attributes the defacement of human figures at Persepolis to "Muslim fanaticism," something that calls for further analysis.

7. Mahomed Kasim Ferishta, *History of the Rise of the Mahomedan Power in India, Till the Year A.D. 1612*, trans. J. Briggs, 4 vols. (London, 1829; reprint, Lahore: Sang-e Meel, 1977), 3:84, dates this to 1573, but epigraphic evidence places this conquest in December 1575; see H. K. Sherwani and P. M. Joshi, eds., *History of Medieval Deccan, 1295–1724*, 2 vols. (Hyderabad: Government of Andhra Pradesh, 1973–74), 1:335.

8. Iqtidar Alam Khan, "The Tazkirat ul-Muluk by Rafi'uddin Ibrahim Shirazi: As a Source on the History of Akbar's Reign," *Studies in History* 2 (1980): 41–55.

9. André Wink, *Al-Hind: The Making of the Indo-Islamic World*, vol. 1, *Early Medieval India and the Expansion of Islam, 7th–11th Centuries* (Delhi: Oxford University Press, 1990), 303–9, esp. 305.

10. Abū al-Ḥasan ʿAlī ibn al-Ḥusayn ibn ʿAlī al-Masʿūdī, *Murūj al-dhahab wa*

ma'ādin al-jawāhir, 4th ed., ed. Muḥammad Muḥyī al-Dīn 'Abd al-Hamīd, 4 vols. (Egypt: al-Maktaba al-Tajāriyya, 1384/1964), 2:262; cf. Mas'ūdī, *Les Prairies d'or*, trans. Barbier de Maynard and Pavet de Courteille, ed. Charles Pellat, Collection d'Ouvrages Orientaux (Paris: Société Asiatique, 1965), 2:547, §1424, corresponding to 4:95–96 in the nineteenth-century edition of the Arabic text by Barbier de Maynard. There are problems in the Arabic text published in Egypt; I have followed the French translators in reading *bidada* rather than *badra* (which would result in "the form of the moon" rather than "in the form of Buddhas"), and Ellora (*Alūrá*) rather than the anomalous MS readings *al-adrī* and *bilād al-ray*. Both Arabic editions are in error, however, in reading *jawārin* ("female slaves," pl. of *jāriya*) in place of *jiwārun* ("resident pilgrims," pl. of *jār*, probably in this case meaning Jain monks); this led the French translators to render the last phrase as "jeunes esclaves destinées aux pèlerins qui viennent de toute l'Inde pour adorer cette idole." From what we know of Ellora under the Rashtrakutas, it would have functioned as a monastery rather than as a massive *dēvadāsī* center.

11. The British traveler Seely, too, was fairly vague about the relations between Hinduism and Buddhism; see J. B. Seely, *The Wonders of Ellora or the Narrative of a Journey to the Temples or Dwellings Excavated out of a Mountain of Granite at Ellora in the East Indies* (London, 1824), 197–98.

12. Abū al-Qāsim Firishta, *Gulshan-i Ibrāhīmī* (Lucknow: Nawal Kishōr, 1281/1864–65), 1:117; Mahomed Kasim Ferishta, *History of the Rise of the Mahomedan Power in India*, 1:210.

13. Banarsi Prasad Saksena, "Qutbuddin Mubarak Khalji," in Mohammad Habib and Khaliq Ahmad Nizami, ed., *A Comprehensive History of India*, vol. 5, *The Delhi Sultanate, (A.D. 1206–1526)* (New Delhi: People's Publishing House, 1970; reprint, 1982), 436.

14. *Aurangabad District, Maharashtra State Gazetteers*, 2d ed. (Bombay: Gazetteers Department, Government of Maharashtra, 1977), 88. This information is apparently drawn from an important modern Urdu history of the Deccan, Muḥammad 'Abd al-Jabbār Mulkapūrī, *Maḥbūb al-waṭan, tazkira-i salāṭīn-i Dakan*, vol. 1, *Dar bayān-i salātīn-i Bahmaniyya* (Hyderabad: Maṭba'-i Fakhr-i Niẓāmī, n.d.), 147–50, which is followed by a lengthy and enthusiastic appreciation of the Ellora caves.

15. Inayatullah Khan Kashmiri, *Kalimat-i-Taiyibat* (Collection of Aurangzeb's Orders), ed. and trans. S. M. Azizuddin Husain (Delhi: Idarah-i Adabiyat-i Delli, 1982), 27 (English), 13 (Persian).

16. Seely, *The Wonders of Ellora*, 150, 165, 202, 245, 345.

17. Catherine B. Asher, *The New Cambridge History of India*, I:4, *Architecture of Mughal India* (Cambridge: Cambridge University Press, 1992), 254. As an example of later sources on Awrangzīb's temple destruction, she notes Jadunath Sarkar, *History of Aurangzib* (Bombay: Orient Longman, 1972), 3:185 (not 285), who cites a Marathi source dated Śaka 1838 (1916 C.E.).

18. Seely's brahmin informants told him "that if Aurungzebe actually did not commit the atrocious act himself, he allowed his court" (241).

19. Haarmann, "Quest," 65. See also Haarmann, ed., *Das Pyramidenbuch des Abū Ǧaʿfar al-Idrīsī (st. 649/1251)*, Beiruter Texte und Studien, 38 (Stuttgart: Franz Steiner, 1991).

20. ʿAbd al-Laṭīf, *Relation de l'Égypte par Abd-allatiph*, trans. Silvestre de Sacy (Paris, 1810), 182, quoted in Gaston Wiet, *L'Égypte de Murtadi fils de Gaphiphe* (Paris: Librairie Orientaliste Paul Geuthner, 1953), introduction, 98.

21. Wiet, *L'Égypte de Murtadi fils de Gaphiphe*, 60.

22. Ibid., 2, 87–88. Further on the Arabic Hermetic histories of pre-Islamic Egypt, see Michael Cook, "Pharaonic History in Medieval Egypt," *Studia Islamica* 57 (1983): 67–104.

23. R. H. Major, ed., *India in the Fifteenth Century, Being a Collection of Narratives of Voyages to India . . .*, Works Issued by the Hakluyt Society, 22 (London: Hakluyt Society, 1857), 20–21; cf. C. A. Storey, *Persian Literature: A Bio-bibliographical Survey*, 2 vols. (London: Luzac, 1927–71), 1:293–98.

24. Maḥmūd ibn Amīr Walī Balkhī, *Baḥr al-asrār fī manāqib al-akhyār*, ed. Riazul Islam (Karachi: Institute of Central and West Asian Studies, 1980), 13–16, 32–38, of the Persian text. See Iqbal Husain, "Hindu Shrines and Practices as Described by a Central Asian Traveller in the First Half of the Seventeenth Century," in *Medieval India I: Researches in the History of India, 1200–1750*, ed. Irfan Habib (Delhi: Oxford University Press, 1992).

25. Haarmann, "Quest," 58.

26. Yohanan Friedmann, *Shaykh Aḥmad Sirhindī: An Outline of His Thought and a Study of His Image in the Eyes of Posterity*, McGill Islamic Studies, 2 (Montreal: McGill-Queen's University Press, 1971), 71.

27. Sāqi Mustʿad [*sic*] Khan, *Maʿāsir-i-ʿĀlamgiri: A History of the Emperor Aurangzib-ʿĀlamgir (reign 1658–1707 A.D.*, trans. Jadu-nath Sarkar, Bibliotheca Indica, no. 269 (Calcutta: Royal Asiatic Society of Bengal, 1947), 145 (passage dated 1094/1683); this translation is superior to that in H. M. Elliot, *The History of India as Told by Its Own Historians*, ed. John Dowson, 8 vols. (London, 1867–77; reprint ed., Allahabad: Kitab Mahal, n.d.), 7:189–90.

28. Muḥammad Dārā Shikūh, *Majmaʿ al-baḥrayn*, ed. Muḥammad Riḍā Jalālī Nā'īnī (Tehran: Nashr-i Nuqra, 1366/1987–88), introduction, v–vi.

29. Ghulam Yazdani, "Fine Arts: Architecture," in Yazdani, ed., *The Early History of the Deccan*, 2 vols. (London: Oxford University Press, 1960), 2:731.

30. Seely, *The Wonders of Ellora*, 230, quoting Lieutenant Colonel Fitzclarence.

31. Ibid., 258.

32. Seely (145–47) was informed that the Ellora caves were excavated by the Pandavas prior to the main action of the Mahabharata.

33. Ibid., 139, 299. Seely also records that "two colossal figures resting on large maces" were called *dewriesdars* (172), apparently from the Hindi term *deorhi* (door) plus the Persian suffix *-dār* (holder); cf. Sarkar in *Maāsir-i- ʿĀlamgiri*, 325. Modern scholars unselfconsciously go back to the classical Sanskrit term *dwarapala* to describe the massive doorkeepers at Ellora (Surendranath Sen, ed.,

Indian Travels of Thevenot and Careri, Indian Records Series [New Delhi: National Archives of India, 1949], 320 n. 6).

34. K. G. Jayne, *Vasco da Gama and His Successors, 1460–1580* (London: Methuen, 1910), 55.

35. Seely, *The Wonders of Ellora*, 156–67. It was particularly representations of the bull (i.e., Nandi) and of serpents that aroused recognition among the "Bombay Siphauees."

36. Ibid., 156–58.

37. Yazdani, *The Early History of the Deccan*, 2:731.

38. T. V. Pathy, *Elura: Art and Culture* (New Delhi: Humanities Press, 1980), 4.

39. James Laine, "The Construction of Hindu and Muslim Identities in Maharashtra, 1600–1810," paper presented at conference on "Indo-Muslim Identity in South Asia," Duke University, May 1995.

40. Seely, *The Wonders of Ellora*, 152.

41. Anquetil du Perron, *Le Zendavesta*, 3 vols. (Paris, 1771), 1:ccxxxiii, cited in Jean-Luc Kieffer, *Anquetil-Duperron: L'Inde en France au XVIIIe siècle* (Paris: Société d'Édition "Les Belles Lettres," 1983), 347–63 (Duperron's map of the caves, with identifications proposed by his informants, is in Bibliothèque Nationale, Nouvelles acquisitions françaises, Fonds Anquetil-Duperron, 8878); Seely, *The Wonders of Ellora*, 205 ff., 238–39.

42. Partha Mitter, *Much Maligned Monsters: History of European Reactions to Indian Art* (Oxford: Clarendon Press, 1977), 107–8.

43. Seely, *The Wonders of Ellora*, 286.

44. L. F. Rushbrook Williams, *A Handbook for Travellers in India, Pakistan, Bangladesh, and Sri Lanka (Ceylon)*, 22d ed. (New York: Facts on File, 1975), 149 n. 1.

45. *The Baburnama: Memoirs of Babur, Prince and Emperor*, trans. Wheeler M. Thackston (Washington, D.C.: Freer Gallery of Art/Arthur M. Sackler Gallery, 1996), 406–7; cf. Ẓahiru'd-Dīn Muḥammad Bābur Pādshāh Ghāzī, *Bābur-nāma* (Memoirs of Bābur), trans. Annette Susannah Beveridge (1922; New Delhi: Oriental Books Reprint Corporation, 1979), 608–13. Beveridge notes that Bābur's destruction amounted to cutting off the heads of the idols, which were restored with plaster by Jains in the locality.

5

Mapping Hindu-Muslim Identities through the Architecture of Shahjahanabad and Jaipur

Catherine B. Asher

As C. J. Fuller has rightly observed, scholars interested in temples and temple ritual tend to focus on South India, where presumably there is relatively little impact of Muslim conquest and rule. As a result, he notes, we know very little about temples in North India, even those at the most important pilgrimage sites on the Gangetic Plain.[1] Slowly we are moving away from this direction; for example, the final volume of the *Encyclopaedia of Indian Temple Architecture* will examine North Indian temples constructed into the fourteenth century.[2] Some scholars have looked at post-Muslim conquest temples in Bengal, and some are now interested in temples built during the Mughal period.[3] With few exceptions, these studies consider temples as individual works of art, never as a focus for ritual activity in a larger social context.

The situation in some ways is not all that different for North Indian Islamic architecture. True, we know a good deal about individual monuments, but to date there has been little attempt to examine how they fit into the larger urban fabric or how they coexisted with contemporary Hindu or other non-Muslim sacred structures—temples, shrines, *dharmashalas*, or schools.[4] In many ways this is understandable, since relatively little was known even about the basic buildings. Events at Ayodhya culminating in the 1992 destruction of the so-called Babri masjid stimulated me, at least, to think increasingly about how Muslims in what were predominately Hindu cities or cities constructed by Hindu rajas, such as Jaipur, understood their built environment and how Hindus in seemingly Muslim cities, such as Shahjahanabad (Delhi), expressed their own religious identity through structures. Much of what I will present here is the result of very recent work that I have just begun.[5]

Even if I am not always yet ready to draw conclusions from the observations I present here, I believe that probing the visible landscape can help us understand the complex issue of Hindu-Muslim identities in premodern and even early modern India.

Little is known about temples in North India built after the Muslim conquest of Delhi; attention tends to be drawn to Islamic monuments, often on those parts constructed from Hindu temples, thus skewing our perceptions of Muslim relations with India's majority population. A rare statement of political victory—for example, the use of temple pillars in Aibek's Jami mosque in Delhi—is seen as a universal Muslim mode of building in India. Archaeological reports repeatedly present mosques that are claimed to consist of elements from destroyed (read wantonly) Hindu temples.[6] Yet examining these monuments at the site—for example, the Jami mosque at Kannauj widely believed to be constructed from reused material—could go a long way in dispelling that view.[7] In fact, it is generally assumed that no temples were constructed in Muslim-ruled domains, whereas Islamic structures were built and survive in great numbers. Ironically, to cite one example, we have about a hundred inscriptions telling about once existing pre-Mughal Islamic monuments in Bihar, but only one survives.[8] By contrast we have about six extant fourteenth-century temples.[9] Such tabulations may help us understand how a Muslim elite or religious devotees perceived themselves, but it does little to further our understanding of identity perception across or among communities. More useful is to look at structures in a larger context. For this purpose I will focus on cities whose original setting is more or less intact: Shahjahanabad, Jaipur, and Amber, among others.

It might be useful to see first what can be gleaned about Hindu-Muslim identity in the built environment before the construction of planned cities such as Shahjahanabad and Jaipur. Since relatively few towns or extensive sites built before the seventeenth century survive intact, an examination of paintings provides insight. The distant backgrounds of some Mughal miniatures give us a sense of a shared Hindu-Muslim landscape. Domes and *shikharas,* possibly mosques and temples, are depicted, although in a rather fuzzy manner.[10] But such depictions hardly can be taken to mean that these are religious structures or that they literally sat side by side, for the Mughal artist painted the known world, not the literally observed world. We may conclude, though, that both Hindu and Muslim monuments were part of the larger landscape.

All the same, we have virtually no surviving temples at Mughal palaces or palace towns, even those as well preserved as Fatehpur Sikri, to suggest what might have been the situation. Rohtas fort, the seat of Raja Man Singh when governor of Bihar, is an exception. There temples and mosques are grouped in separate areas of the hill fort, although this may be as much a result of chronology as it is of community.[11] I have argued elsewhere for a strong sense of Rajput identity in the Mughal governor's palace adjacent to the mosques and tombs there, but the palace has no sectarian overtones—either Hindu or Muslim.[12]

We know that under Akbar the construction of monumental Hindu temples proliferated. A case in point is Vrindaban, where Akbar himself used imperial funds to support the construction and maintenance of Raja Man Singh's Govinda Deva temple, among others.[13] But the site is essentially a temple enclave and a pilgrimage center (*tirtha*); there are no Muslim monuments in town.[14] Thus two other contemporary towns, Amber, Raja Man Singh's *watan jagir* in Rajasthan, and Rajmahal, his capital as Akbar's governor of Bengal,[15] each intended for Kachhwaha residence and administration, might be more useful for understanding issues of Hindu-Muslim identity in the sixteenth and seventeenth centuries.

Amber is famed for its palace built by this raja and further expanded in the seventeenth century by Mirza Jai Singh (1622–1667), but many other contemporary structures grace the site that largely go unnoticed by today's visitors. For example, on the main Delhi road lies a mosque originally constructed in accordance with Akbar's order in 1569–70. It is now rebuilt, but the locale and space occupied remain constant, as is shown on an early eighteenth-century map of Amber.[16] In Rajmahal the Jami mosque, built in this case by Raja Man Singh, is in a similar location, that is, on the main road.[17] The small temple also reputedly provided by Raja Man Singh is behind the mosque, not visible from any distance. How are we to read this placement? Does this mean that Islamic identity always sublimates a Hindu one even in cities built by a Hindu prince? Or does it mean that location of temples to Hindus in premodern North India had a very different meaning than it might today? Some answers may be gleaned by further examining Amber, the Kachhwaha seat of authority until the construction of Jaipur in 1737.

Upon entering Amber's Delhi gate, one encounters a *kos minar,* an official Mughal distance marker, and the very prominent Jami mosque on the main road (fig. 5.1).[18] Yet the town also has temples dedicated to a variety of deities including Jinas, the goddess, Shiva, and Vishnu. Some of these temples predate the Mughal period. They are all small structures (for example, the one dedicated to Ambikeshvara, the town's tutelary deity). The most important of these temples are located close to a large tank, or *kund*, and a small stream. They sit at the edge of a hill—the traditional seat of Rajput retreat and safety—not on the plain of the town. Others spill into the town but are away from the main Delhi road, where the Jami mosque is located.

About 1600 Raja Man Singh added to Amber his magnificent Jagat Siromani temple, but like most other temples it is located in the town's interior close to the palace and an even older Kachhwaha *haveli.*[19] It is not visible to the casual passerby or to those adhering to the main road only. In some ways this arrangement recalls those Jain temples at Abu, Ranakpur, and even in nearby Sanganer designed to resemble mansions; from the outside, they do not look like temples.[20]

There is another model for the post-twelfth-century North Indian temple, one that probably seems more familiar, namely, temples that are prominently and centrally located in an urban setting.[21] This type is not limited to the Rajasthani examples but is found across much of the Doab in the late eighteenth and nineteenth centuries. Pilgrimage maps of premodern India confirm that this type existed widely.[22] If there is a significant distinction between these two basic temple types—one whose presence is overtly manifest and the other more obscured—it remains unclear.

5.1. Jami mosque, Amber.

5.2. Fakhr al-Masajid from street, Shahjahanabad, Delhi.

In some cities, Varanasi or Lucknow, for example, mosques dominate the landscape.[23] Even in Lucknow today, temples are not particularly visible, although many do exist.[24] In Varanasi, of course, deemed by many the Hindu city par excellence, small temples literally dot the ghats and city, although most of them date no earlier than the late eighteenth century.[25] It is particularly interesting that Rani Ahilya Bai Holkar's newly constructed Vishvanath temple, the focal tirtha in all Varanasi, is notably smaller than the adjacent mosque constructed during Aurangzeb's reign from the spoils of an earlier Vishvanath temple.[26] Yet the Rani was a woman of considerable resources, and the temple was built in 1777 when Hindu political power dominated in Varanasi.[27] Had she wished to build a larger temple, rather than one almost lost in the interior gullies of Dasashvamedh Ghat, she could have done so.

To understand this pattern of dominant mosques and small temples, we may turn to Shahjahanabad, where nuance between Hindu and Muslim society is still evident today. Shajahanabad is considered by most scholars an Islamic city; in fact, by many it is believed to have once been the subcontinent's leading Islamic city.[28] One highly visible feature is its mosques commencing with the enormous Jami Masjid, followed only by somewhat smaller ones such as the Fatehpuri mosque, the mosque of Zinat al-Nisa, or the no longer extant Akbarabadi masjid.[29]

There are then those that dot the main roads of every *mahalla*, for example, the Fakhr al-Masajid (fig. 5.2) or even the more humble Muhtasib's mosques.[30] Still today in the overcrowded and overbuilt walled city, these mosques are evident. For example, if one proceeds from Hauz Qazi to Khari Baoli, a distance of less than a mile, on the west one would see the following in this order: the mosque of Mubarak Begum, Sirki Walan's mosque, Sabz Mosque, the mosque of Tahawwar Khan, and a few other small ones.[31] Then veering a little to the right, one of the city's major landmarks, Masjid Fatehpuri, comes into view. One also sees the entrances to havelis—not so much the havelis themselves—but it is the mosques that draw attention.[32] This tour includes structures built from the seventeenth through nineteenth centuries provided by begums, queens, nawabs, and landholders; at any one historical moment the picture would be a little different, but not much. Any major thoroughfare of the city would reveal similar structures. True, before the city was rather radically changed by the British after 1858, there was more space for fewer people and more gardens, and Chandni Chowk from Masjid Fatehpuri to the Red fort was a tree-lined street through whose center ran a canal.[33] The best comparison would probably be contemporary Isfahan.

Before the nineteenth century we have no figures for the breakdown of Delhi's population in terms of Muslims and non-Muslims.[34] In 1845, however, it was about equal,[35] suggesting that the Hindu population since the inception of Shahjahanabad in 1639 was always sizable. Even in Shah Jahan's time, highly desirable plots in the Chandni Chowk vicinity had been allocated to Hindu and Jain bankers and merchants.[36] Wealthy Khattri Hindu merchants and Jains, including one branch of the Jagat Seth family,[37] played a role in the city's economic well-being. So it is not surprising that between 1639 and 1850 Hindus and Jains built over a hundred temples that still survive; others must have been destroyed, for example, in the massive rebuilding of Faiz Bazaar.[38] Yet for the most part, these temples are almost invisible to the casual visitor. The question is why?

These temples, unlike Delhi's mosques and tombs, rarely bear dated inscriptions.[39] Basing my fieldwork on the 1916 *List of Muhammadan and Hindu Monuments: Shahjahanabad*, I have started to study these temples, although a good deal more work still needs to be done.[40] Even though I have yet to establish a chronology based on style, it is apparent to me that a substantial number of these temples were founded in the seventeenth and eighteenth centuries and then rebuilt.[41] I do not think the exact date of each construction or reconstruction is critical to my observations. Rather, location and scale—factors that have remained constant—are important.

It might be useful to consider these temples in light of their better-known contemporary Islamic counterparts, although doing so should not suggest that there were distinctive religious styles or that one was derivative of the other. The eighteenth- and nineteenth-century mosques built throughout the walled city are easily visible from a distance. The largest take up considerable space, while the smaller ones are located on the second story above a main street intended for both vehicular and pedestrian traffic. The very smallest are in gullies and *kunchas* (a linear street similar to a gully). By contrast, as at Amber, temples in Shahjahanabad are not as immediately visible. They are almost never located on a main road. Rather, they are found in the city's interior lanes. Often they are essentially openings in a wall, appearing little different from a shop. Some are so small that one never enters; others are entered and vary in size from a small room to perhaps the size of two rooms. In some mahallas, these temples are inside small private courtyards just off the narrow pedestrian lanes of the city (fig. 5.3). In these courtyard types, the temple area is public, but the dwellings within which they are located are private.[42]

None of these temples is surmounted by a high shikhara (superstructure), which we so often associate with traditional temple construction.[43] Many lack any superstructure, especially those similar to recessed shops. Others with domes are low and small. In fact, most of these temples are only apparent during the timings for *darshan*, that is, when the doors to the courtyards are open, a situation today that probably reflects original use. I found, for example, that as an outsider it was virtually impossible to locate these temples between noon, when darshan ceases, and 5 P.M., when it recommences. Rarely was there an indication that behind a pulled shutter or a locked arched door was a temple, not a house or shop. Moreover, these temples are never very large. Even in areas such as Katra Nil, which always housed a predominant Hindu community, as many as six or seven small obscure temples might be found on a single short lane.[44]

There are areas, according to the *List*, where mosques stand, but there are virtually no premodern temples, for example, in Daryaganj, Bazaar Chitliqabr, and Bazaar Churiwalan. However, rebuilding after 1857 may have distorted the accuracy of this picture, since, as we know, there were havelis of Hindus in some of these areas.[45] All the same, the *List* indicates

5.3. Shivalaya of Dhumi Mal Khanna (*List* 1:359), Katra Nil, Shahjahanabad (Delhi).

that there is no mahalla in which there are temples yet no mosques. An excellent case in point is at the intersection of Khari Baoli and Lal Kuan. A cluster of temples is there,[46] and just to the south is the mosque of Tahawwar Khan, while to the east is the Fatehpuri mosque. The mosques are highly visible; the temples are apparent only if one enters the mahalla's interior. Even in Katra Nil, considered the richest quarter of Delhi in the early nineteenth century,[47] there is a huge concentration of temples, but there is also a small mosque.[48]

The only temples located prominently on a main street are the Digambara Jain temple, called today the Lal Mandir but known until recently as the Urdu or Camp temple, and Gauri Shankar temple next to it. The Gauri Shankar temple was built in 1761 during a period of Maratha supremacy by Appa Gangadhara, a Maratha Brahman in the service of the Scindia family.[49] The temple, like most of them in Delhi, has been considerably enhanced throughout the twentieth century. Its modern shikhara does not reflect its original appearance. The bulk of the Jain Lal Mandir was built between 1835 and the 1870s;[50] portions are more recent, but reputedly its position on this site dates to Shah Jahan's time.[51] Inside the original portion of this restored temple are three white marble Jina images, each dated the equivalent of 1492 C.E.,[52] suggesting veracity to the claim that the site is of considerable antiquity.

While much can be said for this prime location, the relevant question for our purposes is: How visible were these temples and others before the late nineteenth century?[53] Were they the exceptions to the rule in Delhi, or were they as virtually invisible as Delhi's other Hindu and Jain religious edifices? Maps dating between 1751 and 1850 suggest that these temples, no matter their initial construction date, were not part of the visible landscape. The area north and east of the Jami mosque was then residential but leveled after 1857. A map datable to about 1850 indicates a dharmasala where the Jain and Gauri Shankar temples are located, apparently subsuming the two temples under the common term *dharmasala*.[54] They were not sufficiently significant to be separately identified. Illustrations by two British artists, each done in the early nineteenth century, indicate no visible temple on the skyline, but the Fatehpuri mosque is present in each, as is evident in the one reproduced here (fig. 5.4).[55] Even an illustration of Shahjahanabad made by a Kotah artist about 1842–43 does not show these temples, indicating that the dominant appearance they have today is not an original feature.[56]

How can we understand the prominence in Delhi's landscape of construction associated with Islam and the almost invisible presence of structures associated with non-Islamic traditions? Blake, for example, equates the lack of monumental temple building in early eighteenth-century Delhi with the "economic and political impotence of [Delhi's Jain and] Khattri merchants."[57] But if this is the sole reason, then why do we not see much temple building on a main street until about 1900 when we know that they had become powerful in the late eighteenth century and remained so into the early twentieth century? Even around 1900, temples constructed along the British-created Esplanade were small and

5.4. Chandnee Chauk, Delhi. From John Luard, *Views in India, St. Helena and Car Nicobar: Drawn from Nature and on Stone* (London: J. Graf, 1838). Courtesy of the Ames Library, University of Minnesota.

lacked the traditional signifiers indicating temple presence.[58] For example, little differentiates them from any shop facade on the street; there are no shikharas or domes or even large-scale images of deities to draw attention to their sacred status.

To understand the dominance of mosques and the surprisingly low visibility of Shahjahanabad's temples, it is instructive to look at temple and mosque construction in a city planned and ruled by Hindu monarchs, that is, Jaipur in the eighteenth and nineteenth centuries. Commenced by Sawai Jai Singh in 1727, the city today boasts more temples than any other but Varanasi.[59] Most of these date to the eighteenth and nineteenth centuries, that is, exactly contemporary with temples in Delhi's walled city. Let me interject my own story here. I have visited Jaipur numerous times, but never noticed many temples in the city besides the eighteenth-century Govinda Deva temple, actually part of Sawai Jai Singh's City Palace complex, and the modern Birla one. So what, you might say, but I am an art historian, and it is second nature for me to notice monuments. Why did I not see them until I consciously sought them out armed with lists of temples in Jaipur's various bazaars?

Even though Jaipur was built by a Hindu ruler and, many have argued, as a Hindu city,[60] temples are no more visible within the confines of Jaipur's walls than they are in eighteenth- and nineteenth-century Shahjahanabad. Only one inside Jaipur's walls, the Kalkiji temple, built by Sawai Jai Singh in 1740, bears a shikhara.[61] While the entire temple is easily visible from its platform on the second story above shops, it is not readily visible from the busy main street in the major Sireh Deori Bazaar. The other two temples with dominant shikharas visible from a distance probably were not built until the late nineteenth century.[62] The rest are, like those in Delhi, within courtyards. Examples include the Ramachandraji temple (1854) located above shops in Sireh Deorhi Bazaar and Shri Brijraj Behariji's temple (1813) in Tripolia Bazaar.

Today signs in Hindi indicate the presence of some; others have none. For example, there is no indication that an almost unnoticeable entrance off the main Jalab Chowk leads to Shri Brijnandji's temple provided by Maharaja Sawai Pratap Singh in 1792 (fig. 5.5).[63] Of course, we do not know how they were marked at the time of construction, but chances are there were few written indications to tell of the temples' existence.[64] While the temples are larger than those in Shahjahanabad, they are no more visible from the outside. We can therefore conclude after examining temples in Jaipur that the Delhi ones are obscure to those who do not know their location not because their builders and patrons sought to

5.5. Entrance to the Sri Brijnandji Temple, Jaipur.

hide them from Muslim rulers and Muslim neighbors but for some other reason.

What about the situation of mosques in Jaipur?[65] This is a little more difficult to analyze, since almost every mosque has been refurbished recently with a new facade or is currently undergoing remodeling. But if we focus on location and general patterns of appearance, we can attempt to understand mosque construction here. First, though, we need to recognize that Jaipur has a sizable Muslim population. Just as we have no statistics for Delhi's Muslim-Hindu breakdown before the nineteenth century, so the same holds true for Jaipur. Today the Muslim population of Jaipur is about a fifth of the total; this is about the same as in Lucknow, which is so often imagined to be a Muslim city.[66]

Muslim military personnel and craftsmen were employed by Sawai Jai Singh and his successors. For example, in 1788 Tirandaz, a predominately Muslim mahalla of the city, was established within Ramganj Bazaar to house Jaipur's Muslim archers originating from Lahore.[67] Today Muslims live mainly in the areas between Suraj Pol and Johari Bazaar, apparently reflecting patterns since at least the late eighteenth and nineteenth centuries.[68] In this area are a large number of mosques. But Muslims also live around Chand Pol gate. In fact, their businesses and mosques are found throughout much of the city. For example, there is a small mosque adjacent to Ajmeri gate, and the city's Jami mosque occupies prime land where the Bari Chaupar intersects with Johari Bazaar—just a few hundred meters away from the Kachhwaha palace, the seat of the Jaipur Maharaja.[69] Other major mosques line the main street that intersects the city on an east-west axis with most of them nearer the Suraj Pol end of town. Smaller mosques are located on the main streets within the mahallas themselves. In short, just as mosques tend to be located on the main streets of Delhi, some close to the ruler's palace, so the situation seems parallel here, even though Jaipur is the seat of a Hindu prince.

If the location of these mosques follows a pattern similar to the one in Delhi, what about their appearance? In Delhi, we argued, the prominent facades of mosques on the main street made them a highly visible feature of the landscape. It is more difficult to discuss the appearance of mosques in Jaipur, especially those on the main roads, since they have all undergone remodeling. We need to examine those inside lanes and even in *dargahs*, where less damage to the original appearance has been done. For example, although Masjid Maulana Zia al-Din Sahib in Mahalla Hadipura (a subdivision of Ramganj) was being refurbished during my visit in February 1995, it had enough of the original construc-

5.6. Mosque of Maulana Zia al-Din Sahib, Mahalla Hadipura, Jaipur.

tion visible to understand it and other contemporary mosques in the city (fig. 5.6). Similar to contemporary Mughal mosques in Delhi, it is surmounted by three domes. Each dome marks an interior bay. Arches are defined by faceted stucco work; exquisite arabesques are painted on fine *chunam*. I found similar painting elsewhere in Jaipur, for example, on the mosque of Dargah Zia al-Din Sahib (fig. 5.7), which the local inhabitants assured me is one of the oldest mosques in the city.[70]

All the mosques on Jaipur's main thoroughfares have new high facades. Only at the mosque of Bilor Khan on Ghat Darwaza Rasta does

5.7. Interior, mosque at Dargah Zia al-Din Sahib, Jaipur.

any semblance of the original appearance remain. The mosque was originally a three-domed structure, not dissimilar to those on the back streets. The point here is that not only in location but also in overall appearance do the mosques of Jaipur built in the eighteenth and nineteenth centuries relate well to those of Delhi.

What pertains elsewhere in North India? Are dominant mosques and almost invisible temples a consistent pattern? Although my research to date is preliminary, it indicates that the situation in Jaipur and Shahjahanabad is not universal. Certainly in Bengal, where the most innovative and widespread tradition of temple building developed after the sixteenth century, temples continue to be a highly visible part of the landscape vying in competition for visibility with contemporary mosques.[71] The Bengal temples, however, generally are not part of the urban fabric, more often in the domain of a *zamindar* than in Bengal's premier cities. So too in tirtha sites such as Ayodhya or Varanasi, temples are readily seen as are a number of mosques.[72] One issue here, though, is that with some exceptions, for example, Chait Singh's temple in Ramnagar or the famous Vishvanath temple in Varanasi, we do not know enough about these structures to differentiate between those of the eighteenth and nineteenth centuries.

We know that some temples with shikharas were built in the late eighteenth century, for example, the one at Dev ki Nandan ki Haveli in Varanasi.[73] Since the temple is enclosed within high walls, only its shikhara is visible. Others are more elusive: for example, the Jagannath temple reputedly provided by Nawab Asaf al-Daula in a village known as Serai Shekh, about twenty kilometers from Lucknow.[74] The temple is enclosed in a high walled courtyard. A small dome, virtually indistinguishable from those used on mosques and tombs, marks its presence. In short, this eighteenth-century structure is clearly a religious building, but nothing from a distance further defines its sectarian affiliation. So too the domed temple at Chakiya, about forty-five kilometers from Varanasi, resembles a Muslim tomb.[75] Similarly, the famous Kalkaji temple in south Delhi originally had no features that would indicate its religious affiliation, even though it was always a prominent structure.[76] When the temple was first constructed in 1764, it was a flat-roofed twelve-sided structure; the shikhara, now prominent, was not added until 1816, when Mirza Raja Kedar Nath, *peshkhar* of Akbar II, provided it.[77]

Shahjahanabad's neighborhood mosques, regardless of mahalla, almost invariably follow a single pattern. That is, they are single-aisled multi-bayed structures surmounted with domes. Usually they are above shops on a main street, thus enhancing their visibility (fig. 5.2).[78] The temples show a greater variety of types. For example, in Katra Nil most of the temples are small domed Shivalayas situated within an open courtyard (fig. 5.3), while in nearby Balli Maran, Hauz Qazi, and Sita Ram Bazaar, Shivalayas are incorporated into walls almost as if they were shops. I am not sure what conclusions I can draw from this, but the variety of temple types seen from mahalla to mahalla has nothing to do with sect. In the eighteenth and nineteenth centuries, most temples in Delhi were dedicated to Shiva.[79] Many of these are domed. The few dedicated to Vishnu, more specifically to Radha and Krishna, are what I call haveli types.[80] That is, they are flat-roofed temples that are located within high enclosure walls and have an open courtyard in their center recalling a traditional house. One creative example, the Temple of Charan Das, founded by an eighteenth-century Delhi reformer, is essentially a haveli type, but in the open courtyard a domed structure that resembles a typical Shivalaya of the Katra Nil variety serves the *samadhi* (memorial) of Charan Das and enshrines impressions of his footprints, as if they were Vishnu *pada*.[81]

In contrast to the variety of temple types, the high degree of uniformity found in mosques—whether they are in Shahjahanabad, Jaipur, or elsewhere—may reflect a conservative adherence to a pattern of imperial patronage established earlier in the Mughal period. For Hindu temples in Delhi, at least, there had been no recent imperial patronage and so no uniform models to emulate. Thus buildings constructed by prominent individuals in a single mahalla may have served as models for subsequent work, resulting in narrowly localized styles. The reserved appearance and diminished scale of Old Delhi's temples may reflect patterns of use that in turn reflect the sociological and economic makeup of the mahalla. For example, Katra Nil, at least by the early nineteenth century the wealthiest area of the city,[82] had the largest number of temples as well as those that occupy the greatest amount of physical space. Nevertheless, even these temples remain essentially hidden.

Although a number of temple types in Delhi and elsewhere were built throughout the eighteenth and nineteenth centuries, the two most common types in the walled city are the domed circular or polygonal ones (fig. 5.3) and the haveli type (fig. 5.8). How the North Indian temple was transformed from large structures with porches and shikharas that we might perceive as textbook examples to the essentially interiorized haveli or domed Shivalaya type is not clear. The small domed Shivalaya seems to have had a long albeit obscure history. For example, a small domed temple enshrining a lustrated Shiva *linga* is depicted in the 1591 Chunar Ragamala, a manuscript commissioned by the Bundi raja.[83] Since our knowledge of seventeenth-century temples is restricted to a few large-scale ones, the development of the domed Shivalaya is unclear.[84] However, this domed Shivalaya type relates closely to two sorts of memorial structures: the Muslim tomb and the Hindu memorial *chattri*. I am not trying to suggest that Shivalayas are transformed memorials, Hindu or Muslim, but rather that the domed chattri-like structure simply was associated with the visual vocabulary of religion in general.

The haveli temple style in Delhi is particularly interesting for two reasons. One is the origins of its appearance, and the other is its sectarian affiliations. The haveli type probably derives from an imperial audience hall inside which the ruler sits in his throne known as a *jharoka-i darshan*. In a temple, the deity is similarly situated for darshan.[85] A good example of such a figure is the Govinda Deva image installed in the Jaipur temple in 1734; it is probably the first temple of the haveli sort.[86] In Shahjahanabad a haveli-style temple is the one of Charan Das in Hauz Qazi, originally founded in the eighteenth century.[87] A good deal of work

5.8. Interior courtyard of the haveli-style Ladliji temple in Katra Nil, Shahjahanabad, Delhi.

needs to be done on the development of the haveli temple type, but tentatively I am inclined to think that it is closely associated with Jai Singh's concept of regnal authority as validated by the divine.[88] To obtain darshan, be it divine or imperial, it is necessary to approach a structure's threshold.[89] In the case of a ruler, Hindu or Muslim, the jharoka must be approached for darshan; in the case of the divine, the *garbhagriha* (inner sanctum) must be approached.

The haveli temple, at least in Delhi and Jaipur, is associated with Vaishnavism, the sect favored by wealthy Hindu bankers and merchants. What is puzzling is why we have so few Vaishnava temples in the walled city. It is true that they are considerably larger than most Shivalayas; it is also true that the two main ones—the Ladliji temple in Katra Nil (fig. 5.8), claimed to have existed since the seventeenth century,[90] and the eighteenth-century temple of Charan Das in Ballimaran[91]—are in areas long associated with concentrated merchant and banker wealth. Nearby are six Jain temples, each claiming some antiquity.[92] Since many Shivalayas in the city also feature images of Vishnu, his consort, Hanuman, and other deities and since each home would have an interior shrine, very likely dedicated to Krishna, perhaps the seemingly small number is deceiving to modern eyes.[93]

Structures originally associated with Mughal authority (the Diwan-i Aam cum jharoka) and religious commemoration (the domed chattri) become appropriate forms for temples. The surface decoration of temples, too, is similar to contemporary Muslim architecture: for example, there is no difference between the arches and baluster columns on the Charan Das temple and those on the mosque of Tahawwar Khan.[94] They belong to a common visual vocabulary; for example, these architectural features also resemble the ones from an eighteenth-century raja's palace in Dig (Rajasthan).[95] It is clear that identity is not sought through individual architectural members or stylistic components, but rather in the manner that they are combined and, perhaps more significantly, displayed to the faithful.[96]

We now may return to why the temples of Shahjahanabad and Jaipur are essentially invisible to the uninformed. Blake's suggestion that the lack of visible temple construction reflects the economic and political impotence of the merchant class might be true for Delhi in the early eighteenth century, but it does not explain why temples remain obscure in the late nineteenth century, when Delhi's Jain and Khattri bankers are powerful.[97] How, in turn, do we explain the situation in Jaipur, where many of the temples are actually the products of imperial patronage? How do we explain in Varanasi the fact that the city's major temple is small and tucked inside a gully? Instead of a single answer, I would like to suggest that several forces are at play here.

We might recall that the dominant sixteenth-century mosque at Amber was on the main road, while the near-contemporary temples were in the interior. This is similar to the situation both in Jaipur and Delhi later in the eighteenth and nineteenth centuries. Thus I would suggest that the arrangement, location, and prominence of religious structures are factors of community identity—though not communal identity. In fact, if we think back to North Indian temple architecture before the Muslim conquest of Delhi, we must realize that large-scale temples provided imperially such as those at Khajuraho are the exception, not the rule. Temples in North India tend, in fact, to be small and often in areas that today seem distant from well-established centers of population. They, in fact, are often in areas that are intentionally remote, that is, the tirtha sites.[98] Their patronage is unknown; they do not adhere to the more common South Indian patterns of enormous structures sponsored by the king. Today's large prominent temples in North India—for example, the recently constructed Birla one in Jaipur—may reflect modern concepts of Hindu identity, not premodern ones.

Delhi's obscured temples may have yet an additional explanation. Bayly points out the conflict many merchants, especially Khattris and Jains, experienced. Hindu social code demanded a frugal lifestyle, yet a business code with Islamic rulers demanded a display of opulence and wealth.[99] Dual lifestyles developed. For example, the exterior of a haveli might be splendid, but the interior rooms were austere. Jewelry suitable for Mughal court attendance was worn in public, while at home more traditional jewelry and garb were donned. Often money was spent on religious structures, for example, the Jain Digambara Lal Mandir and others within the walled city in Delhi. Their carved and inlaid marble surfaces are covered lavishly with gold gilt.[100] Concurrently, reform movements instigated by men such as Charan Das urged a return to a simpler and more austere form of religion.[101] The tendency to look inward, whether for spiritual purposes or to maintain one's identity in the community, is clear. So I think we can argue that the very form, appearance, and location of Delhi's religious Hindu architecture reflects these same values.

Visible mosques and less visible temples, Hindu or Jain, need not be seen as a matter of Islam subsuming Hindu or other non-Muslim identities. Rather, these patterns of mosque and temple construction in Delhi, Jaipur, and other places in North India follow long-standing practice. Since the construction of its earliest extant monument, the Dome of the Rock, Islam has manifested itself boldly in urban settings. This is not true for North Indian temples, which tend to be situated in those settings deemed ideal by Sanskrit texts—among trees, hills, and bodies of water.[102] In the urban context this would be translated as in a courtyard garden (figs. 5.3 and 5.8). The surrounding walls of the haveli temple or the Shivalaya are the hills, and the potted flowers are the greenery that can only thrive on water. This is the setting, so the *Brhatsamhita* tells, where the gods dwell and frolic.

Notes

1. C. J. Fuller, "The Hindu Temple and Indian Society," in Michael Fox, ed., *Temple in Society* (Winona Lake: Eisenbrauns, 1988), 58.

2. Volumes of the *Encyclopaedia of Indian Temple Architecture* have been produced since 1986 by the American Institute for Indian Studies' Center for Art and Archaeology under the editorship of M. A. Dhaky and Michael W. Meister; later volumes are being produced by M. A. Dhaky.

3. For examples, see George Michell, ed., *The Brick Temples of Bengal* (Princeton: Princeton University Press, 1983); Catherine B. Asher, "The Architec-

ture of Raja Man Singh: A Study of Sub-Imperial Patronage," in Barbara Stoler Miller, ed., *The Powers of Art: Patronage in Indian Culture* (New Delhi: Oxford University Press, 1992), 183–201; Asher, "Authority, Victory, and Commemoration: The Temples of Raja Man Singh," *Journal of Vaisnava Studies* 3 (summer 1995): 25–36; and Asher, "Kachhvaha Pride and Prestige: The Temple Patronage of Raja Man Singh," in Margaret Case, ed., *Govindadeva: A Dialogue in Stone* (New Delhi: Indira Gandhi National Centre for the Arts, 1996), 215–38.

4. One notable exception is the work of Atillio Petruccioli, "Geometry of Power: The City's Planning," in Michael Brand and Glenn D. Lowry, eds., *Fatehpur-Sikri* (Bombay: Marg, 1987), 49–64. Also see his edited issue of *Environmental Design* on "Mughal Architecture: Pomp and Ceremonies," 1–2 (1991).

5. For an even more exploratory article on this work, see my forthcoming article, "Piety, Religion, and the Old Social Order in the Architecture of the Later Mughals and Their Contemporaries," in Richard B. Barnett, ed., *New Perspectives on Early Modern India* (Columbia, Mo.: South Asia Books, forthcoming).

6. A good example is the Arhai Din ka Jhompra Masjid in Ajmer, which is commonly believed to be composed of spolia; however, Michael Meister, "The 'Two and a Half Day' Mosque," *Oriental Art* 18, no. 1 (1972): 57–63, has argued convincingly that the bulk of its columns and ceilings are newly carved. Many other monuments need to be reevaluated in light of Meister's argument.

7. This view was published by 1891 by A. Fuhrer, *The Monumental Antiquities and Inscriptions in the Northwestern Provinces and Oudh*, vol. 12a of the New Imperial Series, Archaeological Survey of India (reprint ed., Varanasi: Indological Book House, 1969), 21, and repeated by James Fergusson, *History of Indian and Eastern Architecture*, vol. 2 (London: John Murray, 1910), 68. These views may seem antiquated, but nothing has been published to reverse them. A case in point is that two leading scholars who finished a draft of an otherwise superb book on Islamic art and architecture had intended to include this mosque and point of view in their survey; luckily, they showed me the draft, and the mosque under discussion was dropped from the text.

8. For the inscriptions, see Qeyamuddin Ahmad, *Corpus of Arabic and Persian Inscriptions of Bihar* (Patna: K. P. Jayaswal Research Institute, 1983), 1–118. Catherine B. Asher, *Islamic Monuments of Eastern India and Bangladesh* (Leiden: Inter Documentation Co. on behalf of the American Committee for South Asian Art, 1991), provides illustrations.

9. See D. R. Patil, *Antiquarian Remains in Bihar* (Patna: K. P. Jayaswal Research Institute, 1963), 134, 139, 141, 213–15, 580–81; and Frederick M. Asher, "Gaya: Monuments of the Pilgrimage Town," in Janice Leoshko, ed., *Bodhgaya: The Site of Enlightenment* (Bombay: Marg, 1988), 77.

10. An example is the background of a depiction of Saint Jerome in Amina Okada and Francis Richard et al., *A La Cour du Grand Moghol* (Paris: Bibliothèque Nationale, 1986), 118.

11. For example, the Rohtas temple is the earliest one and situated so it can be

seen from below. Man Singh built the Harischandra temple next to it for political reasons; on this part of the hill there was inadequate room for a palace. The mosques and tombs are situated near the palace, and even though they predate the palace, this same area likely always was used for habitation. For basic coverage of Rohtas fort, see Muhammad Hamid Kuraishi, *List of Ancient Monuments Protected under Act VII of 1904 in the Province of Bihar and Orissa,* New Imperial Series, vol. 51, Archaeological Survey of India (Calcutta: Government of India, Central Publication Branch, 1931), 146–83. Also see Catherine B. Asher, *Architecture of Mughal India* (Cambridge: Cambridge University Press, 1992), 67–74, 90–92, and "The Architecture of Raja Man Singh," 187–91.

12. Catherine B. Asher, "Sub-Imperial Palaces: Power and Authority in Mughal India," *Ars Orientalis* 23 (1993): 287.

13. Tarapada Mukherjee and Irfan Habib, "Land Rights in the Reign of Akbar: The Evidence of Sale-Deeds of Vrindaban and Aritha," *Proceedings of the Indian History Congress, 50th Session* (Delhi: Indian History Congress, 1989–90), 236–55, and the same authors, "Akbar and the Temples of Mathura and Its Environs," *Proceedings of the Indian History Congress, 48th Session* (Panajim: Indian History Congress, 1988), 234–50.

14. Mons. Victor Jacquemont's comment, "I could not discover in [Vrindaban] a single mosque," in F. S. Growse, *Mathura: A District Memoir* (reprint, Ahmedabad: New Order, 1978), 188. This is an interesting contrast to another tirtha, Pushkar, where there is a mosque near the water's edge.

15. While today Rajmahal is in Bihar, in the Mughal period it was in *suba* Bengal.

16. For the mosque's foundation inscription, see S. A. Rahim, "Nine Inscriptions of Akbar from Rajasthan," *Epigraphia Indica, Arabic and Persian Supplement,* 1969, 55–56. See Susan Gole, *Indian Maps and Plans* (New Delhi: Manohar, 1989), 170, for a portion of a map of Amber in the National Museum, New Delhi [56.92.4] showing the mosque.

17. Kuraishi, *List of Ancient Monuments Protected under Act VII of 1904,* 217–19, for the mosque; the temple is in Asher, "The Architecture of Raja Man Singh," 192.

18. There is little scholarly discussion of Amber. B. L. Dhama, *A Guide to Jaipur and Amber* (Bombay, 1948), 68–82, is a good source for the town. The best map is provided by George Michell, *Buddhist, Hindu, Jain,* vol. 1 of *The Monuments of India* (New York: Viking Press, 1989), 290.

19. B. L. Dhama, *A Memoir on the Temple of the Jagatshiromani at Amber* (Jaipur: Chiranji Lal Sharma, 1977), provides a good description supported by drawings and photographs as well as a map indicating its location. For analysis of the temple's meaning, see Asher, "Kachhvaha Pride and Prestige," 221–26 and plates 10.3–10.24.

20. For example, see Susan L. Huntington, *The Art of Ancient India* (New York: Weatherhill, 1985), 490.

21. See the Jagdish temple in Udaipur in H. B. Pal, *The Temples of Rajasthan* (Alwar and Jaipur: Prakash, 1969), plate 22.

22. Gole, *Indian Maps and Plans*, 172–73, shows pilgrimage towns with such temples depicted on the walls of the Bhojan Shala of Amber palace.

23. For the mosques of Lucknow, see B. N. Tandan, "The Architecture of the Nawabs of Avadh, 1722–1856," in Robert Skelton et al., eds., *Facets of Indian Art* (London: Victoria and Albert Museum, 1986), 66–75. For those in Varanasi, see Pierre-Daniel Coute and Jean-Michael Leger, *Benares* (Paris: Editions Creaphis, 1989), 71–81. Perhaps the most famous drawing of the so-called Alamgir mosque dominating the riverscape is in James Prinsep, *Benares Illustrated* (Calcutta: At the Baptist Mission Press, 1833). I still need to examine the prominence of mosques in cities such as Udaipur or Kotah.

24. Some temples are cited in Yogesh Praveen, *Lucknow Monuments* (Lucknow: Pnar, 1989), 1–23.

25. Diana Eck, *Banaras, City of Light* (Princeton: Princeton University Press, 1982), 90.

26. For a view showing this juxtaposition, see Rajesh Bedi and John Keay, *Banaras, City of Shiva* (New Delhi: Brijbasi Printers, 1987), 37.

27. Coute and Leger, *Benares*, 54; Eck, *Banaras, City of Light*, 120, 248, where the queen is credited with building a temple at the Manikarnika Cremation ghat in Benares. F. M. Asher, "Gaya," 74, indicates she also built the Vishnupad temple in Gaya.

28. For example, see Eckart Ehlers and Thomas Krafft, "Islamic Cities in India? Theoretical Concepts and the Case of Shahjahanabad / Old Delhi," in Ehlers and Krafft, eds., *Shahjahanabad/Old Delhi: Tradition and Colonial Change* (Stuttgart: Franz Steiner, 1993), 9–26, and Jamal Malik, "Islamic Institutions and Infrastructure in Shahjahanabad," 43–64 of the same volume. Also see Stephen P. Blake, *Shahjahanabad: The Sovereign City in Mughal India, 1639–1739* (Cambridge: Cambridge University Press, 1991), for the city as essentially an Islamic one.

29. Blake, *Shahjahanabad*, 51–55, and Asher, *Architecture of Mughal India*, chaps. 5–7 for plates. These mosques were built by queens or high-ranking women.

30. Asher, *Architecture of Mughal India*, 298–99, for plates and text on these two mosques.

31. See *List of Muhammadan and Hindu Monuments: Delhi Province*, 4 vols. (Calcutta: Superintendent, Government Printing, 1916–22), 1:168–225, for these and other structures in the vicinity. Hereafter this work will be known as *List;* the numbers correspond to the catalog number, not the page. See Asher, *Architecture of Mughal India*, 198, 256, for plates of the mosque of Tahawwar Khan and the mosque of Mubarak Begum (Lal Kunwar).

32. Illustrations to the Zeenat Mahal haveli are in Pavan K. Varma and Sondeep Shankar, *Mansions at Dusk: The Havelis of Old Delhi* (New Delhi: Spantech, 1992), 78–80. For a good illustration showing the Fatehpuri mosque in its original state, see Emily Bayley and Thomas Metcalfe, *The Golden Calm: An*

English Lady's Life in Moghul Delhi, ed. by M. M. Kaye (New York: Viking Press, 1980), plate facing p. 168.

33. Blake, *Shahjahanabad*, 55–56, portrays Shahjahanabad through the early eighteenth century. Narayani Gupta, "Military Security and Urban Development: A Case Study of Delhi 1857–1912," *Modern Asian Studies* 5, no. 1 (1971): 61–77, is a good source for changes made after the Uprising of 1857.

34. Blake, *Shahjahanabad*, 174.

35. Naryani Gupta, *Delhi between Two Empires*, 1803–1931 (Delhi: Oxford University Press, 1991), 46.

36. Ibid., 49; Hamida Khatoon Naqvi, "Shahjahanabad: The Mughal Delhi, 1638–1803: An Introduction," in *Delhi through the Ages*, ed. R. E. Frykenberg (Delhi: Oxford University Press, 1986), 144. Also see Susan Gole, "Three Maps of Shahjahanabad," *South Asian Studies* 4 (1988): 14–17, where she discusses a map in the IOL (AL 1762) of Chandni Chowk which gives the names of many Hindus' havelis and quarters.

37. Naqvi, "Shahjahanabad," 144.

38. *List*, 1:33–39; these monuments are in the area formerly called Faiz Bazaar. Gole, "Three Maps," 18–23, cites Hindus' havelis on the IOL map of Faiz Bazaar (AL 1763). Since we know, for example, that the massive Akbarabadi mosque was destroyed after 1857, small temples doubtless were as well.

39. This is only true for premodern additions. Now Hindi inscriptions abound on very recent restorations or constructions of temples in Shahjahanabad.

40. This work was commenced in the summer of 1994 and has been ongoing over subsequent summers.

41. Volume 1 of the *List* cites a number of temples believed to date to the seventeenth or eighteenth centuries. Given the location and antiquity of these structures, I see no reason to doubt this. Blake, *Shahjahanabad*, 111, assumes there are only two temples built before 1707, since only these bear dated inscriptions; however, in general very few temples in North India bear dates; thus this argument lacks substance.

42. Conversation with Sri Dalip Sharma, the son of the *pujari* of a Shivalaya in Katra Nil in February 1995. My treatment upon visiting all these temples would also confirm this—I was always most welcome.

43. In the entire walled city, I saw only one temple with a shikhara that appears to date before 1900; it was in the area of Sitaram Bazaar. Today it is enclosed by walls and appears not to function as a temple. It cannot be examined.

44. Thomas Krafft, "Contemporary Old Delhi: Transformation of an Historical Place," in Eckart Ehlers and Thomas Krafft, eds., *Shahjahanabad/Old Delhi: Tradition and Colonial Change* (Stuttgart: Franz Steiner, 1993), 81; *List*, 1:351–61.

45. Gole, "Three Maps," 18–23.

46. This is Mahalla Nayabans. See *List*, 1:219–21. Temple no. 220 reputedly dates to Shah Jahan's time, although it has been rebuilt in the late nineteenth or

early twentieth century. Consult the map provided at the volume's back for the location of these temples and the following mosques.

47. Gupta, *Delhi between Two Empires*, 23.

48. *List*, 1:355.

49. Ibid., 1:334.

50. Gupta, *Delhi between Two Empires*, 50, and Chakrash Kumar Jain Bijli Wale, "Sri Digambara Jain Lal Mandir, Delhi," in *Grismahkalin Naitik Siksan Sibir* (New Delhi: Digambara Jain Naitik Siksa Samiti, 1995). This three-page contribution to this summer school's souvenir program sums up the oral tradition I had been told in August 1995 by the temple's authorities.

51. *List*, 1:333, and Marie-Claude Mahais, *Délivrance et Convivialité: Le System Culinaire des Jaina* (Paris: Editions de la Maison des Sciences de l'Homme, 1985), 20–22. Mahais, who worked in the temple for some time, is not aware that it was rebuilt in the nineteenth century. This is understandable, since her study has nothing to do with architecture. This information is verified in Balabhadra Jaina, *Bharata ke Digambara Jaina Thirta*, 5 vols. (Bombay: Bharatavarshiya Digambara Jaina Tirthakshetra, 1974–88), 1:288, and by the temple authorities. For a brief description of the temple's history preserved by its authorities, see Bijli Wale.

52. Both the *List*, 1:333 and Bijli Wale state these images are dated *samvat* 1548. The images are kept in a locked glass case with numerous smaller metal images on tiered steps before them; unfortunately, these metal images obscure portions of these donative inscriptions, but I could read enough of the numerical section of date on two of the images to assume that 1548 is correct.

53. This prime location reflects a relationship between the Jain community and the Mughal court, for in this same location lived the jewelers many of whom were Jain. While John F. Richards, "Mughal State Finance and the Premodern World Economy," *Comparative Studies in Society and History* 23 (1981): 285–301, argues that Khattri and Jain merchants were not vital to the Mughal court before the eighteenth century, the location of land allotted to them suggests they played a role of some substance in the maintenance of Mughal culture. I would like to thank John Cort for discussing the role of the Jain community in premodern North India with me.

54. See Gole, "Three Maps," 13–27, and Eckart Ehlers and Thomas Krafft, *Shahjahanabad/Old Delhi*, facsimile map of Shahjahanabad (IOL Records X, 1659).

55. H. H. Wilson, *The Oriental Portfolio: Picturesque Illustrations of the Scenery and Architecture of India* (London: Smith, Elder, 1841), plate: The Chouk, Delhi; John Luard, *Views in India, Saint Helena and Car Nicobar: Drawn from Nature and on Stone* (London: J. Graf, 1838), plate: Chandnee Chauk, Delhi. Luard's illustration also includes the Sunhari mosque.

56. Stuart Cary Welch, *India: Art and Culture, 1300–1900* (New York: Metropolitan Museum of Art, 1985), 429–33.

57. Blake, *Shahjahanabad*, 111. The words in brackets are my additions, for Blake ignores the religious activity of the Jain community, also merchants who lived around Chandni Chowk.

58. There are no published references to or illustrations of these temples, including the Jagannath temple, dated 1864.

59. Ashim Kumar Roy, *The History of the Jaipur City* (New Delhi: Manohar, 1978), 29.

60. Joan L. Erdman, *Patrons and Performers in Rajasthan* (Delhi: Chanakya, 1985), 28, is the only scholar to give a balanced reading indicating Jaipur's debt to Mughal tradition.

61. While this appears true for the temples in the city itself, those on the surrounding hills do bear shikharas including the Ganeshgarh temple with which the Govinda Deva temple and City Palace are aligned. The Surya temple, provided by Jai Singh's minister in 1734, also bears a shikhara. The significance of this is not clear, although it may be that these are not Vishnu / Krishna temples; in Jaipur, Krishna temples are inevitably constructed as haveli type temples. For distant views of the Ganeshgarh temple and others, see Aman Nath, *Jaipur: The Last Destination* (Bombay: India House Pvt. Ltd., 1993), 4–5, 72, 73, 147, 198. See Sten Nilsson, "Jaipur, in the Sign of Leo," no. 1 of *Magasin Tessin* (Lund: Wallin and Dalholm, 1987), plate 32 for a plate of the Surya temple. There is no published photograph of the Kalkiji temple proper, but Nath, *Jaipur: The Last Destination*, 162, illustrates its small fore shrine, and G. H. R. Tillotson, *The Rajput Palaces: The Development of an Architectural Style, 1450–1750* (New Haven: Yale University Press, 1987), 168, shows a view of the bazaar taken from the Hawa Mahal, that is, a structure used by the imperial women; the shikhara visible is that of the Kalkiji temple, but access to this view would have been highly limited. I spent considerable time checking its visibility from the street; its shikhara and only this portion of the temple is visible when standing directly in front of it; it is simply invisible from any other location on the street.

62. These include Ramchandraji's temple in Chandrapole Bazaar, which was built in 1894, and the Lakshmi Narayana temple in Bari Chaupar. This temple may possibly be earlier; since it bears no date, it needs to be analyzed in terms of its style. However, so far there is no systematic understanding of the eighteenth-century North Indian temple and its stylistic development.

63. These temples are listed by Roy, *The History of the Jaipur City*, 229–31, but I know of no published illustrations of them. The exception is a detail of the 1854 Ramchandraji temple's exterior in Nath, *Jaipur: The Last Destination*, 68.

64. Roy, *The History of the Jaipur City*, 125, indicates the general population was illiterate or barely literate until the first half of the twentieth century, suggesting written signs would have little value.

65. This portion of the paper is based solely on fieldwork I did in 1995 and 1996. To date, I have found virtually no secondary information on any of Jaipur's mosques.

66. Savritri Gupta, *Jaipur*, vol. 26 of *Rajasthan District Gazetteers* (Jaipur: Directorate, District Gazetteers, Government of Rajasthan, 1987), 64–65, although Roy, *The History of the Jaipur City*, 104, indicates that in 1901 a quarter of Jaipur's population was Muslim. For the Muslim population of Lucknow, see V. C.

Sharma, *Lucknow*, vol. 37 of *Uttar Pradesh District Gazetteers* (Lucknow: Government of Uttar Pradesh, 1959), 73.

67. Nath, *Jaipur: The Last Destination*, 163.

68. Information given to me by local informants. Also see Roy, *The History of the Jaipur City*, 48.

69. Since I have found no written material on the mosque, I asked every Muslim I met in Jaipur which mosques were the oldest. The unanimous response was the mosque at Amber and then the Jami mosque in Jaipur. It has been completely rebuilt, although its location remains unchanged. Gopal Narayan Bahura and Chandramani Singh, *Catalogue of Historical Documents in Kapad-Dwara Jaipur*, vol. 2: *Maps and Plans* (Jaipur: Maharaja of Jaipur, 1990) published a number of maps of Jaipur, but no mosque or *dargah* was included on them. However, this does not mean that there was no mosque in this position. There is no surviving map of Johari Bazaar, where the Jami mosque is located. Moreover, few Hindu temples are included on any of these Jaipur maps (see nos. 205 and 208 for rare exceptions). No Jain temple, for example is cited on the extant published maps, yet K. C. Kasliwal, *Jaina Grantha Bhandars in Rajasthan* (Jaipur: Shri Digamber Jain Atishaya Kshetra Shri Mahavirji, 1967), 43–59, indicates a number of Jain temples were established in the eighteenth century within the city's walls; many of them are still extant in Johari Bazaar.

70. *Annual Report for Indian Epigraphy*, 1975–76, D. 155 gives the date on entrance to dargah as A.H. 1213/1798–99 C.E. This probably is the same date as the mosque; it is not the oldest dated structure, although it may be the oldest intact one, for D. 154 of the same volume indicates an inscription dated A.H. 1190/1776 C.E. on Jaipur's Rahamiyya mosque. This mosque, situated not far from the city's Jami mosque, has recently been completely remodeled.

71. For examples, see Michell, *The Brick Temples of Bengal*, plates 165, 169, 185, 605–6.

72. See Coute and Leger, *Benares*, 51, 78, for examples.

73. Ibid., 52.

74. Praveen, *Lucknow Monuments*, 17–19, provides a description but no illustrations.

75. Coute and Leger, *Benares*, 55.

76. *List*, 4:13; Sayyid Ahmad Khan, *Asar al-Sanadid* (reprint ed.; Delhi: Central Book Depot, 1965), 337–40; Carr Stephen, *The Archaeology and Monumental Remains of Delhi* (Ludhiana: Mission Press, 1876), 28–29.

77. Stephen, *Archaeology and Monumental Remains*, 29, indicates that he provided the shikhara without much enthusiasm.

78. In addition to examples provided in note 31, see Asher, *Architecture of Mughal India*, 275, 297, 302-5. Imperially sponsored mosques in Delhi are larger and necessarily adhere to a slightly different imperial plan. See Ebba Koch, *Mughal Architecture: An Outline of Its History and Development, 1526–1858* (Munich: Prestel, 1991), 119, for an example.

79. See *List*, vol. 1, for the temples that are almost all primarily dedicated to Shiva. See note 93 of this paper for reference to other deities enshrined with these Shiva *lingas*.

80. The two major ones are the temple of Charan Das (*List*, 1:243) in Hauz Qazi (although the *List* includes it under Balli Maran) and the Ladliji temple in Katra Nil (*List*, 1:357).

81. See Christopher A. Bayly, *Rulers, Townsmen, and Bazaars*, rev. ed. (Delhi: Oxford University Press, 1992), 388; H. H. Wilson, *Hindu Religions* (reprint, Calcutta: Society for the Resuscitation of Indian Literature, 1899), 117–19; A. W. Entwistle, *Braj, Centre of Krishna Pilgrimage* (Groningen: Egbert Forsten, 1987), 213.

82. Gupta, *Delhi between Two Empires*, 23.

83. The manuscript is discussed in Milo Cleveland Beach, *Mughal and Rajput Painting* (Cambridge: Cambridge University Press, 1992), 41, 44–47. However, this particular page is illustrated in Douglas Barrett and Basil Gray, *Painting of India* (Lausanne: Skira, 1963), 143, although the date is incorrectly given. A similar and probably earlier Shivalaya is depicted in an undated illustration of Bhairava Raga in Beach, 47.

84. In Vrindaban are several large temples reputedly erected during the seventeenth century, for example, the Jugal Kishore in Asher, *Architecture of Mughal India*, 164, 166. Pal, *Temples of Rajasthan*, plate 22, provides a view of the mid-seventeenth-century Jagdish Temple in Udaipur.

85. Asher, *Architecture of Mughal India*, 194–96.

86. For a distant view of the temple and its interior image, see Nath, *Jaipur: The Last Destination*, 146–47. Erdman, *Patrons and Performers in Rajasthan*, 37, reiterates a story that the temple was first constructed as Jai Singh's sleeping quarters, but after divine revelation in a dream the king gave the structure over to Krishna as Govinda Deva. It is not possible to trace the antiquity of this belief.

87. *List*, 1:243.

88. See Erdman, *Patrons and Performers in Rajasthan*, 27–44, for the interaction of religion and authority in the city's construction.

89. See Diana L. Eck, *Darshan: Seeing the Divine in India*, 2d ed. (Chambersburg, Penn.: Amina Books, 1985), 3–4.

90. *List*, 1:357. This was confirmed by the *mahant* in August 1994 and again in March 1996. This temple, which belongs to the Lalita Sampradaya, is discussed by Babulala Gosvami, *Lalita Sampradaya: Siddhanta aura Sahitya* (Pilani: Kamala Prakasana, 1991), and Entwistle, *Braj, Centre of Krishna Pilgrimage*, 213.

91. *List*, 1:243; Wilson, *Hindu Religions*, 119. Charan Das was born in 1703, and he died in 1783.

92. See *List*, 1:285, 287, 296, 322, 323, 333.

93. A tabulation of the secondary images included in Shahjahanabad's Shivalayas based on material provided in the *List* indicates that about half of them have Vaishnavite images. John Cort has suggested to me that the Shivalaya

is appropriate for a public shrine but that Krishna worship is more suitable for the private domain, and thus he feels that the home shrine probably was dedicated to Krishna.

94. See Asher, *Architecture of Mughal India*, 299–300, for Tahawwar Khan's mosque.

95. Tillotson, *The Rajput Palaces*, 190.

96. See Asher, "Piety, Religion, and the Old Social Order," forthcoming.

97. Blake, *Shahjahanabad*, 111; Bayly, *Rulers, Townsmen, and Bazaars*, 371–72.

98. Examples would include those Gupta period temples at Maria, Bhumera, and Natchna. Others might include those at Menal, Rajasthan, which is clearly a tirtha site.

99. See Bayly, *Rulers, Townsmen, and Bazaars*, 384–90.

100. Examples include the Naya Mandir in Mahalla Dharmapura (*List*, 1:310) and Jain temple in Kuncha-i Seth (*List*, 1:322). Even today continual restoration of the gold is undertaken in these temples; the authorities tell me with great pride that it is real gold.

101. Bayly, *Rulers, Townsmen, and Bazaars*, 388.

102. Varahamihira, *Brhat Samhita*, 2 vols., trans. M. Ramakrishna Bhat (Delhi and Varanasi: Motilal Banarsidass, 1981), 1:499, 516–38; Varahamihira, *India as Seen in the Brhatsamhita of Varhamihira*, trans. A. M. Shastri (Delhi and Varanasi: Motilal Banarsidass, [1969]), 268–69, 273, 395.

6

Indo-Persian Tazkiras as Memorative Communications

Marcia K. Hermansen and Bruce B. Lawrence

Naqsh faryadi hai kis ki shukhi-yi taḥrir ka
kaghazi hai pairhan, har paikar-i taṣvir ka
[Of whose careless recording does the inscription complain,
For every representation wears a paper shirt.]
Ghālib

In a volume that focuses on Muslim identity in general and Indo-Muslim identity in particular, we have a treasure trove to help us understand how South Asian Muslims identified themselves. It is the *tazkira,* or biographical compendium. The tazkira is a genre of literature produced by elites for other elites. Its primary linguistic expression in the subcontinent is Persian, at least during the Mughal or Indo-Tirmuri period, which we emphasize here. Only in the late Mughal and colonial periods of Indo-Muslim history do we find both Urdu translations of Indo-Persian tazkiras and Urdu sequels, with companion compositions in Punjabi, Sindhi, and Gujarati. The tazkira is a staple of Indo-Muslim cultural production, and as such it demands closer analysis than it has so far received if we are to grasp the relationship between personal authority and place in structuring Indo-Muslim identity.

Or, rather, Indo-Muslim *identities,* since the range of elite literary reflection is very broad, and Indo-Persian tazkiras encompass a wide variety of contexts. Above all, the tazkira traces memory through the lives of heroes, both lyrical and spiritual, and in doing so, it raises a number of interesting theoretical questions. How are its heroes selected, and who gets to tell their story for which audiences? While the heroes may display courage, evoke hope, and elicit loyalty, how do their lives relate to the unheroic, to the everyday, to the lives without traces?

A common complaint by critics has been the lack of any consistent principles of selectivity, critical evaluation of facts, or analytical framework in the tazkira tradition.[1] An anthologist has noted "their seemingly irrelevant style of diction."[2] Some scholars of contemporary third world literature have even suggested that we cannot go beyond describing these texts. They are resistant to critical theory because they are drenched in the minutiae of local detail.

Yet we propose a method of reading tazkiras that acknowledges the ambiguity at their core. As the poet Ghālib implies in the epigraph for this essay,[3] there is *no* "careless recording." Each representation that wears a paper shirt is intended to communicate to others the quality, the cultural residue that commends its content to would-be readers. Tazkiras are not mere mnemonic repetitions. They are conscious remembrances, and therefore they are both cultural artifacts and cultural reconstructions. In Walter Benjamin's language, "the 'after' is precisely not the 'again.'" The "after" requires "the destruction of the illusion of its continuity with the past," for "only thus can the past be 'put to work' in the present as remembrance."[4]

If it is possible for tradition to appear in the guise of cultural history, and if that history is marked above all by narrative forms, then the Indo-Persian tazkiras of South Asia exemplify what could be labeled, in a paraphrastic gloss from Benjamin, "memorative communication."[5] At the vertical level, these memorative communications reflect the divine favor conferred on worthy Indo-Muslim emissaries—in this case, saints and poets—just as these same emissaries reflect the divine impress on their own creatively courageous lives. At the horizontal level, Indo-Persian tazkiras project a collective testimony for others who also locate themselves in the same subcommunity of South Asian Muslims. These are literary works that both remember and communicate. They concentrate the readers' focus on their heroic subjects at the same time that they disperse, or redeploy, that focus to present-day concerns and contingencies. Although they draw from the past, they are *not* commemorative; they do not recall the past for its own sake or for the sake of the heroes whom they exalt. They *are* memorative, relying on memory and remembrance to communicate with the living the legacy of prior Indo-Muslim exemplars.

Indo-Muslim exemplars are Muslim as well as Indian, and so we find that certain general cultural themes typical in Islamic civilization persist in the tazkira genre in Muslim South Asia. For example, the moods of nostalgia or boasting can be traced back even to the Jahiliyya poetry of pre-Islamic Arabs.[6] The genealogical preoccupation of the Arabs merged with the formulation of a sacred history embodied by the early Muslim community in early biographical compendia. Works written in Arabic, such as the *Ṭabaqat* of Ibn Saʿd (ca. 784), feature the practice of extensively listing very ordinary participants in the Muslim community, as if to somehow represent its existence and significance by remembering even the names of who had been present, in other words, to provide a trace for those who otherwise would remain traceless, unacknowledged, forgotten.[7]

But much more important in terms of thematic characteristics is regional and urban location. The nature of Islamic civilization, at least from the perspective of the celebrators of its intellectual vibrancy, had an overwhelmingly urban focus, and we will demonstrate from several cases how the memorialization of cities came to characterize this genre as it expanded into the space of Muslim South Asia.[8] The urban notables who abound in the pages of Indo-Persian tazkiras are rarely rulers, sometimes religious scholars, but more often urban intellectuals. It is, above all, poets and saints who become the principal subjects memorialized in Islamic biographical literature generally but even more frequently in the Indo-Persian tazkiras of South Asia. Common to each entry is attention to the rank, affiliation, profession, and year or century of death of the person remembered. But no less important is the locality of the individual's primary activities, with the double message that the urban setting enhanced the spectrum of possible activity for the deceased at the same time that the achievements of this notable brought to that city a fame or spiritual bounty it did not, or had not, enjoyed before his lifetime.

Nowhere is the accent on place and the reciprocal importance of heroes and homes more pivotal than in a distinctly biographical genre developed in India due to the influence of institutional Sufism. That genre is the *malfuẓat*, or recorded conversations, of spiritual masters. It is developed by the most notable Indo-Muslim brotherhood of the premodern period, the Chishtiya, and from its earliest appearance in North India to its later proliferation throughout Hindustan, it is identified with specific saints whose places shape their audience and whose responses, or question-and-answer sessions with close disciples, enhance the places where they settle and teach, advise and warn, fast and pray, and meditate and eventually (usually after long lives) die.[9] From the major Chishti exemplar of his day, Shaykh Nizam ad-din Awliya (d. 1325), in Delhi to his disciple, Shaykh Burhan ad-din Gharib, in the

Deccan and especially in Burhanpur (named after him), we find the genre of malfuẓat fostering an intensely localized memory, even when it is a "false" memory.

"False" memory? Yes, for as Carl Ernst has noted, we should not approach the malfuẓat only as historical purists. Although many later malfuẓat either were spurious or projected major distortions of their core contents, they still reinforced both the authoritativeness of their saintly subjects and the place where they presided, then expired. What interests us is that both kinds of malfuẓat became included in the canon of South Asian Sufi memory.[10]

The lesson from malfuẓat is extended in the genre of tazkira. It is attention to place, or to relocation of place, from a real or imagined Central Asian or Arabian homeland to a new South Asian primary home, that governs the principle of biographical collection and the inscription of an altered sense of identity. Even the focus on individual heroes is subordinated to a still larger purpose: the collective display of groups of individuals. It is as groups of heroes, sharing a common identity and a convergent legacy, that saints and poets reinforce the value of a Muslim presence in South Asia—not just anywhere in South Asia, but in South Asian urban settings, in premodern cities. It is bards and Sufis together who authorize the cultural symbolism of South Asia as an urban, and also an urbane, Muslim realm.

Especially during one period, the Mughal or Indo-Tirmuri, from the early sixteenth century to the mid-nineteenth century, we find this pronounced tendency to compile tazkiras both to honor heroes and to authenticate Muslim urban spaces. For that reason, while our essay will look at multiple points of the millennial long history of South Asian Islam, we will give particular stress to those poetic and saintly tazkiras that emerged from Mughal India.[11]

Tazkiras, as their name suggests, both memorialize individuals and communicate their legacy to a new generation. They are, to repeat our title, "memorative communications," projecting the worth of individual heroes as icons of urban Indo-Muslim collective identity. If there is a key word for understanding poetic and Sufi tazkiras, it is *memory*. Memory has a long etiology in western thought, which is bound up with its invocation in Islamic contexts. Both need to be considered before applying our analysis to Indo-Persian figures from South Asia.

The Concept of Memory in Muslim South Asia

A study of memory in medieval European culture, *The Book of Memory* by Mary Carruthers,[12] suggests some interesting approaches to looking at memorialization in premodern Muslim South Asia. For example, consider the civilizational context of memory. In developing an Islamic concept of memory, a root image is established by the Qur'anic metaphor of the source of primordial reality in a "preserved tablet."[13] The "pen" that inscribes is also mentioned in the Qur'an (68:1), and this imagery has been drawn upon throughout the interpretive tradition of Muslim Neoplatonic philosophy and in the philosophical and poetic tradition following Ibn Arabi's Sufi metaphysical system.[14] The world itself and human, religious, and political destinies are conceived as a sequence of articulations of what has been written on this primordial preserved tablet (*al-lauḥ al-maḥfuẓ*). Embodied in maḥfuẓ is a double meaning: What has been "preserved" has also been "memorized."

Annemarie Schimmel, discussing "the pen" in a section on "letter symbolism in Sufi literature," notes:

> The mystics have dwelt on another aspect of pen symbolism as well. There is a famous hadith: "The heart of the faithful is between the two fingers of the All-compassionate, and he turns it wherever He wants." This hadith suggests the activity of the writer with his reed pen, who produces intelligible or confused lines; the pen has no will of its own, but goes wherever the writer turns it. . . . The hadith of the pen has inspired the poets of Iran and other countries—they saw man as a pen that the master calligrapher uses to bring forth pictures and letters according to his design, which the pen cannot comprehend. Mirzā Ghālib, the great poet of Muslim India (d. 1869), opened his Urdu Dīwān with a line that expresses the complaint of the letters against their inventor, for "every letter has a paper shirt."[15]

We should not be surprised that the same Aristotelian categories of form and matter which structured medieval European thinking about the process of creation, whether divine or human, were also inherited by the Islamic tradition. The imagery of wax which takes on the shape of the mold or the signet ring was a way of describing the creative process as it was channeled through retrieved memory. Tracing the development of this model in Socrates and Plato, Carruthers observes, "In fact, Socrates is at some pains to say that his way of describing the memory as being like seals made by a signet ring is not new, but really is very old. This is important because it is a model based on how the eye sees in reading, not how the ear hears. In recollection, one *looks* at the contents of memory, rather than hearing or speaking them; the mediator is visual."[16] Coexisting with and sustaining this centrality of memory in classical Islamic civilization were the now almost forgotten technologies of memorizing and then retrieving memorized information in speech and writing.[17]

In the experience of madrasa study, for example, the visual arrangement of text and commentary on the written or printed page was pivotal, as was the tradition of transforming essential texts or principles into rhyme. Al-Ṣuyuṭi's *Alfiyya*,[18] for instance, was composed in order to make the rules of hadith criticism accessible for memorization, and Shah Wali Allah of Delhi undertook a rhyming translation into Persian of the standard manual of rhetoric, the *Ṣarf-i Mir*.[19]

Memory was closely linked to remembrance for South Asian Muslim elites. It included various acts or practices such as *dhikr* (ritualized recitation of pious phrases that are sanctioned by Qur'anic injunctions to remember God in all situations),[20] *yad dasht*,[21] *taṣawwur*,[22] and *ḥifẓ*. In Sufi practice, moreover, memory was ritualized in the recitation of *shajaras* or *khaṭms*.[23] On the occasion of celebrations of a saint's marriage to God (*ʿurs*), or at other notable moments, the lineage of a Sufi order would be ritually recited, with the belief that the spirits of the departed saints would present themselves and bestow blessings on those assembled.

The Sufi ritual of dhikr is a more specialized form of a basic Islamic practice of the remembrance of God through recitation and repetition; its opposite, *ghaflat*, that is, "forgetting" or "negligence," is both a moral shortcoming in terms of religious piety and a personal affront to the beloved in the tradition of poetic love.

This premodern sense of memory in Islamic civilization included an appreciation both of memory as "recollection," which constituted a powerful tool for self-awareness and creativity, and memory as connection, which incorporated the emotional dimension of the act of memorialization. Thus the inscription of memory as a cultural activity involved both an appropriation of power over a space and the creation of an emotional investment in it. It was, in every sense, a memorative communication, not merely a commemoration of bygone saints/poets or nostalgia for their heroism, whether courageous spirituality or lyrical fervor.

Ham parvarish-i lauh-o-qalam karte raheṅge
joo dil peh guzartī hai raqam karte raheṅge

We will safeguard the tablet and the pen,
We will record whatever the heart experiences.

Faiẓ Ahmad Faiẓ[24]

Language and writing then inscribe what is essential; they also project values that must be reappropriated in each successive generation of readers, almost invariably urban elites who descended from other urban elites. "Literature was thought to contribute to the ethical life of the individual and the public memory of society," writes Carruthers in reference to medieval Europe. In the case of South Asian Muslim tazkiras, their writing suggests the further intention and effect of "making Muslim space." From multiple regions of Hindustan, their authors appropriate urban places and authorize them as the sites of Indo-Muslim cultural memory.

In studying the Chishti shrine complex at Khuldabad, for instance, Carl Ernst recounts two stories connected with memory that link the classical Islamic tradition with South Asian tazkira compositions. The Chishti saint Nizam al-Din Auliya' (d. 1325) in commending the efforts of the poetic compiler of his malfuẓat, Ḥasan Sijzi, suggests a parallel to Abu Hurayra (ca. 678), the most prolific transmitter of Prophetic hadith according to the Sunni tradition. "Niẓam al-Din said that the Prophet told Abu Hurayra to extend the skirt of his garment whenever the Prophet spoke, then slowly gather in the garment when the words were finished and place his hand upon his breast; this routine would enable him to memorize Muhammad's words."[25] This same motif of extending the skirt of the garment to collect words of wisdom and guidance is later echoed in another malfuẓat, *Khayr al-Majalis,* where Hamid Qalandar applies this method in recording the sessions of Nizam al-Din's successor, another Delhi Chishti master, Nasir al-Din Chiragh-i-Dihli.[26]

The symbolism of extending and pulling in the skirt of a garment when applied to a literate tradition evokes the process of interpretation through reading inward from the commentaries on the margins of texts to the texts themselves in order to gain access to the core meanings. This also sets up a resonance with the emotional quality of memorizing and preserving the words of an individual. It underscores the link between memory and personal devotion. Grasping the *daman* or skirt of a garment is, in fact, the gesture of the petitioner or supplicant, resonant with the paper shirt worn by the plaintiff of Ghālib's couplet. It also underscores the need of each person in the present to account for the representation offered, that is, to be an active agent in the process of commemorative communication.

Patterns in Poetic and Sufi Tazkiras

The tazkiras of both poets and Sufis evidence the changing shape of Muslim identity in South Asia through their principles of ordering as well as their thematic concerns. We have stressed their commonality, but one might also note their difference. While the role of saints is to sanctify the new soil of Hindustan and, above all, its cities, the function of the poets and poetic tazkiras lies elsewhere. In the case of the poetic tazkiras, the language and imagery of a city's poets inscribes another sort of privileged space; most often it sets the scene for a particular "state of mind" associated with that place,[27] and to understand that link we will examine the poetic tazkiras before turning to their saintly counterparts.

Poetic Tazkiras

So extensive has been the scholarship on tazkira as a genre applied to the lives of Indo-Muslim poets that it merits brief review. Some of the basic work in the literary history of this genre was carried out by the Pakistani scholar Farman Fateḥpuri in a special 1964 issue of the journal *Nigar* and then in a 1972 monograph entitled *Urdu Shuara kê Tazkirê aur Tazkira Nigari*.[28]

Fateḥpuri suggests that the model for subsequent poetic tazkiras was the early Persian biographical compendium *Lubab al-Albab*, composed in A.H. 618/1282–83 C.E. by Muḥammad Awfi.[29] A glance through Awfi's chapter headings indicates that the principle of organization of this tazkira was primarily chronological rather than spatial. E. G. Browne, who edited this work, evaluates it as primarily an anthology and disappointing in biographical particulars.[30]

The early tazkiras in South Asia were written in Persian, even those of Urdu poets. A glance through Fateḥpuri's catalog of tazkiras indicates that the three earliest tazkiras of Urdu poets were written in Persian in the same year, 1165/1752.[31] Perhaps a conclusion might be drawn regarding the connection of tazkira preparation with patronage networks. The Mughal empire at this point was on the verge of takeover by Europeans; it was also experiencing a major shift in its revenue system. One might speculate that part of the motivation for compiling such compendia was to draw the attention of potential patrons and gain reward for the needy litterateur. The prospect of European rule could have also produced another motivation: faced with the loss of social as well as political and economic power, Indo-Persian elites may have intensified their memorative communications, with poets high on the list of those deemed to be endangered species!

According to Fateḥpuri, until the *Ab-i Ḥayat* (Water of life) of Muḥammad Ḥusain Āzād[32] in 1880, most of the tazkiras were written in Persian following the old formula.[33] Āzād's tazkira has been celebrated as a breakthrough or watershed in the genre that, according to Ralph Russell, a noted scholar of Urdu, helped "lay the foundation of modern literary criticism in Urdu." Russell cites Āzād's readiness to learn from the British methods, that is, in employing historical critical standards. He explains how Āzād advanced on the traditional tazkira form, which had been essentially that of a biographical dictionary, providing "the poet's name, his *takhallus* (pen-name), the city of his birth, his patrons, the date of his death, a description of the quality of his poetry, couched in rather conventional terms, and one or two specimen couplets from his ghazals." Āzād's principal contribution was to introduce a periodization of Urdu poetry into five periods based on chronology and the use of language by the poets.[34]

Two scholars of Persian and Urdu have attempted to sort traditional tazkiras according to two rather unrevealing types, the general (in which the time frame is not limited) and the particular (centered on a particular period).[35] Fateḥpuri raises a more interesting tension regarding this tradition by inquiring whether these biographical works were primarily composed as a showcase for the poetry, or whether, in fact, the biographical component was the primary motive for composition.[36]

The French scholar Garcin de Tassy took an interest in the tazkira form, compiling an extensive list of tazkiras available to him in the mid-nineteenth century and making synopses of their notices on Hindu and Muslim poets of Hindustani, together with representative translations of their work in three volumes. He speaks of the poetic notices falling into three basic categories, based primarily on the quality and extent of a poet's production, so that some figures merit only a brief notice, whereas poets at a middle rank who have produced longer collections known as *divans* or *kulliyat* receive an "honorable mention." The highest category, in his estimation, are those notices of poets or authors whose works have been given specific titles.[37]

In exploring the motivations for the composition of tazkiras, Fateḥpuri makes the following proposals:

1. The memorialization of the compiler or others might have motivated tazkira writing.

2. *Biaz nigari*, or the citation of favorite or thematically coherent poetic couplets, might have been the true motivation behind biographical compendia.[38]
3. Another motivation could be the urge to discuss the personal traits and rivalries of poets.
4. There was also appeal of such works during that period of artificiality in speech and imagination; they could appeal as a way of denying political and material decline by retreating to an interior world.
5. One also had to consider the increasing popularity of poetic gatherings (*musha'iras*) and the publication of more and more poetic anthologies based on the couplets recited at a particular one.[39]
6. Finally, they might assist the movement to establish Urdu over against Persian.[40]

By contrast, the contemporary critic Muḥammad Sadiq evaluates tazkiras solely by the standards of historical accuracy.

> The history of the tazkiras reveals a more serious approach and a greater desire for authenticity and fair play as time passed. The earlier tazkiras, for the most part, confined themselves to notes on the poets and drew heavily on their predecessors. Subsequent writers enlarged the sphere of their research by including discussions on prosody, diction, and the history of the Urdu language, some of them discarding the alphabetical order in favor of the chronological. They also tried to establish contact with their contemporary poets, and obtained first-hand information about them from their friends and relatives. We may say, therefore, that the history of tazkiras shows a steady advance in research; and what was once a pastime, a desire for personal recognition, or a means of expressing one's approval or disapproval, became a really responsible undertaking.[41]

Not till very recently, though, have we seen the student of poetic tazkiras shift to the interest of our essay: the use of heroes and homes in a reciprocal form that enhanced the benefit of each for Indo-Muslim urban identity. It is the American linguist Carla Petievich who has traced the organizing principle of locating the Urdu poetic tradition. It has shifted from the space of the *markaz* or city-based circle, centered around an *ustadh* (or master), to the region, which became defined by the scope of princely patronage, before it finally became linked to the school, based on canons of European literature as taught in the new universities modeled on the British system. Ironically, although this latter, accompanied by the inculcation of Victorian literary and moral standards, was an artificial fit with the reality of the South Asian Urdu poetic tradition and its lines of influence, it did become the generally accepted way of distinguishing the "Dihlavi" from the "Lakhnavi."[42] In other words, the very accent on competing traditions legitimated these major North Indian cities as spaces of urbane Indo-Muslim cultural expression.[43]

What resulted was more than an innocent competition of mutually reinforcing minority identities. The intense urban/regional focus of later poetic tazkiras became a crucial marker of regional identity. Tazkiras highlighted linguistic variants, rivalries over poetic eloquence, or even the correctness of local expressions. They thus served to define a certain space in terms of a "state of mind," with Lucknow, for example, seeking the highest ground as the epitome of refinement, "*nazakat*."

Carla Petievich has criticized this "two school" construction of Urdu poetry in the late eighteenth and nineteenth centuries.[44] Lucknow poetry, she observes, is too often represented as decadent: "It is acclaimed as the quintessential symbol of what Muslim culture in India achieved, yet it is simultaneously denounced today for the societal immorality, waste and decadence of its past." She goes on to lament that "in the case of Lakhnavi poetry, most critics have described the society of Lucknow as leisured, pleasure-loving and courtesan pursuing."[45] Other characteristics of Lakhnavi style cited in the critical literature include effeminacy, sensuality, frivolousness, a certain vulgarity, amorous repartee, and a lack of the traditional ambiguity regarding the beloved's gender and whether a divine or human beloved is really the object of the poet's address.[46] Petievich, however, tries to rescue Lucknow from the slanders of its detractors: she analyzes samples of poetry from various cities in order to disprove the applicability of these stereotypes solely to Lakhnavi poetry.

Nor is the shift in cultural memory as represented in the tazkira tradition limited to Lucknow. Another city-based tazkira from the twentieth century is the *Kamilan-i Rampur.* Written by Ḥafiẓ Ali Khan in 1929, it was reissued by the Rampur library in 1986[47] with the addition of a postnationalist preface to the original composition. In this the writer of the new preface, Abid Rida Bédar, develops the concept of Rampuri Urdu poetry as a "third school" aside from Delhi and Lucknow.[48] He evokes symbols of Rampuri identity such as a Rampuri cap (*topi*), a knife, and a particular style of knife fighting. And he also argues for the inclusion of the Ali brothers, activists in the independence movement, who had connections to Rampur but were omitted from the original tazkira. In other words, the tazkira takes on still another urban role: to demonstrate the emergence of a proto-nationalist space within the Muslim memory of particular cities, in this case, Rampur. The principle for inclusion is widened beyond saints and poets to include other notables, especially those identified with the emergence of independent India.

Sufi Tazkiras

Sufi tazkiras provide a genre parallelism to the poetic tazkiras but with some distinct differences. In the case of the Sufi tazkira tradition as in the poetic one, inspiration was drawn from Persian models, in this instance, Aṭṭar's famous *Tazkirat al-Auliya* as well as from the Naqshbandi-inspired models, Abd al-Raḥman Jami's *Nafaḥat al-uns*[49] and Kashifi's *Rashaḥat*.[50]

Also, Sufi tazkiras, like the poetic tazkiras just examined, are closely linked both to the institutional formation and the collective memory of Indo-Muslim elites.

A kind of partial tazkira is suggested by a section of the earlier *Kashf al-Maḥjub* of Hujwiri (d. 1074) that establishes the idea of *ṭariqa* or Sufi order. Subsequently, the schema of fourteen Sufi lineages or families became the organizing feature for most later tazkiras, despite its often poor fit, which generated many anomalous categories. One possibility is to contrast the ṭariqa-based tazkiras with those that attempt to catalog all orders, since multiple affiliation among Sufis had become more common by the sixteenth century.[51] But even more important is to connect the writing of these tazkiras with the places and the contexts, either regional or urban but most often both, that generated the need for memorative communication at the heart of tazkira writing.

It is for this reason that we draw special attention to Indo-Persian production from the high Mughal or Indo-Timuri period. It epitomizes the elite literary activity that we are analyzing throughout this essay, and at the same time it gives an extended case illustration of one of the most powerful processes of cultural production at any point in the history of Islamicate South Asia.

Each Indo-Persian tazkira from premodern South Asia illustrates concern for one's own *silsilah* as the declared motivation for authorship. There is one exception: Abd al-Qadir al-Badauni's *Muntakhab at-tawarikh*, the memorative communication of a pious but independent-minded courtier that throws light on the patronage that shapes the production of other Mughal period Sufi tazkiras.[52] But to understand the rareness of Badauni's project, one must first note other tazkiras that confirm the pattern of privileging one's own order in telling, or retelling, the entire drama of Muslim saintly labor.

Let us consider the ill-fated older son of Shah Jahan, Dara Shikoh (d. 1659). Before he was executed by his younger brother, Aurangzeb, Dara was both a Sufi adept and a Sufi tazkira author. Dara composed not one but two Sufi tazkiras, fulsome dictionaries of antecedent Muslim spiritual heroes. Dara seems to have been motivated by a concern for getting the record straight, but it is a surface concern. Dara's apparent concern masks his overriding goal: not only to affirm Abd al-Qadir Jilani as the foremost Sufi exemplar and the Qadiriya as the paramount Sufi brotherhood but to undergird his own authority vis-à-vis rival claims to Qadiri spirituality. His was not the first Indo-Persian biographical dictionary written by a Qadiri. He was preceded by the formidable scholar of *hadith,* himself a Qadiri adept, Shaykh Abd al-Haqq Muhaddith Dihlawi (d. 1642). Abd al-Haqq's *Akhbar al-akhyar,* completed in 1618, had already gained considerable fame by 1640, and Dara models many of his own entries on Indian saints after the longer, fuller entries of *Akhbar al-akhyar.* Yet in presenting the Qadiriya, he bypasses the lineage traced by Abd al-Haqq, acknowledging only that line of Qadiri affiliation traceable through Abd al-Qadir ath-thani to Abdallah Bhiti to Miyan Mir (d. 1635) and then to his own preceptor, Mulla Shah (d. 1660).

The significance of the Islamic past for Dara Shikoh is functional: its retelling helps to affirm his own status as a Qadiri adept. The tazkira, in his imaginative plane, becomes the ideal tool of memorative communication. Giants of Persian Sufism like Ala al-Dawla Simnani and Jalal al-Din Rumi, when mentioned, are accorded half a page, consisting mostly of a cursory recap of standard biographical, travel, and literary data. While their inclusion affirms Dara Shikoh's awareness of the long tradition in which he stands, their sole purpose is to provide a backdrop for the stage onto which he parades as central exhibit the Qadiriya, especially his own immediate spiritual mentors, and their location in the region of Lahore. Is it mere coincidence that his disagreement with the Delhi author of Sufi tazkiras, Shaykh Abd al-Haqq, has to do with the region of their respective Qadiri affiliations? It would seem that even within the domain of elite Indo-Persian cultural production the importance of space, specifically urban sacred space, was determinative, even if unstated.

Dara Shikoh's *Safinat al-auliya* also contrasts with another biographical dictionary from Mughal India. While much has been written about *Safinat al-auliya*, mention is seldom made of the Chishti master, Shaykh Abd ar-Rahman (d. 1094/1683), or his Sufi tazkira, *Mir'at al-asrar*. Although it appears in several published catalogs, *Mir'at al-asrar* has never generated a fraction of the interest directed to *Safinat al-auliya*, yet the two works merit comparison, if only because their authors were near contemporaries, they employed the same inclusive method of tazkira writing, and, above all, they were both preoccupied with the relationship of personal authority to place.

In *Mir'at al-asrar*, after noting the twelve family clusters into which Sufi brotherhoods may be parceled, Shaykh Abd ar-Rahman reviews no less than twenty-three generations of spiritual exemplars. He brackets the prophet Muhammad and his three immediate successors as the first generation, followed by ʿAli and the other eleven Imams in the second generation. He continues in this manner until he reaches the tenth generation in which the first Chishti master is said to have lived and died in Syria (ca. 328/940). Appearing in the same generation with him were his contemporaries Shibli and Hallaj. By the time of the fourteenth generation when Qutb al-Din Mawdud (d. 537/1132) became the successor at Chisht, he counted among his contemporaries Muhammad and Ahmad Ghazzali as well as Ayn al-Quzzat Hamadani. Successive generations boasted still more illustrious names, so that by the sixteenth generation when Uthman Harvani (d. 607/1210) became the Chishti standard-bearer, he welcomed as fellow *mashaikh* both Abd al-Qadir Jilani and Abu Madyan Maghribi.

Abd ar-Rahman's primary purpose is to retell the saga of Persian/Indo-Persian Sufism as a single dramatic endeavor shaped by the Unseen for the benefit of humankind. Yet from the nineteenth generation on, that is, from the time of Shaykh Farid al-Din Ganj-i Shakar (d. 664/1265), a major Chishti saint in the Sultanate period, to the end of *Mir'at al-asrar*, the Indo-Persian actors begin to overshadow their Persian predecessors. After the eighteenth generation, few if any non-Indian saints are even mentioned, and the reason is directly connected to place and its importance for structuring collective identity. Shaykh Abd ar-Rahman is not only a Chishti master; he is also the incumbent of a shrine in Avadh, well to the east of Delhi in modern-day Uttar Pradesh.

Authenticating Avadh as an urban Muslim realm is as delicate as it is crucial for Shaykh Abd ar-Rahman. He traces his own spiritual lineage back through the Sabiri rather than the Nizami branch of the Chishtiya. That lineage is beset with chronological difficulties that cloud its initial years. Its eponymous founder was one Shaykh Ala al-Din Ali ibn Ahmad Sabir, who died in 691/1291 in Kalyar, a town in northern Uttar Pradesh. He is said to have been identical with the Shaykh Ali Sabir, who is briefly mentioned in *Siyar al-auliya* as a disciple of Shaykh Farid al-Din Ganj-i Shakar. No less an authority than Shaykh Abd al-Haqq, however, questions the conflation of the two names and persons. Even if it were to be accepted, there seems to be more than a generation between Ali Sabir's successor, Shams al-Din Turk Panipati (d. 718/1318), and his successor, Jalal al-Din Panipati (d. 765/1364). Further comprising the historical markings of the lineage is the fact that Ahmad Abd al-Haqq (d. 837/1434), who succeeds Jalal al-Din and is the biological as well as spiritual ancestor of Abd ar-Rahman, was not born until ca. 751/1350.[53]

Yet our concerns with chronological plausibility and historical accuracy were not Abd ar-Rahman's. Instead of lingering on these hiatuses and discrepancies, he paints a colorful canvas of spirituality that includes all the major figures of the Nizami branch of the Chishtiya as part of his own mystical legacy. Unlike Dara Shikoh's brief reminders, these are full, vivid accounts of both Persian and non-Persian saints of earlier eras. The organization by successive *tabaqat* or generations, despite the chronological discrepancies, draws attention to the preeminent Sufi authority (the "axis" or *qutb*) of each age. From the perspective of Abd ar-Rahman's lineage, the qutb of each age, since the appearance of Shaykh Ali Sabir, had to be, and has been, a Sabiri Chishti master. Yet his is not a partisan view arguing for Sabiris over Nizamis, Chishtis over other Sufis, Sufis over other Muslims, or Muslims over Hindus. Instead, he shows a wide acquaintance with classical Persian Sufism and an appreciation for the luster that its exemplars bring to his own generation and to his own place. While each generation is marked by a qutb, he is situated among, not apart from, other Sufi masters. Although he stands at their head, they add to his preeminence. By this ingenious artifice the author of *Mir'at al-asrar* accomplishes a double purpose: (1) he makes clear how vital was the connection to a Persian Sufi tradition for all Sabiri Chishtis while (2) conferring the highest spiritual rank on a handful of obscure saints, most of whom lived and toiled and died in northeastern India, specifically in the region of Avadh.

What is evident in Abd ar-Rahman's wide-ranging account of his saintly forebears is also discernible in the very different project of

Badauni. Although he devotes but one section of his *Muntakhab at-tawarikh* to saintly biographies, it would be hard to overemphasize their significance for him. Not only do they exude a freshness lacking in the comparable section of *Ain-i Akbari*, itself part of the *Akbarnama*, the most famous commissioned history of Mughal India, but they also indicate the variety of spiritual endeavors that were taking place outside the royal court. Unlike the narratives of Shaykh Mustafa, the Mahdavi master whom Derryl MacLean analyzes in a later essay of this volume, none of the endeavors depicted by Badauni were in explicit competition with the imperial cult increasingly focused on Akbar after 1574, that is, for almost the entirety of his reign at Fateḥpur Sikri.

Badauni was a maverick intellect. He had no illusions of obtaining a reward for his book. He did not write to please his powerful patron. At most, he may have entertained the hope of some historical redress. Above all, he wanted to acquit himself at the court of Divine Justice, as is clear from his final supplication: "[If it] please God this work will, for a while, be preserved from the treachery of lack of preservation, of faithlessness, or of evil guardianship . . . and being constantly hidden under the protection of God's guardianship, will receive the ornament of acceptance."[54] Yet, even if one discounts the author's special pleading for the authority of his own experience, the sum total of these individual accounts provides an independent profile of Indo-Muslim identity as shaped through institutional Sufism, and it confirms both the resilience of the orders in their regional manifestations and also the significance of local, often urban Sufi lodges.

For Badauni, the strongest claimants to spiritual authenticity were those Shaykhs who combined a grounding in the traditional religious sciences of Sunni Islam with an attachment to mystical pursuits. Two exemplars from less well known urban sites are Shaykh Nizam al-Din Ambethi and Shaykh Daud of Chati. In both cases Badauni dwells on noble ancestry, pursuit of learning, and calm judgment under fire. The present-voice narrative infuses his account of these and other saints. Both Shaykhs come alive as holy men constantly being tested, whether by jealous notables, a distant sultan, or a persistent visitor. With Shaykh Nizam al-Din, it is Badauni who is the overzealous guest, making a verbal faux pas that seems to doom him never to obtain the saint's favor. But in the case of Shaykh Daud, it is the saint himself who is set up to be the victim of a court conspiracy against Sufi masters (perhaps because of his Mahdavi persuasions). His gracious manners and sound learning not only rescue him. They actually turn the tables on his would-be persecutors and secure fame both for him and for the minor urban location of Chati where he taught and prayed and was buried.

The importance of place in Badauni's Sufi biographies becomes still clearer when his vignettes are intercalated with the acknowledged master of Mughal hagiography, Shaykh Abd al-Haqq Muhaddith Dihlawi, whom we noted above. Abd al-Haqq is himself the subject of one of Badauni's sketches, confirming that the production of saintly biographies was a proven means of securing memorialization in one's own right! Like Badauni, Abd al-Haqq was among the Indo-Persian urban elite of the late sixteenth century: even though he survived well into the reign of Shah Jahan, his most famous tazkira, *Akhbar al-akhyar,* was written during the third phase of the Akbar period, ca. 999/1591. Also like Badauni, he was not beholden to the new imperial ideology constructed by Abul-Fazl and advocated by Akbar in the late 1570s, for although he studied at Fateḥpur Sikri as a teenager, by age twenty-one (1572) he opted to return to Delhi, where he had been born and reared, where his parents still resided, and where he could teach in his father's madrasa.

Unlike Badauni, however, Abd al-Haqq is clearly writing his work for public dissemination. In the light of Badauni's fears, his literary strategy has to be subtly shaped, at once revealing and concealing his true intentions. Unable to disagree with the emperor directly, he also cannot follow the not so subtle pattern of Badauni's clandestine work: to criticize those who were the confidants of the emperor, especially Faizi and Abul-Fazl. Instead, Abd al-Haqq constructs his work in such a way that it both supports Akbar's imperial agenda and offers an alternative set of spiritual authorities. He lauds the Chishti epigones of virtue but does not dwell on Shaykh Salim. Rather, he adopts a diachronic scheme that begins with the Chishtis and so with Muin al-Din and then progresses generationally through the Delhi Sultanate to the Akbari era. The saints who merit most extensive attention and whose biographies mirror Abd al-Haqq's disposition are the later Qadiris. They were the spiritual precursors of his father, Sayf ad-din, and also his own mentor, Abd al-Wahhab. So generous does he appear to be toward all saints that a censor would have been hard-pressed to fault him on either his organizational strategy or his more than 250 individual entries. In short, Abd al-Haqq attempted to be more than a pawn in the grand design for expanding Mughal hegemony that Akbar, with assistance from his courtiers, directed. Yet the Delhi savant could not operate outside the constraints of a bureaucratic structure that dominated, even as it animated, all aspects of the emergent Indo-Persian culture complex, and he himself was prone to privilege those saints whose labor confirmed the region of northern India where he himself lived and labored, prayed and fasted, and died.[55]

The very process of memory and recording had its constraints: Not all Indo-Persian memorative communications had the freshness of Badauni or the comprehensiveness of Abd al-Haqq. While the period of Mughal imperial expansion made possible the concept of a pan-Indian scope in historical writing, as we have seen above,[56] most later tazkiras tended to have a more limited scope, because of the restricted audience for whom their authors were recording as they tried to memorialize the saints of earlier epochs. Rather than the analytical study of tazkiras, which might generate new categories, one too often finds a replication of the genre, still another tazkira of tazkiras rather than a creative or locally derived approach to memorialization.

In the colonial period we find the routinization of tazkira writing taken to new depths of serial logic. The idea of the comprehensive or cataloging tazkira, one which listed Sufis of all orders in tabular form, became prevalent, in part due to the influence of maps and census taking.[57] Examples of such compendia abound, the most notable being the *Masalik al-Salikin: Tazkira al-Waṣilin* of Mirza Muḥammad Abd al-Saṭṭar Baig (Agra: Maṭbaʿ Faiḍ, n.d.) (Urdu) and *Ḥadiqat al-Asrar fi Akhbar al-Abrar* of Imam Bakhsh (Lahore, 1364/1944).

More interesting for our general thesis is the way that Indian cities become Muslim holy spaces for certain Sufi tazkira authors. From an early date Ajmer had been recast as Madina[58] in the biography of Muin al-Din Chishti, but more extensive still was the new topography of holy cities charted in *Kalimat al-Ṣadiqin* of Muḥammad Ṣadiq Dihlavi Kashmiri Hamadani.[59] The work is a tazkira of the Sufis buried in Delhi up to the year 1023/1614. The author, a student of Baqibillah, the Delhi-based Naqshbandī Shaykh, whose prize disciple was Aḥmad Sirhindī, discussed in the next essay by David Damrel, claims to have modeled his work on the *Rashaḥat* of Kashifi. Consider how the author depicts Delhi as Muslim "sacred space." In his preface, he asks God to protect Delhi from calamities, and then continues:

> Know, may God support you with the light of gnosis, that Delhi is a very large and noble city and that certain of the saints of the nation (ummat) have said things about it like, "One in a thousand and very few out of the multitude recognize its greatness." Thus, whoever has the least understanding and the slightest knowledge

will surely recognize that after the two holy cities (of Mecca and Madina), if there is any nobility to be found in a place or greatness in a land, it is in this noble land which is distinguished completely over the rest of cities and is exceptional. Therefore it is said by the common folk that Delhi is a little Mecca and even the elite have no doubt of its greatness. Everyone asserts its exaltedness, whether due to the fact that the great ones of the religion, the ulema among the people of certainty, the great shaikhs, the reputable wise men, the powerful rulers, and the exalted nobles have filled this city and have been buried here, or due to its fine buildings, delightful gardens and pleasant localities. . . .

According to some esteemed personages, since one of the people of mystical intuition said in elaboration, "All of Delhi is declared to be a mosque," all of this city is distinguished from other places by its greatness and nobility. In summary, these verses of Khwāja Khusrau inform us of the greatness of this city and certain of its sites.

Noble Delhi, shelter of religion and treasure,
It is the Garden of Eden, may it last forever.
A veritable earthy Paradise in all its qualities
May Allah protect it from calamities.
If it but heard the tale of this garden,
Mecca would make the pilgrimage to Hindustan.[60]

Yet Delhi was not the sole claimant for divine favor as the urban Muslim capital of South Asia. "Even more than the *Akhbar al-Akhyar*, which is a Delhi-oriented work, *Khazinat al-Aṣfiya* is Lahore directed, including the entire region to the North and North west of Delhi."[61] It was in the late 1800s that Mufti Ghulam Sarwar Lahorī wrote his massive and impressive Sufi tazkira, *Khazinat al-Aṣfiya*. It was a memorative communication that privileged Lahore over all other Indo-Muslim capital cities, and in the postcolonial period Lahore acquired a renewed importance with the creation of Pakistani sacred space. Since Ajmer and, of course, Delhi remained within the Republic of India, the sacral role of Lahore became upgraded through its "patron," ʿAli Hujwiri, whose tomb, the Data Darbar, has been increasingly celebrated during the last half century.

The Data Darbar underscores what has been hinted at but not developed in the literary focus of this essay. Heightening the power of tazkiras to both create and sustain Muslim cultural memory in urban South

Asia was the cemetery. All tazkiras took note not only of death dates but also of burial places, so that the symbolic resonance of the cemetery was crucial for Indo-Muslim urban identity. On the one hand, the tomb-cults were transitional spaces between the higher world and this one, but on the other hand, and with increasing emphasis, they were symbols of a distinctly Muslim identity in the Indian context (since Hindus cremate their dead). Graveyards as sites, then, are both a locus of inscription for local communal memory and the means of this inscription.[62]

Conclusions: Space and Identity

Muslims over time imagined their space in South Asia differently as their sense of identity changed in the light of social and political development. This change may be traced in the organizing and structuring principles of the tazkira genre.

The frame for this genre is memorialization, or better, memorative communication. One key element in this is inscription, which is done through the writing of memory on new spaces whose imagined shape is also subject to reconfiguration. Critical also in the South Asian tazkira tradition is the language of inscription, which serves to define a space even as it is the medium for writing it.

In the course of this process, spaces have expanded from cities to regions to nations, while the principles of affiliation have loosened: no longer direct initiation, or even continuity in space and time, they have relied on a sense of "imagined community," as suggested by Benedict Anderson in his classic study of the construction of nationalist identities.[63]

While the production of books generally encouraged a mnemonic reflex, it went well beyond memorializing dead heroes, whether poets or saints, in the Indo-Persian tazkira genre favored by South Asian urban Muslim elites. Whatever their location or their authors' motivation, the premodern tazkiras laid a claim to Muslim space in South Asia. They did so by Islamicizing the soil, by creating a "new" home, by configuring "new" spiritual and intellectual centers, and also by laying out "new" circuits of pilgrimage.[64]

The late Mughal and early modern period introduced a different tone in tazkira writing. While the urge to celebrate cities did not disappear, it appeared in a new guise. The desire to project memorative communication that is felt in times of expansion takes a different turn in times of crisis or despair. Among Indo-Muslim versifiers it has been reflected in the laments over chaos in the poetic *shahr ashob* tradition.[65]

Is ahd ko na janiyee agla sa ahd Mir
voh daur ab nahin, voh zamin asman nahin
These times are nothing compared to the old days, Mir;
That age has passed, that heaven and earth are no longer.
Mir

Beyond Mir but through his agency, what we discover as the final accent on tazkiras is the possibility of mapping the altered sense and shape of urban Hindustan. Tazkira writers continue to project an inscribed space and identity in the colonial and post-independence periods of South Asian history, but the modern/postmodern reflex traces a more solemn sense of spatial orientation and organization of collective memory in contemporary tazkiras.

The modern/postmodern space is one of aggressive retrieval of memory, for example, the proliferation of translations of old tazkiras from Persian into Urdu in Pakistan, as well as attempts to erase it. In the case of the poetic tazkiras, new canons of literary appreciation[66] and even an altered mode of eloquent expression have rendered them obsolete. In *Ab-i Ḥayat*, Āzād mourns the fact that "the page of history would be turned—the old families destroyed, their offspring so ignorant that they would no longer know even their own family traditions." Pritchett observes, "The critical attitudes and vocabulary used by the tazkiras are all but unintelligible to most scholars—and in fact arouse considerable disdain."[67]

It is, above all, the threat of chaos[68] that looms in the remarks of the late tazkira author Muḥammad Din Kalim.[69] In contrast to the hope of relocation, which marked many of the Indo-Persian tazkiras from Mughal India that we examined above, Kalim sees dislocation, even erasure, as the theme for his own memorative communication. Commenting on the contemporary situation in Lahore, he laments:

> Wherever you see an old grave, the keepers or greedy persons have spent quite a bit of money on fixing it up, popularizing it, and giving it some name which is unknown in the old sources so that they make it a means of earning money. [He then lists several such shrines saying, "God knows who is really buried there."]
>
> Nowadays the style of constructing new tombs has incorporated a lot of use of marble and other expensive stones and even the use of inlaid mirrors in some, so that you don't feel that you are in a graveyard but rather in a Shish Mahal. These tombs have proliferated to the point that they are found in every lane, street, bazaar,

> field, government park, and even in cinemas and government offices etc. even though there is no historical mention of them. . . . For some years I have been shocked by the lamentable situation that certain dissolute persons have pitched tents in the public graveyards out of which they deal in drugs.[70]

In response, Kalim writes of the special features of his work. He personally visited the shrines he writes about, he investigated the accurate names of the persons whom he mentions, and he reports the names of pīrs falsely attributed to shrines when no such individuals were ever known to exist. Even while decrying "the lamentable situation" he confronts, he finds in the act of writing a recuperation of the past for the benefit of responsible mediation in the present; he remains a memorative communicator.

And so there is a link between the oldest and the most recent phases of tazkira writing among South Asian urban Muslim elites. Kalim, as a contemporary tazkira writer, finds himself responding to an imminent threat of chaos, yet his remains a quest for the recovery of history, not a repetition of the past. Like the poet Ghālib, he struggles to understand how the act of erasure still retains its quality of a trace, a reminder, an emberlike hope. As Ghālib himself attests, with the fullness of his own sense of irony and place:

> ya rabb zamana mujh ko miṭata hai kis liʿe
> lauḥ-i jahañ peh ḥarf-i muqarrar nahin huñ maiñ
> O Lord, why is time erasing me?
> I am not a repeated letter on the tablet of this world.

Whether one accents the trace that is never a repeated letter, or bemoans the self erased by time, one acknowledges in both cases the power of the Lord, the One who can both erase and re-create all that is. The poet, like the saint, locates his faith in language and in space. Ghālib implores the Omnipotent through Urdu (or Indo-Persian), and he implores Him from a familiar place, the still sacralized though much reduced Muslim space of Delhi. Memorative communication thus becomes more than a trace. It continues to embody hope; it projects the erased self in a reduced space as the servant before the Lord, the letter of Muslim identity etched not on the tablet of this world but on the Tablet that is both preserved and memorized, *al-lauḥ al-maḥfuẓ*.

Notes

1. M. Garcin de Tassy, *Histoire de la littérature hindouie et hindoustanie* (Paris: A. Labitte, 1870–71); Farman Fateḥpuri, *Nigar,* 1964 Annual (Tazkirah Number).

2. George Morrison, *Persian Literature from the Earliest Times to the Time of Jami* (Leiden: E. J. Brill, 1980), 14.

3. Annemarie Schimmel comments on this and other couplets of Ghālib that are apposite to the present topic in her chapter "Poetry and Calligraphy," in *A Dance of Sparks: Imagery of Fire in Ghālib's Poetry* (Delhi: Vikas, 1979), 112–36.

4. Peter Osborne, *The Politics of Time: Modernity and Avant-Garde* (London: Verso, 1995), 179. There are other aspects of Benjamin's project, especially his dialectical sparring with Marx, Heidegger, and Freud, that lie beyond the scope of our article, but his accent on time as nonlinear, at once disruptive and recuperative, is key to our own project.

5. The actual phrase "memorative communication" is coined by Peter Osborne in trying to distinguish the benefit of Benjamin's approach to tradition from the flawed approaches of Gadamer and Ricoeur. Insofar as "memorative communication" projects historical narrative in its living relationship to the present, the two categories elide, but memorative communication accents the role of the one who both remembers and uses memory to communicate; hence its special benefit for interpreting the catalytic role of the Indo-Persian tazkira.

6. Discussed, for example, in Jaroslav Stetkevych, *The Zephyrs of Najd: The Poetics of Nostalgia in the Classical Arabian Nasib* (Chicago: University of Chicago Press, 1993); and Michael Sells, *Desert Tracings: Six Classical Arabian Odes* (Middletown, Conn: Wesleyan University Press, 1989).

7. Noting here H. A. R. Gibb's statement that "the biographical dictionary is a wholly indigenous creation of the Islamic community": Gibb, "Islamic Biographical Literature," in B. Lewis and P. M. Holt, *Historians of the Middle East* (Leiden: E. J. Brill, 1968), 54. Reflecting on the inclusion of very ordinary persons in the biographical dictionaries (*ṭabaqat*), Gibb further observes that the history of the Islamic community is essentially the contribution of individual men and women to the building up and transmission of its specific culture. That is, it is these persons (rather than the political governors) who represent or reflect the active force of Muslim society.

8. "Urdu literature, almost from its very beginnings, has been concerned with city life. The language has functioned for a long time as an urban-centered, but non-regional language": Leslie Fleming, "Two Pakistani Women Writers View the City: The Short Stories of Bano Qudsiyya and Farkhandah Lodhi," *Journal of South Asian Literature* 25, no. 1 (1990): 1, quoting A. K. Ramanujan, "Towards an Anthology of City Images," in *Urban India: Society, Space, and Images,* ed. Richard G. Fox (Durham, N.C.: Duke University Press, 1970), 224–44.

9. Bruce B. Lawrence, *Notes from a Distant Flute: Sufi Literature in Pre-Mughal India* (Tehran: Imperial Iranian Academy of Philosophy, 1978).

10. Carl W. Ernst, *Eternal Garden: Mysticism, History, and Politics at a South Asian Sufi Center* (Albany: State University of New York Press, 1992), 62–84.

11. A discussion of the inscription of memory on nonwestern sites and the emotional and ephemeral qualities of memories inscribed there may be found in Susanne Kuchler, "Landscape as Memory: The Mapping of Process and Its Representation in a Melanesian Society," in *Landscape Politics and Perspectives*, ed. Barbara Bender (Oxford: Berg, 1996), 85–86.

12. Mary Carruthers, *The Book of Memory: A Study of Memory in Medieval Culture* (Cambridge: Cambridge University Press, 1990).

13. Qur'an 85:22. Annemarie Schimmel's discussion of tablet and pen imagery in the Qur'an, hadith, and poetic tradition is quite helpful here: *Mystical Dimensions of Islam* (Chapel Hill: University of North Carolina Press, 1975), 414–16.

14. For Ibn Arabi's influence in South Asia, see William Chittick, "Notes on Ibn al-Arabi's Influence in the Indian Sub-Continent," *Muslim World* 82 (July–October 1992): 218–41.

15. Schimmel, *Mystical Dimensions of Islam*, 414–15. This is the very couplet cited at the outset of the current chapter.

16. Carruthers, *The Book of Memory*, 21.

17. A work that stimulated scholarly awareness of technologies of memory was Francis Yates, *The Art of Memory* (London: Routledge and Kegan Paul, 1966). On the role of memory in a world of few books and the relationship of trained memory or "memoria" to literacy, see Carruthers, *The Book of Memory*, 7–15, passim.

18. Al-Ṣuyuṭi, *Alfiyya fi Ilm al-ḥadith* (Cairo: al-Babi al-Ḥalabi, 1934).

19. Cited in J. M. S. Baljon, *Religion and Thought of Shah Wali Allah of Delhi, 1703–1762* (Leiden: E. J. Brill, 1986), 12.

20. Qur'an 3:191.

21. Literally, "keeping in mind," or as one Sufi puts it, keeping the heart in the presence of God in all situations (*yad* means "memory"), this refers technically to one of the steps of practice in the Naqshbandiyya Sufi order that might be summarized as remaining aware at all times. See Fritz Meier, *Zwei Abhandlungen über die Naqshbandiyya* (Istanbul: Franz Steiner, 1994), 44–46.

22. The term *taṣawwur* evokes the element of visual memory. The Sufi practice of "taṣawwur-i shaykh" is calling to mind the image of a person's spiritual master. It is also specifically related to the Naqshbandī practice known as "rabiṭa," or developing a bond with the spiritual preceptor. Hamid Algar, "Devotional Practices of the Khalidi Naqshbandis of Ottoman Turkey," in *The Dervish Lodge: Architecture, Art, and Sufism in Ottoman Turkey*, ed. Raymond Lifchez (Berkeley: University of California Press, 1992), 209–27. *Taṣawwur* also means "representation" in terms of the logic of formulating propositional statements, as opposed to a statement of "verificaṭion" (taṣdiq). See Roy Mottahedeh, *The Mantle of the Prophet: Religion and Politics in Iran* (New York: Simon and Schuster, 1985), 72–74, for a brief discussion of this system.

23. These consist of ritualized recitations of rhymed spiritual genealogies of previous saints in a particular Sufi lineage.

24. Cited in V. G. Kiernan, *Poems by Faiẓ* (London: George Allen and Unwin, 1971), 128–29.

25. Ernst, *Eternal Garden*, 67; *Nizam ad-Din Awliya: Morals for the Heart*, trans. Bruce B. Lawrence (New York: Paulist Press, 1992), 214.

26. Ernst, *Eternal Garden*, 69.

27. The phrase was used by Stetkevych in *The Zephyrs of Najd*, 121.

28. Farman Fateḥpuri, *Urdu Shuara kê Tazkirê aur Tazkira Nigari* (Lahore: Majlis-i Taraqqi Urdu, 1972). An earlier work on this topic is Sayyid Muḥammad Abdullah, *Shuara-yi Urdu kê Tazkire awr Tazkirah Nigarika Fann* (Lahore: Maktaba Khiyabane-Adab, 1952).

29. Muḥammad Awfi, *Lubab al-Albab* (Tehran: Kitabkhanah-yi Ibn Sina, 1957), partially translated in R. A. Nicholson, *Studies in Islamic Poetry* (Cambridge: Cambridge University Press, 1969). Fateḥpuri, *Nigar*, 9–11.

30. Edward G. Browne, ed., *Lubab al-Albab*, vol. 2 (London: Luzac, 1906), 12.

31. Fateḥpuri, *Nigar*, 14–15. They were *Nakat ash-Shuara* of Mir Taqi, *Gulshan-i Goftar* of Ḥamid Aurangabadi, and *Tuḥfat ash-Shiʿr* of Afḍal Beg Qaqshal. The latter two were produced in the Deccan, but they mentioned northern poets as well.

32. Muḥammad Ḥusain Āzād, *Ab-i Ḥayat* (Lucknow: Uttar Pradesh Urdu Academy, 1982). Reprint of the 1907 Newal Kishore edition. Āzād as a critic is discussed in Frances Pritchett, *Nets of Awareness: Urdu Poetry and Its Critics* (Berkeley: University of California Press, 1994), 46–59.

33. Fateḥpuri, *Nigar*, 7. A review of previous tazkiras of poets and their possible influence on Āzād is Aslam Farrukhi, *Muḥammad Ḥusayn Āzād: Ḥayat awr Taṣanif* (Karachi: Anjuman-i Taraqqi Urdu, 1965), 2:28–58.

34. Ralph Russell, *The Pursuit of Urdu Literature* (London: Zed Books, 1992), 121–22.

35. Abd al-Saṭṭar Siddikqi, *Oriental College Magazine*, 1927, and Gulchin-i-Maʿani, Aḥmad, *Tarikh-i-Tazkiraha-yi Farsi* (Tehran, 1970).

36. Fateḥpuri, *Nigar*, 19.

37. Garcin de Tassy, *Histoire de la littérature hindouie et hindoustanie*, 57.

38. Pritchett describes "bayaz" as "the ubiquitous little notebook that lovers of poetry carried around with them for recording verses that caught their fancy": *Nets of Awareness*, 66.

39. These collections are known as *guldastas* (bouquets). On the guldasta see Pritchett, *Nets of Awareness*, 74. On mushaʿiras see Pritchett or Carla Petievich, *Assembly of Rivals: Delhi, Lucknow, and the Urdu Ghazal* (Delhi: Manohar, 1992).

40. Fateḥpuri, *Nigar*, 17–21.

41. Muḥammad Sadiq, *History of Urdu Literature*, 2d ed. (Delhi: Oxford, 1984), 40.

42. Petievich, *Assembly of Rivals*, 204.

43. Pritchett also notes the role of tazkiras as being "the most important genre of literary record and commentary that existed in Urdu": *Nets of Awareness*, 74.

44. Two works specifically organized according to this paradigm are Nur ul Ḥasan Hashmi, *Dilli ka Dabistan-i Sha'iri* (Delhi school of poetry) (Lucknow: Uttar Pradesh Urdu Academy, 1971) and A. L. Siddiqi, *Lakhnau ka Dabistan-i Sha'iri* (Lucknow school of poetry) (Lahore: Urdu Markaz, 1955). The paradigm was criticized by Ali Javad Zaidi, *Do Adabi Iskul* (Two literary schools) (Lucknow: U. P. Urdu Academy, 1970), a work which is examined in Petievich, *Assembly of Rivals*, 89–99.

45. Petievich, *Assembly of Rivals*, ix, xiii.

46. Ibid., 13–15.

47. Ḥafiẓ Aḥmad Ali Khan Shauq, *Kamilan-i Rampur* (Patna/Delhi: Khuda Bakhsh Oriental Public Library, 1986).

48. Tajammul Ḥussain Khan, *Urdu Sha'iri ka tisra Skul* (Karachi: Jauhar Academy, 1976); Kalb-i Ali Khan Fa'iq, "Rampur ka Sha'iri Skul," in *Ma'arif*, October 1955, 285–94.

49. Abd al-Raḥman Jami, *Nafaḥat al-uns min ḥaẓarat al-quds* (Tehran: Intisharat-i ittila'at, 1994).

50. Jo-Ann Gross, "Khoja Ahrar: A Study of the Perceptions of Religious Power and Prestige in the Late Timurid Period," Ph.D. diss., New York University, 1982, discusses the tazkira of Ali ibn al-Ḥusayn Kashifi: *Rashaḥat* (Lucknow: Newal Kishore, 1890).

51. Ernst, *Eternal Garden*, 89–90.

52. Abd al-Qadir al-Badauni's *Muntakhab at-tawarikh* (Summation of histories) was translated into English at the turn of the century; see G. S. A. Ranking (vol. 1), W. H. Lowe (vol. 2), and Wolseley Haig (vol. 3) (Calcutta: Asiatic Society of Bengal, 1884–1925; reprint, Delhi: Idarat-Adabiyat-i Delli, 1973). Although volume 3, with which we are concerned here, abounds with infelicities, it is still remarkable to have an English version of this maverick biographical review of Sufi masters provided by Badauni.

53. The problems of this lineage have been traced with singular clarity and characteristic understatement by Simon Digby in "'Abd al-Quddus Gangohi (1456–1537 A.D.): The Personality and Attitudes of a Medieval Indian Sufi," *Medieval India—A Miscellany* 3 (Aligarh, 1975): 4–5.

54. See Badauni, *Muntakhab at-tawarikh*, 3:535–36.

55. The Shaykh's experience at the Mughal court was interrupted by a five-year absence (1587–92), most of it spent on a "pilgrimage of penance" to the Hijaz, where he furthered his own studies of hadith with the Indian alim in exile, Shaykh Abd al-Wahhab Muttaqi, who also receives prominent attention in *Akhbar al-akhyar*. See N. H. Zaidi, "Abd al-Haqq Mohaddeth Dehlavi," in *Encyclopaedia Iranica* (London: Routledge and Kegan Paul, 1982): 1/2: 113–14.

56. Ernst, *Eternal Garden*, 90.

57. For example, the extensive tradition of compiling gazetteers of regions under British control, studied by Robert C. Emmett, "The Gazetteers of India," M.A. thesis, University of Chicago, 1976; Henry Scholberg, *The District Gazetteers of British India* (Zug: Inter Documentation, 1970).

58. Lawrence, *Notes from a Distant Flute*, 20.

59. Muḥammad Ṣadiq Dihlavi Kashmiri Hamadani, *Kalimat al-Ṣadiqin*, ed. Muḥammad Saleem Akhtar (Islamabad: Iran Pakistan Research Center, 1988).

60. Ibid., 5. Amir Khusrau, *Qiran al-Saʿdayn* (Lucknow: Newal Kishore, 1875), 22–23, is the *mathnavi* from which these verses are taken. Other features of Delhi, such as the Friday mosque and minaret, are also praised in the same section.

61. Bruce Lawrence, "Biography and the Seventeenth-Century Qadiriyya of North India," in *Islam and Indian Regions*, ed. Anna Libera Dallapiccola and Stephanie Zengel-Avé Lallemant (Stuttgart: Steiner, 1993), 399–415, 402. The entire chapter has developed some of the points of this essay, but without an appreciation of the crucial role of place, an appreciation that only emerged later, due to the Rockefeller Residency Program on "South Asian Islam and the Greater Muslim World, 1993–1997," convened through the Triangle South Asian Colloquium.

62. A further dimension of the relationship between gardens, tombs, and Islamic cosmology has been explored by art historian Wayne Begley in "The Myth of the Taj Mahal and a New Theory of Its Symbolic Meaning," *Art Bulletin*, no. 61 (March 1979): 7–37.

63. Benedict Anderson, *Imagined Communities: Reflections on the Origin and Spread of Nationalism* (London: Verso, 1991).

64. The incorporation of such pilgrimage circuits into calendars of ritual observances of saints' anniversaries is discussed in Carl W. Ernst, "An Indo-Persian Guide to Sufi Shrine Pilgrimage," in *Manifestations of Sainthood in Islam*, ed. Grace Martin Smith and Carl Ernst (Istanbul: Isis, 1993), 43–68. "Whenever one comes to a town, the first thing one has to accomplish is to kiss the feet of the saints who are full of life, and after that, the honor of pilgrimage to the tombs of saints found there. If one's master's tomb is in that city, one first carries out the pilgrimage to him; otherwise one visits the tomb of every saint shown him" (61). Quoted from Simnani, *Laaʾif al-Ashrafi*.

65. Carla Petievich, "Poetry of the Declining Mughals: The Shahr Ashob," *Journal of South Asian Literature* 25, no. 1 (1990): 99–110.

66. Gauri Vishvanathan, *Masks of Conquest: Literary Study and British Rule in India* (New York: Columbia University Press, 1989); Sara Suleri, *The Rhetoric of English India* (Chicago: University of Chicago Press, 1992).

67. Pritchett, *Nets of Awareness*, 75.

68. In his study of "place" in religion, Jonathan Z. Smith writes concerning the Jewish and Christian understandings of sacred centers in Jerusalem, "For each there was a triumphant, ideological literature that perceived in their construction a cosmogonic act. For each, there was a literature of indigenous lamentation . . . that found, in the destruction or loss of the sites, a plunge into chaos." Smith, *To Take Place: Toward Theory in Ritual* (Chicago: University of Chicago Press, 1987), 3.

69. For Kalim's biography see Naṣr Iqbal Qureishi, "Muʾarrikh-i Lahur Mian Muḥammad Din Kalim Qadiri," *ʿArafat*, Lahore (November/December 1989): 128–38.

70. Muḥammad Din Kalim, *Madinat al-Auliya* (Lahore: Maʿarif, 1982), 78–79.

7

The "Naqshbandī Reaction" Reconsidered

David W. Damrel

The event of the "Naqshbandī reaction" has occupied a special place for a generation of historians of religion seeking an explanatory paradigm for the history of Islam in early seventeenth-century South Asia. There is no question that at the center of this "reaction" stands the prominent Naqshbandī scholar and sufi Shaykh Aḥmad Sirhindī, the *Mujaddid-i alf-i thānī*, "renewer of the second millennium" (d. 1624). But the nature of his movement, its long-term effects, and even the "crisis" that initially prompted the reaction remain subjects of intense controversy.

Aziz Ahmad coined the phrase "Naqshbandī reaction" over thirty years ago in his well-known *Studies in Islamic Culture in the Indian Environment.* There he argued that the Mughal emperor Akbar's neglect of Islam and experiments with "imperial heresy" spurred Sirhindī and the Naqshbandīs to answer with an orthodox reformation of Sufism designed to promote the general "rehabilitation of Islam in India."[1] Fazlur Rahman surely had this in mind when he suggested that "the Sirhindī-led movement was a successful reaction" against Akbar's much-discussed *Dīn-i Ilāhī.* It was also effective in "counteracting the antinomian tendencies" within Indian Sufism.[2] Annemarie Schimmel agreed that the movement was the struggle of the Naqshbandī order against "Akbar's syncretism and against the representatives of emotional Sufism." Expanding on this theme, she asserted that the later Naqshbandiyya played "a remarkable role in all parts of Muslim India," especially as a "defense against syncretism."[3]

It is clear that this issue of syncretism explicitly and implicitly informs much of the writing about the Naqshbandī reaction. In seeking the spiritual and intellectual roots of the movement, many scholars interpret the dramatic rise of the Naqshbandī line at the start of the seventeenth century as a critical moment in a long Indian encounter between two competing Islamic mystical traditions: *waḥdat al-wujūd* (unity of being) and *waḥdat al-shuhūd* (unity of appearance).[4] When paired as opposites, the former esoteric philosophy typically is seen as a door to religious syncretism, while the latter is seen as a defense against syncretic interaction. Fazlur Rahman describes the concept of waḥdat al-wujūd formulated by Ibn al-ʿArabī (d. 1240) as "pantheistic mysticism" and argues that when these ideas were introduced into South Asia they readily found "a strong ally in the Vedantism of orthodox Hinduism."[5] The perceived mutual affinities between these two doctrines—waḥdat al-wujūd and Vedantism—created an arena for syncretistic interaction between mystically minded Muslims and Hindus. Aziz Ahmad argued that Sirhindī feared the syncretism that pantheistic "heterodox Sufism" invited; these "syncretisms" actually threatened "the disintegration of Islam in India and its gradual absorption into Hinduism."[6] In this view, Sirhindī's revitalized doctrine of waḥdat al-shuhūd presented a defensive mystical barrier, even a corrective, to such exchanges between Hindu and Muslim "spiritual athletes." Driven by such concerns, interpretation of the Naqshbandī reaction suddenly involves much more than the dispute between the Mughal Padishahs and a Sufi order over religious practice at court. It becomes a battle between syncretism and exclusivism, religious tolerance and intolerance, and, for some, nothing less than the defining moment in the course of Hindu-Muslim relations to this day.[7]

Our goal is not to revisit these controversies—which comprise for some the central elements of the Naqshbandī reaction—but rather to ask a question more closely related to the issue of Muslim identity in South Asia. Simply put, what are the discernible Naqshbandī elements in Sirhindī's "Naqshbandī reaction"? Can the actions that he took and the attitudes that he held unquestioningly be ascribed to his Naqshbandī persona and not to other spiritual affiliations and religious influences on him? In particular, what effect, if any, did his Chishtī affiliations play in the worldview that he developed in his writings and praxis?

If, painted in such broad strokes, the Naqshbandī-Mujaddidī order that crystallized around Shaykh Sirhindī is seen as the great champion of waḥdat al-shuhūd, then the long-established Chishtī order must be counted to represent the alternative view, that of waḥdat al-wujūd.[8] Notable even in a long tradition of so-called *wujūdī*, Chishtī shaykhs, the famed Chishtī-Ṣābirī Sufi Shaykh ʿAbd al-Quddūs Gangōhī (d. 1537) in particular has long been recognized as "a vigorous advocate of the doctrine of waḥdat al-wujūd."[9] Further, Shaykh ʿAbd al-Quddūs is also identified as a leading Indian Muslim syncretist between Islamic mysticism and Nathapanthi Yogic traditions.[10] At one level then, Shaykh ʿAbd al-Quddūs, the ecstatic wujūdī Chishtī syncretist, could easily be construed as the antithesis of Shaykh Aḥmad Sirhindī, the sober *shuhūdī* Naqshbandī exclusivist. But, as will be explored below, the lives of these two medieval North Indian Sufis contain similarities and convergences that challenge such simplistic constructions of identity and offer insight into the more complex configuration of Sufi identity and praxis in the first century of Mughal rule in India.

This chapter explores certain elements in the identities of these two Sufi shaykhs and attempts to demonstrate a thread of continuity in their actions, attitudes, and behavior that undermines the exaggerated conflicting identities often ascribed to them in later literature. In particular, their attitudes toward Hindus and Hindus in state service will be discussed, as well as certain elements of each man's spiritual beliefs and practices.

Shaykh Quṭb al-ʿAlam ʿAbd al-Quddūs b. Ismāʾīl b. Ṣafī al-dīn Hanafī Gangōhī was born in 1456 in Rudauli, now a village in modern Uttar Pradesh. Born into a family of ulema, ʿAbd al-Quddūs abandoned an agenda of formal studies early on in favor of spiritual pursuits. When he was still quite young, he presented himself to the *sajjāda-nishīn* at the *khānaqāh* of Shaykh Aḥmad ʿAbd al-Ḥaqq Rudaulvī (d. 1434) for mystical instruction. This sajjāda-nishīn was Shaykh Muḥammad, son of Shaykh ʿĀrif and grandson of Shaykh ʿAbd al-Ḥaqq. This Chishtī family represented what became known as the Chishtī-Ṣābirī line, so named because of their spiritual descent from Shaykh ʿAlāʾ al-dīn ʿAlī b. Aḥmad Ṣābir (d. 1291 at Kalyar). Shaykh ʿAlāʾ al-dīn ʿAlī b. Aḥmad Ṣābir was a *khalīfa* of the prominent Chishtī *pīr* Shaykh Farīd al-dīn Ganj-i Shakar (d. 1265 at Pakpattan).[11]

Shaykh ʿAbd al-Quddūs nominally accepted Shaykh Muḥammad as his pīr, but he apparently received much of his spiritual instruction from Shaykh Piyāra, an elder trusted companion of Shaykh ʿĀrif. Moreover, in an episode that hints of a strong Uwaysī influence, ʿAbd al-Quddūs also claimed to have received "spiritual grace" directly from the *rūh* of the deceased Shaykh ʿAbd al-Ḥaqq.[12] These spiritual ties were augmented with family links following his marriage to Shaykh Muḥammad's sister, the granddaughter of Shaykh ʿAbd al-Ḥaqq.

In Rudauli, Shaykh ʿAbd al-Quddūs practiced the rigorous devotions for which he later became famous, including *namāz-i maʿkūs* ("inverted prayer," that is, prayer performed while suspended upside-down) and gained a reputation for asceticism and mystical intoxication. He also developed a substantial following among the Afghan soldiers posted to the Awadh region with the Lōdī armies. Lōdī conflict with the Sharqī dynasty in Jaunpur through the last half of the fifteenth century caused periodic devastation in Rudauli and, in 1489, the town briefly fell into the hands of the Bachgoti Rajputs. Two years later ʿAbd al-Quddūs accepted the invitation of one of his prominent Afghan disciples and left Rudauli entirely, moving himself and his family almost five hundred miles north and west to Shāhābād, in eastern Punjab, near Gangōh. He remained in Shāhābād for over thirty years, strengthening his ties with the Lōdī Afghan nobility while writing and instructing his numerous disciples.

ʿAbd al-Quddūs's intimate links with the Afghans served him poorly in the tense years surrounding Bābur's initial Mughal incursions against Sultan Ibrāhīm Lōdī. Internal dissent led some Lōdī nobles in the Punjab to contact Bābur in Kabul, and the Mughal conquest of northern India began in earnest late in 1525. The Mughal invasion must have been widely anticipated in the Punjab, for even before Bābur's army actually advanced, ʿAbd al-Quddūs relocated to Gangōh, a village some forty miles from Shāhābād and presumably safe from any army marching on Delhi. In 1526, as the Mughal and Lōdī armies assembled for what would be the decisive battle at Panipat, ʿAbd al-Quddūs and his family attempted to flee. But at Kutana, near Panipat, Sultan Ibrāhīm Lōdī prevailed on the elderly shaykh to remain with his army and provide spiritual support. ʿAbd al-Quddūs did so, but he also sent his family south. Following the Lōdī disaster at Panipat—in which Sultan Ibrāhīm himself was killed—Shaykh ʿAbd al-Quddūs was captured by the Mughals and marched forty miles to Delhi.

The length of his captivity in Delhi is unspecified, although it was probably brief. Released in Delhi, ʿAbd al-Quddus returned to Gangōh, where he remained until his death in 1537. During this period of early Mughal rule, ʿAbd al-Quddūs retained contact with his defeated Afghan disciples and cultivated respectful if spare relations with Bābur and then Humāyūn. These relations will be discussed at length below.

Shaykh ʿAbd al-Quddūs's writings are many and diverse. His most important works include *Rushd-Nāma* (*Murshid-Nāma*), a work in Persian for the spiritual preparation of his disciples that contains frequent and detailed allusions to Yogic practice; a no longer extant commentary on Ibn al-ʿArabī's *Fuṣūṣ al-Ḥikam;* and an Arabic commentary on Shihāb al-dīn Suhrawardī's *'Awārif al-Ma'ārif*. There are also two collections of correspondence, the minor *Muntakhab-i Maktūbāt-i Quddūsī* and the much more important *Maktūbāt-i Quddūsī*.[13] Recently, I. H. Siddiqui announced the discovery of another work by 'Abd al-Quddūs, entitled *Sharh-i Risāla-i Lama'āt*.[14] This work is a commentary in Persian on the *Lama'āt* of the widely traveled, ecstatic wujūdī Suhrawardī mystic Shaykh Fakhr al-dīn 'Irāqī (d. 1289). 'Abd al-Quddūs also produced a significant body of verse, including a partial translation into Persian of an Awadhi romance and, in Hindi, several verses that survive mainly as marginalia in the *Rushd-Nāma*. In addition, his son and sajjāda-nishīn Shaykh Rukn al-dīn (d. 1576) left the *Lata'if-i Quddūsī*, a compilation of richly detailed biographical anecdotes about 'Abd al-Quddūs that still serves as the best, if incomplete, introduction to the shaykh's life.[15]

Despite his distinctive and innovative spiritual practices, it is important to note that Shaykh 'Abd al-Quddūs considered himself (and was considered by others) to be impeccable in his observance of the *sharī'a*. As Shaykh Rukn al-dīn declares, perhaps defensively, "It is apparent that in conforming to the example of the Prophet and in the observance of the *shar'* of the Prophet he was so strict that he did not allow the most minute departure from it to be permissible in either exterior or interior matters—as regards himself or others. If he got to know of any departure from the *shar'* by anyone he showed dissatisfaction and wished to avoid his company." Shaykh Rukn al-dīn adds that Shaykh 'Abd al-Quddūs, despite associating "with all kinds of men," was unaffected by "company which was hostile to the faith" and in fact helped return his associates to "the narrow path" through his companionship.[16]

'Abd al-Quddūs's important contact with Yogic thought and practice should also be noted. In his various techniques designed to produce mystical ecstasy, particularly involving breathing exercises, he drew upon Nathapanthi Yogic traditions; in explaining these practices he employed spiritual-physiological constructs that also reveal Yogic origins. He had a lifelong enthusiasm for Hindi love poetry (which often produced ecstatic mystical states in him), and he produced some verse in Hindi under the Hindi pen name Alakhdas, "servant of the Invisible."[17] These borrowings and inspirations from Yogic tradition have earned him a lasting name as a leading syncretist between Hindu and Muslim esotericism.[18]

In sum, Shaykh 'Abd al-Quddūs was an influential North Indian Sufi who left a wide range of writings and numerous initiates. He instilled new vigor into what later became the powerful Ṣābirī line of the Chishtī order, and his life spanned the political transition from the last of the Delhi Sultanates, the Lōdīs, through the early years of Mughal rule. A staunch supporter of waḥdat al-wujūd with an inclination for ecstasy, he was also well versed in the intimacies of Yogic practices. The striking later success of the Chishtīyya-Ṣābirī lineage after Shaykh ʿAbd al-Quddūs need not detain us here, except to note two of his key spiritual descendants. The first was his principal khalīfa, the famous Shaykh Jalāl al-dīn Thaneswarī (d. 1582), who gained prominence in Akbar's reign. A chain of Chishtī-Ṣābirī initiates from Jalāl al-dīn onward has proved important in South Asian Muslim circles ever since.[19] The second important spiritual descendant was a young Sufi who first met ʿAbd al-Quddūs while the great pīr resided at Gangōh. The novice learned *dhikr* from the shaykh but actually took *bay'at* into the Chishtī-Ṣābirī line from Shaykh Rukn al-dīn, ʿAbd al-Quddūs's son and sajjāda-nishīn. This initiate, named Shaykh ʿAbd al-Aḥad (d. 1599), then settled in Sirhind to a life of scholarship and piety.

Shaykh ʿAbd al-Aḥad is, of course, the father of Shaykh Aḥmad Sirhindī. He is also, significantly, Sirhindī's pīr in the Qādirī and the Chishtī-Ṣābirī *turuq*. Sirhindī, born in 1564 in the same Punjabi village where his father had settled, is too well known to deserve more than passing treatment here. However, certain aspects of his life and career require more critical attention in light of his early and persistent connections with the Chishtī-Ṣābirī order.

From his early religious and spiritual education in Sirhind, and through his further studies of *ḥadīth* and *fiqh* in Sialkot, his brief and much debated tenure at Akbar's court in Agra, and his fateful trip to Delhi in 1599, Sirhindī followed the path of a Chishtī Sufi. More than that, in his later years he portrayed himself in this period of his life as an ecstatic mystic who, under the influence of waḥdat al-wujūd, could not distinguish Islam from infidelity.[20] And, although his career as a Chishtī pīr was brief, he did take over the instruction of several of his aging father's disciples, and he actually enrolled several Chishtī disciples of his own. At one point he refers to specific practices he learned from Chishtī mentors: "I also developed a taste for supererogatory works (*nawīfil*), particularly *nafl* prayers, from my father, who got it from his teacher, a Chishtī saint."[21] The sources note that even while he was an active Chishtī pīr, Sirhindī chose not to participate in the *samāʿ* assemblies that are so closely identified with Chishtī practice.[22] Like many of the ulema in North India at the time, Sirhindī was initiated into several orders—the Chishtī, Qādirī, and, by one account, the Suhrawardī—but it is clear that, by choice and family tradition, his Chishtī affiliation was paramount.

The change came in 1599, less than half a year after the death of his father. That year Sirhindī undertook the *Hajj* and visited Delhi en route. There he met the itinerant Naqshbandī Sufi Khwāja Bāqī Billāh Birangī (d. 1603). Following an intense three-month discipleship, he abandoned his pilgrimage and returned home to Sirhind as Bāqī Billāh's Naqshbandī khalīfa. For the next two decades he established himself as a Naqshbandī shaykh, mostly through a substantial literary output that included several short treatises and his famous correspondence, more than five hundred letters collected in three volumes known as the *Maktūbāt-i Imām Rabbānī.* In addition, anecdotal literature about Sirhindī appeared early and continued well after his death, devoting special attention to his miraculous works and political activities.[23]

Based in Sirhind, the *Mujaddid-i alf-i thānī* oversaw a network of *khulafā'* that, according to the Mughal emperor Jahāngīr, was active in every town and city in the empire.[24] The critical events of his public life—such as his precise role in the accession of Jahāngīr in 1605, his spiritual impact on the nobles at the Mughal court, his brief imprisonment by Jahāngīr in 1619, and his subsequent influence on that emperor—still spark controversy and debate. More important for our theme is the emergence of his religious persona and the development of his style of mystical practice.

That Sirhindī asserted and maintained his Chishtī ties even after he became a Naqshbandī is quite clear in his *Maktūbāt*, and from the following it is also clear that he ranked his Naqshbandī affiliation above his membership in both the Qādirī and the Chishtī: "I am a disciple of Muḥammad connected with him through many intermediaries: in the Naqshbandī order there are twenty-one intermediaries in between; in the Qādirī, twenty-five; and in the Chishtī, twenty-seven; but my relationship to God as a disciple is not subject to any mediation, as has already been related."[25]

There are a number of important points on which Shaykh Aḥmad Sirhindī and his Chishtī-Ṣābirī predecessor Shaykh ʿAbd al-Quddūs Gangōhī show remarkable similarity and continuity. The first issue that we will examine is the nature of the correspondence each mystic conducted with the ruling houses of his day.

Shaykh ʿAbd al-Quddūs Gangōhī wrote to various nobles, at first the Lōdī and then the Mughal courts. He also addressed letters directly to

Sikandar Lōdī, Bābur, and Humāyūn during their respective reigns.[26] The earliest of these letters was an appeal to Sikandar Lōdī (reigned 1489–1517). Although he praised his Chishtī-Ṣābirī predecessor Shaykh ʿAbd al-Ḥaqq Rudaulvī for a pointed indifference toward political affairs and patronage, ʿAbd al-Quddūs himself is conspicuous for his willingness to petition the imperial court for financial relief. His letter to Sikandar Lōdī warns of the calamities that will befall the state because of his cancellation of permanent stipends (*wazāʾif*) to the Muslim religious élite.[27] This letter, stressing how generosity to the ulema and Sufis strengthens an empire, is a plea for the emperor to restore his monetary support for the Muslim religious classes; if they are neglected, ʿAbd al-Quddūs obliquely warns, there will be a cry for redress.[28] The emperor's reaction to this letter is unrecorded, but ʿAbd al-Quddūs's interest in matters that are explicitly financial is notable.

In a letter to Bābur soon after his accession in 1526, ʿAbd al-Quddūs reiterates this emphasis on the imperial obligation to nurture the *fuqarāʾ*, the ulema, and the *mashāʾikh*. In this epistle his immediate aim is to end the imposition of *ʿushr*, a tithe that Bābur had enacted on the revenue-producing lands that supported the various Muslim religious classes. And again ʿAbd al-Quddūs warns Bābur of the danger of a "cry for redress" from the fuqarāʾ if their needs are ignored.[29]

This letter is interesting in many ways, for it marks the Chishtī recognition of a new, non-Indian Muslim dynasty that would have had little special reason to honor the Chishtī order. The Mughals, as K. A. Nizami has pointed out, from Timur downwards maintained "an unbroken tradition of respect, devotion and attachment to the Naqshbandī saints."[30] Bābur certainly demonstrates this attachment, and while the *Bāburnāma* is full of repeated and copious notice of the Naqshbandī order and Bābur's own affiliations with Naqshbandī pīrs, there is no mention in the work of the Chishtī *silsila* at all.[31] Indeed, Bābur's sole knowledge of the Chishtī silsila might well have been that members of the order—and onetime Mughal captive Shaykh ʿAbd al-Quddūs himself—had in fact supported the Lōdīs against him. But neither of these experienced political figures was willing to let the circumstances of conquest interfere with the expediencies of rule: ʿAbd al-Quddūs noted with approval Bābur's early provisions to sponsor the religious classes, and Bābur in turn was generous to the religious élite he inherited from Sultan Ibrāhīm Lōdī.[32]

After noting his concerns about the burden of *ʾushr* on the religious classes (*tāʾifa-i ʿulamāʾ*), ʿAbd al-Quddūs then offers Bābur advice on how he should rule in India. Much of his counsel, in the tradition of Islamic polity, is standard and seemingly formulaic: royal justice should prevail, the army should be firm in its attachment to the sharīʿa, *muḥtasibs* should be appointed to inspect the bazaars and enforce order, congregational prayer should be enjoined, and the state should support the people of learning and faith.

ʿAbd al-Quddūs also details who should serve in the Muslim government in India. Muslims "of pure and zealous faith" should occupy posts of authority in the countryside. No non-Muslim (he uses the term *kāfir*) may serve in a Muslim administration or receive an assignment of revenue. Non-Muslims should not be employed in bureaucratic offices, and they should not be tax collectors or local commanders. They should be forced to pay *jizya* and should not be allowed to dress like Muslims or to practice their faith ostentatiously and publicly.[33] ʿAbd al-Quddūs makes no explicit mention of the issue of temple construction, repair, or refurbishment, but his advice to Bābur explicitly calls for a return to the sharīʿa as it was practiced in the time of the *khulafāʾ-i rashīdūn*. There is no record of Bābur's response to this entreaty, and we will return to ʿAbd al-Quddūs's views of non-Muslims in government service shortly.

By contrast, ʿAbd al-Quddūs's letter after Humāyūn's accession to the Mughal throne is brief and ignores the issue of *kuffār* in state service.[34] He once again states the need for the emperor to support the religious classes for the good of the empire and recommends that any revenue-producing lands given to these groups should be in tax-free tenure.[35] ʿAbd al-Quddūs may also have waited on Humāyūn at court in Agra in 1536, and it is reported that Humāyūn may have contributed to the erection of the shaykh's tomb in Gangōh.[36] The Sufi's letter to Humāyūn contained no explicit criticisms of his reign; however, one of ʿAbd al-Quddūs's Afghan disciples, Dattu Sarvani, relates that his pīr told him in a dream that "Humāyūn Pādishāh is plundering Islam" and "makes no distinction between *kufr* and Islam but plunders them all."[37] While this certainly cannot be taken as ʿAbd al-Quddūs's verbatim assessment of Humāyūn, it may well have reflected a private view that he shared within his circle of followers, and indeed express a more general Afghan disaffection with their recent conquerors.

Less than a century later, Shaykh Aḥmad Sirhindī also wrote to Muslim nobles at the Mughal court in a wide-ranging correspondence that briefly touched on the question of non-Muslims in state service. Although Sirhindī occasionally wrote to request specific favors on behalf of his *murīds,* his correspondence with the Mughal élite more often offered spiritual and religious counsel. Unlike the letters of Shaykh ʿAbd al-Quddūs, Sirhindī's epistles rarely express any concern for specifically financial matters.

Both men are in agreement in their opposition to permitting non-Muslims access to state service. Sirhindī sent this advice to various Mughal officials.[38] In one letter to Shaykh Farīd Bukhārī, a Mughal noble with Naqshbandī sympathies, Sirhindī allowed that if it became necessary to assign official posts to non-Muslims, the positions should be minor, and that Bukhārī should not trust his kuffār appointees.[39]

Again like ʿAbd al-Quddūs, Sirhindī was hopeful that the Mughals would impose the jizya on non-Muslims in the empire. He wrote to the Mughal official Lālā Bēg early in Jahāngīr's reign, telling him that "Muslim ways"—including the jizya—needed to be introduced at the beginning of the new rule to help restore the confidence of the Muslims.[40] Further, Sirhindī urged that the Mughals should impose restrictions against overt religious display and enforce rules requiring distinctive dress for non-Muslims: measures that were virtually identical to those that ʿAbd al-Quddūs had called for nearly a century earlier.

The remarkable similarities in the measures that both Sufis felt should order Muslim and non-Muslim relations in India betrays the legalistic orientation and training of the two men. Their views of the appropriate organization of Muslim society vis-à-vis non-Muslims were modeled on a much older, classical legal formulation of the issue that did not speak specifically to the question of Hindus versus other non-Muslims. In their treatment of non-Muslims, both men returned to a central element in their approach to religion: an abiding emphasis on the observance of the sharīʿa.

In the prevailing historiographical image of Sirhindī, it is no surprise that he should adopt this relatively hard line against Hindus in government service. Even the ever judicious Yohannan Friedmann points out what he calls "Sirhindī's deep-seated hatred of the non-Muslims."[41] On the other hand, ʿAbd al-Quddūs's harsh views of Hindus are harder for modern biographers to reconcile. Digby writes, "Throughout his life ʿAbd al-Quddūs's attitudes toward the non-Muslim Indian environment were complex and contradictory—as are those of most educated human beings living in a background of mixed but divergent cultures and communities."[42] Bruce Lawrence, too, notes the seeming anomaly between his intimacy with Hindu religious thought and his call to exclude non-Muslims from government service, and suggests that this was "simply revealing the sober, militantly orthodox side of his multifaceted personality."[43]

Most efforts to locate the source of Shaykh Aḥmad Sirhindī's "militant orthodoxy" do not take into account the complexities of his personality. Rather, they cite his Naqshbandī training and heritage. Aziz Ahmad describes the Naqshbandī order, "with its Central Asian emphasis on simple conformity to religion," as "being closer to orthodoxy than any other Sufi school."[44] Presumably this sober Central Asian mystical tradition is the origin of Sirhindī's insistence on the sharīʿa and uncompromising opposition to allowing non-Muslims into the Mughal administration. Closer inspection, however, reveals problems with this assumption.

First, there is no recorded tradition of Naqshbandī pīrs before Sirhindī having strong opinions one way or the other about non-Muslims in India. Sirhindī's own pīr, Khwāja Bāqī Billāh Birangī, was born in Kabul, and he traveled widely in Central Asia, Kashmir, and the Punjab before settling in Delhi. Noted for his insistence on following the sharīʿa, he had also acquired a reputation for patience, courtesy, and generosity toward Muslims and non-Muslims alike. In the slim collection of his letters and in the hagiographical literature extant about Bāqī Billāh, non-Muslims appear only briefly and evoke no special reaction.[45] The other Naqshbandī pīrs in Sirhindī's silsila before Bāqī Billāh were all Central Asians—Bāqī Billāh's immediate pīr Maulānā Khwājagi Amkingī (d. 1600) being based at Amkina near Samarqand—and would have had little or no experience of Hindus or Hinduism. Although certain roughly contemporary Naqshbandī hagiographical texts note Sufi missionary activity in remoter parts of Central Asia and report the practices of the potential converts, these literary notices are brief, make no mention of the position of non-Muslims in a Muslim state, and are confined to a particular branch of the Naqshbandī silsila separate from that of Bāqī Billāh and Sirhindī.[46] There is simply no evidence for any claim that asserts Sirhindī's strong attitudes toward non-Muslims in India derived from his association with the Naqshbandī tradition. It could also be added that Sirhindī's equally well known and disdainful views of Shīʿism, which by contrast are strongly attested to in Central Asian Naqshbandī literature, appear to have been present even before Sirhindī met Bāqī Billāh and was accepted as his khalīfa.[47]

There is another dimension of the Naqshbandī presence in Mughal India that must be explored in order to appreciate Sirhindī's importance as a Naqshbandī pīr: the roles and attitudes of the largely underreported Naqshbandī Sufis present and active in Mughal India before Sirhindī emerged as the dominant Naqshbandī pīr in India. How did these pioneer Naqshbandīs respond to the new religious situation in the Indian environment that was ushered in with Mughal rule? The Mughal dynasty's ancestral reverence toward various Naqshbandī shaykhs has been noted above, and a number of Central Asian Naqshbandīs entered North India in the company of Bābur or visited him soon after the conquest was completed. As Stephen Dale has shown, a steady stream of Central Asian Naqshbandīs who were spiritual and biological descendants of the famous Khwāja 'Ubaydullāh Aḥrār (d. 1490) presented themselves at the Mughal court throughout Akbar's reign and beyond. Quite apart from the fact that these early Naqshbandīs were almost always well received and accorded great honors and prestigious posts, a pattern of marriages between the Mughal house and these Naqshbandī families further cemented their élite status within the Mughal service nobility.[48]

Yet within this first generation of Central Asian Naqshbandīs in Mughal India there are only a handful of shaykhs with the ability to enroll disciples, and of these few, there is little or no record of their spiritual activities or religious attitudes. As a result we do not know how they viewed Muslim and non-Muslim relations in Mughal India. Note, however, that later generations of the Naqshbandī silsila in India make little or no reference to these pre-Sirhindī Naqshbandīs, with the strong implication that they were held in slight esteem at best. In any case, except for the scant evidence relating to Khwāja Bāqī Billāh, Sirhindī is the first Indian Naqshbandī whose attitudes regarding Muslims and non-Muslims in India can be examined in his own works.[49]

Where, then, are the origins of Sirhindī's strong views vis-à-vis non-Muslims in India? In the absence of any explicit and prior Naqshbandī teachings on the issue, there are several possibilities. He may have developed these views on his own, basing them in part on his formal education in India. He may have reached these opinions and developed his advice in his interactions with other Indian Muslims, in the mosque, the *madrasa*, and the khānaqāh. Finally, he may have accepted these views and the attitudes they imply as part of his spiritual orientation in the Chishtī-Ṣābirī line of his father, going back to Shaykh 'Abd al-Quddūs. Whatever their origins, Sirhindī's views on non-Muslims in India are not original to him. Nor, as shown above, are they part of the Naqshbandī tradition that Bāqī Billāh imparted to Sirhindī. Therefore, it seems safe to say that one of the most discussed and notorious features of Sirhindī's spiritual message—his uncompromising opposition to non-Muslim participation in government and his widely known antagonism toward Indian non-Muslims—more likely comes from his background in Indian Islam rather than from his membership in the imported Central Asian Naqshbandī order.

That some or even much of Sirhindī's mystical thought, practices, and teaching should derive from his education and experience prior to his enrollment as a Naqshbandī shaykh should come as no surprise. His discipleship under Bāqī Billāh was exceptionally brief, and afterwards he benefited from his pīr—through personal visits and correspondence—for only three more years before Bāqī Billāh's death. It seems reasonable then to expect that much of Sirhindī's non-Naqshbandī grounding in Islamic mysticism would come from his association with Indian Sufi orders, particularly the Chishtī-Ṣābirī lineage that connected his father, Shaykh ʿAbd al-Aḥad, with Shaykh ʿAbd al-Quddūs Gangōhī. We now turn to examine some of these mystical themes and practices.

On issues relating more specifically to Sufi practices there are significant differences between the two mystics. Shaykh ʿAbd al-Quddūs, for example, was like many Chishtīs a lifelong proponent of samaāʿ and was himself prone to extended periods of musically induced mystical ecstasy.[50] Shaykh Aḥmad Sirhindī held almost the opposite view, considering spiritual audition "a reprehensible custom" that was unable to produce lasting spiritual progress.[51] As noted above, Sirhindī is said to have disapproved of samāʿ assemblies even before his membership in the Naqshbandī order. Note, however, that other Indian Naqshbandīs were more lenient toward the practice, despite Sirhindī's admonitions.[52]

The two Sufis also diverged in their views of dhikr. Dhikr, meaning "remembrance (of God)," is a type of Sufi spiritual exercise that usually employs the rhythmical repetition of the names of Allāh or ritual formulae in a practice that, in the view of one modern scholar, "signifies a kind of prayer."[53] Regarding this elemental Sufi practice, Sirhindī upheld the distinctive Naqshbandī practice of "silent dhikr" (*dhikr-i qalb* or *dhikr-i khaf*) and would not allow his disciples to practice "vocal dhikr" (*dhikr-i jahr*).[54] Silent dhikr is often identified as one of the Naqshbandī order's trademarks: Schimmel notes that silent dhikr forms "the center of Naqshbandī education," and Hamid Algar considers this technique "normative for the order, various later deviations notwithstanding."[55] Silent dhikr, allegedly first taught by the Prophet himself to Abū Bakr, formed an integral part of early Naqshbandī practice in Central Asia. It was the preferred dhikr of the pivotal Naqshbandī shaykh Khwāja ʿUbaydullāh Aḥrār (d. 1490) in Samarqand, and many of his spiritual descendants within the order—including Bāqī Billāh in Mughal India—followed it exclusively.[56] Yet along with silent dhikr there is also an alternative Naqshbandī tradition of vocal dhikr. Indeed, other Indian Naqshbandīs contemporary with Sirhindī actually practiced both vocal dhikr and the silent variety. Significantly, among these "divergent" Naqshbandīs were some of Bāqī Billāh's murīds and even his two sons, Khwāja ʿUbaydullāh (known as "Khwāja-i Kalān") and Khwāja ʿAbdullāh (known as "Khwāja-i Khurd"). Sirhindī, in several letters to the sons of his pīr, expressed his disappointment in their decision to join in what he considered a *bidʿa* practice.

Shaykh ʿAbd al-Quddūs's views of dhikr are more complex and reflect his own unique contribution. ʿAbd al-Quddūs practiced vocal dhikr, but he also performed a special dhikr that he called *sulṭān-i dhikr*, a term allegedly taken from Ibn al-ʿArabī's *Risāla-i Makkiyya*. This overpowering dhikr, which Shaykh ʿAbd al Quddūs's son Shaykh Rukn al-dīn compared to *wahy* (Prophetic inspiration), is described as at first being a terrifying ordeal for the spiritual novice; with practice, however, the initiate learns to appreciate and seek out the experience. A description of a quality of dhikr more than its technique, it is not clear whether the *sulṭān-i dhikr* is silent or vocal. This dhikr, with its strong emphasis on producing a state of mystical ecstasy, stands in marked contrast with the potent yet controlled silent dhikr that Sirhindī practiced and advocated.[57]

The final point of comparison between the mystical philosophies of the two great shaykhs is their attitude in the "debate" between waḥdat al-wujūd and waḥdat al-shuhūd. Shaykh ʿAbd al-Quddūs's reputation is well known; as a defender and exponent of Ibn al-ʿArabī's teachings in India, including the notion of waḥdat al-wujūd, he had few equals. The hagiographical literature about him contains several instances of his stubborn defense of the doctrine and his tireless efforts to convince his sons and various ulema to accept his views.[58] As for Aḥmad Sirhindī, he is considered the champion of the countervailing notion, waḥdat al-shuhūd, generally acknowledged as being first formulated by the well-known Iranian Kubrāvī mystic ʿAlāʾ al-Dawla Simnānī (d. 1336).[59]

Aziz Ahmad offers the most sweeping judgment on the impact of Sirhindī's theory concerning waḥdat al-wujūd, proclaiming that "the revolution he [Sirhindī] brought about in Indian Sufism negated this position completely." Ahmad then assesses the impact that Sirhindī's "phenomenological monism" had on Indian Islam: "It re-diverted its various streams, orthodox and esoteric, into one channel; it relaxed the tension between the religious law and mystical experience; it resolved whatever conflict there was between the Sūfīs and the *'ulamā'* uniting them in a single synthesis of solidarity."[60]

Yet, as Friedmann has shown, Sirhindī's views on Ibn al-ʿArabī and waḥdat al-wujūd are far more subtle and complex than most biographers allow. While Sirhindī makes specific objections to some of the teachings of the *Shaykh al-Akbar,* he also acknowledges Ibn al-ʿArabī's tremendous contribution to Sufism. "The Sufis who preceded him—if they spoke about these matters at all—only hinted at them and did not elaborate," observes Friedmann. "Most of those who came after him chose to follow in his footsteps and use his terms. We latecomers have also benefitted from the blessings of that great man and learned a great deal from his mystical insights." At another point Sirhindī writes in defense of Ibn al-ʿArabī that "in most assertions about reality *(tahqīqāt)* the Shaykh is in the right and his detractors far from the truth. From the investigation of this matter one ought to learn about the greatness and the profound wisdom of the Shaykh, not refute and condemn him."[61] It seems clear that while Sirhindī took issue with various points of Ibn al-ʿArabī's waḥdat al-wujūd, his was not a categorical rejection of the great Andalusian mystic's work and was never intended to be. Sirhindī certainly believed that later Sufi commentators misunderstood and misinterpreted Ibn al-ʿArabī's writings—sometimes with impious results—but Sirhindī regarded Ibn al-ʿArabī's mystical achievements and writings with great respect and borrowed from them freely.

Summarizing our comparison of the mystical praxis of Shaykh ʿAbd al-Quddūs and Shaykh Aḥmad Sirhindī, the two men diverge widely on samāʿ and dhikr, and although both express admiration for Ibn al-ʿArabī, they also differ as to the validity of waḥdat al-wujūd. It seems obvious that Sirhindī rejects or accepts only with modifications many of the doctrines espoused by Shaykh ʿAbd al-Quddūs and then passed on to Sirhindī's father via the Chishtīyya-Ṣābiriyya. But it is also clear that, with few exceptions, Sirhindī's differences from the Chishtī line do not derive from his Naqshbandī identity. A few examples will suffice.

First, as noted above, there is no Naqshbandī precedent for Sirhindī's opposition to the participation of non-Muslims in state service; indeed, the writings of Shaykh ʿAbd al-Quddūs on this matter may well have influenced Sirhindī in his views more than any Naqshbandī work. Second, it is apparent that Sirhindī' s rejection of samāʿ is his own practice and not that of the Naqshbandī order in general. Even while Sirhindī eschewed participation in samāʿ, the sons of his pīr Bāqī Billāh embraced it openly. As Bāqī Billāh's son Khwāja ʿAbdullāh (Khwāja-i Khurd) expressed it much later, "Although samāʿ is not prevalent in our *tarīqa* and we are not known as those who indulge in samāʿ, we have no repulsion towards it."[62] The ambivalence of the Naqshbandī order toward samāʿ in this period is unmistakable. The other major Naqshbandī shaykh active in Mughal India in Sirhindī's lifetime, Khwāja Khāwand Maḥmūd Naqshbandī (d. 1642), expressed similarly equivocal views on samāʿ. Whatever the source of Sirhindī's rejection of samaāʿ, it cannot be definitively shown to come from the Naqshbandīyya.

The origins of Sirhindī's views on dhikr are equally difficult to pinpoint. Khwāja Bāqī Billāh did not allow vocal dhikr in his presence, although again later his two sons considered it permissible. Presumably, Sirhindī gained his preference for silent dhikr from his pīr. But there was no Naqshbandī consensus on the practice, either among the Naqshbandīyya in Central Asia or in Mughal India. Sirhindī, in choosing silent dhikr, was exercising a choice within the Naqshbandī order and not simply adopting a standard practice. The importance of this element of personal choice within the Indian Naqshbandī order—which in practice allowed the Sufis to choose between silent or vocal dhikr, practicing samāʿ or rejecting it—is often overlooked in the usual descriptions of "normative" Naqshbandī practice.

There is one more intriguing point of similarity between Sirhindī's teachings and the earlier works of the Chishtīyya-Ṣābiriyya. In the *Maktūbāt* Sirhindī developed an elaborate theory of prophetology that seems to have no origins in his Naqshbandī background. Both Friedmann and Schimmel have noted this anomaly and offer interpretations of the Mujaddid's millennialist spiritual hierarchy. Sirhindī, Schimmel argues, posited two individuations *(taʿayyun)* of the prophet Muḥammad: his "bodily human" form and his "spiritually angelic" form. These individuations were represented in the two *mīms* that appear in Muḥammad's name. With the arrival of the millennium the first *mīm*, representing the Prophet's human and physical side, would disappear and be replaced by the letter *alif*, signifying divinity *(ulūhīyat)*. In Sirhindī's own words, "Muḥammad became Aḥmad (*Muḥammad Aḥmad shud*).[63] Schimmel concludes that "it is no accident that the change from

Muḥammad to Aḥmad coincides with the very name of Aḥmad Sirhindī and points to his discreetly hidden role as the 'common believer' called to restore these perfections."[64]

While one is hard-pressed to find any examples of similar mystical speculation in earlier Naqshbandī works, such letter-based conjecture is fairly well known in other medieval Sufi circles. Sa'ad al-dīn Maḥmūd Shabistarī (d. 1320) hints at the theme in his *Gulshan-i rūz:* "The One (*Aḥad*) was made manifest in the *mīm* of Aḥmad. In this circuit the first emanation became the last. A single *mīm* divides Aḥad from Aḥmad. The world is immersed in that one *mīm.*"[65] A very similar interpretation for the letter *mīm* and the names Aḥad and Aḥmad is found in none other than Shaykh ʿAbd al-Quddūs Gangōhī's *Rushd-Nāma (Murshid-Nāma)* in a series of Hindi verses (*dohas*). Digby suggests that the author of these verses is Shaykh Muḥammad, the khalīfa of Shaykh ʿĀrif who was in turn the khalīfa of Shaykh Aḥmad ʿAbd al-Ḥaqq Rudaulvī. Two notes may help with the text; first, "Maḥmad" is a deliberate alternate vocalization of Muḥammad and, second, it is Shaykh Muḥammad who is the "Ladhan" of the final verse:

> The world says Maḥmad, Maḥmad, but nobody understands
> Aḥmad has lost its *mīm;* tell me, how could there be a second?
> Maḥmad is the flower of the eternal; he himself is also the fruit,
> How can the poor wretch know this who has not tasted it?
> Maḥmad is becoming ʿĀrif and ʿĀrif, he is Aḥmad,
> This is the untellable tale of Ladhan; there are few who understand.[66]

The similarities of the wordplay and symbolism employed by Shaykh Muḥammad (the pīr and brother-in-law of Shaykh ʿAbd al-Quddūs) with Shaykh Aḥmad Sirhindī's suggestive speculations a century later are not definitive evidence of a link between the two mystical systems. But they do firmly connect at least part of Sirhindī's post-Naqshbandī esotericism to an older, well-established mystical doctrine to which he, as a Chishtī-Ṣābirī, would have had access. This may be one part of Sirhindī's Chishtī spiritual inheritance that he retained and even expanded upon after his entry into the Naqshbandīyya.

In view of the similarities and differences between Shaykh ʿAbd al-Quddūs and Shaykh Aḥmad Sirhindī described above, what conclusions can be drawn? And how do these conclusions affect our understanding of the Naqshbandī reaction? First, it is apparent that there are certain features in Sirhindī's spiritual makeup that, while absent in

Naqshbandī ethos, have strong parallels with certain traits found in the mystical disposition of Shaykh ʿAbd al-Quddūs and the Chishtī-Ṣābirī line. The analogous perspectives of both Sufis on non-Muslims in India, their only qualified support for the Mughal ruling house, their common if divergent interest in Ibn al-ʿArabī, and a shared system of mystical letter symbolism suggest that Sirhindī may have retained more of Chishtī-Ṣābirī worldview than simply the tarīqa's *nisba*. Second, in terms of praxis, there are relatively few elements in Sirhindī's way that derive *exclusively* from his affiliation with the Naqshbandī order. His opinions and attitudes regarding dhikr and samāʿ mirror those of his pīr, Bāqī Billāh, but they are only two choices in a range of established, if not universally accepted, Naqshbandī practice.[67] Those two preferences in practice alone do not distinguish Sirhindī as a Naqshbandī.

It might be interesting to speculate about Sirhindī's Naqshbandī identity if he had made different choices among the range of Naqshbandī practices available to him. What if he had elected to follow vocal dhikr and to participate in samāʿ and at the same time continued his respectful criticism—which in many ways is more a sympathetic commentary and elaboration—of Ibn al-ʿArabī and waḥdat al-wujūd? Had this been the case, except for the Naqshbandī spiritual nisba, what would have distinguished Sirhindī and his tarīqa from the practices of other Indian Sufi orders, notably the Chishtīyya-Ṣābiriyya?

The striking continuity between Sirhindī's configuration of the Naqshbandī order and some of the elements of Chishtī-Ṣābirī practice suggests some provocative conclusions. In many ways it could be argued that Sirhindī joined certain Chishtī-Ṣābirī concepts with select components of his newfound Naqshbandī discipline. The result was not the submergence of his Chishtī identity into his new position within the Central Asian Naqshbandī tradition. Far from it. Rather, he drew on both mystical traditions to create a new path, recognized by his followers as the Naqshbandīyya-Mujaddidiyya. But this new Indian Naqshbandī branch, as we have seen, is notably out of step with previous Central Asian Naqshbandī practice. Sirhindī's new branch could be viewed as the heir to a Chishtī-Ṣābirī set of attitudes and practices—which may not have been confined to the Chishtī line alone—recast under the name of a new Naqshbandī tarīqa.

There are, finally, two sets of testimony that obliquely support this claim. The first is the dramatic and almost overnight success that Sirhindī and the Naqshbandīyya-Mujaddidiyya found among the Indian Chishtīs. The new order must have appealed to a common set of values and beliefs held by these Sufis. Multiple affiliation, already a common feature of Indian Sufi practice, allowed many individual Sufis to share in a new discipline that bore many similarities with their previous practice. While the Naqshbandīs were skillful in recruiting membership from a number of Sufi orders in South Asia, they found particular success in finding new initiates among the Chishtīs. If this demonstrates how close the Naqshbandīyya-Mujaddidiyya were to the Chishtīyya-Ṣābiriyya, the second bit of evidence shows how far Sirhindī was from his contemporary Naqshbandīs active in India.[68] It is no aberration that these other Naqshbandī leaders—some from Central Asia, as in the case of Khwāja Khawand Maḥmud Naqshbandī, others who were Sirhindī's co-*khulafā'* under Bāqī Billāh, and even the sons of Bāqī Billāh—did not easily accept Sirhindī's claims to authority. Indeed, some of these other Naqshbandī leaders barely considered him an authentic Naqshbandī shaykh at all.[69] They did not recognize Sirhindī's Naqshbandīs, while at the same time Indian Chishtīs appreciated a distinctly fresh orientation within the new branch. The Naqshbandīyya-Mujaddidiyya thus seemed disturbingly new and innovative to Central Asian Naqshbandīs while they appeared at the same time as surprisingly familiar to South Asian mystics, the Chishtī-Ṣābirī in particular. In some ways then, Sirhindī's "Naqshbandī reaction" might actually represent more of a "Chishtī reformation," the survival and elaboration of a particular longstanding South Asian mystical ethos reshaped, restated, yet still recognizable within the Central Asian Naqshbandī tradition.

Notes

Many colleagues graciously have enriched this paper, including Professors Charles Adams, Bruce Lawrence, Derryl MacLean, Naim R. Faruqi, and John Richards. To them I am grateful. News of the death of Ahmad Farokhpay, a longtime friend and generous colleague, came while this essay was being prepared for publication, and with respect and sadness it is humbly dedicated to his memory.

1. Aziz Ahmad, *Studies in Islamic Culture in the Indian Environment* (Oxford: Oxford University Press, 1964), 183. 2. Fazlur Rahman, *Islam*, 2d ed. (Chicago: University of Chicago Press, 1979), 148.

3. Annemarie Schimmel, *Mystical Dimensions of Islam* (Chapel Hill: University of North Carolina Press, 1975), 363–64, 402.

4. Ibid., 368–69; Rahman, *Islam*, 148, 164; Aziz Ahmad, *An Intellectual History of Islam in India*, Islamic Surveys, vol. 7 (Edinburgh: Edinburgh University Press, 1969), 40–41.

5. Rahman, *Islam*, 164.

6. Ahmad, *Studies in Islamic Culture*, 186.

7. Yohannan Friedmann, *Shaykh Aḥmad Sirhindī: An Outline of His Thought and a Study of His Image in the Eyes of Posterity* (Montreal: McGill–Queen's University Press, 1971), xiii, 105–11.

8. Khaliq Ahmad Nizami, *Tarikh-i Mashā'ikh Chisht*, 2 vols. (Delhi: Idarah-yi Adabiyat-i Dilli, 1980, 1984), 1:432–38.

9. Simon Digby, "ʿAbd al-Quddūs Gangōhī (1456–1537 A.D.): The Personality and Attitudes of a Medieval Indian Sufi," *Medieval India: A Miscellany* 3, Aligarh, (1975): 19. See also *Encyclopedia of Islam*, 2d ed., s.v. "Gangōhī," by G. Böwering.

10. Sayyid Athar Abbas Rizvi, *The History of Sufism in India*, 2 vols. (Delhi: Munshiram Manoharlal, 1978–83), 1:336.

11. Digby, *ʿAbd al-Quddūs*, 4; see also *Encyclopedia of Islam*, 2d ed., s.v. "Chishtīyya," by Khaliq Ahmad Nizami, and S. H. Askari, "Hazarat ʿAbdul Quddūs Gangōhī," *Patna University Journal* 11 (1957): 1–31. Shaykh ʿAbd al-Quddūs's life is recorded by many Mughal period authors, most notably by Shaykh ʿAbd al-Ḥaqq Muḥaddith Dihlavī in *Akhbār al-Akhyār ma'a Makūtbāt* (Zila Khayrpur, Pakistan: Faruq Academy, 1977), 221–24.

12. Digby, *ʿAbd al-Quddūs*, 6; see also *Encyclopaedia Iranica*, s.v. "ʿAbd al-Qoddūs Gangōhī," by Bruce Lawrence.

13. The *Rushd-Nāma* (*Murshid-Nāma*) exists in several manuscripts and in a lithographed edition, *Rushd-Nāma Muhashsha*, ed. Ghulam Aḥmad Khan (Jhajjar: Muslim Press, 1896–97). There is also a Hindi translation: see *Rushd Nama*, translated by Alakh Bani, S. A. A. Rizvi, and S. Zaidi (Aligarh: n.p., 1970). A lithographed edition of the *Makūtbāt-i Quddūsī* (Delhi: Aḥmadi Press, 1870) is also available. Digby notes a lithograph of the *Muntakhab-i Maktubat-i Quddūsī* (Delhi: Matbaʿ-i Mujtabaʾ-i, 1894); see Digby, *ʿAbd al-Quddūs*, 16, notes 90–92.

14. Iqtidar Husain Siddiqui, "Resurgence of the Chishtī Silsila in the Sultanate of Delhi during the Lōdī Period (A.D. 1451–1526)," *Islam in India* 2 (1985): 70–71. For ʿIrāqī and the *Lama'āt*, see *Fakhruddin 'Iraqi: Divine Flashes*, trans. William C. Chittick and Peter Lamborn Wilson (New York: Paulist Press, 1982).

15. Shaykh Rukn al-dīn, *Lata'if-i Quddūsī* (Delhi: Mutbaʿ-i Mujtabaʾ-i, 1894). The work is described in S. Nurul Hasan, "*Lata'if-i Quddūsī:* A Contemporary Afghan Source for the Study of Afghan-Mughal Relationships," *Medieval India Quarterly* 1 (1950): 49–57.

16. Digby, *ʿAbd al-Quddūs*, 18.

17. Ibid., 36–51, 57.

18. Rizvi, *History of Sufism in India*, 1:335–48.

19. Although discussion of the Chishtī-Ṣābirī order after the seventeenth century is beyond this essay, it should be mentioned that the spiritual and political careers of many later members of this order often display actions and interests well beyond the typical narrow "wujūdī" characterization of the order. See Nizami, *Tarikh-i Mashā'ikh-i Chisht*, and the life of Shaykh Hajji Imdād Allāh al-

Makkī (d. 1899) in *Encyclopedia of Islam,* 2d ed., s.v. "Imdād Allāh," by A. S. Bazmee Ansari, for examples of Chishtī-Ṣābirī shaykhs engaged in rich and diverse patterns of mystical expression.

20. Friedmann, *Shaykh Aḥmad Sirhindī,* 23–25.

21. M. Abdul Haq Ansari, *Sufism and Sharī'ah: A Study of Shaykh Aḥmad Sirhindī's Effort to Reform Sufism* (Leicester: Islamic Foundation, 1986), 13.

22. Rizvi, *History of Sufism in India,* 2:190.

23. A very brief survey of this literature would include the *Zubdat al Maqāmāt* compiled by Muḥammad Hāshim Kishmī in 1626–27 (printed at Kanpur by Naval Kishor, 1890), Badr al-dīn Sirhindī's *Hadarāt al-Quds* started in 1647–48 (India Office Library ms. D.P. 630, and an Urdu translation printed at Lahore, 1971), and Abū al-Fayḍ Iḥsān's *Rawdat al-Qayyūmiyya,* started after 1740 (ms. in the Library of the Asiatic Society of Bengal, Ivanow, Curzon 82, and an Urdu translation printed at Lahore, 1917). All of these demonstrate consistent and prolonged interest in Sirhindī and Khwāja Bāqī Billāh Birangī in Mughal India.

24. Jahāngīr, *The Tūzuk-i Jahāngīrī, or Memoirs of Jahāngīr,* 2 vols., 2d ed., trans. Alexander Rogers, ed. Henry Beveridge (Delhi: Munshiram Manoharlal, 1968), 2:91–92.

25. Friedmann, *Shaykh Aḥmad Sirhindī,* 27–28.

26. See the *Maktūbāt-i Quddūsī,* 44–46, 335–37, 338–39. See also Digby, *'Abd al-Quddūs,* 32–34, and I'jāz al-Ḥaqq Quddūsī, *Shaykh 'Abd al-Quddūs Gangūhī aur unki Ta'līmāt* (Karachi: Academy of Educational Research, 1961), 437–39.

27. Digby, *'Abd al-Quddūs,* 28–29.

28. *Maktūbāt-i Quddūsī,* 44–46; Digby, *'Abd al-Quddūs,* 32; Quddūsī, *Shaykh 'Abd al-Quddūs Gangōhī,* 438.

29. *Maktūbāt-i Quddūsī,* 335–37; Digby, *'Abd al-Quddūs,* 33; Quddūsī, *Shaykh 'Abd al-Quddūs Gangōhī,* 452–56.

30. Khaliq Ahmad Nizami, "Naqshbandī Influence on Mughal Rulers and Politics," *Islamic Culture* 39 (1965): 42.

31. Bābur, *Bāburnāma: Chaghatay Turkish Text with Abdul-Rahim Khankhanan's Persian Translation,* 3 vols., trans. W. M. Thackston Jr. (Cambridge: Harvard University, Department of Near Eastern Languages and Civilizations, 1993).

32. *Maktūbāt-i Quddūsī,* 335–37; Digby, *'Abd al-Quddūs,* 32–33.

33. *Maktūbāt-i Quddūsī,* 335–37; Digby, *'Abd al-Quddūs,* 33–34.

34. *Maktūbāt-i Quddūsī,* 338–39; Digby, *'Abd al-Quddūs,* 34. The date of this letter is unspecified, and Digby speculates that it was written in either 1531 or 1535.

35. Quddūsī, *Shaykh 'Abd al-Quddūs Gangōhī,* 459.

36. *Encyclopaedia Iranica,* s.v. "'Abd al-Qoddūs Gangōhī," by Bruce Lawrence.

37. Simon Digby, "Dreams and Reminiscences of Dattu Sarvani, a Sixteenth-Century Indo-Afghan Soldier," *Indian Economic and Social History Review* 2 (1965): 57, 71. See also *Lata'if-i Quddūsī,* 79–81.

38. Friedmann, *Shaykh Aḥmad Sirhindī,* 75.

39. Shaykh Aḥmad Sirhindī, *Maktūbāt-i Imām-i Rabbānī*, 6 vols., ed. Nūr Aḥmad Amritsarī (Lahore: Nūr, 1964), 1:93–97, letter #193.

40. Ibid., 2:85–86, letter #81.

41. Friedmann, *Shaykh Aḥmad Sirhindī*, 73.

42. Digby, *'Abd al-Quddūs*, 36.

43. *Encyclopaedia Iranica*, s.v. "'Abd al-Qoddūs Gangōhī."

44. Ahmad, *Studies in Islamic Culture*, 182.

45. Muḥammad Ṣādiq Kashmīrī Hamadānī, *Kalimāt al-Sādiqīn* (Khuda Bakhsh Oriental Public Library, Patna, ms. #202), ff. 97v–110v.

46. The only Central Asian Naqshbandī hagiography I am aware of that mentions conversion is Muḥammad 'Iwaḍ's *Diyā'al-qulūb*, a life of the Naqshbandī shaykh Khwāja Isḥāq Walī, who died probably in 1599–1600 (1008 A.H.). I have consulted an uncataloged manuscript copy graciously provided by the curator of the Houghton Library of the Harvard University Library. It is also noted in Joseph Fletcher, "Confrontations between Muslim Missionaries and Nomad Unbelievers in the Late Sixteenth Century: Notes on Four Passages from the *Diyā'al-qulūb*," in *Tractata Altaica*, ed. W. Heissig, J. R. Krueger, F. J. Oinas, and E. Schutz (Wiesbaden: Otto Harrassowitz, 1976), 167–73.

47. Friedmann dates Sirhindī's famous anti-Shī'ī tract *Risāla dar Radd-i Rawāfiẓ* to before 1599–1600 and considers it "the first manifestation of his Sunni fervour." See Friedmann, *Shaykh Aḥmad Sirhindī*, 4.

48. See Stephen Dale's "Ashraf Sufis: Ahrārī Naqshbandī's in Early Mughal India," paper presented at the 1990 Middle East Studies Association annual meeting in San Antonio, 4–8.

49. An exception to this is Khwāja Khāwand Maḥmūd Naqshbandī (d. 1642), a Central Asian émigré to Mughal Kashmir c. 1600 whose life is relatively well documented; see David Damrel, "Forgotten Grace: Khwāja Khāwand Maḥmūd Naqshbandī in Central Asia and Mughal India," Ph.D. diss., Duke University, 1991.

50. Digby, *'Abd al-Quddūs*, 19–20. For Chishtī attitudes toward samā', see Bruce Lawrence, "The Early Chishtī Approach to *Samā'*," in *Islamic Society and Culture: Essays in Honour of Professor Aziz Ahmad*, ed. Milton Israel and N. K. Wagle (New Delhi: Manohar, 1983), 69–93.

51. Friedmann, *Shaykh Aḥmad Sirhindī*, 68.

52. Sayyid Athar Abbas Rizvi, *Muslim Revivalist Movements in Northern India in the Sixteenth and Seventeenth Centuries* (Agra: Agra University, 1965), 333.

53. See the *Encyclopedia of Religion* (1987–89), s.v. "Dhikr," by William C. Chittick.

54. Friedmann, *Shaykh Aḥmad Sirhindī*, 44.

55. Schimmel, *Mystical Dimensions of Islam*, 366, and Hamid Algar, "The Naqshbandī Order: A Preliminary Survey of Its History and Significance," *Studia Islamica* 44 (1976): 136. Algar also addresses this theme in his "Silent and Vocal *Dhikr* in the Naqshbandī Order," *Akten des VII. Kongresses für Arabistik und*

Islamwissenschaft, Abhandlungen der Akademie der Wissenschaften in Göttingen, philologisch-historische Klasse, series 3, no. 98 (Göttingen, 1976), 44–45. Note, too, Joseph Fletcher's pioneering studies of a Central Asian branch of the *tarīqa* called the Jarhiyya, "a sub-group within the Naqshbandīya proper who practiced a vocal dhikr in addition or in preference to the Naqshbandīya's customary silent one." See Fletcher, "Central Asian Sufism and Ma Ming-Hsin's New Teaching," in Ch'en Chieh-hsien, ed., *Proceedings of the Fourth East Asian Altaistic Conference* (Taipei: National Taiwan University, 1975), 80.

56. Friedmann, *Shaykh Aḥmad Sirhindī,* 44.

57. *Lata'if-i Quddūsī,* 16–18; Digby, *'Abd al-Quddūs,* 22.

58. *Lata'if-i Quddūsī,* 55, 58; Digby, *'Abd al-Quddūs,* 19.

59. Hermann Landolt, "Simnānī on Waḥdat al-Wujūd," in *Collected Papers on Islamic Philosophy and Mysticism,* ed. M. Mohaghegh and H. Landolt (Tehran: McGill University, Tehran Branch, 1971), 93–111.

60. Ahmad, *Studies in Islamic Culture,* 187, 188.

61. Friedmann, *Shaykh Aḥmad Sirhindī,* 62–68, quotes from 65.

62. Rizvi, *Muslim Revivalist Movements,* 333.

63. Friedmann, *Shaykh Aḥmad Sirhindī,* 29.

64. Schimmel, *Mystical Dimensions of Islam,* 369.

65. Sa'ad al-dīn Maḥmūd Shabistarī, *Gulshan-i rūz* (Mystic rose garden), trans. E. H. Whinfield (London, 1880), 2.

66. *Rushd-Nāma Muhashshā,* 20; Digby, *'Abd al-Quddūs,* 65–66.

67. Differing regional interpretations of Naqshbandī practices by members of the order throughout the Muslim world have received only scant scholarly attention. An important exception is Joseph F. Fletcher's work on two rival groups of Naqshbandīs in Central Asia and Northwest China. For these two branches of the order—the Isḥāqiyya (*Qarataghlïq,* the "Black Mountain Khwājas") and the *Āfāqiyya Aqtaghlïq* (the "White Mountain Khwājas")—the question of vocal versus silent dhikr is the defining element of Naqshbandī identity. See Joseph F. Fletcher, "The Naqshbandīyya in Northwest China," in his *Studies on Islamic Inner Asia,* ed. Beatrice Forbes Manz (Great Yarmouth, U.K.: Variorum, 1995), 3–46.

68. Johan G. J. TerHaar "The Naqshbandī Tradition in the Eyes of Aḥmad Sirhindī," in *Naqshbandīs: Cheminements et situation actuelle d'un ordre mystique musulman* (Naqshbandīs: Historical developments and present situation of a Muslim mystical order), ed. Marc Gaborieau, Alexandre Popovic, and Thierry Zarcone (Istanbul: Isis, 1990), 83–93.

69. Damrel, "Forgotten Grace," 155–62.

8

Real Men and False Men at the Court of Akbar

The *Majalis* of Shaykh Mustafa Gujarati

Derryl N. MacLean

The year 982/1574 was an auspicious one for the intellectual history of Muslim India. It was a year which, following the successful Mughal conquest of Gujarat, saw the introduction to the imperial court of the two bitter antagonists, Badaʾuni and Abu al-Fazl, the building of the foundation of the *ʿibadat- khanah* (house of devotion) at Fatehpur Sikri, and the inauguration there of intensive discussions concerning the nature of Islam in India as the emperor Akbar strove to locate an ideology congenial to him personally and to the expanding empire. In the same year, Asaf Khan, the Mir Bakhshi, brought a prisoner from Gujarat to Fatehpur Sikri. His name was Shaykh Mustafa, and he was a Mahdavi of some renown who had already entered into a lengthy correspondence with Shaykh Mubarak, Abu al-Fazl's father, met Akbar himself at Patan during the conquest of Gujarat, and been subjected to a prolonged and strenuous interrogation at Ahmadabad by Mirza ʿAziz Koka, the first Mughal governor of Gujarat and Akbar's foster brother. Shaykh Mustafa would spend over a year at the court of Akbar, meeting Bada'uni, Shaykh ʿAbd an-Nabi, and other Mughal luminaries, and serving as the main course in a series of imperial disputations concerning his movement, the Mahdaviyah. Fortunately for historians, Shaykh Mustafa left an account of five of these sessions (*majalis*), copied in some haste by his son, Faqir Jalal. This little-known source, the subject of this chapter, provides privileged access to the disputation of identity at a critical juncture in Indo-Muslim history.

Shaykh Mustafa belonged to the Mahdaviyah community, which attributes its origins to Sayyid Muhammad Jaunpuri (847–910/1443–

1505), a pious Chishti Sufi from North India who arrived in Ahmadabad in 903/1497 and began teaching a radical Sufi message at the mosque of Taj Khan Salar.[1] Expelled from Ahmadabad for his views on the vision of God and then from Patan for his *takfir* (anathema) of those who desire the world, he settled in Barli, just outside of Patan, where the mixed message of his earlier years was clarified in a divine audition: "You are the promised Mahdi; proclaim the manifestation of your Mahdiship, and do not fear the people."[2] His public proclamation at Barli propelled him from the ranks of those with acceptable Sufi charisma into the more dangerous realm of Mahdi charisma. His increasingly focused rejection of the political and religious status quo coupled with mounting support among the religious and political elite led to his expulsion from Gujarat. Sayyid Muhammad emigrated first to Sind and then, after his expulsion there, to Khurasan where he settled at Farrah and spent the last three years of his life, dying on Monday 19 al-Qaʿdah 910 (23 April 1505).

The death of the Mahdi left the nascent community in considerable disarray. His followers regrouped back in Gujarat, where they began to work out the implications of a Mahdism without a Mahdi or a new scripture. While some Mahdavis claimed to be ʿIsa (Jesus) and others looked for the Dajjal (Antichrist), most of his companions attempted to locate the Mahdi in an eschatological and social context and to provide a blueprint for the guidance of the community.[3] This process involved a series of restructurings and reimaginings of the notions and practices of being Muslim in India.

The early Mahdavis proposed bypassing historically evolved Islam and returning to projected origins. Rejecting the notions of *taqlid* (binding authority of prior jurists) and *naskh* (abrogation of Qur'anic verses), the Mahdavis referred their concerns back to the Qur'an and the prophetic *hadith,* as reread by the Mahdi and his companions, for social and moral directives. This authoritative rereading opened up numerous possibilities. The Mahdavis recovered the notion of emigration (*hijrah*) as a religious duty (*farz*) defining the community of believers. While emigration was from a cluster of physical and social ties (of place, family, status, and wealth), it was also immigration to new residential communes founded by the Mahdavis. Called *da'irahs* (circles) and modeled after Sufi hospices, they consisted of an enclosed compound run as a self-contained joint family system and governed through the consensus of the brotherhood. Within these communes, the Mahdavis practiced breath meditation (*pas-i anfas*) and an extended but silent liturgy (*zikr-i khafi*) fifteen hours a day, forbade its members to earn a living or receive any kind of sinecure, and distributed all legitimate unsought income daily and equally to all commune members. The purpose of these arrangements was to facilitate the removal of all possible mundane obstacles between man and God and, through the various onerous disciplines, achieve the direct vision of God (*didar*) thought to be characteristic of the spiritual perfection (*ihsan*) of true Muslims in the last days.[4]

There were clear political implications in the notion of a Mahdi come to enforce justice at a time of injustice, the emphasis on emigration with its suggestion of subsequent *jihad,* the practice of defensive takfir, and the active proselytization of the political and religious elite looking for ideological clarity at a time of perceived chaos. The challenge to the state was initially articulated by Sayyid Khundmir, the second *khalifah* of the Mahdi, who argued in response to intensified persecution that "it has now become a general religious duty (*farz-i ʿayn*) for all—men and women, slaves and freemen—to unite and defeat the oppressors so that the faithful might be victorious."[5] Khundmir died in battle shortly thereafter (930/1523), but the Mahdavis continued to pursue the victory of the faithful in Gujarat with the conversion of the Afghan Lohanis and Puladis, in Ahmadnagar with the conversion of members of the Nizamshahi dynasty, and in North India with the activities of Shaykh ʿAbd Allah Niyazi and Shaykh ʿAlaʾi.[6] In the confused and highly volatile political situation of the sixteenth century, it seemed for a time as if the Mahdaviyah, with the support of disaffected Afghans, would sweep across India from their base in Gujarat and establish a millennial empire, just as the Qizilbash had done for the Safavids in neighboring Iran.

Shaykh Mustafa Gujarati was born within this charged political and social climate in Patan in 932/1525, shortly after the martyrdom of Sayyid Khundmir. His father, Miyan ʿAbd ar-Rashid, a descendent of Muhammad ibn al-Hanafiyah and a Kubravi, was a first-generation Mahdavi who had converted at the hands of the Mahdi himself and subsequently attached himself to the daʾirah of Sayyid Khundmir.[7] Shaykh Mustafa received a quality Mahdavi education from his father and others, and rapidly mastered Arabic, Persian, Urdu, and Gujarati. Indeed, there is evidence that Mustafa was being hot-housed by the Mahdavis to serve as an intellectual carrier of their position in the many disputations that were breaking out in Gujarat around this time. At an early age, he was selected, along with the older scholar ʿAbd al-Malik Sajavandi, to reply to a series of questions posed to the Mahdavis by Shaykh Mubarak, the father of Abu al-Fazl and a Mahdavi sympathizer.[8]

Mustafa's reply, later known as the *Hujjat al-balighah*, reveals not only a lively intellect, one already well acquainted with the critical proof texts of the Mahdiship, but also a personal inclination to move beyond questions of proofs to matters of community and mysticism.[9] Around the same time, he wrote a short treatise denying the abrogation of any Qur'anic verse and, perhaps somewhat later, a more formidable treatise (*Javahir at-tasdiq*) on the traditional proofs of the Mahdiship, complete with apparatus and the piling on of textual citations.[10] He would subsequently compile his letters while in prison in Ahmadabad.[11]

Mustafa's influence quickly surpassed that of his father, and he established his own da'irah in Andari, in the vicinity of Patan. He married into the family of ʿAlam Khan Suri, the prominent Afghan *jagirdar* of Morabi, and began to attract as *murids* a large following of Afghan maliks, especially the Puladis, who were beginning to make a bid for power and to whom Mustafa was related by marriage.[12] At the time of Akbar's invasion of Gujarat, then, Shaykh Mustafa held a very high political and religious profile, and he almost immediately attracted the attention of the Mughals. The well-known traditionalist of Patan, Muhammad ibn Tahir, an ex-Bohrah and newly returned from Mecca, is said to have used the occasion of the Mughal invasion to enlist the aid of Shaykh ʿAbd an-Nabi, the chief *sadr*, and Qazi Yaʿqub Manakpuri, the chief *qazi*, in his efforts to enforce a juristic orthodoxy in Gujarat.[13] Political events, especially the Puladi threat, led to Mughal troops being sent against Mustafa, who had fled to Murabi and ʿAlam Khan Suri. His Afghan connections proved a liability, and Mustafa's da'irah was pillaged, eight members (including his father) were executed, the women and children were imprisoned, and Mustafa and his son were brought in chains to Ahmadabad. Here he was tortured and then interrogated at length before being summoned to the more congenial court of Akbar at Fatehpur Sikri. He would reside here for almost two years, participating in the newly launched debates at Akbar's court and recording their proceedings in his *Majalis*. Shaykh Mustafa's health rapidly deteriorated—Bada'uni saw him coughing up blood at the home of the painter Khwajah ʿAbd as-Samad—and Akbar ultimately gave him permission to return to Gujarat.[14] He never made it, dying at Bayanah in 983/1576 at the age of fifty-two.

Portions of five of these imperial sessions have been preserved by the Mahdavis and are known variously as the *Majalis- i khamsah*, *Munazarat*, and *Tahqiqat-i Akbari*. The earliest known manuscript begins abruptly without the usual apparatus:

> These are the sessions of Miyan Shaykh Mustafa held in the presence of the emperor Akbar. This fragment (*qatʿi*) concerns the proofs of the Mahdaviyat and took place before the *ʿulamaʾ* and nobles. It begins: "Shaykh Mustafa said: 'When they brought this helpless one in chains into the assembly and the presence of the *vali,* the other nobles, and many ʿulamaʾ, this helpless one greeted them and they responded. They sat this helpless one in the middle of the circle, and the vali began the interrogation: "What is your name?"'"[15]

Two sessions took place at Ahmadabad at the court of Mirza ʿAziz Koka, and three were at the court of Akbar at Fatehpur Sikri. There is a clear difference between the Ahmadabad and Fatehpur sessions. The former took place in the atmosphere of a trial where Mustafa's life was in peril due to a preexisting *fatva* of execution for heresy and by the political stance of his murids, the Puladis. The Fatehpur sessions, in contrast, occurred in the more relaxed atmosphere of court debate far from the conflict in Gujarat. The sessions also reflect the personalities of the conveners. ʿAziz Koka emerges as a witty and learned scholar in his own right, frequently interrupting the participants either to bring the discussion back on track or to interject some Shiʿite interpretation.[16] The Fatehpur sessions, on the other hand, reveal a congenial if slightly dim-witted and naive Akbar who delights in exemplary tales and poetry, especially *dohras* in the vernacular.[17]

The sociopolitical contexts for these sessions seem relatively straightforward. Akbar would appear to be using Mustafa to play tricks on recalcitrant court ʿulamaʾ. This was the beginning of Akbar's Hindustani turn, when he was attempting to legitimate his rule as an Indo-Muslim emperor, and it was not yet clear whether the ʿulamaʾ could be abashed into supporting his agenda.[18] While we need not accept the *Majalis'* insistence that the ʿulamaʾ were routed by the vigor of Mustafa's arguments, clearly Akbar drew some satisfaction from Mustafa's turning the tables on them, especially ʿAbd an-Nabi, the center of Mustafa's opprobrium, and suggesting that it was not Mustafa or the Mahdavis who were on trial but the imperial ʿulamaʾ and their role in the state and society.

It is possible that Akbar was toying with the notion of a Mahdavi-derived millennial state ideology to legitimate Mughal domination, following the well-known Safavid example. That the *ʿibadat-khanah,* the center of Akbar's imperial debates, was built around this time on the hospice quarters of Shaykh ʿAbd Allah Niyazi, a prominent Mahdavi, does suggest an imperial attempt to co-opt Mahdavi charisma.[19] There are other historical and thematic connections between Mahdavi and Akbari millennialism, although it may be preferable to speak of a common millennial climate rather than a specific Mahdavi source.[20] In any case, the Mahdavis were too closely connected with Afghan soldiery by this time to make it a safe power ideology for Akbar. He would look elsewhere, to the Chishtis, to construct a mystique of legitimacy.

As far as the unfortunate Shaykh Mustafa is concerned, he also had a clear agenda, demonstrated both by the *Majalis* and his substantial collection of letters. Mustafa would appear to be concerned with de-emphasizing the political engagement of earlier Mahdavis, the paradigm of Sayyid Khundmir and Shaykh ʿAlaʾi, and portraying the Mahdavi community as a kind of politically benign millennial mystical order, with the Mahdi as a kind of charismatic foundational *pir* and vali not all that dissimilar to Akbar's own Muʿin ud-Din Chishti. "What would you do," Mustafa asks Akbar, "if someone were to say that Shaykh Muʿin ud-Din was sinful and deviant and leading his murids astray?" Akbar replies, not surprisingly, "I would call him a *kafir* and slay him with my own hands." In the same way, continues Mustafa, "The pir of this servant is the Mahdi of the last days."[21]

Shaykh Mustafa performs this difficult balancing feat without sacrificing essential Mahdavi tenets, but by putting a slightly different gloss on them. In the first session at Ahmadabad, Mustafa explains to ʿAziz Koka that the Mahdavi spiritual genealogy is Sufi (*ahl-i tasavvuf*) and that it is the custom (*mazhab*) of this group to consider the denial (*inkar*) of the words of the vali forbidden (*haram*).[22] The Mahdavis are simply following this well-trodden path. It is true, he adds, that the externalists (*ahl-i zahir*) do deny the authority of the valis, but in the process they do injury to both faith (*iman*) and mystical experience (*maʿrifat*). In any case, this leads them to divisive and aggressive confrontations (*mubahathat va mujavalat*) and away from saintly sobriety (*hoshyar*).

The letters of Shaykh Mustafa, compiled in prison in Ahmadabad and intended for a wider audience, provide further evidence of the attempt to mystify the Mahdaviyah. He is quite explicit concerning his motives: "Just as the assembly of ascetics (*majlis-i fuqaraʾ*) does not lack in religious tales (*hikayat-i dinvi*), so these letters do not lack them. They are written to make an impression on the heart. While the writer does not belong to the group of ascetics (*zumrah-yi fuqaraʾ*), he aspires to resemble (*mushabahat*) them. The tradition (*hukm*), 'who resembles a people (*qawm*), belongs to them,' provides grounds for hope in this endeavor."[23] Mustafa is arguing here for a family resemblance between the Sufi and Mahdavi communities. He demonstrates this resemblance in subtle and linguistically exacting letters, full of Sufisms, often expressed in quite stunning poetry in Persian, Arabic, Urdu, and even *rekhtah* (macaronic Persian-Urdu).[24]

Mustafa's attempt "to make an impression on the heart," referred to in the above letter, found a receptive audience among the mystically inclined at Fatehpur Sikri. Bada'uni clearly saw him as one of his own, an ascetic *ʿalim,* referring in his *Muntakhab at-tawarikh* to Mustafa's letters, "full of the odor of exile and annihilation (*ghurbat va fana'*)," and numbering him among the prominent Sufis (*tariqah-yi faqr va fana'*).[25]

Shaykh Mustafa was not the only Mahdavi looking for rapprochement after a half century of political confrontation, and later Mahdavis would adopt a quietist stance toward the state, with the pirs turning inward to the ritual and theology of the private realm of the da'irah.[26] They would not lose their sense of being a chosen community with a larger moral authority, but the activist political implications of Mahdism would be downplayed, and the history of the earlier phase would be rewritten as an ethic of exemplary martyrdom of misunderstood pirs.

But the sessions are not simply evidence for political and social contexts and agenda. They represent transcriptions of public disputations concerning meaning and action, and they imply a community of discourse and attempts to monopolize ways of speaking about the world. As George Zito has observed: "The true apostate *speaks some other language,* foreign to the parent group. This does not occur in heresy. In heresy, the speaker employs *the same language* as the parent group, retains its values, but attempts to order its discourse to some other end."[27]

Mustafa was a formidable ʿalim and shaykh by any standard, a man of consequence. He knew the language and conventions of the pan-Indian juristic and mystical traditions, and he utilized this knowledge to support a Mahdavi reading at the court. The major themes discussed by Mustafa, the authorities invoked in defense of the themes, the technical vocabulary utilized to discuss them, and the interpretive conventions are, for the most part, familiar ones. To a certain extent, then, the *Majalis* appears as a kind of Islamist discourse over the authority to interpret and reduces to the perceived superior grammar, textual citations, and logic of Shaykh Mustafa. The ʿulama' are made to say in some exasperation: "If we, the learned people in the emperor's assembly, hear even a little of his words, we might imagine that he is right, for his words made an impression on our hearts. For this reason, one must not permit *fitnah*."[28] The issue, they explain, is not if Mustafa is right, but that he is engaged in fitnah (actions threatening the stability and power of a Muslim state) and they have a fatva to that effect. It now remains to act on it. This and other passages witness to the concern for the power and danger of words, proper textual citations, and the mastery of the conventions of disputation. Shaykh Mustafa must be silenced, for he speaks the language of the pious ʿulamaʾ.

But while the *Majalis* can be read as a public transcript disputing the location of heresy, there are elements in it that suggest a hidden transcript of the Gujarati Mahdavis, with its own codes and conventions. This is particularly evident when Mustafa seems to depart from pan-Indian norms of comportment in the disputation, the charge of gynemimesis against Akbar's court ʿulamaʾ is raised, and discursive slippage results.

In the course of the first surviving session at Fatehpur Sikri, the participants broke for the midday prayer. Shaykh ʿAbd an-Nabi, the chief sadr, served as the prayer leader (*imam*) for the group, but Shaykh Mustafa declined to follow his lead in the prayer. ʿAbd an-Nabi was quick to draw the implications of Mustafa's action, asking him why he was calling Muslims kafir. Akbar added, more specifically, "O Shaykh Mustafa, these shaykhs and *mullas* are pious persons showing the way for the people. Why did you not pray behind them?"[29] In a rather startling justification, Shaykh Mustafa explained that he was calling them not kafirs but transvestites or effeminates:

> The Messenger, on whom be peace, has said: "The pursuer of the world is effeminate (*mukhannath*), the pursuer of the next world is feminine (*mu'annath*), and the pursuer of the Lord is masculine (*muzakkar*)." This means that the pursuers of this world are effeminates, the pursuers of the next world are women, and the pursuers of God are men. Likewise, God Almighty has said: "Men (*rijal*) whom neither trade nor sale keeps from the remembrance of God and prayer" [Qur'an 24:37]. This means men who are not occupied in trade nor buying and selling and renounce the world hearing only the *zikr* of God and the *bayan* of the Qur'an and act on that. They are the only real men (*mardan*); the rest are false men (*namardan*). O emperor, exercise justice (*insaf*) and ask ʿAbd an-Nabi and those in the assembly to produce even a single support (*masalah*) from the literature (*kutub*) where the imam might be ef-

> feminate and it is permissible for real men to follow him [in the prayers]. It is overwhelmingly clear from the literature that the *imamat* of the effeminate is not permissible, and for that reason I did not pray behind him.[30]

The Arabic term used by Mustafa here is *mukhannath*, which means transvestite in hadith and effeminate in lexicography.[31] Mustafa renders this in Persian as *na-mard* (false man) and contrasts it with *mard* (real man). He does not employ the term *hijra* (the Indian community of transvestites), the most obvious translation of *mukhannath* in an Indian context, but perhaps the participants would have made the connection.[32]

Despite the outraged reaction to this charge, Shaykh Mustafa does not leave the matter alone but tells Akbar a tale of real men who were sitting in an assembly speaking of the rewards of pilgrimage.[33] An envious effeminate heard them and resolved to proceed to Mecca. After traveling a few miles from his home, he spotted a large shade tree and lay down beneath it, "sighing like a woman." A real man passed by, and the effeminate asked how far it was to Mecca. The man replied, "Many months the way you are going," and told him of the many difficulties of the journey: "O effeminate one, you are here and Mecca there; return home for when you see the sea you will surely perish." The effeminate, alarmed by these words, quickly returned home and, again "sighing like a woman," threw himself down on the cushions. His family were not surprised to find him back, since pilgrimage, they inform him, is "the affair of real men."

In case Akbar may have missed the point, Mustafa carefully draws out the moral of the tale. Real men practice *taqva* (fear of God) and *tavakkul* (trust in God), while false men appear before the king, flatter him and his nobles, and accept his largesse (*vazifat*). Like the effeminate who never reached Mecca, they are caught in a life of comfort and ease and will never reach God. "Go, O effeminate one, this is not the place to pray; for the love of God is not the affair of the effeminate."[34]

Shaykh Mustafa returns to the subject in the next session when the debate addresses the topic of the witness of truth. Mustafa quotes the Qur'an (2:282), "Call to witness two witnesses from your men (*rijal*)," and points out that God specified in this verse real men (*mardan*) and not false men (*na-mardan*).[35] He then cites the previously mentioned hadith of the effeminate pursuers of the world and concludes that since the court ʿulamaʾ are not real men, they are not legitimate witnesses to whether the Mahdi will come or has come and gone. Real men act on their knowledge, he explains, while the false men of the ʿulamaʾ are like asses who carry books on their backs but cannot use them.[36] Flies buzzing around human excrement, he concludes, are more beautiful than the ʿulamaʾ and *fuqaha*ʾ who buzz around the door of the emperor out of greed and wordly-mindedness. How can such persons sight the Mahdi? "The sun has appeared in the sky; what is the profit of sightless eyes?"[37]

Clearly, Mustafa's colorful charge surprised Akbar and the ʿulamaʾ. Indeed, Akbar's initial response was to laugh before turning to the ʿulamaʾ and saying, "See, he does not pray behind you, because you are effeminate and prayer behind the effeminate is not permissible."[38] Akbar then asks Mustafa for a proper answer, but Mustafa does not understand why Akbar is laughing and persists for the remainder of the session in drawing out the charge. Mustafa is not telling a joke for the entertainment of the imperial court.

What should we make of this? At the simplest level, it seems legitimate to consider it part of a strategy to emasculate the court ʿulamaʾ. They are not male, not female, but a third and confused gender. Real men are potent, whereas false men are impotent.[39] And moral authority belongs to real men who think independently and act decisively on their thoughts; false men dither and scurry off to the Hijaz for their opinions. This is not an argument that privileges Arab Islam. Mustafa pillories the ʿulamaʾ who accept the fatvas of the Hijaz rather than create their own in India. The court jurists justify acting on the Meccan fatva of execution of the Mahdavis: "We do not possess the knowledge of the ʿulamaʾ of Mecca. It is not our place to protest or object to their words, but simply to accept the binding authority (*taqlid*) of their words and act on them."[40] Shaykh Mustafa vehemently objects to this contemporary taqlid of Indian scholars to the Meccans, accepting only taqlid to the Qurʾan and the Prophet. Indian Muslims are capable of producing, indeed, are required to produce in his view, an Islam as authentic and legitimate as in the central heartlands. It is the effeminate impotent false Muslims and not the masculine potent real Muslims who practice this illegitimate foreign taqlid in India.

The incident also reveals something of the Gujarati Mahdavi mentality and conceptual resources. The Gujarati Mahdavis of the period tended to think in terms of triads reduced to dyads for the purpose of critical resonance. We have seen how Mustafa employed the triad masculine/feminine/effeminate, but then dropped the feminine, reducing the critical realm of gender to the dyad of real men and false men. Indeed, in both subsequent citations of the hadith of the effeminate, the middle element, the feminine, is not even mentioned.[41] Similarly, the triad real Muslim/real kafir/false Muslim drops the real kafir, the Hindu or Jain, and reduces the actionable political and religious world to the dyad of real Muslims and false Muslims. Hindus or Jains are as irrelevant to this dyad as women were irrelevant to the other.

The secondary literature on the Mahdaviyah has tended to read it as a mass revitalization movement directed against the Hinduizing Islam of the subcontinent. It is seen as part of a larger Muslim "orthodox" reaction with a genealogy extending from the Mahdavis through the Mujaddidi Naqshbandis, perhaps even up to Pakistan. That it ultimately failed, Bazmee Ansari tells us, was only because "the immoderate teachings of the *Mahdi* could not stand up to the mature, sober and Islamically creative message of the Mujaddid."[42] To the extent that a Mahdavi identity is located by modern historians, it is found in a series of reactions to an indigenizing or Hinduizing Indian Islam.

There is very little in Mahdavi primary sources to commend this view. The customs (*rasm*), habit (*'adat*), and innovations (*bid'at*) criticized so soundly by the Mahdi were contaminants not from the non-Muslim environment but from the Muslim.[43] In any case, Mustafa's straw men are the Arabizing, not the indigenizing, 'ulama' of the imperial court. The Mahdavi charge is against false Muslims who do not take Islam seriously, and their solution is a radical millennial space on Indian earth: the faithful, real men, who through constant *zikr* and trust in God obtain within the communes the vision of God with their own eyes. The Mahdavis construct an identity as a righteous Muslim community within Islam and within India, and not as a defense against the non-Muslim environment. It is not an identity constructed in opposition to a Hindu "other."

The modern reading of the Mahdaviyah movement also resonates within larger historiographic assumptions. Like national character, Indo Muslim identity is usually read as dyadic, symbiotic, and oppositional in nature. It is dyadic in the sense that it is paired with some other group, symbiotic in that it feeds off a cluster of identifications of the other group, and oppositional in that it exists within a context of confrontations. In the case of Indian Islam, the dyad, symbiote, and opposition are usually thought to be the Indian environment read as Hindu. Elements of this assumption are shared by those who emphasize the Islamic or the Indian in the Indo-Islamic, and it implies the existence and importance to identity of what Wilfred Cantwell Smith has termed "the crystallization of religious communities."[44] Smith would place this development squarely in the Mughal period and relate it to empire, while others would place it much later and relate it to imperial decline, colonialism, or modernity.

While the Mahdavi evidence supports the notion of a series of self-aware Muslim communities within premodern India (sometimes cohering, sometimes conflicting), it contradicts the notion that identity as a community is necessarily formed in opposition to the Hindu or indigenized environment. It is not an essence but a community that is being constructed, and there is no demonic Hindu "other" lurking in the background definition. This should not be taken, however, as evidence for some kind of benign Indo-Muslim apartheid, where Muslims inhabit India but are not part of it. Shaykh Mustafa himself frequently shifted registers and codes from Arabic to Persian to Urdu and back again, even producing some startling mixed Persian-Urdu rekhtah, and he did this without apology.[45] His descendants, the Mustafa'iyan, along with other Mahdavis, continued this process of straddling speech communities. The expanded repertoire of terms and symbols exists without apparent conflict or crisis of conscience: *prem* and *prit* alongside *ʿishq* and *mahabbat; jap* with *zikr; prana* with *ruh; mitra* with *maʿshuq* or *dost; purush* with *insan; patti* with *khudavand.*[46] Real Muslims can employ both terms, within varying contexts. Linguistic hybridization does occur, as other genres are revoiced within a Mahdavi context, but it is neither oppositional nor syncretist. The symbolic repertoire expands in a complementary fashion and not by a series of essential exclusions.

What seems to be distinctive about premodern Indo-Muslim identity, as evidenced by the *Majalis,* is the degree to which it departs from assumptions that emerged and became reified during the modern period. To a major extent, colonial modes of "knowing" Islam, reproduced in nationalisms, have contaminated our understanding of Muslim identity formation and maintenance in premodern India. By contrast, the Mahdavi instance suggests that Indo-Muslim identity was embedded within a larger number of discrete primary communities with shared symbolic and social resources, and was not yet objectified in terms of an oppositional Hindu "other." These primary communities could be regional, but more often in imperial polities they spanned regions. The multiplex nature of these communities is noteworthy, as is the plasticity of their interplay. They conjoined or clashed for the purposes of material or symbolic exchange, but the cultural product that emerged varied with the idiom and social location brought to the exchange. The social fabric was complex and changeable, and the signs bearing it were multiplex. Thus, while Mahdavi identity was constructed and maintained through the unique space and rituals of the da'irah and personified in a Mahdi ushering in an end-game of time to validate that identity, the Mahdavis also represented or transmitted their identities variously, depending on the social or cultural location of the exchange and of its participants, coresiding and code-switching in turn as the need occurred. Dissonance could occur and frequently did. At times, as in the *Majalis*, Muslims spoke the same language and shared similar views of the world; at other times, they diverged and spoke past each other. One group saw a joke, but Shaykh Mustafa was not laughing.

Notes

This essay is based on research funded in part by a Canada Research Fellowship and a President's Research Grant. I am indebted to the Mahdavis of Hyderabad and Palanpur, especially Sayyid Khuda Bakhsh Khundmiri and Sayyid Da'ud ʿAlim Palanpuri, for their hospitality and generous access to sources. Naturally, the views expressed in this essay are my own.

1. The biography of the Mahdi given here is reconstructed from the earliest collections of traditions, assembled by Bandagi Miyan Vali ibn Yusuf (d. after 955/1548), *Insaf-namah* (Hyderabad: Shamsiyah, 1947), and the first cohesive biography by Bandagi Miyan Shah ʿAbd ar-Rahman (d. after 950/1543), *Sirat-i Imam Mahdi Mawʿud khalifat allah* (Hyderabad: Jamʿiyat-i Mahdaviyah, 1948). Later Mahdavis wrote prodigious biographies of the Mahdi, but these are less useful for the historical Mahdi than for subsequent developments. See, e.g., the most important of the Mughal period biographies, Bandagi Miyan Sayyid Burhan ud-Din (d. 1062/1651), *Shavahid al-vilayat* (Hyderabad: Jamʿiyat-i Mahdaviyah, 1959).

2. Vali, *Insaf-namah*, p. 12.

3. The companions of the Mahdi sought consensus (*ijmaʿ*) in a series of authoritative *mahzars* that summarized their agreement on the Mahdi's position or sayings on specific issues. They normally were signed by all those present. For the process, see Vali, *Insaf-namah*, p. 3. A well-known example is preserved as the *Mahzar-i Shah Dilavar* (Hyderabad: Aʿzam Steam Press, 1941).

4. The process of community definition was protracted and contested. The earliest attempt to define essentials belonged to Bandagi Miyan Sayyid Khundmir (d. 930/1523), *Umm al-ʿaqaʾid* (Hyderabad: Jamʿiyat-i Mahdaviyah, n.d.), and Mughal era formulations of community rules (*ahkam*) can be found in Bandagi Miyan Sayyid Burhan ud-Din (d. 1062/1651), *Hadiqat al-haqaʾiq haqiqat al-daqaʾiq: daftar duvum*, ms., Kutub-khanah-yi Sayyid Da'ud ʿAlim Palanpuri, 2:182–84, and Bandagi Miyan Shah Qasim Mujtahid (d. 1043/1633), *Jamiʿal-usul* (Hyderabad: Jamʿiyat-i Mahdaviyah, 1944). Also see the modern Urdu discus-

sion by Sayyid Qutb ud-Din Khub Miyan Khundmiri Palanpuri, *Risalah-yi hudud-i da'irah-i Mahdaviyat* (Hyderabad: Idarah-yi Tabligh-i Mahdaviyah, 1990).

5. Khundmir argues (Vali, *Insaf-namah*, p. 206) that the legal (*shar'*) position here is equivalent to a case where Muslim cities have been attacked and a defensive jihad becomes incumbent on all Muslims. The ensuing conflict is formalized by Mahdavis as the incident of *qatalu wa-qutilu* (meaning "they fought and were slain") and read as a fulfillment of Qur'an 3:195. See Vali, *Insaf-namah*, pp. 205–10, and Miyan Sayyid Husayn ʿAlim Sayyidan Miyan (d. after 1106/1694), *Tazkirat as-salihin* (Hyderabad: Jamʿiyat-i Mahdaviyah, 1961), pp. 57–98.

6. The political sympathizers of the Mahdaviyah are segregated into four separate chapters of Malik Muhammad Sulayman (d. 1232/1816), *Khatam-i Sulaymani*, ms., Kutub-khanah-yi Sayyid ʿAbd al-Karim Yadillahi, vol. 4, ff. 356–497.

7. Biographical information for Shaykh Mustafa and his family comes primarily from Sulayman, *Khatam-i Sulaymani*, vol. 3, ff. 95, 213–36. Also see Bandagi Miyan Shah Qasim Mujtahid (d. 1043/1633), *Asami-yi musaddiqin* (Hyderabad: Jamʿiyat-i Mahdaviyah, 1972), pp. 6–7, and *Fazilat afzal al-qawm* (Hyderabad: Jamʿiyat-i Mahdaviyah, 1970), and the non-Mahdavi ʿAbd al-Qadir Bada'uni (d. ca. 1024/1615), *Muntakhab at-tawarikh*, ed. Maulvi Ahmad ʿAli (Calcutta: Asiatic Society of Bengal, 1865–1869), 3:50–51. Bada'uni tells us that Mustafa's father was a Bohrah, but this is not confirmed by Mahdavi sources. Mustafa's unnamed mother was the daughter of Qutb-i Jahan, a prominent Sufi of Patan.

8. Bandagi Miyan ʿAbd al-Malik Sajavandi (d. 981/1574), *Minhaj at-taqwim* (Hyderabad: Jamʿiyat-i Mahdaviyah, 1951); Bandagi Miyan Shaykh Mustafa Gujarati (d. 983/1576), *Risalah al-hujjat al-balighah* (Hyderabad: Jamʿiyat-i Mahdaviyah, 1958). Mubarak's queries are preserved in Persian in both works, although Sajavandi responds in Arabic and Mustafa in Persian. While Mustafa does not mention Mubarak by name, Sajavandi does (p. 3), and there seems little reason to doubt the Mahdavi tradition that both works are in response to Mubarak.

9. Mustafa Gujarati addresses such matters as mystical audition, dress, and ritual in *Risalah al-hujjat al-balighah*, pp. 32–50.

10. Mustafa Gujarati, *Risalah dar bahth-i nasikh va mansukh* (Hyderabad: Jamʿiyat-i Mahdaviyah, 1982); *Javahir at-tasdiq* (Hyderabad: Jamʿiyat-i Mahdaviyah, 1988). The latter, with its careful listing of texts and authorities, is useful in locating the textual and conceptual resources of Mahdavis of the period.

11. Mustafa Gujarati, *Makatib* (Hyderabad: Jamʿiyat-i Mahdaviyah, 1957). Bada'uni refers to these letters in his *Muntakhab* (3:51).

12. The Puladis (aka Fuladis) are discussed in Sulayman, *Khatam-i Sulaymani*, vol. 4, ff. 436–44, and Qasim, *Asami*, p. 6. Malik Shah Muhammad Puladi was the nephew of Shaykh Mustafa. The Puladi role in Gujarati politics is noted in all standard Mughal histories. See, e.g., Khvajah Nizam ud-Din Ahmad (d. 1003/

1594), *Tabaqat-i Akbari,* trans. B. De (Calcutta: Asiatic Society of Bengal, 1927–39), 3:394–414.

13. Sulayman, *Khatam-i Sulaymani,* vol. 4, ff. 95, 221–26. For a non-Mahdavi view of Muhammad ibn Tahir, see Shaykh ʿAbd al-Haqq Muhaddith Dihlavi, *Akhbar al-akhyar* (Delhi: Muhammad Mirza Khan, 1866), p. 268.

14. Bada'uni, *Muntakhab,* 3:51.

15. When I cite the *Majalis* of Mustafa Gujarati, I am referring to the untitled manuscript preserved in the Kutub-khanah-yi Sayyid Da'ud ʿAlim Palanpuri. A marginal note indicates that it was copied by Mustafa's son, Faqir Jalal. There are two lithograph traditions: the older *Tahqiqat-i Akbari* (n.p.: Shin-Pa, n.d.), and the much reprinted *Majalis-i khamsah* (Hyderabad: Jamʿiyat-i Mahdaviyah, 1946). The manuscript differs from both lithographs in the order and length of the sessions and the sequence and substance of the questions and answers. While retaining the abrupt quality of the work, the lithographs have polished Mustafa's prose, improved the citations, and added some formulaic aspects required of disputations (*munazarat*).

16. See, e.g., *Majalis,* ff. 9–12b.

17. The sessions with Akbar contain all of the *dohras* of the text (95.23b–24) and, in contrast to the Ahmadabad sessions, Arabic is usually carefully translated into Persian for Akbar's benefit, although the Hindi *dohras* are not.

18. The best discussion of the various phases remains Iqtidar Alam Khan, "The Nobility under Akbar and the Development of His Religious Policy," *Journal of the Royal Asiatic Society* (1968): 29–36. Also note the suggestive comments of Bruce Lawrence, "The City as an Intellectual Center," in *Fatehpur-Sikri,* ed. Michael Brand and Glenn D. Lowry (Bombay: Marg, 1987), pp. 83–92.

19. Badaʿuni, *Muntakhab,* 2:201.

20. A crucial conduit of Mahdavi ideas into Akbar's court would have been Shaykh Mubarak and his sons, Abu al-Fazl and Fayzi, major architects of Akbar's political millennialism. While Abu al-Fazl would ultimately gloss over his father's well-known Mahdavi episode (Shaykh Abu al-Fazl ʿAllami [d. 1011/1602], *Seh daftar* [Lucknow: Bayt as-Sultanat, 1853], pp. 242–44), clearly Mubarak was a sympathizer and his sons would have been well acquainted with Mahdavi perspectives. Not only is Mubarak's correspondence with Mahdavis preserved (see note 8 above), but Sayyid Yusuf wrote a biography of his great-grandfather, the Mahdi, at the request of Fayzi himself. See Bandagi Miyan Sayyid Yusuf (d. 1026/1617), *Matlaʿ al-vilayat,* ms., Kutub-khanah-yi Sayyid Muhammad Asadullah Ishaqi. Common elements in Mahdavi and Akbari millennialism include the attack on taqlid, the concern with the eschatological properties of the year 1000, the emphasis on authoritative *vilayat,* and the use of elusive experimental poetry as expressive of that vilayat.

21. *Majalis,* f. 17b.

22. *Majalis,* ff. 3–3b.

23. *Makatib,* pp. 38–39.

24. See, e.g., *Makatib*, pp. 141–42, for a long *rekhtah*.

25. Bada'uni, *Muntakhab*, 3:50–51. Bada'uni expands on his complex understanding of the Mahdaviyah in his *Najat ar-rashid*, ed. Sayyid Mu'in al-Haqq (Lahore: Idarah-yi Tahqiqat-i Pakistan, Danishgah-yi Panjab, 1972), pp. 77–82.

26. Around this time, a tradition was circulated to the effect that Humayun had become a Mahdavi supporter (*mu'taqid*) while in exile in Gujarat and that he had left written instructions to his descendants to follow his example. See Burhan ud-Din, *Shavahid*, p. 151.

27. George V. Zito, "Toward a Sociology of Heresy," *Sociological Analysis* 44 (1983): 125 (original emphasis).

28. *Majalis*, ff. 9–9b.

29. *Majalis*, f. 17b.

30. *Majalis*, ff. 17b–18.

31. Everett K. Rowson, "The Effeminates of Early Medina," *Journal of the American Oriental Society* 111 (1991): 671–93.

32. For a discussion of India's third gender, see Serena Nanda, *Neither Man nor Woman: The Hijras of India* (Belmont, Calif.: Wadsworth, 1990).

33. *Majalis*, ff. 18b–19.

34. *Majalis*, f. 18b.

35. *Majalis*, ff. 23–25.

36. *Majalis*, ff. 23b–24. Mustafa's frequent reference to the 'ulama' as asses or as riding on asses might evoke for literate Muslims the traditional image of the one-eyed Dajjal riding an ass at the end of time.

37. *Majalis*, f. 24b.

38. *Majalis*, f. 18.

39. In a somewhat similar manner, Mustafa's father, 'Abd ar-Rashid, earlier had used the analogy of judicial divorce (*tafriq*) for physical impotence to justify the right of Mahdavis to divorce their spiritually impotent teachers (*ustadan*). In both cases, any dishonor (*'ayb*) involved in the divorce belonged to the impotent and not the potent. See Bandagi Miyan 'Abd ar-Rashid (d. 980/1572), *Naqliyat* (Hyderabad: Jam'iyat-i Mahdaviyah, 1955), pp. 13–14.

40. *Majalis*, f. 9b.

41. *Majalis*, ff. 19, 23.

42. A. S. Bazmee Ansari, "Sayyid Muhammad Jawnpuri and His Movement," *Islamic Studies* 2 (1963): 60.

43. Vali, *Insaf-namah*, p. 10.

44. Wilfred Cantwell Smith, *On Understanding Islam: Selected Studies* (Delhi: Idarah-i Adabiyat-i Delli, 1981), pp. 177–96.

45. Letter 46 of his *Makatib*, e.g., begins in Arabic, follows with a Persian verse, returns to Arabic, then proceeds to a Hindi dohra. Letter 74 contains a long Persian-Urdu *tarji'band*. Also see Sulayman, *Khatam-i Sulaymani*, vol. 3, ff. 226–27, for a *khayal* of Mustafa.

46. The Mahdavi contribution to early Urdu literature is discussed in an important article by Mahmud Sherani, "Da'irah ke Mahdaviyun ka Urdu adab ke ta'mir men hissah," *Oriental College Magazine* 17 (November 1940): 27–92; 17 (February 1941): 3–38. Also see Sayyid Shams ud-Din Mustafa'i, *Istiqamat fi ud-din* (Karachi: Sayyid Kamal ud-Din, 1977), a Mahdavi rejoinder to Sherani, and Sayyid Nusrat Mahdi Yadillahi, *Urdu adab men Mahdaviyun ka hissah* (Hyderabad: I'jaz Printing Press, 1984).

9

Shari'a and Governance in the Indo-Islamic Context

Muzaffar Alam

The relevance of *shari'a* for the discussion of medieval Indian politics cannot be denied. But many modern historians have used the term only in its juristic sense and thus have overlooked the varieties of its use in nonjuridical literature. Even in the juristic *shari'a*, there is a measure of flexibility. The accepted doctrine of diversity (*ikhtilaf*), resulting in the plurality of the schools of jurisprudence, and above all, the diversity within the schools in the specific verdicts (*fatwas*) of the theologians, testify to this flexibility. However, I am not concerned here with the latitude allowed to the jurist in practice. This remained confined within the ambit of accepted juridical principles. When jurists tolerated a non-*shari'a* act, they still regarded it as an offense and suggested its expiation (*kaffara*). I have in mind, rather, the differing senses in which the Muslim philosophers and intellectuals used the term in their politico-cultural writings. Although originating often as works of dissent, many of these writings were gradually integrated into the larger body of Islamic literature. Thus, like the *shari'a* of the jurist, the *shari'a* of these philosophers and intellectuals deserves equal notice for a fuller appreciation of the nature of medieval Muslim politics. If we accept an uncompromisingly fixed juridical meaning for the *shari'a*, we concede not simply the theologians' construction of the term but also their criteria for evaluating the medieval past and for evaluating religion as a matter simply of religiosity or irreligiosity.

For political philosophers, and also for rulers, the term *shari'a* carried different meanings in different contexts. In some political writings—as in those of Zia-ud-Din Barani, the noted historian and political theorist of pre-Mughal India who carried forward in a measure the Perso-Turkic tradition in the Islamic East—*shari'a* was seen as totally opposed to "secular" state legislation, which was tolerated primarily only as a device for the *shari'a*'s final glory. On the other hand, in some post-Mongol texts on political norms, notably the portions of *akhlaq* digests dealing with governance, "secular" legislation was integral to the enforcement of *shari'a*. One explanation of this, as we will see below, was that the authors of these texts used the term *shari'a* in two different senses. I will try to discuss these two sets of political writings, and their view of *shari'a*, with a view to understanding some of the principles and practice of governance under the sultans of Delhi and in Mughal India and the implications of these for Islamic identity.

The two sets of writings, it must be noted at the outset, represent two different traditions, but they have often been mentioned as examples of "mirrors of the princes" literature without any regard for the distinction between the two.[1] Some of the *akhlaq* texts illustrate the appropriation in the medieval Muslim intellectual world of non-Islamic and, strictly juristically, even anti-Islamic ideas. The effort in the writings was, as we will see below, to provide a philosophical, nonsectarian, and humanistic solution to the emergent problems that Muslim society encountered. There is a redefinition of *shari'a* in a measure in these texts, while in other texts on the principles of governance, the narrow legalistic sense of the term has generally been accepted uncritically. With a radical meaning given to *shari'a*, these *akhlaq* digests signified a protest against such a strictly legalistic approach. This protest was, however, not meant to provoke the theologians. While it encouraged dissidence, it also paved the way for an alternative definition of *shari'a* to become part of the generally acceptable and "orthodox" Islam.

Shari'a in Early Islamic Writings

The first notable work that cleverly integrated the demands of the *shari'a* with the heritage of the classical Islamic past, and at the same time manipulated current opinion, was *al-Ahkam al-Sultaniya* of Abul Hasan al-Mawardi (974–1058). For Mawardi, the authority of the caliph was supreme, and among his important duties were defense of *shari'a*, dispensation of justice according to *shari'a*, and organization of *jihad*.[2] Nizam al-Mulk Tusi was another notable political theorist of the eleventh century. He wrote his *Siyasat Nama* or *Siyar al Muluk* in the time of Malik Shah Saljuq (1027–92). The ideals and the models to which Nizam al-Mulk appealed were most often ancient Persian ones. The caliph for him and for his Saljuq master was simply like a pension holder.[3] Even for institutions for which one could have found precedents in the classical Islamic period, Nizam al-Mulk looked to ancient Persia. While Mawardi, for instance, legitimated hereditary rulership from the case of Umar's nomination by Abu Bakr,[4] Nizam al-Mulk did so from the examples of ancient Persia.[5] But for Nizam al-Mulk, too, defense of *shariʿa* and keeping the true faith alive were among the most important duties of the king. Thus he characterized the Batinis, the Qarmaties, and others as "heretics" and as "enemies of state and Islam," and made a strong plea for their ruthless suppression.[6]

Between Mawardi's apologia for the Caliphate and Nizam al-Mulk's appeal to Persian kingship was Ghazali's (1058–1111) position of compromise in his celebrated *Nasihat al-Muluk,* written around the same time and also addressed to a Saljuq sultan, Sanjar bin Malik Shah (1105–18).[7] "Constituent authority," in Ghazali's view, belonged to the sultan, but the validity of the sultan's government depended on his oath of allegiance to the caliph and the latter's appointment of him. Ghazali's principal concern was the execution of the *shariʿa,* but his ideas were also influenced by Sufi ethics.[8] What is of greater significance for our purpose is the fact that along with the maintenance of the *shariʿa,* Ghazali lays equal emphasis on the practical duties of the ruler, according to the principles of justice.[9]

In a measure, Ghazali laid down theoretical grounds to support the positions of those writers who later justified the ordinary duties of the king on grounds of political expediency.[10] However, the debate on political norms had so far been governed by the demands of *shariʿa* only in its narrow juridical sense. Many political actions juristically in opposition to *shariʿa* were tolerated only as necessary evils. There was no attempt at giving *shariʿa* a meaning different from the one developed in law books.

The early Indo-Islamic political theory enunciated in Fakhr-i Mudabbir's *Adab-al-Harb wash Shujaʿa,* and more pronouncedly in Zia-ud-Din Barani's *Fatawa-i Jahandari,* was just an extension of this tradition. As a matter of fact, in the hostile and "infidel" Indian environment, where early Muslim rulers were uncertain of their position, the limitations of this tradition were evident, as we will see below.

Fakhr-i Mudabbir's *Adab-al-Harb*

Fakhr-i Mudabbir's book is not strictly an Indo-Turkic text, but it has a strong bearing on the early Muslim state in northern India.[11] The book comprises more than thirty-five chapters. Twenty-seven of these chapters pertain principally to warfare, army organization, the drawing of battle lines, and weaponry. Seven chapters, which have also been edited and published separately as *Ain-i-Kishwardari,* relate to the norms of governance.[12] Right at the opening of the book, the author emphasizes the finality of Islam. The mission of the prophets, 124,000 in all, was to retrieve humanity from "the darkness of infidelity to the light of Islam." With the advent of Muhammad, the last and most revered of the prophets, the world finally was embellished with *shari'a-i-Islamia;* all other faiths were canceled. In the subsequent sections of the text, Islam provides the structure within which Fakhr-i Mudabbir locates the various categories of battles. The most "sacred" battles were those fought against infidels for the glory of Islam; those killed in these "holy" battles were martyrs (*shahids*) and those who survived were *ghazis.* All other battles, whether fought against other Muslims for superior power, to ensure the smooth flow of revenue, or to subdue criminals, were inferior and avoidable.[13]

Fakhr-i-Mudabbir's emphasis on the overwhelming responsibility of upholding Islam is shown in his devoting an entire chapter to the merits of *jihad.* Again, chapter 26 of the book details the manner in which *jizya* was to be collected from the *zimmis.* "The people of the *zimma* should not ride on horses, should not wear clothes like Muslims or live like Muslims."[14] Mudabbir adds that those Muslims who turn away from Islam become renegades. If they stick to heresy for three days, they should first be persuaded to come back to Islam, but if they refuse to return to the Faith, they should be executed. Apostates should also lose their claim to property, regaining it only if they come back to Islam. He was more charitable to women. He declared that if a woman turns apostate she should not be killed but imprisoned until she repents and embraces Islam again.[15]

Mudabbir recommends state offices only for religious, pious, and God-fearing Muslims, whose primary concern was to protect and promote the rights of the Muslims (*haqq-i Musalmani*) and to avoid circumstances in which Muslims were liable to be offended (*azar-i dil-i Musalman*). But in the final analysis, it is the personal religiosity of an official that determines his ability to discharge his responsibility as promoter of Islam.[16] This is illustrated in Mudabbir's chapter on justice. Here, the qualities that he lists for the *amir-i-dad* are revealing. This was an important office, next only to the exalted position of king, and thus it was fitting that the person adorning this office be appointed from among the princes and the sons of high nobles, Saiyids, and other members of noble lineage. It was equally important, however, that he be kind to the people and familiar with *shari'a*. Mudabbir stressed that during court petitions the *amir-i-dad* should take all possible care that the rights of Muslims be not violated.[17] To underscore that all "virtues" rest ultimately in the followers of Islam, Mudabbir recommended that the judiciary be peopled with God-fearing Muslims alone. Those who presented the cases of petitioners and respondents to the office of the *amir-i-dad* were also required to be good Muslims. This was the only way to ensure the efficient functioning of the judicial apparatus, to benefit the Muslims.[18]

Even if emulating the examples of the ancient Sassanid kings, Fakhr-i Mudabbir's king was thus to manage the state for the sole purpose of protecting and promoting the interests of the Muslims and their *shari'a*.

Zia Barani's *Fatawa-i Jahandari:* Construction of the Past

Zia-ud-Din Barani is one of the most widely read authors of pre-Mughal India. He was not simply a continuer of the Nizam al-Mulk/Ghazali tradition. He built his own theory in the new Indian context with a view to protecting and promoting the interests of *shari'a*. In a modern evaluation, he has been adjudged "the first theoretician to justify secular laws among the Mussalmans."[19] This assessment seems to me anachronistic. We need to scrutinize Barani's political views and the adoption of such laws in context. Significantly, there were for Barani despicably sinful repercussions for the Musalmans who enacted or lived with these laws. I have tried to study his thought here in the light of his *Fatawa-i Jahandari*, recognizing that without examining his history and other works, this assessment of Barani's ideas must remain tentative.

The *Fatawa* is principally a text on abstract principles, but discussion on principles is usually followed in the text by detailed historical anecdotes to illustrate and legitimatize these principles. The discussion on almost every theme is thus divided into two parts, intimately woven into each other. Each shapes the other, and together they bring into relief Barani's political thought. We cannot come to a proper understanding of Barani's political doctrine if we separate his sections on historical anecdotes, "authentic" or otherwise, from those on abstract principles. By choosing and selecting his historical characters, Barani attempted to resolve, in theory at least, the problems of governance of his own time. He created the past with a purpose.

In this context I would like to add that in the available English translation of the text much of Barani's construction of the past has been dismissed summarily. The translator, Mrs. Afsar Salim Khan, justifies her dismissals on the grounds that the events described are based on sources of dubious authenticity and that there are obvious chronological discrepancies and errors. She rejects a large part of the historical part of the text as "fallacious," "fictitious," a "figment of Barani's imagination," "historically impossible," and stemming from Barani's "stupendous" and "frightful ignorance" of history and geography.[20]

But it is difficult to accept Mrs. Khan's views. Barani was not an ordinary writer. He was, in fact, one of the most literate historians and theorists of his time. As a courtier adviser (*nadim*) of Muhammad bin Tughlaq, a most literate ruler of pre-Mughal India, he could not have afforded to be ignorant of the documented, and what Mrs. Khan considers the authentic, historical past. He compiled a biography of the prophet Muhammad (*Na'ṭ-i Muhammadi*) and translated an Arabic history of the Barmaki *wazirs* of the Abbasids (*Tarikh-i-Baramika*). His original plan was to write a world history, which he abandoned because he believed the task had been performed successfully by his predecessor, Minhaj-us-Siraj, in his *Tabaqat-i-Nasiri*. He later decided to resume the thread where Minhaj had left off. Amir Khurd and Shams Siraj Afif, Barani's two eminent junior contemporaries, admired his knowledge of history and literary brilliance.[21] It seems likely, therefore, that Barani exercised choice not only in what he included in his *Fatawa* but also in the ways that he presented and projected the events of the past in the text. His al-Mamun, the illustrious Abbasid Caliph, for instance, emerges in the *Fatawa* as a protector of Sunni Islam and an admirer of orthodox religious scholars like Imam Ahmad bin Hanbal and Imam Yahya. Evidently Barani's portrayal of al-Mamun is contrary to what we know from the "authentic" histories of the time about the caliph's Muʿtazilite leanings and the two Imams' indignation over this. In Barani's view, however, Sunni orthodox Islam achieved brilliance in al-Mumun's time. The caliph therefore is his hero and should be in the company of the Imams he adored, and under no circumstances associated with the Muʿtazilites, whom Barani despised and regarded as heretics.[22]

Barani's portrayal of Mahmud illustrates best how his theory is linked to the history he creates. His Mahmud was inspired right from childhood with the desire to extirpate infidelity and idolatry, and he launched campaigns into India to annihilate the Brahmans, the leaders of the false religion. Mahmud, as depicted by Barani, was not influenced by the love of wealth; instead, the desire for martyrdom always illuminated his noble soul. He never accepted presents from non-Muslims to spare their lives. If only he were able to launch one more campaign in India, Barani writes, he would have exterminated all the Hindus with his holy sword. Barani's Mahmud, like Barani, detested the Muʿtazalites and the philosophers, and considered them to be the worst enemies of the "True Faith." If only Bu Ali Sina, the progenitor of Greco-Hellenic philosophy in Islamic lands, had fallen into Mahmud's hands, he would have torn him to pieces and served his flesh to the kites. Mahmud never missed any of his congregational prayers. One of the most powerful rulers of his age, Qadr Khan of Khita, embraced Islam at his hands.[23]

There is little purpose in looking for evidence for this Mahmud in the "authentic" accounts of Mahmud's contemporaries. Barani's Mahmud is possibly close to the traditions and legends that had surrounded the memory of the sultan. But in the *Fatawa*, Mahmud is used as a model ruler of the ideal Muslim state that Barani wished to be built in Hindustan. The Muslim king should not be content with merely levying the *jizya* and *kharaj* from the Hindus. He should, like Mahmud, establish the supremacy of Islam by overthrowing infidelity and by slaughtering its leaders (*imams*), who in India are the Brahmans.[24] Justice was to be the hallmark of this state, and in Barani's view, justice could only be ensured by a strong, religion-protecting (*din-parwar*) Muslim ruler.[25]

Barani's definition of the ideal Muslim ruler, of course, drew on a number of sources. An anecdote mentioned in the *Fatawa* is particularly helpful to illustrate this. It relates to the conflict between two political figures, Yaqub Lais and Ismaʿil Samani, for control of Baghdad, then capital city of the Islamic world. For Barani, Yaqub was not a Muslim in the true sense of the word because he had created problems for the caliph in Baghdad. On the other hand, Ismaʿil Samani was a good Muslim because he had delivered the caliph and the city of Baghdad from the terrors Yaqub Lais unleashed in the capital. Moreover, Ismaʿil Samani was endeared to Barani because he took pride in the fact that he never violated the injunctions of *shariʿa*.[26] A political, nonreligious event was thus used as a historical precedent to shape the definition of the ideal Muslim ruler.

But history, though frequently invoked by Barani, is not always easy for Barani to deal with. He is uncomfortable with the influence on Muslim history of the non-Islamic Sassanid state system. Throughout his *Fatawa* an unmistakable uneasiness prevails. In fact, the whole text, including the portions where he takes up the discussion of "secular principles," appears to be an attempt to check and undo this malaise. Unlike Fakhr-i Mudabbir, Barani does not simply inherit a tradition and pass it on. He intervenes instead to try to resolve the dilemma posed by the conflict between the concrete realities of Muslim politics and the theory of the *shariʿa*. Theorists in the past had also attempted to resolve this dilemma. But this had been done either by silently accepting and accommodating the non-Islamic, as in the political commentary of Nizam al-Mulk Tusi, or, as in the case of Ghazali, by reinterpreting the *shariʿa* to adjust it to the non-Islamic presence. Barani reacts to this problem by repudiating outright the non-Islamic. The Iranian pattern of governance, or *padshahi*, is to Barani a sin; the ruler who practices this system of governance is a sinner. True religion, according to Barani, consists only in following in the footsteps of the prophet Muhammad, son of Abdullah Quraishi. Barani concedes that the ruler who desires to govern effectively may have to follow the policies of the ancient Iranian kings. But since "between the traditions of the Prophet and his mode of life and living, and the customs of the Iranian emperors, and their mode of life and living, there is a complete contradiction and total opposition," appropriation of the latter by a Muslim ruler is an offense to the law.[27] To atone for the offense and provide for his own salvation, the sultan's only recourse is to continue to perform religious duties in an exaggerated manner.

Barani thus tampers with a developing political tradition in the Islamic world, and he justifies his position by consigning the antecedents of this tradition to the political rather than to a religious domain. He is forced to do this because the theologian in him surfaces each time he theorizes on a political doctrine. Despite his realization of the benefits of drawing on the political precedents of the past, he is skeptical of their long-term value for the upholding of Islam. But his attitude creates more problems than it solves. It defines more rigidly the schism between the political and the religious, and it reduces the scope for political maneuverability. Barani sketches a rather impracticable framework for governance, and yet the ruler who does not follow it does not deserve, in his eyes, to be called a Muslim.[28]

In Barani's world there were, in fact, only two diametrically opposed life patterns, one in conformity with *shariʿa*, as theologians understood the term, and another against it. Even the normal, universal, human qualities are slotted by him into binary opposition, as either Islamic or anti-Islamic, *sharaʿi* or *ghair-sharaʿi*. This is indicated in the chapters in the *Fatawa* on royal will (*azm*), tyranny and despotism (*satihash-o-istibdad*), and justice (*'adl*). For Barani, royal will has no independent character of its own; it is determined by the nature of the objective it aims at achieving. A political act intended to promote the interests of Muslims is to him laudatory, however detrimental it may be to others. No royal action taken in the cause of Islam can be conceived as despotic. The royal resolve that offends, ignores, or overlooks the demands of Sunni Islam is nothing but tyranny.[29] Likewise, according to Barani, only a pious Muslim ruler can deliver justice to the people. To justice, too, he denies independent existence. Justice is to be sought because its enforcement creates conditions in which "molesters of the Faith (*din*) and *shari'a* are disgraced and overthrown, . . . the glory of Islam is raised." Justice flows only in the situation when the king truthfully follows the commands of religion.[30]

Barani is familiar with Plato and Aristotle, the two oft-cited Greek philosophers in Islamic literature, but he only hints at the importance of reason and rationality. He also draws on the prevailing memory of the legendary justice of the Sassanid ruler, Anushirwan. But he quickly balances this by describing anecdotes of justice associated with Umar bin Khattab, the Second Pious Caliph of Islam. What is more significant is that he is uneasy with the fact that it was Anushirwan, a Sassanid (non-Islamic) ruler, whose image was as the ideal just ruler. He thus postulates a formula to resolve this problem. He divides justice into two categories: justice that guarantees universal equality (*adl-i musawat-talabi-ye am*) and justice that ensures only a special or limited equality (*adl-i musawat-i talabi-ye khass*). The former is the justice represented by the Islamic caliph Umar; here the ruler obliterates the distinction between the ruler and his subjects and imparts justice by mingling with them as one of them. The latter form of justice is represented by the Sassanid Anushirwan—a system in which the king retains his distinguished regal status and delivers justice to the people from that exalted position. The ruler thus ensures here only the equality of all litigants.[31] Justice that guarantees universal equality is Islamic, and even though this ended with the Pious Caliphs, a Muslim ruler should have this justice as his ideal, not that of Anushirwan. This superior model of justice was not easy to emulate, but it was to be preferred because it could be used also as a mechanism to convince people of the finality and truth of the Faith.[32]

The chapter on justice, while emphasizing the ultimate superiority of the Islamic politico-judicial tradition, draws also a close nexus between *dindari* and *jahandari*. The two are not separate, and their combination is seen as facilitating the ideal conditions for the spread of Islam. Barani's discussion of principles of governance revolves around *shari'a, kufr, jihad,* and *jizya;* all that is good originates from Islam and a non-Muslim is nothing but evil embodied. Regrating, for instance, the practice of hoarding goods to sell at higher prices, was a bad practice as such, but since it was practiced generally by the Hindus who dominated trade, Barani attributed it to their religion. Regrating was to be suppressed not because it was bad for the people, irrespective of their faith, but because by suppressing it the Muslim ruler would deprive the Hindus of the wealth and honor they obtained through this practice and thus serve the cause of Islam.[33]

On grounds of necessity, however, Barani also advised that non-Muslims be taken into Muslim state service to some degree. The existence of non-Muslim soldiers in the army of his eponymous hero, Mahmud, fighting the enemies of Islam, was enough of a reason for him not to abhor their presence. But Barani hastens to point out the disadvantages of this measure also.[34] The logic of necessity extends to his argument about the *zawabit,* or the secular state regulations framed by the ruler. He makes it very clear that *zawabit* can only be justified on the grounds of political necessity, emanating from the inability of Muslim rulers in the prevailing circumstances to implement *shari'a* in full. But the *zawabit* were to reinforce *shari'a,* to reinvigorate and complement it; they were not to work separately or contrary to it.[35] In this context, Barani's description of a meeting between Sultan Mahmud and Qadr Khan, the ruler of Khita, in which the two rulers discussed the success of their laws, is revealing. As Mrs. Khan rightly points out, this anecdote is clearly a construction, since Mahmud died in 1030 and the kingdom of Khita (or Kara Khita) was not founded till 1123.[36] But Mahmud's justification to Qadr Khan of the success of his own *zawabit* is nevertheless a telling statement of Barani's views: "We belong to Mohammed's Faith; he was the last of the prophets. In every law I frame concerning the affairs of my state, my real object is the enforcement of the Prophet's *shari'at* to which my laws are not opposed. The first law of my government is this. Thirty-eight years have passed since I became king, and it has been my strong resolve and firm determination ever since my accession to put the opponents of the Prophet's religion to the sword, to take the orders of the Muslim *shari'at* to the ends of the earth and to illuminate all territories with the light of Islam. I assign the duty of enforcing the orders of the *shari'at* to pious, religious and God-fearing men."[37]

Barani's emphasis on high birth, heredity, and class generally is seen by some scholars as a secular/irreligious feature of his political theory. For Barani, such merits as political acumen, administrative skill, and statesmanship are not acquired traits but genetic ones. He attributes the longevity of the rule of Sassanids, for example, to the fact that they upheld the principle of heredity when allocating positions to their officials.[38] However, it is important to keep in mind that the discussions on heredity by Barani are all geared toward ensuring the stability of Islamic regimes. The principal aim is not to build legitimacy for a "class state."[39] The interests of the Muslim community define the contours of his ideas on the heredity question.

In fact, Barani's narrow horizons on the issue of heredity can be located in the historical developments of his age. Barani covers about a century and a half in his history. This was a particularly unnerving period for him. During this long period, Islam and the rule of *shari'a* should ideally have been firmly established in India. Instead, this was a period rocked by political revolutions and ethnic strife. Muslim ruling families were continuously under challenge. This bothered Barani, and he saw the principle of heredity as the only solution to put an end to this strife and ensure stability. Long passages in Barani's works read like pathetic sermons highlighting how instability has led to the ruination of illustrious Muslim families. He therefore pleads with Muslims to "think of a policy (*tadbir*) owing to which Mussalmans . . . and their families and followers may not be deprived of their lives and properties."[40] Barani's invocation of the principle of heredity, although a principle rooted in non-Islamic, Iranian, and Indian tradition, was a conscious choice exercised by him to serve the narrow sectarian interests of the early Islamic regime in India.

From Mawardi to Nizam al-Mulk to Ghazali and then, in India, to Barani, the theory and practice of governance (*jahandari*) and its adjustment with *shari'a*, or *dindari*, thus evolved over a long period. All advocated the maintenance of the *shari'a* and its defense against its enemies. For Mawardi, the caliph defended *shari'a* the best; for Nizam al-Mulk the king was its best guarantee; Ghazali struck a compromise. For Barani, kingship with all its attendant attributes was a sin for which the king must make compensation (*kaffara*). In the process, bigotry, or narrow religious sectarianism, became integral to his political theory. There was not much impact of the "Islamized" Greco-Hellenic writings on their discussions of statecraft. Further, they all saw the king as a Muslim ruler, to manage in the first place the interests of the Muslims. This was, however, only one tradition which influenced the formation of the Indo-

Islamic principles of governance, particularly in the early phases of the Muslim rule.

The extent to which practice under the Delhi sultans conformed to or deviated from this theory is an altogether different question. Our aim here has been principally to assess what we generally identify as the political ideas of the early Indo-Muslim political philosophers. We know that these ideals barely influenced the policies of the early Turkish rulers in India. Shams-ud-Din Iltutmish (1210–36) took the plea that the Muslims, in terms of strength, were still like salt in a dish and were thus unable to wage an all-out war either to force the infidels to accept Islam or to exterminate them in case of their refusal. Ghiyas-ud-Din Balban, who dominated Delhi politics as a powerful faction leader and then as sultan between 1246 and 1287, kept theologians and theorists like Barani at a distance by dismissing them as mere seekers of narrow mundane gains (*ulama-i dunya).* Ala-ud-Din Khalji (1296–1316) did have a discussion with his *qazi,* but in practice he followed the rule that, in his calculation, best served the interest of his power and people. Muhammad bin Tughlaq (1324–51), far from degrading Hindus, accorded them high positions, while his successor, Firuz Tughlaq (1351–88), showed interest in Hindu traditions and monuments. Sikandar Lodi (1489–1517), even if sometimes remembered as a bigot, encouraged Hindus to learn Persian for their fuller participation in state management.[41] Such being the practice, Barani's *Fatawa* represented just a point of view and can only be wrongly called, as the title of Mrs. Khan's English translation suggests, "The Political Theory of the Delhi Sultanate."

Shari'a in Nasir-ud-Din Tusi's *Akhlaq*

Although in some respects Nizam al-Mulk and Barani represented dissent, in religious matters they adhered to Sunni orthodox traditions. They used the term *shari'a* in its conventional juristic sense. But there were simultaneous movements of religious dissent that, rejecting existing power structures as tyranny, developed alternative norms and principles.[42] Their theories were based largely on Greco-Hellenic ideas that had been appropriated by the Muslims. In the beginning, these ideas found favor with extreme groups of deviationists, but gradually they came to influence almost all Islamic writings on social and political organization. For an evaluation of this process, Khwaja Nasir-ud-Din Tusi's *Akhlaq-i Nasiri* deserves special notice.[43] Through this book, and especially through the section on state and politics, many of the ideas of the erstwhile dissenters gradually entered the general fabric of Sunni political Islam. And significantly, *shari'a* continued to be a touchstone for their political theorizing.

Tusi was a philosopher and a scientist, with more than eighteen books to his credit. He built the celebrated observatory and the library at Maraghah, Azarbaijan, in 1259. He organized a large number of scientists around the observatory and compiled the *Zij-i Ilkhani*.[44] He first published *Akhlaq-i-Nasiri* in Persian in 1235,[45] at the request of the Isma'ili prince Nasir-ud-Din Abd-ur-Rahim bin Abi Mansur, the wali of Quhistan during the reign of Ala-ud-Din Muhammad (1221–55) of Alamut, who had commissioned the author to translate from Arabic Ibn Miskawaih's *Tahzib al-Akhlaq* or *Kitab al-taharat*. But the book was much more than a mere translation. Besides the first discourse, which was a summary arranged anew of Ibn Miskawaih's *Tahzib*, Tusi added two new discourses based on the writings of the celebrated philosophers Farabi and Ibn Sina: on household and family management (*tadbir-i manzil*), and on politics (*siyasat-i mudun*) as part of practical wisdom (*hikmat-i amali*). The result was a skillful blending of the Greek philosophical and scientific tradition with the author's "Islamic" view of man and society. The synthesis represented "a subtle transcending of both," in Wickens's words.[46] The king, for Tusi, was the sustainer of existing things and the one who completes that which is incomplete. Since men (*insan*) by their nature (*uns-i taba'i*) were social beings and needed other men, it was necessary that an agreement should be made for the right working of their relationships. An individual who had attained perfection through equipoise (*itidal*) and a perception of union with the Supreme Being was selected for kingship. The ideal king should aim to help his subjects to "reach potential wisdom by the use of their mental powers." Tusi followed Farabi's classification of civil society (*tamaddun*) into the ideal and the excellent city or state (*al-madinat al-fazilah*) and the bad and unrighteous city. Unrighteous cities could again be divided into three categories: the misguided city (*al-madinat al-zallah*), the evil-doing city (*al-madinat al-fasiqah*), and the ignorant city (*al-madinat al- jahilah*).[47] Like Farabi, Tusi considered that it was possible for the ideal city to be composed of men of different sects and social groups.[48] The leader of the ideal city should be the philosopher king under whose supervision each person, kept in his appropriate place, would engage himself to achieve perfection.[49]

Akhlaq-i Nasiri is a work of theory, idealistic and normative in character. It is difficult to take the text as evidence of actual circumstances. Still, the book was composed at a time when the rulers' religious views did not correspond with those of a number of their subjects. In 1235 Tusi dedicated the book to an Isma'ili prince in a region that in Nizam al-Mulk's *Siyasat Nama* had been described as especially disturbed and misguided.[50] Later, when the edifice of Islamic culture was shaken by the Mongols, Tusi wrote a new preface dedicating his work, without changing its contents, to the non-Muslim Mongol ruler. It was in such a situation that Tusi envisaged the need for an ideal ruler to ensure harmony and the coordination of the diverse groups making up the state. The crisis the Muslim world faced in the wake of the Mongol disaster created favorable conditions for the acceptance of Tusi's idea. This is not to suggest that in Tusi's ideal state, or in the ideas of the authors that followed him, there was no important place for religion or *shari'a*. At least once, Tusi suggests that the divine institute (*namus-i ilahi*), first of the three essentials for the maintenance of a civic society, is expressed in *shari'a*.[51] The divine institute that is the pre-Islamic Greco-Hellenic notion of *nomos* and the *shari'a* in Nasirean ethics appear to be the same in Nasirean *akhlaq* writings. The divergence between the two the writers of these digests then explained (*tawil*) in terms of the difference between real inner meanings (*batin*) and apparent words (*zahir*).[52] At the same time, these authors invoked *shari'a* and illustrated their discourses with anecdotes from the classical Islamic period when such stories supported their ideals. This was also an effective device to enhance the acceptability of their views in orthodox circles.

Tusi's *Akhlaq* in Mughal India

There is not much in the available medieval Indian intellectual and literary history to indicate the exact time and place of the first entry of Tusi's *Akhlaq* into the subcontinent. The book was, however, widely read in Mughal India; it shaped in very large measure Abul Fazl's religious and political views.[53] One can surmise that the book entered through Gujarat or the Deccan, where several Persian scholars—including some disciples of Jalal-ud-Din Dawwani, who had prepared a recension of the book as *Akhlaq-i Jalali* in the late fifteenth century—had migrated in the late fifteenth and early sixteenth centuries. Sikandar Lodi is reported to have invited one Mir Saiyid Rafi-ud-Din, a disciple of Diwwani from Gujarat.[54] But it must be noted that both Dawwani and Rafi-ud-Din were primarily theologians and that the latter lent active support to the orthodox Sunni sectarian *ulama* in India.[55] It is very likely that the Mughals received and appropriated the Nasirean ethics as part of the legacy of Babur, the founder of their rule in India, who in turn received it from the Timurids of Herat after their extirpation at the hands of the Shaibanis. Sultan Husain Bayqara (1470–1506), the last great Timurid in Herat, even though a Sunni, seems to have disapproved of his government being run exclusively on narrow Sunni Islamic norms.[56] It matched his policies that at least two versions of Tusi's work, the *Akhlaq-i Muhsini* of Mulla Husain Wa'iz al-Kashifi and the *Dastur al-Wizarat* of Qazi Ikhtiyar-ud-Din al-Husaini, were prepared at his behest.[57] Of these two, Ikhtiyar al-Husaini's work in particular helps us to understand the reasons for Tusi's special status in the Mughal Persian reading list.

Ikhtiyar-ud-Din Hasan bin Ghiyas-ud-Din al-Husaini, the chief *qazi* of Herat and a *wazir* in the time of the Timurid sultan Husain Bayqara, came from an eminent family of the ulama of Turbat-i Jam, who held high positions in Timurid Central Asia. He compiled *Dastur al-Wizarat*, apparently in the time of Sultan Abu Sa'id Mirza (1459–69), for the young prince Husain Mirza, better known as Sultan Husain Bayqara, who was then the chief support of the sultanate and acted virtually like the *wazir*. Later, after the collapse of Timurid power in Herat, Ikhtiyar al-Husaini, lucky to escape the fate ("imprisonment and execution") of many of his contemporaries, chose a life of retirement in his hometown, Turbat. Then a day came when he heard that "the lamp of the illustrious Timurid house" had again been set ablaze in Kabul by Zahir-ud-Din Muhammad Babur. He arrived at the court of Babur, accompanied by several "princes and great men of Herat." Babur impressed him with his unusual accomplishments, support for learning, and active interest in learned discourses. Ikhtiyar himself had long discussions with Babur on diverse branches of the sciences and, in particular, on the laws and norms (*qawanin-o-adab*) of government. The result, as he claims in the preface of his book, was a treatise the title of which was suggested by Babur, possibly after his favorite son, Humayun: the *Akhlaq-i Humayuni*.[58]

In the *Akhlaq-i Humayuni*, the author claims that he has summed up in simple and elegant language "the subtle, abstruse, complex and convoluted" discourses of numerous books, in particular, those by Ibn Miskawaih and Nasir-ud-Din Tusi on human nature, family, household, and government. The book is divided into three parts, called *qanuns* (laws), each being divided further into two sections, called *qaidas* (rules), which again are each divided into two chapters called *bahs* (debates, inquiries).

Part one of the book is on the ethics of correction of disposition (*tahzib-i akhlaq wa farhang*), with discussions on virtues and vices and on the methods of their acquisition and removal, respectively. In part two, the author proposes in the introduction to discuss family and the regulation of households and properties, but in the text he discusses only the regulation of properties (*tadbir-i amwal*). Part three, especially significant for our purpose, discusses the principles of rulership (*taqwim-i ri'aya wa mamlikat-dari*) and has one section on the king's servants, with discourses on the nobles and the army in two separate chapters. Section two of this part considers the ruler's ordinary (*awam*) and accomplished (*khawas*) subjects (*ri'aya*).[59]

The book is very likely a version of the treatise the author had earlier compiled for Prince Husain Mirza. At any rate, Husaini is very conscious of the value of his work, which he takes to be a guide for Babur and for his illustrious descendants (*aulad-i amjad*).[60]

Babur's "illustrious descendants," however, did not much relish Ikhtiyar al-Husaini's simplified recension of the works of Ibn Miskawaih and Tusi. Introduced as they now were to these works through the *Akhlaq-i Humayuni*, they preferred to read and understand by themselves the fuller, if "convoluted," original texts. Tusi's *Akhlaq* was among the favorite readings of the Mughal political elites. It was among the five most important books that Abul Fazl wanted to have read regularly to the emperor Akbar. The emperor, in turn, issued instructions to his officials to read Tusi.[61] Further, in the discourses on justice, *itidal*, harmony, *siyasat*, reason, religion, and norms of governance that filled Mughal political digests, imperial edicts, and missives, the imprint of the tradition to which Tusi's *Akhlaq* belonged is unmistakable. Tusi's *Akhlaq* is an indisputable source of Abul Fazl's nonsectarian ideology. In Baqir Khan Najm-i Sani's *Mau'izah-i Jahangiri*, a book on the art of governance compiled for and presented to Jahangir, religion occupied little space in matters of government.[62] Jahangir also commissioned a Persian translation, perhaps the first, of Ibn Miskawaih's celebrated *al-Hikmat al-Khalida*, which was to be used as a reference manual (*dastur al-amal*) for his officials. This book, originally written in Arabic, consisted of maxims of the Greeks, the Persians, the Indians, and the Arabs. Taqi-ud-Din Muhammad bin Shaikh Muhammad al-Arjani al-Tushtri rendered it into Persian under the title of *Jawidan Khirad* (the eternal wisdom).[63] It was a measure of its popularity that later in 1655, Haji Sahms-ud-Din Muhammad Husain Hakim prepared a compact recension of the book on Shayista Khan's instruction. This version is known as *Intikhab-i Shayista Khani*.[64]

The Mughals thus inherited the Nasirean norms of governance, in a measure, from a branch of Central Asian Timurids. These norms contested the norms we noticed above in Barani's *Fatawa;* they also proved to be an important support to facilitate stable and enduring Mughal rule in the specific multi-religio-cultural conditions in India. By appropriating Nasirean norms as a base of their politics, the Mughals also emphatically demonstrated their dissociation from the ambience of yet another Central Asian political code. This was the code developed in the early sixteenth century by Fazlullah bin Ruzbihani Isfahani under the influence of the Uzbeks, the avowed enemies of the Mughals in the region. Ruzbihani's *Suluk al-Muluk* was intended to be a guide for the ruler in matters relating to high Islamic offices, such as *qazi, muhtasib*, and *shaikh al-Islam;* taxes such as *sadaqat, zakat, ushr, khums, kharaj, jizya;* observance of the rites of Islam, such as *jihad, zimmi, kafirs;* and questions of punishment, such as the penalties for adultery, drinking, robbery, and false accusation. All were to be adjudged strictly according to Sunni Islam within the limits of the schools of jurisprudence (*fiqh*) of Shafiʿi and Abu Hanifa.[65] The book is virtually a manual on Islamic jurisprudence, its ambit in political terms narrow, much narrower, in fact, than in the works of Nizam al-Mulk, Ghazali, or Barani. The author, Ruzbihani, obsessed with his own Hanafi/Shafiʿi brand of Sunni Islam, regards Shiʿites as apostates and believes that an all-out war (*jihad*) against the Safavid Shiʿites of Iran was obligatory. The Safavid ruler and his Qizilbash followers, according to him, had deviated from the path of Islam (*rifz*), were outright heretics (*ilhad*), and had raised the *fitna* of apostasy (*irtidad*) in the same way as had some of the tribes in the time of the First Pious Caliph Abu Bakr. Cut off from Islam, they had turned the mosques of Transoxiana into places of heresy and centers of propagation of hatred against the holy companions of the Prophet.[66]

The Mughals refused to rule with such an approach to Islam. On the contrary, the Mughal ruler Jahangir (1605–26) prided himself on the fact that in his domain the followers of diverse religions lived in peace—or at least this was the ideal he sought to achieve. What was particularly abhorrent for the Mughals was the portrayal by Ruzbihani of Babur, the founder of their power in India. In spreading heresy in Transoxiana, Babur had played, in Ruzbihani's view, a role as detestable as the Iranian Shiʿi leaders. With the region afire with *fitna*, Babur had accepted the help of the Qizilbash in his fight against the Uzbeks to recover Samarkand and Bukhara. And, but for the gallant *jihad* of the Uzbek king, Ubaidullah Khan, the rites of the true Faith would have been totally routed out.[67]

A politico-religious code like the one laid down in Ruzbihani's *Suluk* thus failed to find favor with the Mughals, even with ordinary Mughal officeholders, who would have been unlikely to welcome something their masters disapproved of. With the unprecedented dissemination of Persian learning in the seventeenth century, the reading of Tusi's *Akhlaq* was not confined only to members of the royal household and high nobility. *Akhlaq-i Nasiri* was integral to the *madrasa* syllabi, and the Nasirean code of life began to be appropriated even by the ordinary *qasba* gentry. Chandra Bhan Brahman, the noted *munshi* and poet of Shahjahan's court (1626–56), advised his son, Khwaja Tej Bhan, to make it a habit to study Tusi's *akhlaq* digest, together with other Persian texts. It was by imbibing the code of life enshrined in these texts, he wrote, that the average learned man in Mughal India prepared himself to earn the wealth of knowledge and good moral conduct (*sa'adat-i ilm ba amal*).[68]

Political Norms in Nasirean Ethics

The Nasirean *akhlaq* digests generally begin with a discussion on human disposition and the necessity of its disciplining and sublimation. Although this discussion is interspersed with Qur'anic verses and the traditions of the Prophet, the reference point is unequivocally the human being, irrespective of his religion or ethnicity (*bashar, insan, bani adam*), his living (*amr-i ma'ash*), or the world he lives in (*alam, afaq*). The perfection of man, according to the authors of these texts, is to be acquired through adulation of Divinity, but it cannot be achieved without a peaceful social organization, where each could earn his living by cooperation and helping each other. "He who seeks help from the other, will spend all his life arranging just a part of his food and clothing. The affairs of living thus must be administered through cooperation (*shirkat-o-mu'awanat*) which depends on justice (*'adl*). If *'adl* disappears, each will then follow his own desire. Therefore there has to be a rule (*dastur*) and a balancing agency (*mizan*) to ensure cooperation. *Shari'a*, the protectors of which have been the prophets (*anbiya wa rusul*), serves this purpose. But *shari'a* can be administered only by a just king, who performs his duty of governing principally with affection and favors (*rafat-o-imti-*

nan)."[69] The goal in Nasirean discourse on political organization is thus "cooperation," achieved through justice (*'adl*) promoted by the king, whose principal instrument of control should be affection and favors, not command and obedience (*amr-o-imtisal*). The *shari'a* here does not strictly connote Islamic law. The reader is reminded of the Qur'anic verse that there is a single God who has sent prophets to different communities, with *shari'as* to suit their times and climes.

Justice (*'adl*) emerges as the cornerstone of social organization. But the fundamental need for "cooperation" can be gauged from Tusi's initial suggestion that mutual love (*mahabbat*) is the most powerful guarantor of this cooperation. Justice was second only to *mahabbat;* it was an artificial way to social balance, as it could be attained only through the coercive means of government machinery: "Justice leads to artificial union, whereas love generates natural unity; and the artificial, in comparison to the natural, comes from force and compulsion. The artificial succeeds the natural, and thus it is obvious that the need for justice, even as it is the most perfect of human virtues, arises when love is unavailable. If love prevailed, *insaf* (justice) would not have been needed. Literally, [the word] *insaf* is derived from *nasf* (taking the half, reaching the middle). The dispenser of justice (*munsif*) divides the disputed object into two equal parts (*munasafah*); division into halves (*tansif*) implies multiplicity (*takassur*) whereas oneness is the product of love."[70]

The Nasirean *akhlaq* literature recommends that men be evaluated and treated on the strength and level of their natural goodness or maladies (*khair-o-sharr-i tab'i*).[71] The rights of the *ri'aya* do not follow from their religions; Muslims and *kafirs* both enjoy the Divine compassion (*rahmat-i Haqq*). The true representative and the shadow of God on earth here is the king, who guarantees the undisturbed management of the affairs of his (God's) "slaves," so that each could achieve perfection (*kamal*) according to his competence and class. This pattern of governance is *siyasat-i fazila* (the ideal politics), which establishes on a firm foundation the leadership (*imamat*) of the king. There is also a flawed and blemished politics (*siyasat-i naqisa*), against which the ruler is warned to guard himself, for faulty and perfunctory politics leads eventually to the ruination of the country and the people.[72] "The man of ideal politics is always on the right path, considers the *ri'aya* as his sons and friends, and controls his greed and desire (*hirs-o-shahwat*) through his intellect. The man of faulty politics resorts to coercion, takes the *ri'aya* as his slaves, nay even as women, while he himself is a slave of greed, desire, and lust for wealth."[73]

Discussions on and around the meanings of justice figure prominently in these *akhlaq* texts, but the tenor of these discussions was altogether different from those in Barani's *Fatawa*. In the Nasirean *akhlaq* texts, justice is defined as social harmony, the coordinated balance of the conflicting claims of diverse interest groups, which might well in an ideal state belong to more than one religion. The ruler, like a good physician, must know society's diseases, their symptoms, and their correct treatment. Since society is composed of groups of diverse interests and of individuals of conflicting dispositions, the king must take all possible care for justice to work smoothly, to maintain the body politic and the society in good health and equipoise (*itidal*). This is how all members of society can be brought together into a single unit, irrespective of their creed and community. Deviation from the path of justice leads groups and individuals to fight for their rights by themselves and thus leads the entire body politic to destruction. None should get less or more than he deserves. Excess (*ifrat*) and deficiency (*tafrit*) both disturb unity and relations of companionship.[74]

The intention of the king, who emerges in these texts as the all powerful center of societal organization, is critical. "If his [the king's] intention is justice," writes Husain Waʿiz al-Kashifi, "the result will be blessing and [the country] will become populous and well-managed; but if, God forbid, the contrary is the case, blessing will depart, the revenues will cease to grow, and the people will be in a quandary."[75] A just king is the shadow of God, the source of all that is good for the society. The emphasis was on maintenance of balance in the society, not on the eradication of infidelity and idolatry.

Justice was the primary goal; it served a real public interest. The religion of the ruler was secondary. A non-Muslim but just ruler would serve society better than an unjust Muslim sultan. The inherent excellence of justice and its intrinsic strength kept the ancient Sassanid kings firmly entrenched in power for well over five thousand years, even though they all were fire worshipers and infidels.[76] Human reason (*ʿaql*), not adherence to a religious legal code, determined the quality of the ruler's performance. This view of justice echoed the early Muʿtazilite theory of values. In the early Abbasid period, two principal theories of values opposed each other. The Muʿtazilites held that values such as justice and goodness have a real existence, independent of anyone's will, while to the Ashʿarites all values were determined by the will of God, who decides what shall be just, good, or otherwise.[77] Following intense competition between these two doctrines, that of the Ashʿarites finally prevailed in most Sunni theological writings. The Mu'tazilite position survived as a dissent, but in the course of time, mediated through the *akhlaq* texts, it triumphantly entered the Sunni *madrasas*.

Moreover, terms like *namus* or *nomos*, a non-Islamic concept, and *shari'a* (or *shari'a* of the prophets) were often used in these texts interchangeably. The identification of *namus* with *shari'a* comes out clearly, for example, in a treatise compiled in line with Tusi's *Akhlaq* in the Deccan in the seventeenth century. The objective of the state (*sultanat*), according to its author, is to fulfill the human needs of this world, but since human beings, because of their varied temperaments and social milieu, follow diverse religions, conflict (*niza'*) in this endeavor is inevitable. "To avoid this conflict there is thus the need of a perfect person, God-sent and God-supported. The philosophers call him *namus* and the method [he adopts] is called *namus-i Ilahi*. To the ulama of Islam, he is known as *rasul*, *nabi* and *shari*, and the method as *shari'a*."[78]

Clearly, this meaning of *shari'a* indicated a rejection in matters pertaining to the state of the jurists' normal usage of their term. Even for the jurists, however, the term *shari'a* sometimes admitted alien social practices. From the early Islamic period there were cases of legislation in matters of police, taxation, and criminal justice for the sake of *siyasat*, even though in general such legislation was often rejected as *siyasiyyah* as distinct from *shara'iyyah*. *Shari'a* also allowed some consideration for common usages and customs (*'urf*, *'adat*), even though this also was justified only by a resort to *qiyas*, or reasoning by analogy. These foreign social practices thus did not have the same sanctity or authority as those more clearly grounded in *shari'a*.[79] Nonetheless, categories like *qiyas*, *'urf*, and *'adat* introduced and reinforced resilience and ambiguity in *shari'a*, which in turn facilitated the entry into the orthodox Islamic realm of a political code like the one in Nasirean ethics.

Shari'a in the Mughal Tradition

Together with the liberal traditions of Sufism and Persian poetry, Nasirean political norms provided the Mughal rulers, Akbar and Jahangir in particular, with support for a nonsectarian approach to religion. Akbar's ideologue Abul Fazl prepared a working manual (*dastur al-amal*) for his officials with advice on how to protect the principles of justice and equity (*itidal*) and of noninterference in matters of the faith of the people. "And you [the state officials] should not interfere (*ta'arruz*) in any person's religion. For, if a wise person in a transient mundane matter does not go for a thing that harms, how can he then choose loss in a matter of faith, which pertains to the world of eternity? If he is right then [when you interfere in his religion] you oppose the truth; and if you have the truth with you and he is unwittingly on the wrong side, he is a victim of ignorance and [therefore] deserves compassion and help, not interference and resistance. You should be kind, beneficent and friendly to all."[80]

It is difficult to know the extent to which Abul Fazl's advice was followed at lower levels. Some of the high officials did show concern for harmony and yet maintained that they were true Muslims. Shayista Khan, for instance, is described as a true Muslim monotheist and true follower of the prophet (*muwahhid* and *tabi'i Rasul*), and yet totally free from bigotry, advocating peace with all (*sulh-i kul*). He saw all as his possible friends and allies, whatever their personal faiths and religions. Shayista Khan's *dindari* thus was in total harmony with his liberal and open-ended approach in public matters.

But not all high Mughal officials practiced *sulh-i kul*. Two contemporary observations help to give us some idea of the extent to which the Mughal state followed or disregarded the *shari'a*. One of these is a remark of Abd al-Qadir Badaoni, the noted historian of Akbar's time, about the reception accorded in India to Mir Muhammad Sharif Amuli, the Nuqtawi leader, who had to flee Iran for fear of persecution. Badaoni, as we know, was a narrow-minded, bigoted Sunni. He detested the nonorthodox ideas of Amuli and disapproved of the prevailing situation in which even men like Amuli were welcome. He writes, "Hindustan is a wide place, where there is an open field for all licentiousness, and no one interferes with another's business, so that every one can do just as he pleases."[81]

The second comes from the French traveler François Bernier, who visited India decades later in Aurangzeb's time. After commenting disapprovingly on "strange" Hindu beliefs and rituals regarding an eclipse, he remarks, "The Great Mogol, though a Mahometan, permits these ancient and superstitious practices; not wishing, or not daring, to disturb the Gentiles in the free exercise of their religion."[82] Even in matters like *sati*, he observed, the Mughals intervened only indirectly: "They [the Mughals] do not, indeed, forbid it [*sati*] by a positive law, because it is a part of their policy to leave the idolatrous population, which is so much more numerous than their own, in the free exercise of its religion; but the practice is checked by indirect means."[83]

This does not mean that the Mughals were unconcerned with the maintenance of *shari'a*. Consolidation of the community (*tasis-i millat*) and enforcement of *shari'a* (*tarwij-i shari'at*) have been enumerated among the significant achievements of Jahangir's reign.[84] But it was the *shari'a* of the tradition of Nasirean *akhlaq* which the Mughals encouraged and promoted. The Mussalmans thus found a way out after the closure of the so-called door of *ijtihad*. It was not simply that the infidels, like all the sects of the Muslims, had freedom of belief in the regime of this *shari'a*. They were not even treated as the people of ordinary *zimma*. In the regime of this *shari'a*, infidels, like Muslims, could build their own places of worship and could even demolish mosques, even as this implied for the theologians and the jurists the weakness of Islamic rule and a threat to Islam.

Shaikh Ahmed Sirhindi, the famous Naqshbandi saint-theologian, expressed his exasperation with these policies:

> The spread of the illustrious *shari'a* comes from the efficient care and good administration of the great sultans, which has lately slackened causing inevitable weakness of Islam. The infidels of India [thus] fearlessly destroy mosques and build their own places of worship in their stead. In Thanesar in the Krukhet tank there was a mosque and a shrine of a saint. Both have been destroyed by the infidels and in their place they have now built a big temple. Again, the infidels freely observed the rituals of infidelity, while the Muslims are unable to execute most of the Islamic ordinances. On the day of *Ekadshi* when the Hindus abstain from eating and drinking, they see to it that no Muslim bakes or sells bread or any other food in the bazaar. On the contrary, in the blessed month of Ramzan they cook and sell food openly. Due to the weakness of Islam nobody can stop them from doing this. Alas, a thousand times alas![85]

Nonetheless, the Mughal rulers, in whose times Sirhindi thought the *shari'a* ebbed so low, took pride in calling themselves the majesty and the light of the faith (Jalal-ud-Din = Akbar, Nur-ud-Din = Jahangir). The *qazi* and the *sadr*, as in all other Islamic states, had high politico-religious positions; the Muslim divines, among others, had land or cash grants to pray for the stability of the empire and to keep aloft the symbols of Islam (*sha'air-i Islami*). The periodic dispatch with *hajj* delegates of rich donations for the holy cities, Mecca and Medina, continued. What is significant is that even some important religious divines saw the reigning ruler, Jahangir, not only as a man of piety and justice but also as someone who ensured compliance with the ordinances of the *shari'a*.[86] In a Chishti sufi assessment, the Mughals ensured the supremacy of Faith by their exaggerated concern for social harmony (*mashrab-i i'tidal*). In Mughal India, unlike Uzbek Central Asia and Safavid Iran, the followers of all religions (*adyan-o-mazahib*) lived in peace and performed their rituals freely. And yet the Mughals acted in complete accord with the injunctions of their Faith (*nusus*).[87] Clearly in these two assessments of the Mughals' concern for *shari'a*, the implications of the term were not the same. For Sirhindi, like Barani, the rule of *shari'a* meant not only total dominance of the Muslims but also humiliation of infidelity and infidels, if not their annihilation. To the Chishti sufi and the Mughals, the most important task of the *shari'a* was to ensure the balance of conflicting interests of groups and communities, with no interference in their personal beliefs.

We have examined some features of the making of the medieval Indian state and its relationship with the *shari'a*, suggesting as well how developments in India were connected to developments in the larger Islamic world. State building in India drew strength from the appropriation of different cultural strands, not all of which were compatible with textual or juristic Islam. Interaction with non-Arab cultures strongly influenced the development of the *shari'a*, which in course of time came to acquire more than one meaning. While Barani used the *shari'a* in its juristic sense, a nonjuristic meaning of the term was introduced into Mughal India through the Nasirean *akhlaq* digests. This meaning was informed by a strong political tradition of accommodation.

But this does not mean that the forces to contest this tradition were not active in Mughal India. In the seventeenth century, the Mughal ruler Jahangir, unlike Ala-ud-Din Khalji in the fourteenth century, did not have to contend with the views of a Qazi Mughis, but such views still carried considerable weight. These views expressed themselves, in a measure, in the compilation of the *Fatawa* under Aurangzeb (1658–1707) and again in the demand of an eighteenth-century *qazi* that the entire resources of the state be earmarked for the maintenance of theologians and religious establishments.

Further, while the Nasirean *akhlaq* tradition acted generally as an agent for the assimilation of differing cultural views, some texts concerned largely with Islamic legal and juristic matters were also circulated during the Mughal period as *akhlaq* digests. One such text was *Akhlaq-i Hakimi* by Hasan Ali bin Ashraf al-Munshi al-Khaqani, the chief secretary of Akbar's half brother, Mirza Hakim. In Jahangir's time, Khaqani's grandson, Nur-ud-Din Qazi al-Khaqani, prepared an expanded and enlarged edition of this work under the title of *Akhlaq-i Jahangiri*.[88] For both Hasan Ali and Nur-ud-Din, an agreeable disposition was identical with Islamic faith (*iman*). Both exhorted the sultan above all to maintain justice for Muslims.[89] They held up the Mongol ruler, Ghazan Khan, for example, as a ruler who had promoted justice simply by accepting Islam and propagating it among his community.[90] The concept of justice in these texts was thus quite different from that in the Nasirean *akhlaq* tradition, as was the concept of *siyasat*. In the treatises in the Nasirean tradition, the term *siyasat* was used to denote discipline, control, and administration; the ruler is advised to first discipline his own self in order to acquire the legitimacy and moral power necessary to control others by means of rewards or punishments. The ruler must be strong enough to overawe the bad and fulfill the expectations of the good.[91] But for Hasan Ali, there were two principal categories of *siyasat:* first was the propagation of the Faith (*din*) and the strengthening of the community of believers (*Mumin* and Muslim) by launching incessant war against the enemies of Faith; second was maintaining control over the ambitions of high officials and keeping common servants overawed.[92]

Further, a significant section of the Muslim elite still regarded books like *Zakhirat al-Muluk* of Saiyid Ali Hamadani as the true guide for Muslim rulers. Hamadani's book was intended to provide to Muslim kings and rulers an ideal model of governance, a model aimed largely toward setting right matters of the Faith (*umur-i din*).[93] The principal concern of the state for Hamadani was the enforcement of the institutes of the *shari'a*, in the sense of providing justice to the Muslims, rewarding and honoring them in proportion to their level of excellence in faith (*iman*). Hamadani divides the *ra'iyat* into *Kafir* and *Muslim* and dwells only on the categories of the latter (*ahl-i iman*).[94] The rights of the *ri'aya*, according to him, were determined by their religions.

Although some theologians thus appropriated the *akhlaq* tradition as a vehicle to defend their own views, their position was, in fact, contested in the community. The meaning of the *shari'a* that I have tried to read in the texts on Nasirean ethics had still to contend in Mughal India with forces that undermined its strength.

Notes

1. See, e.g., E. I. J. Rosenthal, *Political Thought in Medieval Islam: An Introductory Outline* (Cambridge, 1958); A. K. S. Lambton, *Theory and Practice in Medieval Persian Government* (London, 1980); Sajida Sultana Alvi, ed. and trans., *Advice on the Art of Governance; Mau'izah-i Jahangiri of Muhammad Baqir Khan Najm-i Sani: An Indo-Islamic Mirror for Princes* (New York, 1989), introduction.

2. Abul Hasan Ali ibn Muhammad al-Mawardi, *Al-Ahkam al-Sultaniya*, ed. Muhammad Badr al-Din al-Na'sani (Cairo, 1909), 3–18; H. A. R. Gibb, "Al-Mawardi's Theory of the Caliphate," in *Studies on the Civilization of Islam*, ed. Stanford Shaw and William Polk (London, 1962), 151–65.

3. Nizam al-Mulk, *Siyasat Nama*, ed. Hubert Darke (Tehran, 1962), 13–16, 41.

4. *Al-Ahkam al-Sultaniya*, 7–8.

5. *Siyasat Nama*, 151.

6. Ibid., 74–75.

7. Ghazali wrote the text in Persian, which was later translated into Arabic. Most manuscripts of the Arabic version bear the title of *al-Tibr al-Masbuk fi Nasihat al-Muluk*. The Persian text has been edited by Jalal Humai, and an Arabic text has been published by H. D. Isaacs. Compare the introduction to F. R. C. Bagley's English translation, *Counsel for Kings* (London, 1964).

8. Bagley, *Counsel for Kings*, 51–56.

9. Ibid., 45–47; A. K. S. Lambton, "The Theory of Kingship in Nasihat ul-Muluk of Ghazali," in *Theory and Practice in Medieval Persian Government*, chap. 5.

10. Ghazali was also notable for the impact of Greek writings on his political theory. Even in *Nasihat* he cites Aristotle in support of the essential qualities he recommends for kings. He writes: "Aristotle was asked, 'What great man is worthy to be called king, or is God alone (worthy)?' He answered, 'The man in whom you will find certain things, however lacking he be in other qualities.' Then he continued, 'First of all knowledge, and (then) forbearance, compassion, clemency, generosity and the like; because great men owe their greatness to the divine effulgence and to their radiance of soul, pureness of body, and breadth of intellect and knowledge, as well as the dominion which has long been in their family.'"

11. Fakhr-ud-Din Muhammad bin Mubarak Shah (Fakhr-i Mudabbir), *Adab-al-Harb wash-Shuja'a*, ed. Ahmad Suhaili Khwansari (Tehran, 1968).

12. *Ain-i-Kishwardari*, ed. Muhammad Sarwar Maulai (Tehran, 1976).

13. Fakhr-i Mudabbir, *Adab-al-Harb*, 336.

14. Ibid., 388–97; for jihad, 404–5.

15. Ibid., 405.

16. *Ain-i-Kishwardari*, 25, 30, 33.

17. Ibid., 38.

18. Ibid., 39–40.

19. Muhammad Habib, "Life and Thought of Ziauddin Barani," *Medieval India Quarterly* 4 (January–April 1958), reprinted in Muhammad Habib and Afsar Salim Khan, *Political Theory of the Delhi Sultanate* (including a translation of Zia-ud-Din Barani's *Fatawa-i Jahandari*) (Allahabad, n.d.), 117–72.

20. M. Habib and A. Salim Khan, *Political Theory,* 7, 67.

21. Shams Siraj Afif, *Tarikh-i Firuz Shahi,* ed. Maulvi Wilayat Husain (Calcutta, 1890), 29–30, 177; Amir Khurd Kirmani, *Siyar al-Auliya* (Delhi, 1884–85), 312–13.

22. Zia-ud-Din Barani, *Fatawa-i Jahandari,* ed. Afsar Salim Khan (Lahore, 1972), 125–30.

23. Ibid., 15–20, for instance.

24. Ibid., 165–66; English trans., 46.

25. Ibid., preface, 1–2.

26. Ibid., 5–9.

27. Ibid., 139–40; English trans., 39.

28. Ibid., 142–43; English trans., 40.

29. Ibid., 50–51; English trans., 13–14, 15.

30. Ibid., 68; English trans., 17.

31. Ibid., 184–87.

32. Ibid., 75–81.

33. Ibid., 136–37; English trans., 37–38.

34. Ibid., 104–5; English trans., 25.

35. Ibid., 217; English trans., 64.

36. English trans., 67, notes.

37. Ibid., 228–31; English trans., 69–70.

38. Ibid., 305; English trans., 93.

39. Irfan Habib, "Barani's Theory of the History of the Delhi Sultanate," *Indian Historical Review,* 7.1–2 (1980–81): 99–115.

40. Compare *Fatawa-i Jahandari,* 309; English trans., 104.

41. See K. A. Nizami, *Some Aspects of Religion and Politics in India during the Thirteenth Century* (Delhi, 1974), 152, 315–16; A. B. M. Habibullah, *The Foundation of Muslim Rule in India* (Allahabad, 1976), 264–76.

42. Bernard Lewis, *The Assassins: A Radical Sect in Islam* (London, 1967); P. J. Vatikiotis, *The Fatimid Theory of State,* 2d ed. (Lahore, 1981); Wilfred Madelung, *Religious Trends in Early Islamic Iran* (Albany, 1988).

43. Several editions of Tusi's *Akhlaq-i Nasiri* are available. I have used the edition prepared by Mujtaba Minavi and Ali Raza Haidari (Tehran, 1976); G. M. Wickens translated the text into English as *The Nasirean Ethics* (London, 1964).

44. Edward G. Browne, *Literary History of Persia,* 4 vols. (Cambridge, 1969), 2:485–86; Abdus Salam Nadvi, *Hukama-i Islam,* 2 vols. (Urdu) (Azamgarh, n.d.), 2:256. For an account of the Maraghah Observatory, see Aydin Sayilli, *The Observatory in Islam* (Ankara, 1960), 189–223.

45. The book was reissued with a second preface wherein Tusi is severely critical of the religious milieu in which it is originally written. Tusi alludes to his

enforced service with the Isma'ilis and his rescue from them by the Mongols. (See Panjab University Lahore Press, Lahore, 1955.) This was, however, as G. M. Wickens points out, only to cover a revised preface and dedication.

46. G. M. Wickens in *Encyclopedia Iranica.*

47. M. M. Sharif, ed., *A History of Muslim Philosophy*, 2 vols. (Wiesbaden, 1963–66), 1:704–14.

48. *Akhlaq-i Nasiri*, 286–87. "The People of the Virtuous City, however, albeit diversified throughout the world, are in reality agreed, for their hearts are upright one towards another and they are adorned with love for each other. In their close-knit affection they are like one individual": Wickens, *Nasirean Ethics*, 215.

49. *Akhlaq-i Nasiri*, 286, 288.

50. *Siyasat Nama*, 262–67, for the Qaramitas and the Batinis in Quhestan.

51. *Akhlaq-i Nasiri*, 134.

52. M. M. Sharif, ed., *A History*, 1:544–64, 592–616, for an illustration from Ibn Rushd's *Tahafat al-tahafat* (Repudiation of the Repudiation), which he wrote in reply to Ghazali's *Tahafat al-Falasifah.*

53. S. A. A. Rizvi, *Religious and Intellectual History of the Muslims in Akbar's Reign (1556–1605), with Special Reference to Abul Fazl* (Delhi, 1975), 197, 355–56, 366–69.

54. Ibid., 42, 80.

55. Ibid., 42.

56. Jean Calmard has recently shown that Bayqara discouraged strict legalistic Sunni Islam, had Shi'ite leanings, and also proposed to proclaim Shi'ism as the state religion. See "Les Rituels Shi'ite et le Pouvoir: L'imposition du Shi'ism Safavide, eulogies et maledictions canoniques," in J. Calmard, ed., *Etudes Safavides* (Paris-Tehran, 1993), 113.

57. Kashifi's *Akhlaq-i Muhsini* is available in print; among its several editions is the one published from Bombay in 1890. Husaini's *Dastur al-Wizarat* has not been published; two manuscript copies (nos. 767 and 768) are preserved in the Bibliothèque Nationale, Paris (BNP). Edgar Blochet, *Catalogues de Manuscripts Persans* (Paris, 1912), 2:37–38. An early manuscript is also preserved in the library of Jamia Millia, New Delhi. I have discussed Husaini's text in my paper, "Akhlaq-i Humayuni of Ikhtiyar al-Husaini and the Indo-Persian Norms of Governance," presented at a seminar on the evolution of medieval Indian culture, Jawaharlal Nehru University, New Delhi, 14–16 February 1994.

58. See Khwandmir, *Habib al-Siyar*, 4 vols., Khayyam ed. (Tehran, 1984), 4:355–56; preface in *Akhlaq-i Hamayuni*, BNP ms. no. 767. However, Khwandmir says that the Shaibani ruler, Abul Fath Muhammad, retained him in the office of qazi. He was dismissed after the ruler's death and then he retired to Turbat.

59. BNP ms. no. 767, ff. 6a–8a.

60. Ibid., f. 6a.

61. Muhammad Amin bin Isra'il, *Majma' al-Insha*, BNP ms. no. 708, f. 38a; see also *Insha-i Abul Fazl* (Lucknow, 1863), 57–58.

62. Muhammad Baqir Khan Najm-i Sani, *Mau'izah-i Jahangiri: Advice on the Art of Governance,* trans. Sajida Sultana Alavi (Albany, 1989).

63. British Museum, London, ms. or. 457.

64. India Office Library, London ms. 2210.

65. British Museum, London ms. or. 253 the face. See also Muhammad Aslam's English translation as *Muslim Conduct of State* (University of Islamabad Press, 1974), 31–32.

66. Ibid., f. 3a; English trans., 33–34.

67. Ibid., ff. 3b-4a; English trans., 33–34, 37–46.

68. Chandra Bhan, *Char Chaman* and Brindaban Das Khwushgo, Tazkira, cited in S. M. Abdullah, *Adabiyat-i Farsi men Hinduon ka Hissa* (Lahore, 1967), 240–42. For a discussion on the dissemination of Persian learning in Mughal India, see M. Alam, "The Pursuit of Persian: Language in Mughal Politics," *Modern Asian Studies* 32.2 (1998): 317–49.

69. Ikhtiyar al-Husaini, *Akhlaq-i Humayuni,* BNP ms. 767, ff. 2.

70. *Akhlaq-i Nasiri,* 258–59; see also 251–74 for further elaboration and a discussion on different categories of love. See also Wickens, *The Nasirean Ethics,* 195–211.

71. *Akhlaq-i Humayuni,* BN ms. no. 767, ff. 37b-38b.

72. Ibid., f. 28b.

73. Ibid., f. 29a.

74. Ibid., ff. 30.

75. Husain Wa'iz al-Kashifi, *Akhlaq-i Muhsini* (Bombay, 1890), 56–57.

76. Nur-ud-Din Qazi al-Khaqani, *Akhlaq-i Jahangiri,* 2207, f. 274b.

77. G. F. Hourani, *Reason and Tradition in Islamic Ethics* (Cambridge, 1985), 57–58.

78. Ali bin Taifur al-Bistami, *Akhlaq-i Badshahi, Tuhfa-i Qutb-Shahi,* Bodleian Library, Oxford, ms. 1471, ff. 6b-7a.

79. Fauzi M. Najjar, "*Siyasa* in Islamic Political Philosophy," in Michael E. Marmura, ed., *Islamic Theology and Philosophy* (Albany, 1984), 92–110.

80. Amin bin Isra'il, *Majma' al-Insha,* f. 39b; *Insha-i Abul Fazl,* 1:60.

81. Abd al-Qadir Badaoni, *Muntakhab al-tawarikh,* English trans. W. H. Lowe (1899; reprint, Delhi, 1973), 2:253; see also Riazul Islam, "Akbar's Intellectual Contacts with Iran," in Milton Israel and N. K. Wagle, eds., *Islamic Society and Culture: Essays in Honour of Aziz Ahmad* (Delhi, 1983), 351–73. For Nuqtavis, see K. A. Nizami, *Akbar and Religion* (Delhi, 1989), 54–61.

82. François Bernier, *Travels in the Mogul Empire, 1656–1668,* trans. A. Constable (reprint, New Delhi, 1972), 303.

83. Ibid., 306.

84. Muhammad Baqir Najm-i Sani, *Mau'izah-i Jahangiri,* 2.

85. *Maktubat-i Imam Rabbani,* vol. 2 (reprint, Istanbul, 1977), letter no. 92 to Mir Muhammad Nu'man, 233–44; see also Yohannan Friedmann, *Shaykh Ahmad*

Sirhindi: An Outline of His Thought and a Study of His Image in the Eyes of Posterity (Montreal, 1971), 82.

86. *Maktubat-i Imam Rabbani,* 2:233.

87. Abd-ur-Rahman Chishti, *Mir'at-al-Asrar,* British Museum, Or. 216, f. 507a.

88. India Office Library (IOL), London, mss. 2203 and 2207.

89. IOL ms. 2203, ff. 34 and 35a; ms. 2207, ff. 264a-268b.

90. IOL ms. 2203, f. 46b; ms. 2207, f. 273a.

91. *Akhlaq-i Humayuni,* ff. 31b-32a.

92. IOL ms. 2203, f.96a.

93. *Zakhirat al-Muluk,* Bibliothèque Nationale, Paris ms. 760, ff. 2, 6a, and 19b. The citations in this article are from this manuscript only.

94. Ibid., ff. 19b and 92.

10

Temple Desecration and Indo-Muslim States

Richard M. Eaton

Framing the Issue

In recent years, especially in the wake of the destruction of the Baburi Mosque in 1992, much public discussion has arisen over the political status of South Asian temples and mosques, and in particular the issue of temples desecrated or replaced by mosques in the pre-British period. While Hindu nationalists have endeavored to document a pattern of wholesale temple destruction by Muslims in this period,[1] few professional historians have engaged the issue, even though it is a properly historical one. This essay aims to examine the evidence of temple desecration with a view to asking: Which temples were desecrated in India's premodern history? When, and by whom? How, and for what purpose? And above all, what might any of this say about the relationship between religion and politics in premodern India? This is a timely topic, since many in India today are looking to the past to justify or condemn public policy with respect to religious monuments.

Much of the contemporary evidence on temple desecration cited by Hindu nationalists is found in Persian material translated and published during the rise of British hegemony in India. Especially influential has been the eight-volume *History of India as Told by Its Own Historians*, first published in 1849 and edited by Sir Henry M. Elliot, who oversaw the bulk of the translations, with the help of John Dowson. But Elliot, keen to contrast what he understood as the justice and efficiency of British rule with the cruelty and despotism of the Muslim rulers who had preceded that rule, was anything but sympathetic to the "Muhammadan" period of Indian history. As he wrote in the book's original preface:

> The common people must have been plunged into the lowest depths of wretchedness and despondency. The few glimpses we have, even among the short Extracts in this single volume, of Hindus slain for disputing with Muhammadans, of general prohibitions against processions, worship, and ablutions, and of other intolerant measures, of idols mutilated, of temples razed, of forcible conversions and marriages, of proscriptions and confiscations, of murders and massacres, and of the sensuality and drunkenness of the tyrants who enjoined them, show us that this picture is not overcharged.[2]

With the advent of British power, on the other hand, "a more stirring and eventful era of India's History commences . . . when the full light of European truth and discernment begins to shed its beams upon the obscurity of the past."[3] Noting the far greater benefits that Englishmen had brought to Indians in a mere half century than Muslims had brought in five centuries, Elliot expressed the hope that his published translations would "make our native subjects more sensible of the immense advantages accruing to them under the mildness and the equity of our rule."[4]

Elliot's motives for delegitimizing the Indo-Muslim rulers who had preceded English rule are thus quite clear. Writing on the pernicious influence that this understanding of premodern Indian history had on subsequent generations, the eminent historian Mohammad Habib once remarked, "The peaceful Indian Mussalman, descended beyond doubt from Hindu ancestors, was dressed up in the garb of a foreign barbarian, as a breaker of temples, and an eater of beef, and declared to be a military colonist in the land where he had lived for about thirty or forty centuries. . . . The result of it is seen in the communalistic atmosphere of India today."[5] Although penned many years ago, these words are especially relevant in the context of current controversies over the history of temple desecration in India. For it has been through a selective use of Elliot and Dowson's selective translations of premodern Persian chronicles, together with a selective use of epigraphic data, that Hindu nationalists have sought to find the sort of irrefutable evidence—one of Sita Ram Goel's chapters is entitled "From the Horse's Mouth"—that would demonstrate a persistent pattern of villainy and fanaticism on the part of premodern Indo-Muslim conquerors and rulers.

In reality, though, each scrap of evidence in the matter requires careful scrutiny. Consider an inscription dated 1455 and found over the doorway of a tomb-shrine in Dhar, Madhya Pradesh, formerly the capital of Malwa. The inscription, a Persian *ghazal* of forty-two verses, mentions the destruction of a Hindu temple by one ʿAbdullah Shah Changal during the reign of Raja Bhoja, a renowned Paramara king who ruled over the region from 1010 to 1053. In *Hindu Temples: What Happened to Them?* Goel accepts the inscription's reference to temple destruction more or less at face value, as though it were a contemporary newspaper account reporting an objective fact.[6] Unlike Goel, however, the text is concerned not with documenting an instance of temple destruction but with narrating and celebrating the fabulous career of ʿAbdullah Shah Changal, the saint who is buried at Dhar. A reading of a larger body of the text reveals, in fact, a complex historiographical process at work:

> This centre became Muhammadan first by him [i.e., ʿAbdullah Shah Changal], (and) all the banners of religion were spread. (I have heard) that a few persons had arrived before him at this desolate and ruined place. When the muazzin raised the morning cry like the trumpet-call for the intoxicated *sufis*, the infidels (made an attack from) every wall (?) and each of them rushed with the sword and knife. At last they (the infidels) wounded those men of religion, and after killing them concealed (them) in a well. Now this (burial place and) grave of martyrs remained a trace of those holy and pious people.
>
> When the time came that the sun of Reality should shine in this dark and gloomy night, this lion-man [ʿAbdullah Shah Changal] came from the centre of religion to this old temple with a large force. He broke the images of the false deities, and turned the idol-temple into a mosque. When Rai Bhoj saw this, through wisdom he embraced Islam with the family of all brave warriors. This quarter became illuminated by the light of the Muhammadan law, and the customs of the infidels became obsolete and abolished.
>
> Now this tomb since those old days has been the famous pilgrimage-place of a world. Graves from their oldness became leveled (to the ground), (and) there remained no mount on any grave. There was also (no place) for retirement, wherein the distressed *darvish* could take rest. Thereupon the king of the world gave the order that this top of Tur [Mount Sinai] be built anew. The king of happy countenance, the Sultan of horizons (i.e., the world), the

> visitors of whose courts are Khaqan (the emperor of Turkistan) and Faghfur (the emperor of China), ʿAla-ud-din Wad-dunya Abu'l-Muzaffar, who is triumphant over his enemies by the grace of God, the Khilji king Mahmud Shah, who is such that by his justice the world has become adorned like paradise, he built afresh this old structure, and this house with its enclosure again became new.[7]

The narrative divides a remembered past into three distinct moments. The first is the period before the arrival of the Hero, ʿAbdullah Shah Changal. At this time a small community of Muslims in Malwa, with but a tenuous foothold in the region, were martyred by local non-Muslims, their bodies thrown into a well. The narrative's second moment is the period of the Hero, who comes from the "centre of religion" (Mecca?), smashes images, transforms the temple into a mosque, and converts to Islam the most famous king of the Paramara dynasty—deeds that collectively avenge the martyred Sufis and (re)establish Islam in the region. The narrative's third moment is the period after the Hero's lifetime when his grave, although a renowned place of pilgrimage, has suffered from neglect. Now enters the narrative's other hero, Sultan Mahmud Khalaji, the "king of the world" and "of happy countenance," to whose court the emperors of China and Central Asia pay respect, and by whose justice the world has become adorned like paradise. His great act was to patronize the cult of ʿAbdullah Shah by (re)building his shrine, which we are told at text's end included a strong vault, a mosque, and a caravanserai. The inscription closes by offering a prayer that the soul of the benevolent sultan may last until Judgment Day and that his empire may last in perpetuity.

Although Indo-Muslim epigraphs are typically recorded soon after the events they describe, the present one is hardly contemporary, as it was composed some four hundred years after the events to which it refers. Far from being a factual account of a contemporary incident, then, the text presents a richly textured legend elaborated over many generations of oral transmission until 1455, when the story of ʿAbdullah Shah Changal and his deeds in Malwa became frozen in the written word that we have before us. As such, the narrative reveals a process by which a particular community at a particular time and place—Muslims in mid-fifteenth-century Malwa—constructed their origins. Central to the story are themes of conversion, martyrdom, redemption, and the patronage of sacred sites by Indo-Muslim royalty, as well as, of course, the destruction of a temple. Whether or not any temple was actually destroyed four hundred years before this narrative was committed to writing, we cannot know with certainty. However, it would seem no more likely that such a desecration had actually occurred than that the renowned Raja Bhoja had been converted to Islam, which the text also claims.

In any event, it is clear that by the mid-fifteenth century the memory of the destruction of a temple, projected into a distant past, had become one among several elements integral to how Muslims in Malwa—or at least those who patronized the composition of this *ghazal*—had come to understand their origins. The case thus suggests that caution is necessary in interpreting claims made in Indo-Muslim literary sources to instances of temple desecration. It also illustrates the central role that temple desecration played in the remembered past of an Indo-Muslim state or community.

Early Instances of Temple Desecration

It is well known that, during the two centuries before 1192, which was when an indigenous Indo-Muslim state and community first appeared in North India, Persianized Turks systematically raided and looted major urban centers of North India, hauling immense loads of movable property to power bases in eastern Afghanistan.[8] The pattern commenced in 986, when the Ghaznavid sultan, Sabuktigin (r. 977–997), attacked and defeated the Hindu Shahi raja who controlled the region between Kabul and northwest Punjab. According to Abu Nasr 'Utbi, the personal secretary to the sultan's son, Sabuktigin "marched out towards Lamghan [located to the immediate east of Kabul], which is a city celebrated for its great strength and abounding in wealth. He conquered it and set fire to the places in its vicinity which were inhabited by infidels, and demolishing the idol-temples, he established Islam in them."[9] Linking religious conversion with military conquest—with conquest serving to facilitate conversion, and conversion to legitimize conquest—'Utbi's brief notice established a rhetorical trope that many subsequent Indo-Muslim chroniclers would repeat, as for example in the case of the 1455 inscription at Dhar, just discussed.

Notwithstanding 'Utbi's religious rhetoric, however, subsequent invasions by Sabuktigin and his more famous son, Mahmud of Ghazni (r. 998–1030), appear to have been undertaken for purely material reasons. Based in Afghanistan and never seeking permanent dominion in India, the earlier Ghaznavid rulers raided and looted Indian cities, including their richly endowed temples loaded with movable wealth, with a view to financing their larger political objectives far to the west in Khurasan.[10] The predatory nature of these raids was also structurally integral to the Ghaznavid political economy: their army was a permanent, professional one built around an elite core of mounted archers who, as slaves, were purchased, equipped, and paid with cash derived from regular infusions of war booty taken alike from Indian and Iranian cities.[11] From the mid-eleventh century, however, Mahmud's successors, cut off from their sources of military manpower in Central Asia first by the Seljuqs and then by the Ghurids, became progressively more provincial, their kingdom focused around their capital of Ghazni in eastern Afghanistan with extensions into the Punjab. And, while the later Ghaznavids continued the predatory raids of the Indian interior for booty, these appear to have been less destructive and more sporadic than those of Sabuktigin and Mahmud.[12]

The dynamics of North Indian politics changed dramatically, however, when the Ghurids, a dynasty of Tajik (eastern Iranian) origins, arrived from central Afghanistan toward the end of the twelfth century. Sweeping aside the Ghaznavids, Ghurid conquerors and their Turkish slave generals ushered in a new sort of state quite unlike that of the foreign-based Ghaznavids. Aspiring to imperial dominion over the whole of North India from a base in the middle of the Indo-Gangetic plain, the new Delhi Sultanate signaled the first attempt to build an indigenous Indo-Muslim state and society in North India. With respect to religious policy, we can identify two principal components to this project: (a) state patronage of an India-based Sufi order, and (b) a policy of selective temple desecration that aimed not, as earlier, to finance the military machine of a vast and distant empire but to delegitimize and extirpate defeated Indian ruling houses. Let us consider these in turn.

Sufism and State Building

"The world is bound up closely with that of the men of faith," wrote the Bahmani court poet ʿAbd al-Malik ʿIsami in 1350. "In every country, there is a man of piety who keeps it going and well. Although there might be a monarch in every country, yet it is actually under the protection of a fakir [Sufi shaikh]."[13] Here we find a concise statement of the medieval Perso-Islamic conception of how religion and politics interrelate. In ʿIsami's view, what had saved the Delhi Sultanate from Mongol conquest was the respect showed by Sultan Muhammad bin Tughluq (r.

1325–51) for the memory of the founder of the Chishti order in India, Shaikh Mu'in al-Din Chishti (d. 1236), to whose tomb in Ajmer the sultan had made a pilgrimage just after engaging with a Mongol army.[14] 'Isami also felt, however, that the decline of Delhi, and of the Tughluq empire generally, had resulted in large part from the demise in 1325 of Nizam al-Din Auliya, Delhi's most renowned shaikh. Conversely, he considered that the arrival in the Deccan of one of Nizam al-Din Auliya's leading spiritual successors, Burhan al-Din Gharib (d. 1337), was the cause of that region's flourishing state at midcentury.[15]

Among all South Asian Sufi orders, the Chishtis were the most closely identified with the political fortunes of Indo-Muslim states, and especially with the planting of such states in parts of South Asia never previously touched by Islamic rule. The pattern began in the first several decades of the fourteenth century, when the order's rise to prominence among Delhi's urban populace coincided with that of the imperial Tughluqs. The two principal Persian poets in India of that time, Amir Hasan and Amir Khusrau, and the leading historian, Zia al-Din Barani, were all disciples of Nizam al-Din Auliya. As writers whose works were widely read, these men were in effect publicists for Nizam al-Din and his order. And since the three were also patronized by the Tughluq court, the public and the ruling classes alike gradually came to associate dynastic fortune with that of the Chishti order.[16] Moreover, as the spiritual power of a charismatic Sufi was believed to adhere to his tomb, shrines at such tombs were patronized by Indo-Muslim rulers just as they were frequented by Muslim devotees. And since the tomb-shrines of the greatest shaikhs of this order were located within South Asia, and not in distant Central Asia or the Middle East as was the case with those of other orders, a ruling dynasty's patronage of Chishti shrines could bolster its claims to being both legitimately Islamic and authentically Indian.

Thus Chishti shaikhs repeatedly participated in the launching of new Indo-Muslim states. At the core of 'Isami's narrative of the Bahmani Revolution, which in 1347 successfully threw off Tughluq overlordship and launched an independent Indo-Muslim state in the Deccan, is a narrative of the passing of the Prophet Muhammad's own mantle (*khirqa*) from Abu Bakr, the first caliph, down to Burhan al-Din Gharib's leading disciple, Zain al-Din Shirazi (d. 1369). It was from that very mantle—"by whose scent one could master both worlds"—that the founder of the Bahmani Sultanate, Sultan Hasan Bahman Shah (r. 1347–58), was said to have received his own power and inspiration.[17] We see the same pattern in Bengal, another former Tughluq province that asserted its independence from Delhi in the mid-fourteenth century. The earliest known monument built by the founder of Bengal's Ilyas Shahi dynasty (1342–1486) was a mosque dedicated in 1342 to Shaikh ʿAla al-Haq (d. 1398), a Sufi shaikh whose own spiritual master was—like Zain al-Din's spiritual master—a disciple of Nizam al-Din Auliya (d. 1325). What is more, the political ascendancy of the Ilyas Shahi dynasty coincided exactly with the spiritual ascendancy of Shaikh ʿAla al-Haq and his own family. Down to the year 1532, fully fourteen successive sultans of Bengal enlisted themselves as disciples of the descendants of this shaikh, while the tomb-shrine of ʿAla al-Haq's own son and successor, Nur Qutb-i ʿAlam, became in effect a state shrine to which subsequent sultans made annual pilgrimages.[18]

In short, within the space of just five years, between 1342 and 1347, founders of independent Indo-Muslim dynasties in both Bengal and the Deccan patronized local Chishti shaikhs whose own spiritual masters had migrated from Delhi, where they had studied with the imperial capital's preeminent Sufi shaikh, Nizam al-Din Auliya. The pattern was repeated elsewhere, as the Tughluq empire continued to crumble, giving rise to more provincial successor-states. In 1396, the Tughluq governor of Gujarat, Muzaffar Khan, proclaimed his independence immediately after marching to Ajmer, where he paid his devotions to the tomb of Muʿin al-Din Chishti, the "mother-shrine" of the Chishti order in India.[19] In 1404, soon after proclaiming his own independence from Delhi, the former Tughluq governor of Malwa, Dilawar Khan, described himself as "the disciple of the head of the holy order of Nasir Din Mahmud."[20] The reference here was to Nizam al-Din Auliya's most eminent disciple to have remained in Delhi—Shaikh Nasir al-Din Mahmud (d. 1356), over whose grave Sultan Firuz Shah Tughluq (r. 1351–88) had raised a magnificent tomb several decades earlier.[21]

Nor did the pattern cease with the launching of Tughluq successor states. On entering Delhi in 1526, Babur prayed at the shrine of India's second great Chishti shaikh, Bakhtiyar Kaki (d. 1235), and the new emperor's brother-in-law rebuilt the tomb of Nizam al-Din Auliya. In 1571 Akbar built a tomb for his father, Humayun, near Nizam al-Din's shrine and in the same year began building his new capital of Fatehpur Sikri at the hospice-site of Salim Chishti, the shaikh who had predicted the birth of the emperor's son. Toward the end of his life, this same shaikh tied his turban on the head of that son, the future Jahangir, and pronounced him his spiritual successor. As emperor himself, Jahangir built gates and other buildings at or near the foundational Chishti shrine at Ajmer, as did Shah Jahan as part of his victory celebrations after defeating the raja of Mewar. That emperor's daughter, Jahan Ara, even wrote a biography of Muʿin al-Din Chishti. Shah Jahan's son and successor, Aurangzeb, who sought to build another pan-Indian empire on the Tughluq model, visited and made sizable contributions to Chishti tombs in former Tughluq provinces such as at Gulbarga or Khuldabad, in addition to tombs in Ajmer and Delhi. Even the later Mughals patronized those Chishti shrines to which they still had access in their dwindling domains, as when ʿAlamgir II repaired and made additions to the tomb of Nizam al-Din Auliya. Bringing the pattern full circle, the last Mughal emperor, Bahadur Shah II (deposed 1858), built his own mansion adjacent to the shrine of Bakhtiyar Kaki, the very site where Babur had prayed more than three centuries earlier.[22]

In sum, rulers of the entire Mughal dynasty, believing that the blessings of Chishti shaikhs underpinned their worldly success, vigorously patronized the order. Two of Akbar's fourteen pilgrimages to the shrine of Muʿin al-Din Chishti at Ajmer, those of 1568 and 1574, were made immediately after conquering Chittor and Bengal, respectively.[23] Discussing his military successes with the historian ʿAbd al-Qadir Badauni, Akbar remarked, "All this (success) has been brought through the Pir [Muʿin al-Din]."[24] Vividly dramatized by Akbar's pilgrimages from Agra to Ajmer, several of them made by foot, the Mughal-Chishti partnership even survived the collapse of the Mughal state. In a sense it persists to this day. The ceremonies, the terminology, and the protocol still found at Chishti shrines generally, and at the Ajmer shrine particularly, reflect the extraordinary intrusion of Mughal courtly culture into that of the Chishti order.[25]

Temple Desecration and State Building

By effectively injecting a legitimizing "substance" into a new body politic, royal patronage of Chishti shaikhs contributed positively to the process of Indo-Muslim state building. Equally important to this process was its negative counterpart: the sweeping away of all prior political authority in newly conquered and annexed territories. When such authority was vested in a ruler whose own legitimacy was associated with a royal temple—typically one that housed an image of a ruling dynasty's state deity, or *raṣṭra-devatā* (usually Vishnu or Śiva)— that temple was normally desecrated, redefined, or destroyed, any of which would have had the effect of detaching a defeated raja from the most prominent manifestation of his former legitimacy. Temples that were not so identified, or temples formerly so identified but abandoned by their royal patrons and thereby rendered politically irrelevant, were normally left unharmed. Such was the case, for example, with the famous temples at Khajuraho south of the Middle Gangetic Plain, which appear to have been abandoned by their Candella royal patrons before Turkish armies reached the area in the early thirteenth century.[26]

It would be wrong to explain this phenomenon by appealing to an essentialized "theology of iconoclasm" felt to be intrinsic to the Islamic religion. While it is true that contemporary Persian sources routinely condemned idolatry (*but-parastī*) on religious grounds, it is also true that attacks on images patronized by enemy kings had been, from about the sixth century A.D. on, thoroughly integrated into Indian political behavior. With their lushly sculpted imagery vividly displaying the mutual interdependence of kings and gods and the commingling of divine and human kingship, royal temple complexes of the early medieval period were thoroughly and preeminently political institutions. It was here that, after the sixth century, human kingship was established, contested, and revitalized.[27] Above all, the central icon housed in a royal temple's "womb-chamber" and inhabited by the state deity of the temple's royal patron expressed the shared sovereignty of king and deity. Moreover, notwithstanding that temple priests endowed a royal temple's deity with attributes of transcendent and universal power, that same deity was also understood as having a very special relationship, indeed a sovereign relationship, with the particular geographical site in which its temple complex was located.[28] As revealed in temple narratives, even the physical removal of an image from its original site could not break the link between deity and geography.[29] The bonding between king, god, temple, and land in early medieval India is well illustrated in a passage from *Bṛhatsaṃhitā*, a text from the sixth century A.D.: "If a Śiva linga, image, or temple breaks apart, moves, sweats, cries, speaks, or otherwise acts with no apparent cause, this warns of the destruction of the king and his territory."[30] In short, from about the sixth century on, images and temples associated with dynastic authority were considered politically vulnerable.

Given these perceived connections between temples, images, and their royal patrons, it is hardly surprising that early medieval Indian history abounds in instances of temple desecration that occurred amidst interdynastic conflicts. In A.D. 642, according to local tradition, the Pallava king, Narasimhavarman I, looted the image of Ganesha from the Chalukyan capital of Vatapi. Fifty years later, armies of those same Chalukyas invaded North India and brought back to the Deccan what appear to be images of Ganga and Yamuna, looted from defeated powers there. In the eighth century, Bengali troops sought revenge on King Lalitaditya by destroying what they thought was the image of Vishnu Vaikuntha, the state deity of Lalitaditya's kingdom in Kashmir. In the early ninth century, the Rashtrakuta king, Govinda III, invaded and occupied Kanchipuram, which so intimidated the king of Sri Lanka that he sent Govinda several (probably Buddhist) images representing the Sinhala state. The Rashtrakuta king then installed these in a Śaiva temple in his capital. About the same time the Pandyan king, Srimara Srivallabha, also invaded Sri Lanka and took back to his capital a golden Buddha image—"a synecdoche for the integrity of the Sinhalese polity itself"—that had been installed in the kingdom's jewel palace. In the early tenth century, the Pratihara king, Herambapala, seized a solid gold image of Vishnu Vaikuntha when he defeated the Sahi king of Kangra. A few years later, the same image was seized from the Pratiharas by the Candella king, Yaśovarman, and installed in the Lakshmana temple of Khajuraho. In the early eleventh century, the Chola king, Rajendra I, furnished his capital with images he had seized from several prominent neighboring kings: Durga and Ganesha images from the Chalukyas; Bhairava, Bhairavi, and Kali images from the Kalingas of Orissa; a Nandi image from the Eastern Chalukyas; and a bronze Śiva image from the Palas of Bengal. In the mid-eleventh century, the Chola king, Rajadhiraja, defeated the Chalukyas and plundered Kalyani, taking a large black stone door guardian to his capital in Thanjavur, where it was displayed to his subjects as a trophy of war.[31]

While the dominant pattern here was one of looting royal temples and carrying off images of state deities,[32] we also hear of Hindu kings destroying the royal temples of their political adversaries. In the early tenth century, the Rashtrakuta monarch, Indra III, not only destroyed the temple of Kalapriya (at Kalpa near the Jamuna River), patronized by the Rashtrakutas' deadly enemies, the Pratiharas, but they took special delight in recording the fact.[33]

In short, it is clear that temples had been the natural sites for the contestation of kingly authority well before the coming of Muslim Turks to India. Not surprisingly, Turkish invaders, when attempting to plant their own rule in early medieval India, followed and continued established patterns. Table 10.1 (pp. 274a–d) gives dates and places, which are keyed to three maps (pp. 272–74). These cannot give the complete picture of temple desecration after the establishment of Turkish power in Upper India. Undoubtedly, some temples were desecrated, but the facts were never recorded, or the facts were recorded but the records themselves no longer survive. Conversely, later Indo-Muslim chroniclers, seeking to glorify the religious zeal of earlier Muslim rulers, sometimes attributed acts of temple desecration to such rulers even when no contemporary evidence supports the claims.[34] As a result, we shall never know the precise number of temples desecrated in Indian history. Nonetheless, by relying strictly on evidence found in contemporary or near-contemporary epigraphs and literary evidence spanning more than five centuries (1192–1729), one may identify eighty instances of temple desecration whose historicity appears reasonably certain. Although this figure falls well short of the 60,000 claimed by some Hindu nationalists,[35] a review of these data suggests several broad patterns.

First, acts of temple desecration were almost invariably carried out by military officers or ruling authorities; that is, such acts that we know about were undertaken by the state. Second, the chronology and geography of the data indicate that acts of temple desecration typically occurred on the cutting edge of a moving military frontier. From Ajmer—significantly, also the wellspring of Chishti piety—the post-1192 pattern of temple desecration moved swiftly down the Gangetic Plain as Turkish military forces sought to extirpate local ruling houses in the late twelfth and early thirteenth centuries (see table 10.1 and map 10.1: nos. 1–9). In Bihar, this included the targeting of Buddhist monastic establishments at Odantapuri, Vikramasila, and Nalanda. Detached from a Buddhist laity, these establishments had by this time become dependent on the patronage of local royal authorities, with whom they were identified. In the 1230s, Iltutmish carried the Delhi Sultanate's authority into Malwa (nos. 10–11), and by the onset of the fourteenth century the Khalaji sultans had opened up a corridor through eastern Rajasthan into Gujarat (nos. 12–14, 16–17).

Delhi's initial raids on peninsular India, on which the Khalajis embarked between 1295 and the early decades of the fourteenth century (nos. 15, 18–19), appear to have been driven not by a goal of annexation but by the Sultanate's need for wealth with which to defend North India from Mongol attacks.[36] For a short time, then, peninsular India stood in the same relation to the North—namely, as a source of plunder for financing distant military operations—as North India had stood in relation to Afghanistan three centuries earlier, in the days of Mahmud of

Ghazni. In 1323, however, a new North Indian dynasty, the Tughluqs, sought permanent dominion in the Deccan, which the future Sultan Muhammad bin Tughluq established by uprooting royally patronized temples in western Andhra (nos. 20–22). Somewhat later Sultan Firuz Tughluq did the same in Orissa (no. 23).

From the late fourteenth century, as the tide of Tughluq imperialism had receded from Gujurat and the Deccan, newly emerging successor states sought to expand their own political frontiers in those areas. This, too, is reflected in instances of temple desecration, as the ex-Tughluq governor of Gujarat and his successors consolidated their authority there (see table 10.1 and map 10.2: nos. 25–26, 31–32, 34–35, 38–39, 42), or as the Delhi empire's successors in the south, the Bahmani sultans, challenged Vijayanagara's claims to dominate the Raichur doab and the Tamil coast (nos. 33, 41). The pattern was repeated in Kashmir by Sultan Sikandar (nos. 27–30) and in the mid-fifteenth century when the independent sultanate of Malwa contested renewed Rajput power in eastern Rajasthan after Delhi's authority there had waned (nos. 36–37). In the early sixteenth century, when the Lodi dynasty of Afghans sought to reassert Delhi's sovereignty over neighboring Rajput houses, we again find instances of temple desecration (nos. 43–45). So do we in the later sixteenth and early seventeenth centuries, when the Bahmani kingdom's principal successor states, Bijapur and Golconda, challenged the territorial sovereignty of Orissan kings (nos. 55, 59; maps 10.2 and 10.3), of Vijayanagara (no. 47), and of the latter's successor states—especially in the southern Andhra country (nos. 50–51, 53–54, 60–61; maps 10.2 and 10.3).

Unlike the Deccan, where Indo-Muslim states had been expanding at the expense of non-Muslim states, in North India the Mughals under Babur, Humayun, and Akbar—that is, between 1526 and 1605—grew mainly at the expense of defeated Afghans. As non-Hindus, the latter had never shared sovereignty with deities patronized in royal temples, which probably explains the absence of firm evidence of temple desecration by any of the early Mughals, in Ayodhya or elsewhere.[37] However, when Mughal armies pushed beyond the frontiers of territories formerly ruled by the Delhi sultans and sought to annex the domains of Hindu rulers, we again find instances of temple desecration. In 1661 the governor of Bengal, Mir Jumla, sacked the temples of the raja of Kuch Bihar, who had been harassing the northern frontiers of Mughal territory (no. 64; map 10.3). The next year, with a view to annexing Assam to the imperial domain, the governor pushed far up the Brahmaputra Valley and desecrated temples of the Ahom rajas, replacing the principal one at Garhgaon with a mosque (nos. 65–66).

All of these instances of temple desecration occurred in the context of military conflicts when Indo-Muslim states expanded into the domains of non-Muslim rulers. Contemporary chroniclers and inscriptions left by the victors leave no doubt that field commanders, governors, or sultans viewed the desecration of royal temples as a normal means of decoupling a Hindu king's legitimate authority from his former kingdom, and more specifically, of decoupling that former king from the image of the state deity that was publicly understood as protecting the king and his kingdom. This was accomplished in several ways. Most typically, temples considered essential to the constitution of enemy authority were destroyed. Occasionally, temples were converted into mosques, which more visibly conflated the disestablishment of former sovereignty with the establishment of a new one.[38]

The form of desecration that showed the greatest continuity with pre-Turkish practice was the seizure of the image of a defeated king's state deity and its abduction to the victor's capital as a trophy of war. In February 1299, for example, Ulugh Khan sacked Gujarat's famous temple of Somnath and sent its largest image to Sultan ʿAla al-Din Khalaji's court in Delhi (no. 16; map 10.1). When Firuz Tughluq invaded Orissa in 1359 and learned that the region's most important temple was that of Jagannath located inside the raja's fortress in Puri, he carried off the stone image of the god and installed it in Delhi "in an ignominious position" (no. 23). In 1518, when the court in Delhi came to suspect the loyalty of a tributary Rajput chieftain in Gwalior, Sultan Ibrahim Lodi marched to the famous fortress, stormed it, and seized a brass image of Nandi evidently situated adjacent to the chieftain's Śiva temple. Brought back to Delhi, it was installed in the city's Baghdad Gate (no. 46; map 10.2). Similarly, in 1579, when Golconda's army, led by Murahari Rao, was campaigning south of the Krishna River, Rao annexed the entire region to Qutb Shahi domains and sacked the popular Ahobilam temple, whose ruby-studded image he brought back to Golconda and presented to his sultan as a war trophy (no. 51). Although the Ahobilam temple had only local appeal, it had close associations with prior sovereign authority, since it had been patronized and even visited by the powerful and most famous king of Vijayanagara, Krishna Deva Raya.[39]

In each of these instances, the deity's image, taken as war trophy to the capital city of the victorious sultan, was radically detached from its former context and transformed from a living to a dead image. However, sacked images were not invariably abducted to the victor's capital. In 1556, the Gajapati raja of Orissa had entered into a pact with the Mughal emperor, Akbar, the distant adversary of the sultan of Bengal, Sulaiman Karrani. The raja had also given refuge to Sulaiman's more proximate adversary, Ibrahim Sur, and offered to assist the latter in his ambitions to conquer Bengal and overthrow the Karrani dynasty. As Sulaiman could hardly have tolerated such threats to his stability, he sent an army into Orissa that went straight to the Gajapati kingdom's state temple of Jagannath and looted its images. But here the goal was not annexation but only punishment, which might explain why the Gajapati state images were not carried back to the Bengali capital as trophies of war.[40]

Whatever form they took, acts of temple desecration were never directed at the people but at the enemy king and the image that incarnated and displayed his state deity. A contemporary description of a 1661 Mughal campaign in Kuch Bihar, which resulted in the annexation of the region, makes it clear that Mughal authorities were guided by two principal concerns. The first was to destroy the image of the state deity of the defeated raja, Bhim Narayan. And the second was to prevent Mughal troops from looting or in any way harming the general population of Kuch Bihar. To this end, we are informed that the chief judge of Mughal Bengal, Saiyid Muhammad Sadiq,

> was directed to issue prohibitory orders that nobody was to touch the cash and property of the people, and he should go personally and establish order everywhere. He was asked to confiscate the treasure of Bhim Narayan, break the idols and introduce the laws of Islam. Sayyid Sadiq issued strict prohibitory orders so that nobody had the courage to break the laws or to plunder the property of the inhabitants. The punishment for disobeying the order was that the hands, ears or noses of the plunderers were cut. Sayyid Sadiq busied himself in giving protection to the life and property of the subjects and the destitutes.[41]

In newly annexed areas formerly ruled by non-Muslims, as in the case of Kuch Bihar, Mughal officers took appropriate measures to secure the support of the common people, who after all created the material wealth upon which the entire imperial edifice rested.

Temple Protection and State Maintenance

If the idea of conquest became manifest in the destruction of those temples associated with former enemies, what happened once the land and the subjects of those former states became successfully integrated into an Indo-Muslim state? On this point, the data are quite clear: pragmatism as well as time-honored traditions of both Islamic and Indian statecraft dictated that temples lying within such states be left unmolested. We learn from a Sanskrit inscription, for example, that in 1326, thirteen years after the northern Deccan had been annexed to the Tughluq empire, Sultan Muhammad bin Tughluq appointed Muslim officials to repair a Śiva temple in Kalyana (in Bidar District), thereby facilitating the resumption of normal worship that had been disrupted by local disturbances.[42] According to that sultan's interpretation of Islamic law, anybody who paid the poll tax (*jizya*) could build temples in territories ruled by Muslims.[43]

Such views continued to hold sway until modern times. Within several decades of Muhammad bin Tughluq's death, Sultan Shihab al-Din (1355–73) of Kashmir rebuked his Brahman minister for having suggested melting down Hindu and Buddhist images in his kingdom as a means of obtaining quick cash. In elaborating his ideas on royal patronage of religion, the sultan referred to the deeds of figures drawn from classical Hindu mythology. "Some [kings]," he said,

> have obtained renown by setting up images of gods, others by worshiping them, some by duly maintaining them. And some, by demolishing them! How great is the enormity of such a deed! Sagara became famous by creating the sea and the rivers. . . . Bhagiratha obtained fame by bringing down the Ganges. Jealous of Indra's fame, Dushyanata acquired renown by conquering the world; and Rama by killing Ravana when the latter had purloined Sita. King Shahvadina [Shihab al-Din], it will be said, plundered the image of a god; and this fact, dreadful as Yama [death], will make the men in future tremble.[44]

About a century later, Muslim jurists advised the future Sikandar Lodi of Delhi (r. 1489–1517) that "it is not lawful to lay waste ancient idol temples, and it does not rest with you to prohibit ablution in a reservoir which has been customary from ancient times."[45]

The pattern of post-conquest temple protection, and even patronage, is especially clear when we come to the imperial Mughals, whose overall views on the subject are captured in official pronouncements on Sultan Mahmud of Ghazni, one of the most controversial figures in Indian history. It is well known that in the early eleventh century, before the establishment of Indo-Muslim rule in North India, the Ghaznavid sultan had made numerous, and very destructive, attacks on the region. Starting with the writings of his own contemporary and court poet, Firdausi (d. 1020), Mahmud's career soon became legend, as generations of Persian poets lionized Mahmud as a paragon of Islamic kingly virtue, celebrating his infamous attacks on Indian temples as models for what other pious sultans should do.[46] But the Ghaznavid sultan never undertook the responsibility of actually governing any part of the subcontinent whose temples he so wantonly plundered. Herein lies the principal difference between the careers of Mahmud and Abu'l-fazl, Akbar's chief minister and the principal architect of Mughal imperial ideology. Reflecting the sober values that normally accompany the practice of governing large, multiethnic states, Abu'l-fazl attributed Mahmud's excesses to fanatical bigots who, having incorrectly represented India as "a country of unbelievers at war with Islam," incited the sultan's unsuspecting nature, which led to "the wreck of honour and the shedding of blood and the plunder of the virtuous."[47]

Indeed, from Akbar's time (r. 1556–1605) forward, Mughal rulers treated temples lying within their sovereign domain as state property; accordingly, they undertook to protect both the physical structures and their Brahman functionaries. At the same time, by appropriating Hindu religious institutions to serve imperial ends—a process involving complex overlappings of political and religious codes of power—the Mughals became deeply implicated in institutionalized Indian religions, in dramatic contrast to their British successors, who professed a hands-off policy in this respect. Thus we find Akbar allowing high-ranking Rajput officers in his service to build their own monumental temples in the provinces to which they were posted.[48] His successors went further. Between 1590 and 1735, Mughal officials repeatedly oversaw, and on occasion even initiated, the renewal of Orissa's state cult, that of Jagannath in Puri. By sitting on a canopied chariot while accompanying the cult's annual car festival, Shah Jahan's officials ritually demonstrated that it was the Mughal emperor, operating through his appointed officers (*manṣabdār*), who was the temple's—and hence the god's— ultimate lord and protector.[49] Such actions in effect projected a hierarchy of hybridized political and religious power that descended from the Mughal emperor to his *manṣabdār*, from the *manṣabdār* to the god Jagannath and his temple, from Jagannath to the subimperial king who patronized the god, and from the king to his subjects. For the Mughals, politics within their sovereign domains never meant annihilating prior authority. It meant appropriating authority within a hierarchy of power that flowed from the Peacock Throne to the mass of commoners below.

Such ideas continued into the reign of Aurangzeb (1658–1707), whose orders to local officials in Benares in 1659 clearly indicate that Brahman temple functionaries there, together with the temples at which they officiated, merited state protection:

> In these days information has reached our court that several people have, out of spite and rancor, harassed the Hindu residents of Benares and nearby places, including a group of Brahmans who are in charge of ancient temples there. These people want to remove those Brahmans from their charge of temple-keeping, which has caused them considerable distress. Therefore, upon receiving this order, you must see that nobody unlawfully disturbs the Brahmans or other Hindus of that region, so that they might remain in their traditional place and pray for the continuance of the Empire.[50]

By way of justifying this order, the emperor noted, "According to the Holy Law and the exalted creed, it has been established that ancient temples should not be torn down." On this point, Aurangzeb aligned himself with the theory and practice of Indo-Muslim ruling precedent. But then he added, "Nor should new temples be built"—a view that broke decisively from Akbar's policy of permitting his Rajput officers to build their own temple complexes in Mughal territory.[51] Although this order appears to have applied only to Benares—many new temples were built elsewhere in India during Aurangzeb's reign[52]—one might wonder what prompted the emperor's anxiety in this matter.

Temple Desecration and State Maintenance

It seems certain that Indo-Muslim rulers were well aware of the highly charged political and religious relationship between a royal Hindu patron and his client-temple. Hence, even when former rulers or their descendants had been comfortably assimilated into an Indo-Muslim state's ruling class, there always remained the possibility, and hence the occasional suspicion, that a temple's latent political significance might be activated and serve as a power base to further its patron's political aspirations. Such considerations might explain why it was that, when a subordinate non-Muslim officer in an Indo-Muslim state showed signs of disloyalty—and especially if he engaged in open rebellion—the state often desecrated the temple(s) most clearly identified with that officer. After all, if temples lying within its domain were viewed as state property, and if a government officer who was also a temple's patron demonstrated disloyalty to the state, from a juridical standpoint ruling authorities felt justified in treating that temple as an extension of the officer and hence liable for punishment.

Thus in 1478, when the Bahmanis' garrison in Kondapalle mutinied, murdered its governor, and entrusted the fort to Bhimraj Oriyya, who until that point had been a Bahmani client, the sultan personally marched to the site and, after a six-month siege, stormed the fort, destroyed its temple, and built a mosque on the site (no. 40). A similar event occurred in 1659, when Shivaji Bhonsle, the son of a loyal and distinguished officer serving the ʿAdil Shahi sultans of Bijapur, seized a government port on the northern Konkan coast, thereby disrupting the flow of external trade to and from the capital. Responding to what it considered an act of treason, the government deputed a high-ranking officer, Afzal Khan, to punish the Maratha rebel. Before marching to confront Shivaji himself, however, the Bijapur general first proceeded to Tuljapur and desecrated a temple dedicated to the goddess Bhavani, to which Shivaji and his family had been personally devoted (no. 63; map 10.3).

We find the same pattern with the Mughals. In 1613 while at Pushkar, near Ajmer, Jahangir ordered the desecration of an image of Varaha that had been housed in a temple belonging to an uncle of Rana Amar of Mewar, the emperor's archenemy (see table 10.1 and map 10.3: no. 56). In 1635 his son and successor, Shah Jahan, destroyed the great temple at Orchha, which had been patronized by the father of Raja Jajhar Singh, a high-ranking Mughal officer who was at that time in open rebellion against the emperor (no. 58). In 1669, there arose a rebellion in Benares among landholders, some of whom were suspected of having helped Shivaji, who was Aurangzeb's archenemy, escape from imperial detention. It was also believed that Shivaji's escape had been initially facilitated by Jai Singh, the great-grandson of Raja Man Singh, who almost certainly built Benares's great Vishvanath temple. It was against this background that the emperor ordered the destruction of that temple in September 1669 (no. 69).[53] About the same time, serious Jat rebellions broke out in the area around Mathura, in which the patron of that city's congregational mosque had been killed. So in early 1670, soon after the ringleader of these rebellions had been captured near Mathura, Aurangzeb ordered the destruction of the city's Keshava Deva temple, and he built an Islamic structure (*ʿīd-gāh*) on its site (no. 70).[54] Nine years later, the emperor ordered the destruction of several prominent temples in Rajasthan that had become associated with imperial enemies. These included temples in Khandela patronized by refractory chieftains there, temples in Jodhpur patronized by a former supporter of the emperor's brother and arch rival, and the royal temples in Udaipur and Chitor patronized by Rana Raj Singh after it was learned that that Rajput chieftain had withdrawn his loyalty to the Mughal state (nos. 71–74).

Considerable misunderstanding has arisen from a passage in the *Ma'athir-i ʿAlamgiri* concerning an order on the status of Hindu temples that Aurangzeb issued in April 1669, just months before his destruction of the Benares and Mathura temples. The passage has been construed to mean that the emperor ordered the destruction not only of the Vishvanath temple at Benares and the Keshava Deva temple at Mathura but of all temples in the empire.[55] The passage reads as follows: "Orders respecting Islamic affairs were issued to the governors of all the provinces that the schools and places of worship of the irreligious be subject to demolition and that with the utmost urgency the manner of teaching and the public practices of the sects of these misbelievers be suppressed."[56] The order did not state that schools or places of worship be demolished; rather, it said that they were *subject* to demolition, implying that local authorities were required to make investigations before taking action.

More important, the sentence immediately preceding this passage provides the context in which we may find the order's overall intent. On 8 April 1669, Aurangzeb's court received reports that in Thatta, Multan, and especially in Benares, Brahmans in "established schools" (*mudāris-i muqarrar*) had been engaged in teaching false books (*kutub-i bāṭila*) and that both Hindu and Muslim "admirers and students" had been traveling over great distances to study the "ominous sciences" taught by this "deviant group."[57] We do not know what sort of teaching or "false books" were involved here, or why both Muslims and Hindus were attracted to them, although these are intriguing questions. What is clear is that the court was primarily concerned, indeed exclusively concerned, with curbing the influence of a certain mode of teaching (*ṭaur-i dars-o-tadrīs*) within the imperial domain. Far from being, then, a general order for the immediate destruction of all temples in the empire, the order was responding to specific reports of an educational nature and was targeted at investigating those institutions where a certain kind of teaching had been taking place.

In sum, apart from his prohibition on building new temples in Benares, Aurangzeb's policies respecting temples within imperial domains generally followed those of his predecessors. Viewing temples within their domains as state property, Aurangzeb and Indo-Muslim rulers in general punished disloyal Hindu officers in their service by desecrating temples with which they were associated. How, one might then ask, did they punish disloyal Muslim officers? Since officers in all Indo-Muslim states belonged to hierarchically ranked service cadres, infractions short of rebellion normally resulted in demotions in rank, while serious crimes like treason were generally punished by execution, regardless of the perpetrator's religious affiliation.[58]

No evidence, however, suggests that ruling authorities attacked public monuments like mosques or Sufi shrines that had been patronized by disloyal or rebellious officers. Nor were such monuments desecrated when one Indo-Muslim kingdom conquered another and annexed its territories. To the contrary, new rulers were quick to honor and support the shrines of those Chishti shaikhs that had been patronized by those they had defeated. As we have seen, Babur, upon seizing Delhi from the last of the city's ruling sultans, lost no time in patronizing the city's principal Chishti tomb-shrines. The pattern was repeated as the Mughals expanded into the provinces formerly ruled by Muslims. Upon conquering Bengal in 1574, the Mughals showered their most lavish patronage on the two Chishti shrines in Pandua—those of Shaikh ʿAla al-Haq (d. 1398) and Shaikh Nur Qutb-i ʿAlam (d. 1459)—which had been the principal object of state patronage by the previous dynasty of Bengal sultans.[59] And when he extended Mughal dominion over defeated Muslim states of the Deccan, the dour Aurangzeb, notwithstanding his reputation for eschewing saint cults, made sizable contributions to those Chishti shrines in Khuldabad and Gulbarga that had helped legitimize earlier Muslim dynasties there.

Temples and Mosques Contrasted

Data presented in the foregoing discussion suggest that mosques or shrines carried very different political meanings than did royal temples in independent Hindu states or temples patronized by Hindu officers serving in Indo-Muslim states. For Indo-Muslim rulers, building mosques was considered an act of royal piety, even a duty. But all actors, rulers and ruled alike, seem to have recognized that the deity worshiped in mosques or shrines had no personal connection with a Muslim monarch. Nor were such monuments thought of as underpinning, far less actually constituting, the authority of an Indo-Muslim king. This point is illustrated in a reported dispute between the emperor Aurangzeb and a Sufi named Shaikh Muhammadi (d. 1696). As a consequence of this dispute, in which the shaikh refused to renounce views that the emperor considered theologically deviant, Shaikh Muhammadi was ordered to leave the imperial domain. When the Sufi instead took refuge in a local mosque, Aurangzeb claimed that this would not do, since the mosque was also within imperial territory. But the shaikh only remarked on the emperor's arrogance, noting that a mosque was the house of God and therefore only His property. The standoff ended with the shaikh's imprisonment in Aurangabad fort—property that was unambiguously imperial.[60]

This incident suggests that mosques in Mughal India, though religiously potent, were considered detached from both land and dynastic authority and hence politically inactive. As such, their desecration could have had no relevance to the business of disestablishing a regime that had patronized them. Not surprisingly, then, when Hindu rulers established their authority over territories of defeated Muslim rulers, they did not as a rule desecrate mosques or shrines, as when Shivaji established a Maratha kingdom on the ashes of Bijapur's former dominions in Maharashtra, or when Vijayanagara annexed the former territories of the Bahmanis or their successors.[61] In fact, the rajas of Vijayanagara, as is well known, built their own mosques, evidently to accommodate the sizable number of Muslims employed in their armed forces.

By contrast, monumental royal temple complexes of the early medieval period were considered politically active, inasmuch as the state deities they housed were understood as expressing the shared sovereignty of king and deity over a *particular* dynastic realm.[62] Therefore, when Indo-Muslim commanders or rulers looted the consecrated images of defeated opponents and carried them off to their own capitals as war trophies, they were in a sense conforming to customary rules of Indian politics. Similarly, when they destroyed a royal temple or converted it into a mosque, ruling authorities were building on a political logic that they knew placed supreme political significance on such temples. That same significance, in turn, rendered temples just as deserving of peacetime protection as it rendered them vulnerable in times of conflict.

Temple Desecration and the Rhetoric of State Building

Much misunderstanding over the place of temple desecration in Indian history results from a failure to distinguish the rhetoric from the practice of Indo-Muslim state formation. Whereas the former tends to be normative, conservative, and rigidly ideological, the latter tends to be pragmatic, eclectic, and nonideological. Rhetorically, we know, temple desecration figured very prominently in Indo-Muslim chronicles as a necessary and even meritorious constituent of state formation.[63] In 1350, for example, the poet-chronicler ʿIsami gave the following advice to his royal patron, ʿAla al-Din Hasan Bahman Shah, the founder of the Bahmani kingdom in the Deccan: "If you and I, O man of intellect, have a holding in this country and are in a position to replace the idol-houses by mosques and sometimes forcibly to break the Brahmanic thread and enslave women and children—all this is due to the glory of Mahmud [of Ghazni]. . . . The achievements that you make to-day will also become a story to-morrow."[64] But the new sultan appears to have been more concerned with political stability than with the glorious legacy his court poet would wish him to pursue. There is no evidence that he converted any temples to mosques. After all, by carving out territory from lands formerly lying within the Delhi Sultanate, the founder of the Bahmani state had inherited a domain void of independent Hindu kings and hence void, too, of temples that might have posed a political threat to his fledgling kingdom.

Unlike temple desecration or the patronage of Chishti shaikhs, both of which appear in the contemporary rhetoric on Indo-Muslim state building, a third activity, the use of explicitly Indian political rituals, occupied no place whatsoever in that rhetoric. Here we may consider the way Indo-Muslim rulers used the rich political symbolism of the Ganges River, whose mythic associations with imperial kingship had been well established since Mauryan times (321–181 B.C.). Each in its own way, the mightiest imperial formations of the early medieval peninsula—the Chalukyas, the Rashtrakutas, and the Cholas—claimed to have "brought" the Ganges River down to their southern capitals, seeking thereby to legitimize their claims to imperial sovereignty. Although the Chalukyas and the Rashtrakutas did this symbolically, probably through their insignia, the Cholas literally transported pots of Ganges water to their southern capital.[65] And, we are told, so did Muhammad bin Tughluq in the years after 1327, when that sultan established Daulatabad, in Maharashtra, as the new co-capital of the Delhi Sultanate's vast, all-India empire.[66] In having Ganges water carried a distance of forty days' journey from North India "for his own personal use," the sultan was conforming to an authentically Indian imperial ritual. Several centuries later, the Muslim sultans of Bengal, on the occasion of their own coronation ceremonies, would wash themselves with holy water that had been brought to their capital from the ancient holy site of Ganga Sagar, located where the Ganges River emptied into the Bay of Bengal.[67]

No Indo-Muslim chronicle or contemporary inscription associates the use of Ganges water with the establishment or maintenance of Indo-Muslim states. We hear this only from foreign visitors: an Arab traveler in the case of Muhammad bin Tughluq, a Portuguese friar in the case of the sultans of Bengal. Similarly, the image of a Mughal official seated in a canopied chariot and presiding over the Jagannath car festival comes to us not from Mughal chronicles but from an English traveler who happened to be in Puri in 1633.[68] Such disjunctures between the rhetoric and the practice of royal sovereignty also appear, of course, with respect to the founding of non-Muslim states. We know, for example, that Brahman ideologues, writing in chaste Sanskrit, spun elaborate tales of how warriors and sages founded the Vijayanagara state by combining forces for a common defense of *dharma* from assaults by barbaric (*mleccha*) Turkic outsiders. This is the Vijayanagara of rhetoric, a familiar story. But the Vijayanagara of practical politics rested on very different foundations, which included the adoption of the titles, the dress, the military organization, the ruling ideology, the architecture, and the political economy of the contemporary Islamicate world.[69] As with Indo-Muslim states, we hear of such practices mainly from outsiders—merchants, diplomats, travelers—and not from Brahman chroniclers and ideologues.

Conclusion

One often hears that between the thirteenth and eighteenth centuries, Indo-Muslim states, driven by a Judeo-Islamic "theology of iconoclasm," by fanaticism, or by sheer lust for plunder, wantonly and indiscriminately indulged in the desecration of Hindu temples. Such a picture cannot, however, be sustained by evidence from original sources for the period after 1192. Had instances of temple desecration been driven by a "theology of iconoclasm," as some have claimed,[70] such a theology would have committed Muslims in India to destroying all temples everywhere, including ordinary village temples, as opposed to the strategically selective operation that seems actually to have taken place. Rather, the original data associate instances of temple desecration with the annexation of newly conquered territories held by enemy kings whose domains lay in the path of moving military frontiers. Temple desecrations also occurred when Hindu patrons of prominent temples committed acts of treason or disloyalty to the Indo-Muslim states they served. Otherwise, temples lying within Indo-Muslim sovereign domains, viewed normally as protected state property, were left unmolested.

Finally, it is important to identify the different meanings that Indians invested in religious monuments and the different ways these monuments were understood to relate to political authority. In the reign of Aurangzeb, Shaikh Muhammadi took refuge in a mosque believing that the structure—being fundamentally apolitical, indeed above politics—lay beyond the Mughal emperor's reach. Contemporary royal temples, on the other hand, were understood as highly charged political monuments, a circumstance that rendered them fatally vulnerable to outside attack. Therefore, by targeting for desecration those temples that were associated with defeated kings, conquering Turks, when they made their own bid for sovereign domain in India, were subscribing to, even while they were exploiting, indigenous notions of royal legitimacy. Contemporary Sanskrit inscriptions never identified Indo-Muslim invaders in terms of their religion, as Muslims, but most generally in terms of their linguistic affiliation (most typically as Turk, "turushka"). That is, they were construed as but one ethnic community in India amidst many others.[71] In the same way, B. D. Chattopadhyaya locates within early medieval Brahmanical discourse an "essential urge to legitimize" any ruling authority so long as it was effective and responsible. This urge was manifested, for example, in the perception of the Tughluqs as legitimate successors to the Tomaras and Cahamanas; of a Muslim ruler of Kashmir as having a lunar, Pandava lineage; or of the Mughal emperors as supporters of Ramarajya (the "kingship of Lord Rama").[72] It is likely that Indo-Muslim policies of protecting temples within their sovereign domains contributed positively to such perceptions.

In sum, by placing known instances of temple desecration in the larger contexts of Indo-Muslim state building and state maintenance, one can find patterns suggesting a rational basis for something commonly dismissed as irrational, or worse. These patterns also suggest points of continuity with Indian practices that had become customary well before the thirteenth century. Such points of continuity in turn call into serious question the sort of civilizational divide between India's "Hindu" and "Muslim" periods first postulated in British colonial historiography and subsequently replicated in both Pakistani and Hindu nationalist schools. Finally, this essay has sought to identify the different meanings that contemporary actors invested in the public monuments they patronized or desecrated, and to reconstruct those meanings on the basis of the practice, and not just the rhetoric, of those actors. It is hoped that the approaches and hypotheses suggested here might facilitate the kind of responsible and constructive discussion that this controversial topic so badly needs.

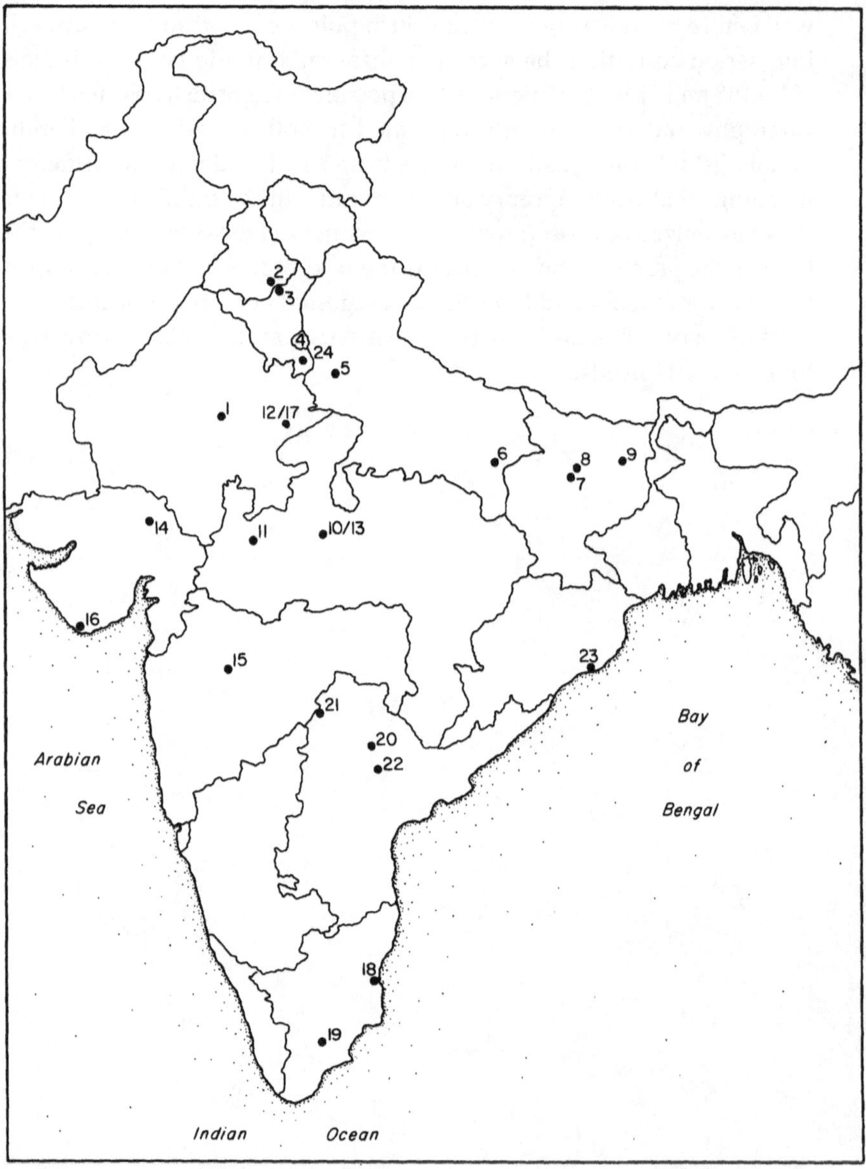

Map 10.1. Temple Desecrations, 1192–1394: Imperialism of the Delhi Sultanate [Note: Numbers are keyed to the table.]

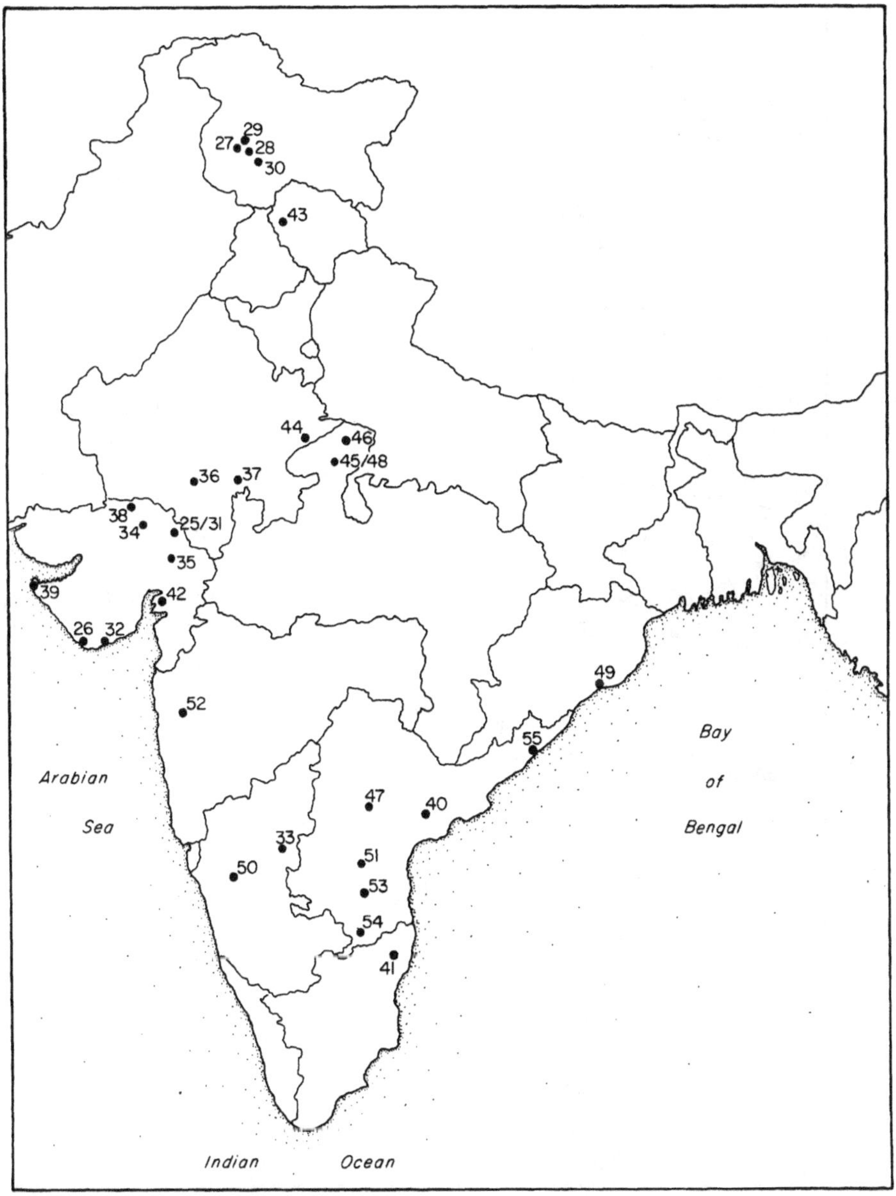

Map 10.2. Temple Desecrations, 1394–1600: The Growth of Regional Sultanates

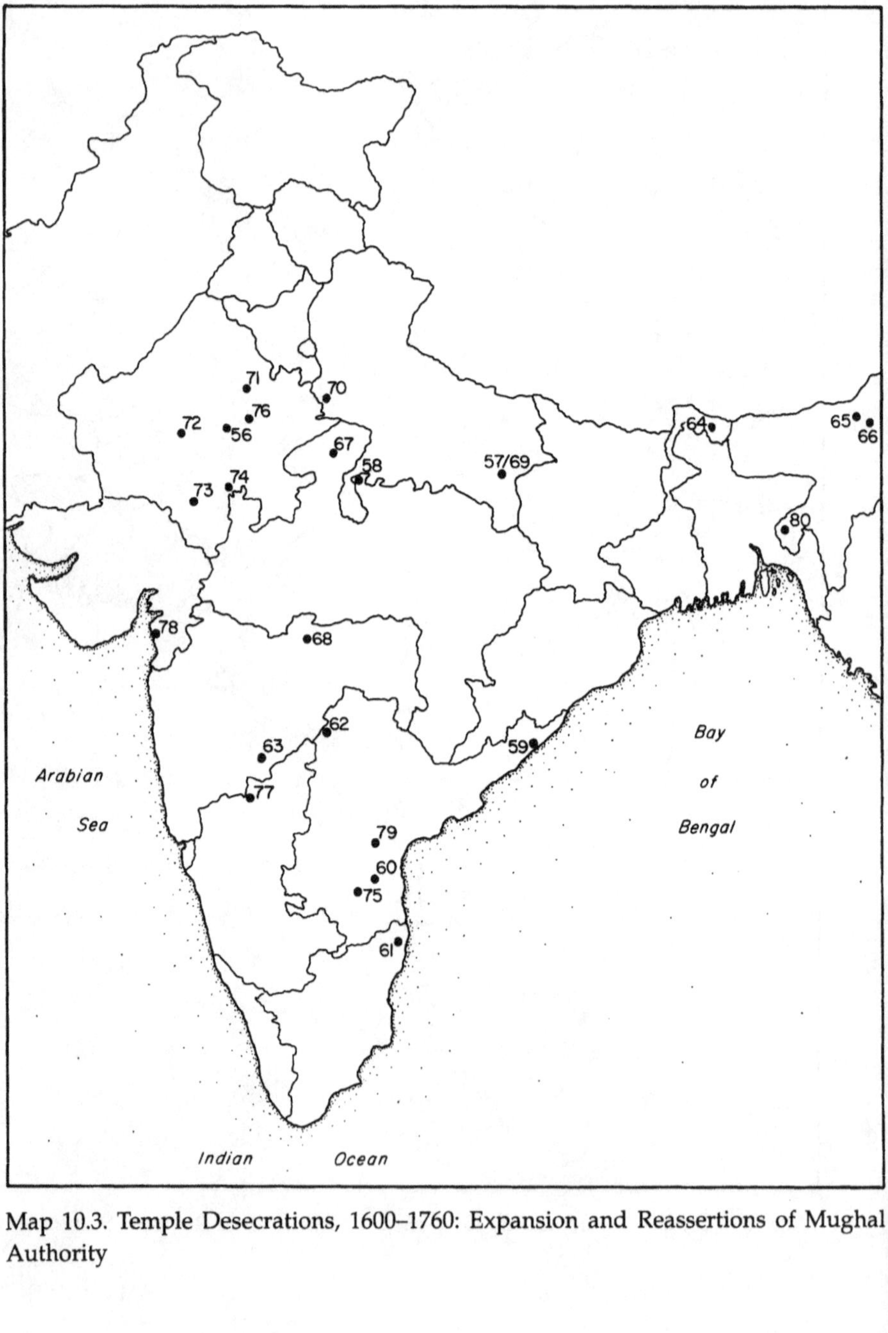

Map 10.3. Temple Desecrations, 1600–1760: Expansion and Reassertions of Mughal Authority

Table 10.1. Instances of Temple Desecration, 1192–1760

(e) = emperor; (s) = sultan; (g) = governor; (c) = commander; (p) = crown prince
For numbers 1–24, see map 10.1.
For numbers 25–55, see map 10.2.
For numbers 56–80, see map 10.3.

No.	Date	Site	District	State	Agent	Source
1	1193	Ajmer	Ajmer	Rajast.	Md. Ghuri (s)	23:215
2	1193	Samana	Patiala	Punjab	Aibek	23:216–17
3	1193	Kuhram	Karnal	Haryana	Aibek (g)	23:216–17
4	1193	Delhi		U.P.	Md. Ghuri (s)	1(1911):13; 23:217, 222
5	1194	Kol	Aligarh	U.P.	Ghurid army	23:224
6	1194	Benares	Benares	U.P.	Ghurid army	23:223
7	c. 1202	Nalanda	Patna	Bihar	Bakhtiyar Khalaji (c)	20:90
8	c. 1202	Odantapuri	Patna	Bihar	Bakhtiyar Khalaji	22:319; 21:551–52
9	c. 1202	Vikramasila	Saharsa	Bihar	Bakhtiyar Khalaji	22:319
10	1234	Bhilsa	Vidisha	M.P.	Iltutmish (s)	21:621–22
11	1234	Ujjain	Ujjain	M.P.	Iltutmish	21:622–23
12	1290	Jhain	Sawai Madh.	Rajast.	Jalal al-Din Khalaji (s)	27:146
13	1292	Bhilsa	Vidisha	M.P.	ʿAla al-Din Khalaji	27:148
14	1298–1310	Vijapur	Mehsana	Gujarat	Khalaji invaders	2(1974):10–12
15	1295	Devagiri	Aurangabad	Mahara.	ʿAla al-Din Khalaji (g)	24:543
16	1299	Somnath	Junagadh	Gujarat	Ulugh Khan (c)	25:75
17	1301	Jhain	Sawai Madh.	Rajast.	ʿAla al-Din Khalaji (s)	25:75–76
18	1311	Chidambaram	South Arcot	Tamilnad	Malik Kafur (c)	25:90–91
19	1311	Madurai	Madurai	Tamilnad	Malik Kafur	25:91
20	c. 1323	Warangal	Warangal	A.P.	Ulugh Khan (p)	33:1–2
21	c. 1323	Bodhan	Nizamabad	A.P.	Ulugh Khan	1(1919–20):16
22	c. 1323	Pillalamarri	Nalgonda	A.P.	Ulugh Khan	17:114
23	1359	Puri	Puri	Orissa	Firuz Tughluq (s)	26:314
24	1392–93	Sainthali	Gurgaon	Haryana	Bahadur K. Nahar (c)	3(1963–64):146
25	1394	Idar	Sabar-K.	Gujarat	Muzaffar Khan (g)	14–3:177
26	1395	Somnath	Junagadh	Gujarat	Muzaffar Khan	6–4:3
27	c. 1400	Paraspur	Srinagar	Kashmir	Sikandar (s)	14–3:648
28	c. 1400	Bijbehara	Srinagar	Kashmir	Sikandar	34:54

No.	Date	Site	District	State	Agent	Source
29	c. 1400	Tripuresvara	Srinagar	Kashmir	Sikandar	34:54
30	c. 1400	Martand	Anantnag	Kashmir	Sikandar	34:54
31	1400–1	Idar	Sabar-K.	Gujarat	Muzaffar Shah (s)	14–3:181
32	1400–1	Diu	Amreli	Gujarat	Muzaffar Shah	6–4:5
33	1406	Manvi	Raichur	Karn.	Firuz Bahmani (s)	2(1962):57–58
34	1415	Sidhpur	Mehsana	Gujarat	Ahmad Shah (s)	29:98–99
35	1433	Delwara	Sabar-K.	Gujarat	Ahmad Shah	14–3:220–21
36	1442	Kumbhalmir	Udaipur	Rajast.	Mahmud Khalaji (s)	14–3:513
37	1457	Mandalgarh	Bhilwara	Rajast.	Mahmud Khalaji	6–4:135
38	1462	Malan	Banaskantha	Gujarat	ʻAla al-Din Suhrab (c)	2(1963):28–29
39	1473	Dwarka	Jamnagar	Gujarat	Mahmud Begdha (s)	14–3:259–61
40	1478	Kondapalle	Krishna	A.P.	Md. II Bahmani (s)	6–2:306
41	c. 1478	Kanchi	Chingleput	Tamilnad	Md. II Bahmani	6–2:308
42	1505	Amod	Broach	Gujarat	Khalil Shah (g)	1(1933):36
43	1489–1517	Nagarkot	Kangra	Him. P.	Khawwas Khan (g)	35:81
44	1507	Utgir	Sawai Madh.	Rajast.	Sikandar Lodi (s)	14–1:375
45	1507	Narwar	Shivpuri	M.P.	Sikandar Lodi	14–1:378
46	1518	Gwalior	Gwalior	M.P.	Ibrahim Lodi (s)	14–1:402
47	1530–31	Devarkonda	Nalgonda	A.P.	Quli Qutb Shah (s)	6–3:212
48	1552	Narwar	Shivpuri	M.P.	Dilawar Khan (g)	4(June 1927):101–4
49	1556	Puri	Puri	Orissa	Sulaiman Karrani (s)	28:413–15
50	1575–76	Bankapur	Dharwar	Karn.	ʻAli ʻAdil Shah (s)	6–3:82–84
51	1579	Ahobilam	Kurnool	A.P.	Murahari Rao (c)	6–3:267
52	1586	Ghoda	Poona	Mahara.	Mir Md. Zaman (?)	1(1933–34):24
53	1593	Cuddapah	Cuddapah	A.P.	Murtaza Khan (c)	6–3:274
54	1593	Kalihasti	Chitoor	A.P.	Iʻtibar Khan (c)	6–3:277
55	1599	Srikurman	Visakh.	A.P.	Qutb Shahi general	32–5:1312
56	1613	Pushkar	Ajmer	Rajast.	Jahangir (e)	5:254
57	1632	Benares	Benares	U.P.	Shah Jahan (e)	31:36
58	1635	Orchha	Tikamgarh	M.P.	Shah Jahan	7:102–3
59	1641	Srikakulam	Srikakulam	A.P.	Sher Md. Kh. (c)	3(1953–54): 68–69
60	1642	Udayagiri	Nellore	A.P.	Ghazi ʻAli (c)	8:1385–86
61	1653	Poonamalle	Chingleput	Tamilnad	Rustam b. Zulfiqar (c)	1(1937–38):53n2

No.	Date	Site	District	State	Agent	Source
62	1655	Bodhan	Nizamabad	A.P.	Aurangzeb (p,g)	1(1919–20):16
63	1659	Tuljapur	Osmanabad	Mahara.	Afzal Khan (g)	16:9–10
64	1661	Kuch Bihar	Kuch Bihar	W. Beng.	Mir Jumla (g)	9:142–43
65	1662	Devalgaon	Sibsagar	Assam	Mir Jumla	9:154, 156–57
66	1662	Garhgaon	Sibsagar	Assam	Mir Jumla	36:249
67	1664	Gwalior	Gwalior	M.P.	Mu'tamad Khan (g)	10:335
68	1667	Akot	Akola	Mahara.	Md. Ashraf (c)	2(1963):53–54
69	1669	Benares	Benares	U.P.	Aurangzeb (e)	11:65–68; 13:88
70	1670	Mathura	Mathura	U.P.	Aurangzeb	12:57–61
71	1679	Khandela	Sikar	Rajast.	Darab Khan (g)	12:107; 18:449
72	1679	Jodhpur	Jodhpur	Rajast.	Khan Jahan (c)	18:786; 12:108
73	1680	Udaipur	Udaipur	Rajast.	Rahullah Khan (c)	15:129–30; 12:114–15
74	1680	Chitor	Chitorgarh	Rajast.	Aurangzeb	12:117
75	1692	Cuddapah	Cuddapah	A.P.	Aurangzeb	1(1937–38):55
76	1697–98	Sambhar	Jaipur	Rajast.	Shah Sabz 'Ali (?)	19:157
77	1698	Bijapur	Bijapur	Karn.	Hamid al-Din Khan (c)	12:241
78	1718	Surat	Surat	Gujarat	Haidar Quli Khan (g)	1(1933):42
79	1729	Cumbum	Kurnool	A.P.	Muhammad Salih (g)	2(1959–60):65
80	1729	Udaipur	West	Tripura	Murshid Quli Khan	30:7

Sources:

1. *Epigraphia Indo-Moslemica.*
2. *Epigraphia Indica, Arabic and Persian Supplement.*
3. *Annual Report of Indian Epigraphy.*
4. *Indian Antiquary.*
5. Jahangir, *Tuzuk-i-Jahangiri,* vol. 1, trans. A. Rogers (Delhi, 1968).
6. Firishta, *Tarikh-i Firishta,* trans. J. Briggs, *History of the Rise of the Mahomedan Power in India* (Calcutta, 1971), 4 vols.
7. Kanbo, *'Amal-i Salih* (Lahore, 1967), vol. 2.
8. A. Butterworth and V. Chetty, *A Collection of the Inscriptions on Copper-Plates and Stones in the Nellore District* (Madras, 1905), vol. 3.
9. Khafi Khan, *Khafi Khan's History of 'Alamgir,* trans. S. Moinul Haq (Karachi, 1975).
10. A. Cunningham, *Four Reports Made during 1862–65* (Varanasi, 1972).
11. S. N. Sinha, *Subah of Allahabad under the Great Mughals* (New Delhi, 1974).
12. Saqi Must'ad Khan, *Maasir-i 'Alamgiri,* trans. J. Sarkar (Calcutta, 1947).
13. Saqi Must'ad Khan, *Maasir-i 'Alamgiri* (Calcutta, 1871).
14. Nizamuddin Ahmad, *Tabaqat-i Akbari,* trans. B. De (Calcutta, 1973), 3 vols.

15. Ishwardas Nagar, *Futuhat-i 'Alamgiri*, trans. T. Ahmad (Delhi, 1978).
16. Surendranath Sen (ed. and trans.), *Siva Chhatrapati* (Calcutta, 1920), vol. 1.
17. P. Sreenivasachar, ed., *Corpus of Inscriptions in the Telingana Districts of H.E.M. the Nizam's Dominions*, pt. 2 (Hyderabad, 1940).
18. Shah Nawaz Khan, *Maathir-ul-Umara*, vol. 1, trans. H. Beveridge (Patna, 1979).
19. Z. A. Desai, *Published Muslim Inscriptions of Rajasthan* (Jaipur, 1971).
20. G. Roerich, trans. *Biography of Dharmaswamin* (Patna, 1959).
21. Minhaj-i Siraj, *Tabakat-i Nasiri*, vol. 1, trans. H. Raverty (New Delhi, 1970).
22. Debiprasad Chattopadhyaya, ed., *Taranatha's History of Buddhism in India* (Calcutta, 1980).
23. Hasan Nizami, *Taj al-maasir*, in Henry M. Elliot and John Dowson, eds., *The History of India as Told by Its Own Historians* (Allahabad: Kitab Mahal, n.d.), vol. 2.
24. Amir Khusrau, *Miftah al-futuh* in Elliot and Dowson, *History of India*, vol. 3.
25. Amir Khusrau, *Khaza'in al-futuh*, in Elliot and Dowson, *History*, vol. 3.
26. Shams-i Siraj, *Tarikh-i Firuz Shahi*, in Elliot and Dowson, *History*, vol. 3.
27. Zia al-Din Barani, *Tarikh-i Firuz Shahi*, Elliot and Dowson, *History*, vol. 3.
28. Khwajah Ni'mat Allah, *Tarikh-i Khan-Jahani wa makhzan-i-Afghani* (Dacca, 1960), vol. 1.
29. Sikandar bin Muhammad, *Mirat-i Sikandari*, in E. C. Bayley, *Local Muhammadan Dynasties: Gujarat*, ed. N. Singh (New Delhi, 1970).
30. Azad al-Husaini, *Nau-Bahar-i Murshid Quli Khani*, trans., Jadu Nath Sarkar, *Bengal Nawabs* (1952; reprint, Calcutta, 1985).
31. 'Abd al-Hamid Lahori, *Badshah-nama*, in Elliot and Dowson, *History*, vol. 7.
32. *South Indian Inscriptions* (New Delhi: Archeological Survey of India).
33. George Michell, "City as Cosmograph," *South Asian Studies* 8 (1992).
34. Jonaraja, *Rajatarangini*, ed. S. L. Sadhu, trans. J. C. Dutt (New Delhi, 1993).
35. Iqtidar Husain Siddiqui, trans., *Waqi'at-e-Mushtaqui of Shaikh Rizq Ullah Mushtaqui* (New Delhi, 1993).
36. Jagadish Narayan Sarkar, *Life of Mir Jumla* (Calcutta, 1952).

Notes

1. See Sita Ram Goel, *Hindu Temples: What Happened to Them?* vol. 1, *A Preliminary Survey* (New Delhi: Voice of India, 1990); vol. 2, *The Islamic Evidence* (New Delhi: Voice of India, 1991).

2. Henry M. Elliot and John Dowson, trans. and eds., *The History of India as Told by Its Own Historians,* 8 vols. (1849; Allahabad: Kitab Mahal, n.d.), 1:xxi.

3. Ibid., 1:xvi.

4. Ibid., 1:xxii, xxvii.

5. K. A. Nizami, ed., *Politics and Society during the Early Medieval Period: Collected Works of Professor Mohammad Habib,* 2 vols. (New Delhi: People's Publishing House, 1974), 1:12.

6. Goel, *Hindu Temples,* 2:115–16. Goel does, however, consider it more likely that the event took place during the reign of Raja Bhoja II in the late thirteenth century than during that of Raja Bhoja I in the eleventh century.

7. G. Yazdani, "The Inscription of the Tomb of 'Abdullah Shah Changal at Dhar," *Epigraphia Indo-Moslemica* (1909): 1–5.

8. A good summary of the political history of this period is found in André Wink, *Al-Hind: The Making of the Indo-Islamic World,* vol. 2: *The Slave Kings and the Islamic Conquest, 11th–13th Centuries* (Leiden: Brill, 1997), 111–49.

9. 'Utbi, *Tarikh-i Yamini,* in Elliot and Dowson, *History of India,* 2:22. For a Persian translation of 'Utbi's original Arabic, made in 1206, see Abu Sharaf Nasih al-Jurfadqani, *Tarjuma-yi Tarikh-i Yamini* (Tehran: Bangah-i Tarjomeh va Nashr-i Kitab, 1926–27), 31.

10. C. E. Bosworth, *The Later Ghaznavids, Splendour and Decay: The Dynasty in Afghanistan and Northern India, 1040–1186* (1977; reprint, New Delhi: Munshiram Manoharlal, 1992), 32, 68.

11. Mahmud did not hesitate to sack Muslim cities. His plunder of the Iranian city of Ray in 1029 brought him 500,000 dinars' worth of jewels, 260,000 dinars in coined money, and over 30,000 dinars' worth of gold and silver vessels. India, however, possessed far more wealth than the more sparsely populated Iranian plateau. Somnath alone brought in twenty million dinars' worth of spoil. C. E. Bosworth, *The Ghaznavids: Their Empire in Afghanistan and Eastern Iran, 994–1040* (Edinburgh: Edinburgh University Press, 1963), 78.

12. 'Ali Akbar Fayyaz, ed., *Tarikh-i Baihaqi* (Mashshad: University of Mashshad, 1971), 517. The contemporary historian Baihaqi recorded the first attack on Benares conducted by a Muslim army, carried out in 1033 by the Ghaznavid governor of Lahore. "He marched out with his warriors and the army of Lahore," wrote Baihaqi, "and exacted ample tribute from the Thakurs. He crossed the river Ganges and went down the left bank. Unexpectedly (*nā-gāh*) he arrived at a city which is called Banāras, and which belonged to the territory of Gang. Never had a Muslim army reached this place. . . . The markets of the drapers, perfumers, and jewelers were plundered, but it was impossible to do

more. The people of the army became rich, for they all carried off gold, silver, perfumes, and jewels, and got back in safety." Baihaqi, *Tarikh-i Baihaqi,* in Elliot and Dowson, *History of India,* 2:123–24.

13. "Jahān-rā ki asās-i matīn basta-and, bi iqdām-i mardān-i dīn basta-and. Bi har kishwarī hast ṣāḥib-dilī, bi har 'arṣat hast bā ḥāṣilī. Bi har mulk garchi amīrī būd, walī dar panāh-i faqīrī būd." 'Abd al-Malik 'Isami, *Futuhus-salatin by Isami,* ed. A. S. Usha (Madras: University of Madras, 1948), 455; Agha Mahdi Husain, ed. and trans., *Futuhu's Salatin, or Shah Namah-i Hind of 'Isami,* 3 vols. (Bombay: Asia Publishing House, 1967), 3:687.

14. Ibid., text, 466; trans. 3:702.

15. Ibid., text, 456, 458; trans., 3:689, 690–92. "As soon as that holy man of virtue [Nizam al-Din Auliya] departed from Delhi to the other world," he wrote, "the country, in general, and the city, in particular, fell into a turmoil and were subjected to ruin and destruction."

16. See Simon Digby, "The Sufi Shaikh as a Source of Authority in Mediaeval India," in Marc Gaborieau, ed., *Islam and Society in South Asia,* in *Purusartha* 9 (Paris: Ecole des Hautes Etudes en Sciences Sociales, 1986), 69–70.

17. 'Isami, *Futuhus-salatin,* text, 7–8; trans., 1:11–13.

18. Richard M. Eaton, *The Rise of Islam and the Bengal Frontier, 1204–1760* (Berkeley: University of California Press, 1993), 86, 91.

19. Muhammad Qasim Firishta, *Tarikh-i Firishta,* trans. John Briggs, in *History of the Rise of the Mahomedan Power in India,* 4 vols. (1829; reprint, Calcutta: Editions Indian, 1966), 4:4.

20. Zafar Hasan, "The Inscriptions of Dhar and Mandu," *Epigraphia Indo-Moslemica* (1909), 12 (murīd-i shaikh-i ṭarīqat-i Naṣīr-i Dīn Maḥmūd, ki būd maljā'-i autād wa marjā'-i abdāl).

21. Iqtidar Husain Siddiqui, "The Early Chishti Dargahs," in Christian W. Troll, ed., *Muslim Shrines in India: Their Character, History, and Significance* (Delhi: Oxford University Press, 1989), 21.

22. Catherine B. Asher, *Architecture of Mughal India,* vol. I:4 of *The New Cambridge History of India* (Cambridge: Cambridge University Press, 1992), 34–35, 51, 100, 134, 174, 215, 260, 293, 307, 310.

23. P. M. Currie, *The Shrine and Cult of Mu'in al-Din Chishti of Ajmer* (Delhi: Oxford University Press, 1992), 100.

24. 'Abd al-Qadir Badauni, *Muntakhab al-tawarikh,* vol. 2, trans. W. H. Lowe (1899; reprint, Delhi: Idarah-i Adabiyat-i Delli, 1973), 243.

25. It has been noted recently that the *qawwālī* protocols observed during the annual *'urs* ceremonies at Ajmer, which commemorate the death of Mu'in al-Din Chishti, "betray the impact of Mughal court etiquette. The diwan, dressed Mughal fashion, represents in fact the Mughal king rather than a religious dignitary, and comes escorted by the torch-bearers and mace-bearers wearing Mughal costumes. He takes his seat on the cushion (*gadela*) under a special tent (*dalbadal*) erected for the occasion. . . . On his arrival in the shrine the diwan kisses the tomb and offers flowers, and then one of the khadims, who happens to be his

wakil, like the other pilgrims, ties a *dastar* (turban) over his head, spreads the cloth sheet over his bowed head, prays for him, and then gives him *tabarruk*, consisting of flowers, sandal and sweets. . . . Then he [the diwan] sits down and the *fatiha khwans*, who are permanently and hereditarily employed, recite the fatiha, as well as prayers for the sovereign (*badshah-i Islam*), the diwan, the mutawalli and other officials, and for the general public." Syed Liyaqat Hussain Moini, "Rituals and Customary Practices at the Dargah of Ajmer," in Christian Troll, ed., *Muslim Shrines in India: Their Character, History, and Significance* (Delhi: Oxford University Press, 1989), 72, 74.

26. Wink, *Al-Hind*, 2:324.

27. "The need to link one's royal origins to religious and divine forces led to the extraordinary temple building of this period." B. D. Chattopadhyaya, "Historiography, History, and Religious Centers: Early Medieval North India, circa A.D. 700–1200," in Vishakha N. Desai and Darielle Mason, eds., *Gods, Guardians, and Lovers: Temple Sculptures from North India, A.D. 700–1200* (New York: Asia Society Galleries, 1993), 40.

28. Michael Willis suggests that one of the reasons the imperial Pratiharas did *not* build great monumental temple complexes was precisely their determination to avoid the localization of sovereign power that temples necessarily projected. According to this reasoning, the most active patrons of temple construction in this period were subordinate kings who did not have such vast imperial pretensions as did the Pratiharas. Willis, "Religion and Royal Patronage in North India," in Desai and Mason, eds., *Gods, Guardians, and Lovers*, 58–59.

29. Richard H. Davis, *Lives of Indian Images* (Princeton: Princeton University Press, 1997), 122, 137–38. Davis here cites David D. Shulman: "A divine power is felt to be present *naturally* on the spot. The texts are therefore concerned with the manner in which this presence is revealed and with the definition of its specific attributes." Shulman, *Tamil Temple Myths: Sacrifice and Divine Marriage in the South Indian Saiva Tradition* (Princeton: Princeton University Press, 1980), 48. Emphasis mine.

30. Cited in Davis, *Lives*, 53.

31. Davis, *Lives*, 51–83, passim. The same pattern continued after the Turkish conquest of India. In the 1460s, Kapilendra, the founder of the Suryavamshi Gajapati dynasty in Orissa, sacked both Śaiva and Vaishnava temples in the Kaveri delta in the course of wars of conquest in the Tamil country. See Phillip B. Wagoner, *Tidings of the King: A Translation and Ethnohistorical Analysis of the Rāyavācakamu* (Honolulu: University of Hawaii Press, 1993), 146. Somewhat later, in 1514, Krishna Deva Raya looted an image of Bala Krishna from Udayagiri, which he had defeated and annexed to his growing Vijayanagara state. Six years later he acquired control over Pandharpur, where he seems to have looted the Vittala image and carried it back to Vijayanagara, with the apparent purpose of ritually incorporating this area into his kingdom. Davis, *Lives*, 65, 67.

32. In the late eleventh century, the Kashmiri king, Harsha, even raised the plundering of temples to an institutionalized activity, and in the late twelfth and

early thirteenth centuries, while Turkish rulers were establishing their rule in North India, kings of the Paramara dynasty were attacking and plundering Jain temples in Gujarat. See Romila Thapar, Harbans Mukhia, and Bipan Chandra, *Communalism and the Writing of Indian History* (Delhi: People's Publishing House, 1969), 14, 31.

33. Willis, "Religion and Royal Patronage," 59.

34. In 1788, for example, the author of the *Riyaz al-salatin* claimed that Muhammad Bakhtiyar demolished local temples after he conquered Bengal in 1204, although no contemporary evidence suggests that he did so. Ghulam Hussain Salim, *Riyazu-s-Salatin: A History of Bengal*, trans. Abdus Salam (1903; reprint, Delhi: Idarah-i Adabiyat-i Delli, 1975), 64. Even contemporary sources could make false claims. An inscription on a mosque in Bidar, dated 1670, claims that the Mughal governor, Mukhtar Khan, had destroyed a temple and built the mosque on its site. "But as a matter of fact," noted the epigraphist who published the inscription, "the mosque is a new construction, and the Hindu shrine [to the lion-god Narasimha] which existed inside the rock does not seem to have been disturbed, for it still survives." *Epigraphia Indo-Moslemica, 1927–28* (Calcutta: Government of India, 1931), 32.

35. Entry for the date 1688 in "Hindu Timeline," *Hinduism Today* (December 1994), cited in Cynthia Talbot, "Inscribing the Other, Inscribing the Self: Hindu-Muslim Identities in Pre-Colonial India," *Comparative Studies in Society and History* 37, no. 4 (October 1995): 692.

36. In 1247, Balban, the future sultan of Delhi, had recommended raiding Indian states for precisely this purpose. See Minhaj-i Siraj Juzjani, *Tabakat-i Nasiri*, 2 vols., trans. H. G. Raverty (1881; New Delhi: Oriental Books Reprint Corp., 1970), 2:816.

37. The notion that Babur's officer Mir Baqi destroyed a temple dedicated to Rama's birthplace at Ayodhya and then got the emperor's sanction to build a mosque on the site—the notorious Baburi Masjid—was elaborated in 1936 by S. K. Banerji. However, the author offered no evidence that there had ever been a temple at this site, much less that it had been destroyed by Mir Baqi. The mosque's inscription records only that Babur had ordered the construction of the mosque, which was built by Mir Baqi and was described as "the place of descent of celestial beings" (*mahbiṭ-i qudsiyān*). This commonplace rhetorical flourish in Persian can hardly be construed as referring to Rama, especially since it is the mosque itself that is so described, and not the site or any earlier structure on the site. See S. K. Banerji, "Babur and the Hindus," *Journal of the United Provinces Historical Society* 9 (1936): 76–83.

38. For example, a 1406 inscription records that after Sultan Firuz Shah Bahmani had defeated the forces of Vijayanagara in the much-contested Raichur doab region, "a mosque has been converted out of a temple as a sign of religion." It then records that the sultan himself had "conquered this fort by the firm determination of his mind in a single attack (lit. on horseback). After the victory, the chief of chiefs, Safdar (lit. the valiant commander) of the age, received (the

charge of) the fort." *Epigraphia Indica, Arabic and Persian Supplement, 1962* (Delhi: Manager of Publications, 1964), 57–58.

39. Briggs, *Rise of Mahomedan Power,* 3:267. The temple's political significance, and hence the necessity of desecrating it, would have been well understood by Murahari Rao, himself a Marathi Brahman.

40. Khwajah Niʿmat Allah, *Tarikh-i Khan Jahani wa Makhzan-i-Afghani,* ed. S. M. Imam al-Din (Dacca: Asiatic Society of Pakistan, 1960), 1:413–15; Abu'l-fazl, *Akbar-nama,* trans. Henry Beveridge (reprint, New Delhi: Ess Ess, 1979), 2:381–82, 480.

41. S. Moinul Haq, trans., *Khafi Khan's History of ʿAlamgir* (Karachi: Pakistan Historical Society, 1975), 142–43.

42. P. B. Desai, "Kalyana Inscription of Sultan Muhammad, Saka 1248," *Epigraphia Indica* 32 (1957–58): 165–68.

43. Ibn Battuta, *Travels in Asia and Africa, 1324–1354,* trans. H. A. R. Gibb (1929; New Delhi: Oriental Books Reprint Corp., 1986), 214.

44. S. L. Sadhu, ed., *Medieval Kashmir, Being a Reprint of the Rajataranginis of Jonaraja, Shrivara, and Shuka,* trans. J. C. Dutt (1898; reprint, New Delhi: Atlantic Publishers and Distributors, 1993), 44–45.

45. Nizamuddin Ahmad, *Tabaqat-i-Akbari,* trans. B. De, 3 vols. (Calcutta: Bibliotheca Indica, 1927–39), 1:386.

46. A useful discussion of Mahmud, his legend, and the question of iconoclasm prior to the establishment of Islamic states is found in Davis, *Lives,* chaps. 3 and 6.

47. Abu'l-fazl ʿAllami, *A'in-i Akbari,* 2d ed., vol. 3, trans. H. S. Jarrett, ed. Sir Jadunath Sarkar (Calcutta: Asiatic Society of Bengal, 1927; New Delhi: Oriental Books Reprint Corp., 1977–78), 377.

48. Catherine B. Asher, "The Architecture of Raja Man Singh: A Study of Sub-Imperial Patronage," in Barbara Stoler Miller, ed., *The Powers of Art: Patronage in Indian Culture* (Delhi: Oxford University Press, 1992), 183–201.

49. P. Acharya, "Bruton's Account of Cuttack and Puri," *Orissa Historical Research Journal* 10, no. 3 (1961): 46.

50. *Journal of the Asiatic Society of Bengal* (1911): 689–90. Order to Abu'l-Hasan in Benares, dated Feb. 28, 1659. My translation. The "continuance of the empire," of course, was always forefront on the minds of the Mughals, regardless of what religious functionary was praying to which deity.

51. "Az rū-yi sharʿ-i sharīf wa millat-i munīf muqarrar chunīn ast, ki dair-hāyi dīrīn bar andākht nashavad, wa but-kada-hā tāza banā nayābad." Ibid., my translation.

52. See Eaton, *Rise of Islam,* 184–85, 263.

53. Surendra Nath Sinha, *Subah of Allahabad under the Great Mughals* (New Delhi: Jamia Millia Islamia, 1974), 65–68; Asher, *Architecture,* 254, 278; Saqi Mustʿad Khan, *Ma'athir-i ʿAlamgiri* (Calcutta: Bibliotheca Indica, 1871), 88.

54. Saqi Mustʿad Khan, *Maasir-i ʿAlamgiri,* trans. Jadunath Sarkar (Calcutta, 1947), 57–61; Asher, *Architecture,* 254.

55. See Goel, *Hindu Temples*, 2:78–79, 83; Sri Ram Sharma, *The Religious Policy of the Mughal Emperors*, 2d ed. (London: Asia Publishing House, 1962), 132–33; Athar Ali, *The Mughal Nobility under Aurangzeb* (Bombay: Asia Publishing House, 1966), 98n.

56. Saqi Must'ad Khan, *Ma'athir-i 'Alamgiri*, text, 81. My translation. "Aḥkām-i Islām-niẓām ba nāẓimān-i kull-i ṣūbajāt ṣādir shud ki mudāris wa mu'ābid-i bīdīnān dast-khwash-i inhidām sāzand, wa ba ta'kīd-i akīd ṭaur-i dars-o-tadrīs wa rasm-i shayū'-i madhāhib-i kufr-āyīnān bar andāzand." Cf. Saqi Must'ad Khan, *Maasir-i 'Alamgiri: A History of the Emperor Aurangzeb-'Alamgiri*, trans. Sir Jadunath Sarkar (Lahore: Suhail Academy, 1981), 51–52.

57. Saqi Must'ad Khan, *Ma'athir-i 'Alamgiri*, 81. "Ba 'arẓ-i khudāvand-i dīn-parvar rasīd ki dar ṣūba-yi Thatta wa Multān khuṣūṣ Banāras brahminān-i baṭṭālat-nishān dar mudāris-i muqarrar ba tadrīs-i kutub-i bāṭila ishtighāl dārand, wa rāghibān wa ṭālibān az hunūd wa musulmān musāfat-hāyi ba'īda ṭaiy numūda, jihat-i taḥṣīl-i 'ulūm-i shūm nazd-i ān jamā'at-i gumrāh mīāyand." Cf. Sir Jadunath Sarkar, trans., *Maasir-i 'Ālamgīri*, 51.

58. Consider the swift and brutal punishment of Baha al-Din Gurshasp, a high-ranking officer in Tughluq imperial service and a governor in the Deccan. In 1327, Gurshasp joined forces with the raja of Kampila in an unsuccessful rebellion against Sultan Muhammad bin Tughluq. When captured, the raja, who had never sworn allegiance to Tughluq authority, got the relatively light punishment of a beheading. But the rebel governor, who was not only a former Tughluq officer but the emperor's first cousin, was spat upon by his female relatives and flayed alive; then his skin was stuffed with straw and paraded throughout the imperial provinces as a cautionary tale to the public, while his body was mixed with rice and fed to elephants. See 'Isami, *Futuhu's-salatin*, trans., 3:658–89; Mahdi Husain, trans., *The Rehla of Ibn Battuta (India, Maldive Islands, and Ceylon)* (Baroda: Oriental Institute, 1953), 96. As a final indignity to Gurshasp, we are told by Ibn Battuta that the elephants refused to eat the meal that had been mixed with the rebel's body.

59. Eaton, *Rise of Islam*, 176–77.

60. Muzaffar Alam, "Assimilation from a Distance: Confrontation and Sufi Accommodation in Awadh Society," in R. Champakalakshmi and S. Gopal, eds., *Tradition, Dissent, and Ideology: Essays in Honour of Romila Thapar* (Delhi: Oxford University Press, 1996), 177n.

61. Examples of mosque desecrations are strikingly few in number. In 1697–98 in Sambhar, in Rajasthan's Jaipur District, Shah Sabz 'Ali built a mosque on the site of a temple. In the reign of Shah 'Alam (1707–12), however, non-Muslims came to dominate the region and demolished the mosque, which was subsequently rebuilt in the reign of Farrukh Siyar. See Z. A. Desai, *Published Muslim Inscriptions of Rajasthan* (Jaipur, 1971), 157. Similarly, there is evidence that in 1680, during Aurangzeb's invasion of Rajasthan, the Rajput chief Bhim Singh, seeking to avenge the emperor's recent destruction of temples in Udaipur and

elsewhere, raided Gujarat and plundered Vadnagar, Vishalnagar, and Ahmedabad, in the latter place destroying thirty smaller mosques and one large one. See *Rāja-sumudra-prasasti*, ch. 22, verse 29, an inscription composed ca. 1683, which appears in Shyamaldas Kaviraj, *Vir Vinod* (Udaipur: Rajayantralaya, 1886); cited in R. C. Majumdar, ed., *The Mughal Empire* (Bombay: Bharatiya Vidya Bhavan, 1974), 351.

62. One can hardly imagine the central focus of a mosque's ritual activity, the prayer niche (*miḥrāb*), being taken out of the structure and paraded around a Muslim capital by way of displaying Allah's co-sovereignty over an Indo-Muslim ruler's kingdom, in the manner that the ritual focus of a royal temple, the image of the state deity, was paraded around many premodern Hindu capitals in elaborate car festivals.

63. Aiming to cast earlier invaders or rulers in the role of zealous and puritanical heroes, later chroniclers occasionally attributed to such figures the desecration of staggering numbers of temples. Mahmud of Ghazni, for example, is said to have destroyed 10,000 temples in Kanauj and 1,000 in Mathura, his grandson Ibrahim 1,000 in the Delhi Doab and another 1,000 in Malwa, Aibek 1,000 in Delhi, and Muhammad Ghuri another 1,000 in Benares—figures that Hindu nationalists like Sita Ram Goel have accepted at face value. Goel, *Hindu Temples*, 269.

64. 'Isami, *Futuhu's Salatin*, trans., 1:66–67.

65. Davis, *Lives*, 71–76.

66. Husain, *Rehla of Ibn Battuta*, 4.

67. Sebastião Manrique, *Travels of Fray Sebastien Manrique, 1629–1643*, trans. E. Luard and H. Hosten, 2 vols. (Oxford: Hakluyt Society, 1927), 1:77.

68. Acharya, "Bruton's Account of Cuttack and Puri," 46.

69. See Phillip B. Wagoner, "'Sultan among Hindu Kings': Dress, Titles, and the Islamicization of Hindu Culture at Vijayanagara," *Journal of Asian Studies* 55, no. 4 (November 1996): 851–80; Wagoner, "Harihara, Bukka, and the Sultan: The Delhi Sultanate in the Political Imagination of Vijayanagara," in this volume.

70. See Wink, *Al-Hind*, 2:294–333.

71. See Talbot, "Inscribing the Other," 701.

72. Brajadulal Chattopadhyaya, *Representing the Other? Sanskrit Sources and the Muslims* (New Delhi: Manohar, 1998), 49–50, 53, 60, 84.

11

The Story of Prataparudra

Hindu Historiography on the Deccan Frontier

Cynthia Talbot

A sense of shared history is one of the central elements in any form of group identity. In various parts of the world, members of a particular ethnic or national community may or may not speak the same language, may or may not live in the same region, and may or may not profess a common religious faith. But the feeling of belonging together can still be strong and is derived from the belief that their ancestors were one, that their people have the same historical roots and shared past experiences. In the imagining of a community, therefore, the construction of a common past is a vital means for creating a sense of unity, particularly in situations where other commonalities are lacking.

Typically, in modern nationalisms, a great antiquity is imputed to the group whose existence is thus represented as inherent to the natural order of things. Hindu nationalists follow this pattern in portraying Hindus as a primordial community having its origins in the misty beginnings of time.[1] In recent years, the definition of Hindu has also been broadened to effectively include all past and present inhabitants of the subcontinent—whether Buddhist, Jain, tribal, or untouchable—except for those who follow(ed) the Islamic faith. The desire to place a united and continuous Hindu community at center stage is the primary impulse behind recent Hindutva revisionist writings on the origins of Indian civilization, explaining why these works recast Aryans as indigenous Indians and claim the Harappan culture for them.[2] Conversely, the distinctiveness of the Hindu community must be emphasized and sharp lines drawn between it and others, and so Muslims are depicted as the implacably alien substance that the Hindu/Indian body politic cannot digest.[3] Since identity formation proceeds along the twofold lines of stressing the unity of the in-group while simultaneously accentuating the boundaries against outsiders, it is no coincidence that Hindu nationalist historians concentrate on the two topics of protohistoric origins and precolonial Hindu-Muslim relations.

In contrast to the primordialist bent of Hindu nationalism, several prominent scholars of modern Indian history have asserted that broadly based Hindu and Muslim identities arose only in the late nineteenth century, stimulated in large part by British policies that differentiated communities on religious grounds.[4] Along similar lines, Partha Chatterjee charts the emergence of a nationalist historiography during the course of the nineteenth century in his article "History and the Nationalization of Hinduism."[5] He compares the *Rajabali,* a Bengali history of India written in 1808 by Mrityunjay Vidyalankar, with Tarinicharan Chattopadhyay's influential *History of India,* published in 1878. While the former can be characterized as a "puranic" history because it merely narrates the history of kings, the latter tells the story of the people/nation-state. Only with the development of modern forms of historiography like Chattopadhyay's work in the late nineteenth century, Chatterjee concludes, was the very concept of Hindutva or Hinduness possible. Similarly, other historians of the colonial era have asserted that the supralocal affinities of caste or common language were products of the nineteenth century.[6]

I propose instead a position somewhere in between the two just described. The nationalist claim that a Hindu community existed since the beginning of historic time is clearly untenable, for reasons that others have already explained in detail.[7] Yet I also disagree strongly with the stance that supralocal identities came into being only under colonial rule. Certainly, the conception of the people as the nation, whose boundaries could be clearly delineated and whose numbers could be definitively counted, may be a construction of the nineteenth century. But this does not mean that precolonial Indians could not and did not ever envision themselves as members of communities that extended beyond the locality or the subcaste. Nor can all non-Muslim historiographic writing of the precolonial period be dismissed as irrelevant to the construction of community identities. I believe rather that supralocal identities were articulated with increasing force by regional political elites after A.D.

1000 and that historical traditions played a critical role in this process of identity formation. One possible stimulus for the growth of a historical consciousness was the Muslim presence in the subcontinent, and not only because Islamic tradition provided models for historical writing. The Muslim challenge to Indic polities may also have heightened the elite awareness of self and led to efforts to codify the past. The sense of a shared history that resulted might not have encompassed all social classes, but there is no doubt that some segments of the medieval Indian population engaged in the imagining of the past and the inventing of tradition.

I cannot offer a comprehensive defense of my thesis, for the non-Muslim historical writings of medieval India have received scant attention. Due to their fulsome praise of kings, frequent mythological allusions, and chronological inaccuracies, scholars have generally regarded Indic royal biographies and dynastic chronicles as ahistorical and unworthy of study. But I hope to demonstrate my points through a close analysis of one text, the *Prataparudra Caritramu*.[8] Although the title literally means the deeds or acts of Prataparudra (r. 1289–1323), the last Kakatiya king of Andhra, this Telugu prose work actually narrates the story of the entire Kakatiya dynasty from its alleged genesis onward. It is considered the earliest historiographic composition in Telugu; Andhra did not produce any similar works prior to the fifteenth or sixteenth centuries even in Sanskrit (unlike the situation in neighboring Karnataka). Because the military activities of the Delhi Sultanate were responsible for the fall of the Kakatiya kingdom, the *Prataparudra Caritramu* provides an opportunity to assess the impact of the Muslim presence on non-Muslim conceptions. Accordingly, I will return to the broader issue of Hindu historiography as an aspect of identity formation toward the end of the essay.

The Story of Prataparudra

The *Prataparudra Caritramu* can be divided into three main sections, with each one becoming progressively more detailed: the origins of the dynasty (eleven printed pages); an account of the "historic" Kakatiya rulers before Prataparudra (twenty-three pages); and the life of Prataparudra (thirty-six pages, or about half the text). The work as a whole is not a consistent, tightly woven narrative. On first reading, especially, it strikes one as being full of abrupt transitions and without a clear focus.

Only when we get to the last segment, on Prataparudra himself, does the narrative seem to settle down. However, the two earlier sections are integral to the work's objective—explaining Prataparudra's greatness and ultimate fate. A brief summary of them is therefore in order.

Beginning with the standard genealogy of kings descended from the moon, the text moves on quickly to a series of kings in the Deccan, the last of whom dwelt in a town called Kandaramu on the Godavari River. This king, Somadeva, loses his life and his cattle herd to the Lord of Cuttack (Kataka Vallabha), who proceeds to pursue Somadeva's fleeing wife into the town of Hanumakonda (in modern Warangal district, Andhra Pradesh). Hidden by the brahmins of Hanumakonda, Somadeva's pregnant queen evades capture and gives birth to a son, Madhava Varma. Madhava Varma goes on to win the favor of the goddess Padmakshi, who gives him a divine sword and shield plus a large army, which he uses to defeat the Lord of Cuttack and recover his father's herds. Seven of Madhava Varma's descendants are then briefly mentioned. In the introductory portion of the text, the greatness of the Kakatiyas is thus traced back to Madhava Varma, who obtained royal boons from the goddess and a promise that his descendants would be invincible for a thousand years.

The second section of the *Prataparudra Caritramu* chronicles the lives of Prataparudra's five predecessors, beginning with Kakatiya Prola (II). The main event occurring in the reign of Prola is the discovery of a touchstone that could transform iron into gold. The touchstone explains both the prosperity of the Kakatiyas and the founding of their second capital, Warangal (Orugallu, literally "one-stone"; also known as Ekasilanagara or "one-rock town" in Sanskrit), built for the sole purpose of housing the fabulous touchstone at its very center. More details are provided about the exploits of the next four Kakatiya rulers (Rudradeva, Mahadeva, Ganapati, and Rudrama-devi), some relating to military campaigns that are corroborated by epigraphic testimony. Excepting Mahadeva, whose reign was very short, each of the Kakatiya rulers is said to have launched a successful expedition against the Lord of Cuttack.

The last section begins with Prataparudra in the womb and the prophecies of his future greatness. Crowned king at the age of sixteen, Prataparudra embarks on that requisite of royal status, the *dig-vijaya*, or conquest of the four quarters. He starts in the east with a campaign against the Lord of Cuttack, moves southward to Pandya territory, then to Karnataka and other regions in the west, and finally completes the circumambulation with an alleged victory in the Gangetic north. After proving himself in this manner, Prataparudra returns to his kingdom and we are given many details about his daily schedule, the realm's boundaries, the tribute owed to the royal treasury, and an enumeration of the houses, temples, and ritual offerings in the capital city of Warangal.

The final eleven pages of the *Prataparudra Caritramu* deal with Prataparudra's prolonged struggle against the Delhi Sultanate and his ultimate defeat at its hands. Four sustained episodes of armed conflict are narrated in the text, corresponding to four out of the five expeditions against the Kakatiyas described by Indo-Muslim chroniclers.[9] The first two campaigns were ordered by Ala-ud-din Khilji—one led by Malik Naib Kafur that reached the Kakatiya capital Warangal in A.D. 1310 and another led by Khusrau Khan in 1318. Both of these Sultanate expeditions were successful in extracting tribute. The third campaign, initiated in 1321 by Ulugh Khan, the son of Ghiyas-ud-din Tughluq, was unsuccessful despite a six-month siege of Warangal. Ulugh Khan, who soon thereafter ascended the throne with the name Muhammad bin Tughluq, regrouped his forces and returned for a second siege that culminated with the capture of Warangal in 1323.

Although both the Indo-Muslim chronicles and the *Prataparudra Caritramu* focus on these four main phases of conflict, the kind of military strategy and action they highlight is quite different. The emphasis is on siege warfare in the Indo-Muslim narratives, with the mobile Turkic armies repeatedly confronting the immobilized Telugu warriors taking refuge within Warangal fort.[10] The *Prataparudra Caritramu*, on the other hand, describes coalitions of armed forces assembling at some distance from the capital and fighting in the open. In each of the four conflicts, there are three arenas of battle within which the same two enemies encounter each other time and again. The most important of these battlefields lies to the north of the capital, where the Sultanate's main army is encamped and against whom are sent the standing army of the Kakatiyas themselves. The seventy-seven Padmanayakas, the chief warrior subordinates of the Kakatiya political network, do not fight with the main Kakatiya army but are instead dispatched west of the capital, where they face off against the Turkic Lord of the West, a person differentiated from the Delhi sultan. The final arena of combat is situated to the northeast of Warangal, where the Lord of Cuttack's army threatens the kingdom. The Lord of Cuttack, an independent king allied with the

Sultanate, is opposed by his equivalent on the Kakatiya side, the ruler of Vijayanagara city called the Narapati, or Lord of Men.

According to the *Prataparudra Caritramu,* the friendly relationship between the Vijayanagara king and the Kakatiyas is a long-standing one, initiated by a marriage alliance several generations in the past and consolidated more recently when Prataparudra visited Vijayanagara during the course of his *dig- vijaya.* In stark contrast, the Lords of Cuttack are portrayed as the hereditary enemies of the Kakatiya dynasty virtually from its very inception, for it was a Lord of Cuttack who not only killed Somadeva but tried to extinguish his lineage. This old hostility was reenacted in subsequent generations as successive Kakatiya rulers sent armies against Cuttack (Kataka), a town in southern Orissa. It was only natural, in the *Prataparudra Caritramu*'s perspective, that the traditional rivals of the Kakatiyas would join up with its new enemies, the Muslim polities based outside of Andhra. The text thus lays out the scenario of a Deccan divided into two basic coalitions: the Kakatiyas and Vijayanagara on one side, versus the combined forces of the Delhi Sultanate, a Deccani Sultanate, and the Orissan lord, on the other.[11]

Historical anachronisms abound in this supposed depiction of the early fourteenth century. Vijayanagara was not founded, at the very earliest, until more than a decade after the fall of Warangal in 1323. The Turkic Lord of the West is also clearly from a slightly later period, a time after the establishment of the first sultanate in the Deccan—that of the Bahmanis—in 1347. Even the figure of the Lord of Cuttack may be anachronistic, for it seems to refer to a later dynasty situated to the northeast of Warangal rather than to the Eastern Ganga contemporaries of the Kakatiyas.[12] By conventional measures of historicity, such glaring chronological inaccuracies would render the text highly suspect and provide yet another illustration of the notorious lack of historical consciousness in Hindu India. But rather than evaluate the *Prataparudra Caritramu* against some absolute standard of veracity, it is more fruitful to approach it as the cultural product of a later era, an era in which many of the details of the Kakatiya period would have been sociologically irrelevant. In the words of a recent work on social memory: "The natural tendency of social memory is to suppress what is not meaningful or intuitively satisfying in the collective memories of the past and interpolate or substitute what seems more appropriate or more in keeping with their particular conception of the world."[13] In other words, historical memories are often altered in order to make the past more comprehensible from the perspective of the present, as well as to strengthen the sense of continuity between the past and the present. This is a logical attempt to order the social universe, not a manifestation of disorderly or irrational thought processes.

Let us return to the *Prataparudra Caritramu*'s geopolitical worldview keeping in mind the point that historical memories are generally transformed for a reason. If we subtract the two actual combatants of the early fourteenth century, the Kakatiyas and the Delhi Sultanate, from the picture, we are left with three main contenders—a Deccani Sultanate (Turkic Lord of the West), an Orissan power (Lord of Cuttack), and Vijayanagara (Narapati). Such a tripartite struggle between the Orissan power, the Vijayanagara empire, and the Sultanate(s) did indeed occur, though not in Kakatiya Prataparudra's lifetime. The three-way contest for power was instead representative of conditions in Andhra between approximately 1450 and 1540. What we have, therefore, is a scenario from the late fifteenth or early sixteenth century, transposed on to more distant times. Since the best estimates of the *Prataparudra Caritramu*'s composition range from ca. 1490 to ca. 1550, it appears that the political realities of its own period were merged with those of the early fourteenth century to form a composite image of the past.[14]

But what was the purpose behind the casting backwards of present-day conditions into the Kakatiya past? If we accept that the *Prataparudra Caritramu*'s historical anachronisms have a conscious intent, then we must try to establish who sought meaning, in the present, from events that had allegedly taken place two centuries earlier. Unfortunately, we have little information on the conditions of the text's production and transmission. All we can say with fair certainty is that it was composed and preserved in the Telangana region of northwestern Andhra, and probably more specifically in the vicinity of the former Kakatiya capital, Warangal.[15] The text's patrons—the people who both financed and circulated it—are also not known. But there is one group, the Padmanayaka warrior subordinates, who are consistently glorified in the narrative. They are said to be warriors personally recruited by Prataparudra for their superior qualities, and they justify that choice by remaining loyal to the Kakatiya cause down to the bitter end. As Prataparudra prepares for death, he bestows his blessings on the assembled Padmanayakas, saying, "You have served your lord on the lion throne faithfully. Now become independent and continue on as the kings and chiefs of the territories (already) given to you!"[16] Because the *Prataparudra Caritramu* legitimizes the status of Telugu warrior lineages who flourished in the post-Kakatiya period, it is likely that its patrons were drawn from this social category.[17]

Aside from creating a link between the Telugu warriors of the present day and the brave Kakatiya warriors of the past, the *Prataparudra Caritramu* also suggests a continuity between the Vijayanagara empire of its time and the long-gone Kakatiya kingdom. The commonality of the two is indicated in their joint alliance against the Delhi Sultanate, but the text implies an even greater connection. After Prataparudra's death, the Kakatiya throne is entrusted to his son Virabhadra. But the Vijayanagara king is forced to withdraw from Warangal and attend to matters in his own realm, where Sultanate troops have been wreaking havoc in his absence. Once deprived of Vijayanagara support, Virabhadra loses Warangal to the Delhi Sultanate, goes off to coastal Andhra where he joins the chiefs of Kondavidu, and is never seen again. Meanwhile, Vijayanagara's vigorous resistance not only keeps Sultanate armies at bay north of the Krishna River but eventually compels the sultan to become a tributary. Hence, although the Kakatiya kingdom is extinguished, the torch is kept lit, so to speak, by Vijayanagara. In that sense, Vijayanagara is the bearer of the Kakatiya legacy, the true successor to the Kakatiya state.

During the second half of the fifteenth century, Vijayanagara's control over southern Andhra was hotly contested by the Gajapati kingdom to the northeast (extending over the borders of Andhra and Orissa) and the Bahmani Sultanate and its offshoots, based to the west of Andhra—that is, the *Prataparudra Caritramu*'s Lord of Cuttack and Turkish Lord of the West, respectively. This was an era of intense competition and protracted warfare, ending only in the early sixteenth century after Vijayanagara's Krishnadeva Raya inflicted a decisive defeat on the Gajapatis. The next fifty years, until the victory of the combined Deccani Sultanate armies over Vijayanagara in the 1565 Battle of Talikota, were the heyday of Vijayanagara power and influence within Andhra, a time when many Telugu warriors were incorporated into the Vijayanagara polity. The affinity for Vijayanagara expressed in the *Prataparudra Caritramu* is understandable in this historical context. But Vijayanagara was not originally an Andhra state, nor were all Telugu warriors part of its political network, for Telangana, in particular, was always outside its compass. In these conditions, the Kakatiyas continued to be an important symbol of Telugu warriorhood.

Much of Kakatiya Prataparudra's significance for later generations seems to derive from his elevation of many men of humble background to warrior status. Although it was his predecessor, Rudrama-devi, who actually initiated the trend, along with the awarding of *nayankara* assignments over land in return for military service, historical memory credits Prataparudra with this innovation.[18] As the first dynasty to create a large-scale political network composed of *nayaka* military leaders, the Kakatiyas were thus implicated in the very origins of Telugu warrior society. Prataparuda's reign was a period of dramatic transformation in another sense as well, for it was while he was king that Muslim armies first appeared in the Deccan and irretrievably shattered the existing political networks. Henceforth, Andhra was never again united under the political rule of a single dynasty.

From the perspective of the sixteenth century, therefore, Prataparudra stood at the very threshold of the contemporary world, a world of dispersed Telugu warriors in which Muslim polities were an inescapable fact. Prataparudra's appeal was the appeal of the lost Golden Age, the era when Telugu warriors were supposedly united and unchallenged. But his life and his story were more meaningful if understood in terms of current circumstances, that is, if the political tensions and conflicts of his era were thought to resemble that of the present day. There was indeed a reason for Prataparudra's memory to be preserved in a particular manner, a purpose in the form through which the new was encompassed by the old. Through this reimagining of the Kakatiya past, Telugu warriors of subsequent centuries could at the same time enhance their sense of linkage to bygone times and their sense of community with each other.

Hindu Historiography

The Kakatiyas were not the only dynasty displaced by the moving military frontier of the Delhi Sultanate, nor is the *Prataparudra Caritramu* the only Indian language composition dealing with such events. Most famous are the narratives revolving around the figure of Prithviraja III, the Cahamana king of Ajmer whose defeat at the battle of Tarain in 1192 paved the way for the founding of the Delhi Sultanate. Two kings conquered at about the same time as Kakatiya Prataparudra, Hammira of Ranasthambhapura (modern Ranthambhor) and Kanhadade of Jalor in southern Marwar, are both commemorated in works bearing their names, the *Hammira Mahakavya* and the *Kanhadade Prabandha*. Elsewhere in peninsular India, we have the *Madhura Vijaya*, a Sanskrit work narrating the reconquest of Madurai in the mid-fourteenth century by the Vijayanagara prince Kumara Kampana.[19] If we expand our search to all historical traditions in Indian languages involving some military conflict between medieval Muslim and Hindu kings, the number of works we could cite would be numerous. Although the topic has never been systematically studied, it seems clear that there was an outpouring of historiographic writing among non-Muslim Indians in the centuries after the establishment of Muslim rule in North India.

One factor accounting for the increased interest in historical narratives on the part of Hindu political elites may very well be the existence of a flourishing Indo-Muslim historiographic tradition. But even if we accept that Indo-Muslim culture exerted a strong influence on non-Muslims, there must have been more internal reasons motivating patrons to sponsor the composition of historical works. Sheldon Pollock's recent work is suggestive in this regard, for he has identified two changes in Indic literary practice that similarly occurred after the military intrusion of Turkic Muslims into the Indian subcontinent. The first is the political valorization of the Rama story, which from the twelfth century onward became "a central organizing trope in the political imagination of India."[20] The second is the emergence of comprehensive collections (*nibandha*) of Hindu law beginning in the eleventh century, which Pollock describes as "totalizing conceptualizations of society."[21] In both instances, Pollock believes that there were two forces at work: an atmosphere of uncertainty and doubt created by the military challenge of Turkic armies, plus the self-consciousness produced by the presence of a radically different culture and society.[22] In other words, the confrontation with an alien Other made it possible to formulate a contrasting self-identity and provided a strong incentive to do so. By extension, we could attribute the growth of historiographic writing in Indian languages to the same interrelated set of causes.

Because the insecurity experienced by Hindu political elites was so closely tied in to the threat posed by Muslim military force, it is not easy to determine how much the alien character of the Muslim was responsible, in and of itself, for a heightened awareness of the past. But enmity between Hindu and Muslim is widely considered to be the primary stimulus in medieval literary production. As Aziz Ahmad notes, "Muslim impact and rule in India generated two literary growths: a Muslim epic of conquest, and a Hindu epic of resistance and of psychological rejection."[23] In his article "Epic and Counter-Epic in Medieval India," Ahmad describes a body of North Indian literature celebrating Rajput heroes who fight Muslims, including two narratives about Prithviraja (the Sanskrit *Prithviraja Vijaya* and the vernacular *Prithviraj Raso*) as well as the afore-mentioned *Hammira Mahakavya*. Although it is not mentioned by Ahmad, we can also classify *Kanhadade Prabandha* in this group, for it too features the military resistance of an Indic king to Turkic conquest. Moreover, both Kanhadade and Hammira are said to be Cauhan Rajputs and thus allegedly descendants of the Cahamana king Prithviraja.[24] Unlike the works categorized as counter-epics by Ahmad, however, the *Prataparudra Caritramu* is not characterized by a discernibly anti-Muslim stance. It neither demonizes the Turkic warriors nor uses pejorative language in referring to them. There is, in fact, no differentiation made between them and the Hindu enemies of the Kakatiyas. If anything, greater hostility is displayed toward the Lords of Cuttack, who are always cast as foes and whose recurring conflicts with the Kakatiyas pervade the text. In contrast, the *Kanhadade Prabandha* explicitly equates Muslims with the *asura* demons of puranic myth, the perennial enemies of the gods. Furthermore, Kanhadade is represented as the savior of the god Somanatha of Gujarat, whose temple the Khilji armies had desecrated and whose image they were carrying back to Delhi when the conflict between them and Kanhadade's forces first erupted. The gulf between Muslim and Hindu is emphasized in the story of the sultan's daughter, who is in love with Kanhadade's son and wishes to be his wife. But Kanhadade takes the sultan's marriage proposal as a mortal insult, for he would never thus sully the honor of his lineage even if it were the only means to survival.

Let us look a little more closely at the *Kanhadade Prabandha*, for there are certain points of resemblance with the *Prataparudra Caritramu* as well. It too was written in a vernacular language, described as either Old Gujarati or Old Rajasthani. Both texts were composed well after the nearly contemporaneous events they purport to describe. The *Kanhadade Prabandha*, dated 1455, concerns the struggle between Ala-ud-din Khilji's armies and the "Rajput" chief Kanhadade of Jalor fort between approximately 1295 and 1310, while the sixteenth-century *Prataparudra Caritramu* ends with the Tughluq conquest of the Kakatiyas in 1323. In both cases, the direct cause of the kings' defeat is treachery among their ranks—warrior subordinates are bribed to retreat from the battlefield in the Kakatiya instance, while a petty official is promised control of Jalor fort in return for leading Sultanate armies into it. But more profound and foreordained reasons are also adduced for their defeat. The thousand years of Kakatiya glory promised by the goddess was coming to an end, as graphically illustrated by the spontaneous disintegration of her sword and shield boons as well as the abrupt cessation of the touchstone's ability to turn iron into gold. The *Kanhadade Prabandha*'s explanation is less straightforward, but it involves the waning of the karmic repercussions that brought the main characters together in the first place.[25] Finally, both texts contain a vision of the sleeping sultan as an incarnation of a Hindu god, which in *Kanhadade Prabandha* prevents his assassination by Kanhadade's nephew.[26]

The similarities between the two texts are intriguing, particularly in the ways that they attempt to account for the downfall of their heroes and in the assertion that the Muslim king was a divinity, just as much as the Hindu one. They suggest that literary strategies for making sense of the Turkic military success were circulating throughout the subcontinent, some of which represented attempts to assimilate Muslims into the natural (i.e., Hindu) order of things. Even a narrative that is overtly hostile to Muslims, like the *Kanhadade Prabandha,* thus consists of complex layers of both rejection and appropriation.[27] The disparity between a so-called epic of resistance such as the *Kanhadade Prabandha* and the more conciliatory *Prataparudra Caritramu* may therefore not be quite as great as it first appears. Nor was the *Prataparudra Caritramu* the only Indic historical text lacking an anti-Muslim polemic, for Ahmad states that "the Rajput epic of internecine chivalry is generally neutral to the Muslims," and he cites the *Alha Khand* as an example.[28] The accounts of the founders of Vijayanagara, Harihara and Bukka, analyzed by Phillip B. Wagoner in this volume are a further illustration of this point. A repudiation of Muslims was clearly not an invariable feature of medieval Hindu historiography.

Indeed, there is evidence from outside of India that a sense of loss and decline among members of a group can be sufficient impetus for the emergence of historical writing. In her book *Romancing the Past,* Gabrielle Spiegel analyzes the French prose chronicle, a form of historical writing that first appeared in the thirteenth century.[29] The patrons who financed these prose chronicles were Flemish aristocrats, a community whose privileged position was being steadily undermined. The agricultural revenues that sustained them were losing value in an increasingly commercialized economy, and at the same time the French king was building up his strength at their expense. In an unsatisfactory present, when trends were adversely affecting the Flemish aristocracy, they thus turned to the past in a quest for lost power and a search for future solutions. Their historical chronicles both authenticated the legitimacy of aristocratic society and established its superiority over other classes.

In the course of affirming its own identity, the aristocratic community of medieval France was, to be sure, implicitly distancing itself from royalty as well as merchants. Identity formation always involves these two aspects of what Thomas Hylland Eriksen has aptly called "us-hood" and "we-hood," the demarcation of boundaries between groups and the highlighting of shared elements within a group.[30] But at any given time, one or the other of these complementary processes could be in the ascendant. While the presence of Turks and other participants in the alien civilizational complex of the Islamic world may have inspired greater self-awareness on the part of the non-Muslim elites of India, I believe we are focusing too much on the single dimension of boundary-marking and neglecting the other side of the coin, the representations of community that emphasize internal features of solidarity. It is in this category that we can place the *Prataparudra Caritramu*, a text whose main thrust is not the demonization of Muslims but the construction of a common genealogy for all Telugu warriors stemming from their alleged past military service to the Kakatiya kings.

The prevailing geopolitical conditions at the time of the *Prataparudra Caritramu*'s composition may also be a factor in its acceptance of Muslim power. Elsewhere, both Wagoner and I have argued that the time span from roughly 1400 to 1565 constituted a phase of Hindu-Muslim collaboration and acculturation in the southern Deccan.[31] The *Prataparudra Caritramu* was written in what can be called an "open" frontier, a zone of interaction in which neither of the two cultures was clearly dominant and in which power was equally distributed amongst Hindu and Muslim polities. Furthermore, a good number of Telugu warrior lineages were either allied with or nominally subordinate to a Deccani Sultanate. In that context, there was little differentiation between Muslim and Hindu warriors, whether in literary texts or in inscriptions. Although the fifteenth century was a period of relative Muslim weakness in Rajasthan and elsewhere in North India, both Rajput society and polity seem to have been in a more defensive posture than was the case among the Hindu political elites of the Deccan. But there are undoubtedly other factors accounting for the differing depictions of Muslims, possibly related to their differing audiences. Only after looking far more carefully at the conditions of textual production and the communities responsible for their dissemination will we be able to say anything definitive about such issues.

Conclusion

In this essay, I have suggested that historical writing in Indian languages flourished in the centuries after A.D. 1000. A genre of Sanskrit literature that can be regarded as historiographic in nature—the royal biography—had its beginnings even earlier, with the seventh-century *Harsha Carita* of Bana. This genre persisted into the second millennium as evidenced by works such as the *Vikramankadeva Carita* of Bilhana composed in late eleventh-century Karnataka and Jayanaka's *Prithviraja Vijaya*, written before the Prithviraja's defeat in 1192 at the hands of the Ghurid chief Shihab-ud-din Muhammad. As the volume of historical writing grew larger, its characteristic features changed. Several of the later works, like the *Prataparudra Caritramu*, *Kanhadade Prabandha*, and *Hammira Mahakavya*, were composed a hundred years or more after the events they supposedly record, unlike the royal biographies written to flatter the poet's current patron. Because the vernacular languages were increasingly the medium of composition, rather than Sanskrit, we can infer that the later texts circulated among a different, more localized audience. Finally, a new sensibility begins to emerge in the late medieval histories. While not totally discarding what we might call puranic elements, such as the intervention of deities or the cyclic repetition of events, there is an enhanced interest in the particular and the unique: when a battle occurred, who was leading a specific campaign, what kind of tribute was exacted, who died as a consequence, and the like.[32]

Underlying the rise of historical writing, I would argue, is the proliferation of various supralocal identities as the regional societies of medieval India continued to mature. In the case of medieval Andhra, we witness repeated appropriations of the Kakatiyas in constructions of the past found in later inscriptions, literature, and folk traditions, aside from the *Prataparudra Caritramu*. Since no group in Andhra claimed to be their direct descendants, historical traditions relating to the Kakatiyas were not preserved for the sake of elevating any single lineage's reputation. Although their memory remained most salient among the warrior elite, constructions of the past in which the Kakatiyas play a part eventually circulated among village officials as well as land-controlling peasants.[33] One can therefore not assume, as Partha Chatterjee seems to, that the histories of kings were meaningful only to kings. The Kakatiya example demonstrates that historical narratives centering on kings were capable of mobilizing large-scale communities around them. Other medieval historical traditions of Hindu India should similarly be understood as strategies for the formation or consolidation of group identities, since the history of their leaders could then, just as now, symbolize the shared past of a people. And it is through agreeing on who we were before that we celebrate the unity of who we are today.

Notes

1. For an analysis of the characteristics and development of Hindu nationalist historical writing, see two of Gyanendra Pandey's essays: "The New Hindu History," *South Asia* 17, special issue: *After Ayodhya* (1994): 97–112; and "Which of Us Are Hindus?" in *Hindus and Others: The Question of Identity in India Today*, ed. G. Pandey (New Delhi: Viking, 1993).

2. Influential revisionist histories include David Frawley, *The Myth of the Aryan Invasion of India* (New Delhi: Voice of India, 1994); K. D. Sethna, *The Problem of Aryan Origins*, 2d ed. (New Delhi: Aditya Prakashan, 1992). Hindu nationalist writing also often pushes back the accepted dates for the Vedic literature by several millennia, thus displacing China's historiographic status as the oldest continuous civilization in the world in favor of India. See, for example, the timeline published in the December 1994 issue of the monthly newspaper *Hinduism Today* or Shrikant G. Talageri, *The Aryan Invasion Theory: A Reappraisal* (New Delhi: Aditya Prakashan, 1993), 1.

3. Sita Ram Goel is the most prolific of the Hindu nationalist writers on Hindu-Muslim relations. See *Hindu Temples: What Happened to Them?* pt. 2, *The Islamic Evidence* (New Delhi: Voice of India, 1991) or *Defence of Hindu Society*, 3d ed. (New Delhi: Voice of India, 1994).

4. Most notably Gyanendra Pandey, *The Construction of Communalism in Colonial North India* (Delhi: Oxford University Press, 1992).

5. Partha Chatterjee, "History and the Nationalization of Hinduism," *Social Research* 59.1 (1992): 111–49.

6. For caste, see Bernard S. Cohn, "The Census, Social Structure, and Objectification in South Asia," *Folk* 26 (1984): 25–49; Poul Pederson, "Khatri: Vaishya or Kshatriya, an Essay on Colonial Administration and Cultural Identity," *Folk* 28 (1986): 19–31; Rashmi Pant, "The Cognitive Status of Caste in Colonial Ethnography: A Review of Some Literature on the Northwest Provinces and Oudh," *Indian Economic and Social History Review* 24.2 (1987): 145–62. On language, see David Washbrook, "'To Each a Language of His Own': Language, Culture, and Society in Colonial India," in *Language, History, and Class*, ed. Penelope J. Corfield (London: Blackwell, 1991); David Lelyveld, "The Fate of Hindustani: Colonial Knowledge and the Project of a National Language," in *Orientalism and the Postcolonial Predicament*, ed. Carol A. Breckenridge and Peter van der Veer (Philadelphia: University of Pennsylvania Press, 1993).

7. For example, Romila Thapar, "Imagined Religious Communities? Ancient

History and the Modern Search for a Hindu Identity," *Modern Asian Studies* 23.2 (1989): 209–31.

8. C. V. Ramachandra Rao, ed., *Ekamranathuni Prataparudra Caritramu* (Hyderabad: Andhra Pradesh Sahitya Akademi, 1984).

9. For a description of the Muslim expeditions against Warangal, see N. Venkataramanayya, *The Early Muslim Expansion in South India* (Madras: University of Madras, 1942), 23–24, 31–43, 83–85, 99–108, 115–19.

10. For instance, excerpts from Amir Khusrau's *Khazain al-Futuh*, in H. M. Elliot and John Dowson, *The History of India as Told by Its Own Historians*, vol. 3 ([1871], reprint, New York: AMS Press, 1966), 77–85; and from Zia-ud-din Barani's *Tarikh-I-Firoz Shahi*, in ibid., 201–4, 231–34.

11. An almost identical tripartite division of the Deccan appears in the *Rayavacakamu*. Although it is a Telugu work composed around 1600, most probably in the Nayaka kingdom of Madurai, it purports to record events during the reign of the famous Vijayanagara king Krishnadeva Raya in the early sixteenth century. The text recognizes three major kingdoms in the Deccan of Krishnadeva Raya's time: those of the Lord of Horses from Delhi, the Lord of Elephants from Orissa, and the Lord of Men from Vijayanagara (Phillip B. Wagoner, *Tidings of the King: A Translation and Ethnohistorical Analysis of the Rāyavācakamu* [Honolulu: University of Hawaii Press, 1993], 60–69). These titles also figure in several Andhra inscriptions from the fifteenth and sixteenth centuries (Cynthia Talbot, "Inscribing the Other, Inscribing the Self: Hindu-Muslim Identities in Pre-Colonial India," *Comparative Studies in Society and History* 37.4 [1995]: 707–10).

12. Eastern Ganga kings rarely attempted to extend their influence beyond the northeastern corner of modern Andhra Pradesh, and in their day the town Cuttack was known as Varanasi-Kataka. The name was shortened to Kataka during the time of the Gajapati dynasty, who were far more aggressive about encroaching on Andhra territory than the Eastern Gangas had been (C. V. Ramachandra Rao, *Administration and Society in Medieval Andhra*, A.D. *1038–1538* [Nellore: Manasa, 1976], 30, 75).

13. James Fentress and Chris Wickham, *Social Memory* (Oxford: Blackwell, 1992), 58.

14. On the dating of the text, see K. Laksmiranjanam, *Sri Siddhesvara Caritramu of Kase Sarvappa* (Hyderabad: Andhra Racayitala Sanghamu), iii-vi; and Ramachandra Rao, *Prataparudra Caritramu*, 6–12.

15. This judgment is based on internal references to the area around Warangal in the text as well as the distribution of the story.

16. Ramachandra Rao, *Prataparudra Caritramu*, 69.

17. Historians have generally identified the Padmanayakas as members of the Velama caste-cluster, but no such caste or community existed during the Kakatiya period. Nor does the term *Padmanayaka* appear before the sixteenth century, at which time people alleging membership in a variety of different lineages and clans (*gotra*) used this label. In my opinion, Padmanayaka was a social

designation adopted by a number of unrelated warrior families of Telangana origin in the post-Kakatiya period.

18. Cynthia Talbot, "Political Intermediaries in Kakatiya Andhra, 1175–1325," *Indian Economic and Social History Review* 31.3 (1994): 270–84.

19. For a discussion first of *Madhura Vijaya* and then of *Kanhadade Prabandha*, see Richard H. Davis, *Lives of Indian Images* (Princeton: Princeton University Press, 1997), 115–22, 191–94.

20. Sheldon Pollock, "Ramayana and Political Imagination in India," *Journal of Asian Studies* 52.1 (1993): 263.

21. Sheldon Pollock, "Deep Orientalism? Notes on Sanskrit and Power beyond the Raj," in *Orientalism and the Postcolonial Predicament*, 105–6.

22. Pollock, "Ramayana and Political Imagination," 286; "Deep Orientalism," 98, 105–6.

23. Aziz Ahmad, "Epic and Counter-Epic in Medieval India," *Journal of the American Oriental Society* 83 (1963): 470.

24. Prithviraja played an important role in later Cauhan Rajput constructions of history, as evidenced in the *Hammira Mahakavya*, which commences with the origin of the Cauhans and soon moves on to an account of Prithviraja's reign. (For an English summary of Nayachandra Suri's *Hammira Mahakavya*, see Nilkanth Janardan Kirtane's 1879 introduction republished in the 1968 edition [Jodhpur: Rajasthan Oriental Research Institute].) *Kanhadade Prabandha* is rather unusual in not starting off with a genealogy, but it does contain passing references to both Prithviraja and Hammira (see translation by V. S. Bhatnagar [New Delhi: Aditya Prakashan, 1991], 62, 64). What we have here, therefore, is a connected body of material forming a single historiographic tradition.

25. The previous lives of Kanhadade and his son were closely intertwined with the lives of the sultan (Ala-ud-din Khilji) and his daughter. She is explicitly said to have been born a Turk due to sins committed in a previous life (Bhatnagar, *Kanhadade Prabandha*, 63–67).

26. While the sultan is identified as Siva, Kanhadade is said to be an incarnation of Vishnu (Bhatnagar, *Kanhadade Prabandha*, 42, 56, 60–61, 65–66). Conversely, the Muslim king is Vishnu and the Hindu king is Siva in the *Prataparudra Caritramu*—this episode is translated in Phillip B. Wagoner's contribution to this volume; for another version of the story, see Wagoner, *Tidings of the King*, 122–23.

27. Here I am thinking especially of the subplot concerning the unrequited love of the sultan's daughter for Kanhadade's son, said to have been her husband in their previous few lives. This is a reversal of the common motif in Muslim narratives of the love of a Muslim hero for a Hindu princess.

28. Ahmad, "Epic and Counter-Epic in Medieval India," 474.

29. Gabrielle Spiegel, *Romancing the Past: The Rise of Vernacular Prose Historiography in Thirteenth-Century France* (Berkeley: University of California Press, 1993).

30. Thomas Hylland Eriksen, "Nationalism, Mauritian Style: Cultural Unity and Ethnic Diversity," *Comparative Studies in Society and History* 36.3 (July 1994): 566–67.

31. Phillip B. Wagoner, "Understanding Islam at Vijayanagara," paper presented at the Association for Asian Studies annual meeting, Boston, 1994; Talbot, "Inscribing the Other, Inscribing the Self," 704–10.

32. This is particularly noticeable in the *Kanhadade Prabandha,* which dispenses with the traditional genealogical opening and jumps straight into the details of the escalating military conflict. It describes the components of the various armies, identifies the weapons used, and lists the names of warriors involved in specific campaigns—giving it a far greater air of historicity than is the case in earlier accounts of battles in Indian languages.

33. For details, see the chapter "The Kakatiyas in Telugu Historical Memory" in my forthcoming book, *Precolonial India in Practice* (New York: Oxford University Press).

12

Harihara, Bukka, and the Sultan

The Delhi Sultanate in the Political Imagination of Vijayanagara

Phillip B. Wagoner

Harihara and Bukka belonged to a family of five brothers, all sons of Sangama. They were at first in the service of [the Kākatīya king] Pratāparudra, but after the Muslim conquest of his kingdom in 1323 they went over to Kampili. When Kampili also fell in 1327, they became prisoners and were carried off to Delhi where, because they embraced Islam, they stood well with the sultan. Now, once again, they were sent to the province of Kampili to take over its administration from Malik Muhammad and to deal with the revolt of the Hindu subjects. What really happened after their arrival in the South does not emerge clearly from the conflicting versions of Muslim historians and Hindu tradition. Both are agreed, however, that the two trusted lieutenants of the sultanate very soon gave up Islam and the cause of Delhi, and proceeded to set up an independent Hindu state which soon grew into the powerful empire of Vijayanagara. They started by doing the work of the sultan, their former connexion with Anegondi making their task easy, though their Muslim faith set some people against them. They followed a policy of conciliation which pacified the people, and only used force where it was absolutely necessary. . . . Then, Hindu tradition avers, the brothers met the sage Vidyāraṇya and, fired by his teaching, returned to the Hindu fold and accepted the mission of upholding the Hindu cause against Islam.

K. A. Nilakanta Sastri, ***A History of South India from Prehistoric Times to the Fall of Vijayanagar***

I

To explain the origins of the medieval South Indian state of Vijayanagara, a narrative similar to Nilakanta Sastri's is appealed to in the majority of standard surveys and reference works on Indian history. Although the precise details offered may vary, these accounts are in broad agreement in suggesting that the rise of Vijayanagara is best understood in terms of the vicissitudes of Harihara and Bukka's experience with Islam, as they undergo first conversion and then apostasy. Thus, we learn that Harihara and Bukka are local Hindus who are taken to Delhi and forcibly converted to Islam; that they are rewarded for their conversion with an appointment as provincial governors; that they are then enabled by the Advaitin ascetic Vidyāraṇya to apostatize and return to the Hindu fold; and finally—and most important—that they give political expression to this act of apostasy by founding the Vijayanagara kingdom. Vijayanagara is thus construed as a great counterpolity to the Delhi Sultanate, which has arisen through an act of resistance to Delhi's southward thrust. Clearly, much of the appeal of this narrative lies in its power to confirm the communally inspired image of Vijayanagara as a Hindu state, dedicated to the containment of Islam and the preservation of the traditional Hindu cultural order in the south.

But what exactly is the basis for this narrative of Vijayanagara's founding? If we pause to examine the primary sources upon which this modern historical interpretation rests, we find a confusing array of sources that differ greatly both in terms of their status as historical documents and in terms of the substance of the testimony they offer. The first body of evidence is the only one that consists of actual contemporary documents—donative inscriptions issued directly by the first rulers of the Vijayanagara state—and significantly, these contemporary documents do not refer at all to the founding of the state. A second body of evidence is likewise contemporary (or very nearly so) with the events of Vijayanagara's founding, but the sources in this category are not "documents" in the strict sense but narrative "histories" composed by three authors working in an Islamicate tradition of historiography: ʿIṣāmī's *Futūḥ al-Salāṭīn*, written at the newly formed Bahmani court in Gulbarga between 1347 and 1350;[1] Baranī's *Ta'rīkh-i Fīrūz-Shāhī*, written at the Sultanate court of Delhi by an intimate of Sultan Fīrūz Tughluq;[2] and the *Riḥlah* or *The Travels of Ibn-Baṭṭūṭa*, transcribed in Morocco by Muhammad Ibn Juzayy from Ibn-Baṭṭūṭa's dictation in 1354 after the traveler's return from India.[3] None of these three narratives presumes to address the origins of the Vijayanagara kingdom, but two of them (ʿIṣāmī and Ibn Baṭṭūṭa) do refer in passing to a "Harip" or "Haryab," who from the context is clearly Vijayanagara's Harihara.[4] Moreover, all three authors make significant allusions to converts and apostates in the fourteenth-century Deccan; although none of the fourteenth-century authors ever identifies any of these converts or apostates explicitly as Harihara or Bukka, modern historians have taken the passages in question as referring to the founders of Vijayanagara.[5] The third group of sources is considerably later than the founding of Vijayanagara and consists of a number of historiographic narratives in Sanskrit that are datable to the sixteenth and early seventeenth centuries, including the *Rājakālanirṇaya*, *Vidyāraṇya-kālajñāna*, *Vidyāraṇya-vṛttānta*, and *Vidyāraṇya-śaka* (discussed in detail below). These texts are separated from the events they purport to describe by over two hundred years, but they are the earliest available sources to present a detailed and coherent account of Harihara and Bukka's capture by the sultan of Delhi, and it is these works which have been used by modern historians as the narrative blueprint for emplotting their own account of Vijayanagara's founding. Nearly all of the details of the modern interpretation are present in these texts, from the names of the brothers Harihara and Bukka and the identities of the Deccani kings they had earlier served, to the episodes of their being captured and taken to Delhi, sent back to the Deccan, and meeting with Vidyāraṇya. Indeed, the only substantial details that are missing from these texts are those of the brothers' supposed conversion and apostasy—which, as we have seen, are of central importance to the modern interpretation.[6]

It is ultimately to N. Venkataramanayya that we owe the modern interpretation of Vijayanagara's founding in its religiously configured form.[7] In a series of important contributions beginning in 1929, Venkataramanayya in effect combined the testimony of the second and third bodies of evidence, so that the deficiencies present in each group of sources were compensated for by the complementary strengths possessed by the other.[8] Thus, the fourteenth-century accounts of the Persian and Arabic histories were seen to possess a considerable degree of reliability, since they were nearly contemporaneous with the events they described, but at the same time they were decidedly oblique and lacking in detail. On the other hand, the sixteenth-century Sanskrit accounts were considerably later and thereby carried less inherent authority as historical sources, but their accounts seemed to be in general agreement with those of the earlier sources, and moreover, they provided many of the details that were lacking in the earlier accounts. Because the two categories of evidence thus appeared to be mutually reinforcing, Venkataramanayya did not hesitate to combine their testimony to produce what was in effect a composite narrative, which he believed to be a fuller and more accurate account of the events that had surrounded Vijayanagara's founding. The coherent and detailed narrative framework of Harihara and Bukka's peregrinations and capture by the sultan was provided by the later Sanskrit historiographic texts, while a reassuring measure of historical reliability and the all-important suggestion of the two brothers' conversion and apostasy—without which, Venkataramanayya felt, the sultan's actions were inexplicable[9]—were contributed by the otherwise more meager accounts of the fourteenth-century Muslim writers.

Venkataramanayya had worked out the details of his composite construction by 1946, when he presented it in its classic form in his introduction to the compilation *Further Sources of Vijayanagara History.*[10] Carefully argued, his presentation includes a detailed discussion of the full range of evidence and how its often conflicting claims may be reconciled. The impact of Venkataramanayya's construction was expanded significantly the following year, when Nilakanta Sastri included his more compact and popularly oriented retelling (the story with which this essay opens) in his widely influential *History of South India.* Nilakanta Sastri made his version of the story more accessible—and more authoritative and resistant to critical analysis—by presenting Venkataramanayya's conclusions as historical facts, without any discussion of the nature of the sources or the line of reasoning Venkataramanayya had followed in constructing the account. In 1960, Venkataramanayya redacted his own popular version of the story for the chapter on Vijayanagara that he contributed to volume 6 of the Bharatiya Vidya Bhavan *History and Culture of the Indian People;*[11] if anything, this version is still more seamless and unassailable than Nilakanta Sastri's. Small wonder, then, that the story has found its way into the majority of standard surveys and reference works on Indian history that have appeared since the publication of Nilakanta Sastri's and Venkataramanayya's popularizations. In one form or another, the religiously configured story of Vijayanagara's founding may be found in such diverse works as Percival Spear's *India: A Modern History,* Romila Thapar's *History of India,* Stanley Wolpert's *New History of India,* Joseph Schwartzberg's *Historical Atlas of South Asia,* and the fourth edition of Vincent Smith's *Oxford History of India.*[12]

What is most remarkable about the popularization of Venkataramanayya's account is the way in which the substance of his modern construction has come to interfere with our perception of the contents of the actual medieval textual sources. In particular, there has been a tendency for subsequent writers to assume that the later Sanskrit accounts of Harihara and Bukka's capture by the sultan actually describe the two brothers' experiences in terms of conversion and apostasy, notwithstanding the fact that Venkataramanayya himself openly and frankly recognized that this was not the case.[13] Already in 1947, we find Nilakanta Sastri suggesting unambiguously that both the "Muslim historians and Hindu tradition" agree that "the two trusted lieutenants of the sultanate very soon gave up Islam"; he even reiterates this point a second time, stating that "Hindu tradition avers" that the two brothers met Vidyāraṇya, whose teaching inspired them to "return to the Hindu fold."[14] More recently, Hermann Kulke and Burton Stein have both rejected the account of Harihara and Bukka's conversion and apostasy as an accurate record of "what actually happened" in the mid-fourteenth century, but even in rejecting the narrative's contents, they have nonetheless assumed that such a tale of conversion and apostasy is indeed recorded in Vijayanagara-period historiographic texts, apparently not realizing that the motif of conversion and apostasy was combined with the narrative of Vijayanagara's founding only through Venkataramanayya's labors in the early twentieth century.[15]

Why should such a seemingly minor misinterpretation be cause for concern? Quite simply because the persistence of this misunderstanding impedes our ability to comprehend the nature of the medieval sources, which are our only avenue to understanding "what really happened" in the period of Vijayanagara's origins. Given the importance of the Sanskrit narrative of Harihara and Bukka's capture and the pivotal role it has played in formulating our current understanding of Vijayanagara, there is a real need to return to the actual Sanskrit textual sources and reexamine them on their own terms, not as evidence of what occurred in the fourteenth century but rather as evidence of an indigenous historiographic discourse about that past. Before asking how these texts may (or may not) accurately reflect that past, we must first attempt to understand the particular forms and contents of their representation according to their own cultural logic. If the medieval narrative of Harihara and Bukka's capture was not originally conceived and deployed as a tale of conversion and apostasy, then what, we must ask, were its real meaning and purpose?

To answer this question, what is needed is a broad, contextual reading of the narrative, first in comparison with episodes from other medieval South Indian historiographic texts that similarly revolve around the motif of capture, transfer to Delhi, and release, and then in comparison with the specific historical background of the period in which the Harihara and Bukka narrative was produced—that of the sixteenth century, by which time independent evidence indicates that the elite culture of Vijayanagara had become heavily Islamicized. Ultimately, what we will find from such a contextual reading is that the narrative of Harihara, Bukka, and the sultan is not at all the account of defiant subversion it has been taken to be. To the contrary, it must be understood as a political foundation myth, an ideological attempt to represent the authority of the Vijayanagara state as deriving directly *from that of the Sultanate.* In the eyes of the redactors of this tradition, at least, we shall see that Vijayanagara thus takes its place alongside a host of regional sultanates, spread across North India and into the Deccan, which arose as local "successor" states to the Delhi Sultanate. Recognition of this fact should give us cause to reevaluate our own communally charged characterization of Vijayanagara as a Hindu bulwark against the advancing tide of Islam, and to question the degree to which this modern image of the state is actually in accordance with the medieval reality.

II

The late Vijayanagara historiographic narrative of Harihara and Bukka's capture by the sultan of Delhi figures prominently in at least four Sanskrit texts dating to the sixteenth and early seventeenth centuries. To my knowledge, none of these texts has ever been published in its entirety—let alone been made available in a complete translation—but extracts of the episode in question, together with translations or synopses, have been published from three of them, *Rāja-kālanirṇaya, Vidyāraṇya-kālajñāna,* and *Vidyāraṇya-vṛttānta.* Extracts from the first two texts, based on manuscripts preserved in the Mackenzie Collection, were included as an appendix to N. Venkataramanayya's 1929 study, *Kampili and Vijayanagara,* and their contents were discussed briefly in the body of the essay. The compilation *Further Sources of Vijayanagara History* reproduced a passage from *Vidyāraṇya-vṛttānta,* as well as a longer extract from *Vidyāraṇya-kālajñāna* than Venkataramanayya had earlier printed; additionally, the third volume of this work provided translations of these extracts (3:9–15). Venkataramanayya opines that the *Rāja-kālanirṇaya* was composed at the beginning of the seventeenth century[16] and that "the earliest recension of the *Vidyāraṇya-kālajñāna* seems to have been composed before the close of the 15th century" (this date is clearly a printer's error for "16th century").[17] He does not discuss the date of the *Vidyāraṇya-vṛttānta.* The fourth work, *Vidyāraṇya-śaka,* is one of a collection of short, related works contained in a single manuscript preserved in the collection of the Oriental Research Institute of the University of Mysore.[18] This text is datable to the last two decades of the sixteenth century. Although unpublished, this manuscript was the subject of a detailed discussion in the *Annual Report of the Mysore Archaeological Department for the Year 1932,* which appeared in 1935. This report included translated extracts of a number of passages relating to the founding and early history of Vijayanagara, including the story of Harihara, Bukka, and the sultan.[19] With regard to this episode at least, the four texts appear to represent only slightly varying redactions of what must have been a common body of historiographic tradition.[20] I have based the following translation on the version of the *Vidyāraṇya-kālajñāna* text printed in *Further Sources of Vijayanagara History;* points of difference with the other three texts are signaled in the notes. The narrator of the passage is the ascetic Vidyāraṇya, who himself enters into the narrative in the first person toward the end:

> Two guardians[21] of the treasury of king Vīrarudra [i.e., Kākatīya Pratāparudra] came from Silāpura [i.e., Warangal], friendless and chased by the Yavanas [i.e., the forces of the Delhi Sultanate], and took up service with Rāmanātha[22] [of Kampili] as guardians of the royal treasury. They bore the marks of sovereignty, these broad-chested and big-armed men.[23] But again in battle, that king was slain by the warriors of Mahāndhēśvara and the two were captured by the sultan's soldiers and brought back to his city.[24]
>
> One evening, in the confusion of a torrential storm as the night roared with thunder, the sultan awoke and noticed that [another] prisoner had escaped, but saw that his two captives remained standing near the open door. "What is this?" he asked them. "How is it that you two remain standing here?"[25] The wise sultan recognized them to be trustworthy indeed, and so he bestowed a province upon them, giving them the Karnāta country.
>
> Thus commanded by the sultan, the two heroes went quickly to the Kṛṣṇavenī, and crossed the river in a boat. They did battle with [the Hoysaḷa] king Ballāḷa,[26] but he defeated them. Exhausted, they went and sat down at the foot of a tree in the middle of the forest. Harihara was very tired and fell asleep in his brother's lap. Just then, the yogi Revaṇa appeared to him in a dream and gave to that lord of the earth a linga of mystic power, named Candramaulīśvara. The great being said, "Henceforth, this shall make you ever victorious, and will cause your prosperity to increase. Soon, you will behold Vidyāraṇya, and you will gain lordship over a lion-throne, there is no doubt about it."
>
> As soon as he had finished saying this, the yogi disappeared, and Harihara awoke from the dream, telling everything to his brother. The two famous brothers were elated. At that very moment, their scattered army reassembled around them, and to their great delight, I myself, Vidyāraṇya, appeared before them. They bowed to

me and joyfully offered me praise, and then I blessed them and dismissed them to go and fight again with Ballāḷa. This time they defeated him, and found a lion-throne that was buried there in the battlefield itself. Thus did the two heroes begin to rule over the kingdom they had acquired.[27]

Three points will be immediately clear from reading this narrative. In the first place, as I have already suggested, this account says nothing about conversion or apostasy; in fact, in the first half of the story up until the brothers meet the yogi Revaṇa, the narrative has nothing to do with religion at all. Instead, the language used in the text clearly and consistently emphasizes political relationships. Thus, the brothers "take up service" with Rāmanātha (*rāmanātham siṣevāte*); they are "endowed with the marks of sovereignty" (*sāmrājya-lakṣaṇa-hitau*); they impress the sultan with their display of "trustworthiness" (*satyasaṃdhau*); the sultan "gives them a province" (*deśam datvā*) and they leave to rule it, "commanded" (*ājñāptau*) by the sultan. Second, once they have arrived back in the Deccan, Vidyāraṇya's actions—as well as those of Revaṇa, who has been completely written out of the story by modern scholars such as Nilakanta Sastri—serve to *confirm* the charge that the brothers have been given by the sultan, not to counter it as the modern construction holds. Thus, Revaṇa presents Harihara with a talismanic *linga*, and Vidyāraṇya pronounces benedictions that enable the two brothers to be "ever victorious." Finally, the text is very clear that the brothers' conflict is not with some communal Muslim foe but rather with the Hoysaḷa ruler Ballāḷa, who is the last remaining Indic king in the region where Harihara and Bukka are to establish their kingdom.

To further refine our understanding of the meaning and significance of Harihara and Bukka's encounter with the sultan, it will be useful to turn for comparison to other medieval South Indian narratives that similarly juxtapose an Indic hero with the alien figure of the sultan of Delhi. Not surprisingly, there are a number of such narratives, which appear to have been generated in response to the campaigns waged in South India by Sultanate forces during the three decades from 1296 to 1327. Collectively, these narratives may be seen to represent an attempt to come to terms with the intrusion of Delhi's power into the southern peninsula and, in particular, to make sense out of the widespread cultural disorder that ensued. One such narrative centers on Kākatīya Pratāparudra (who, it will be recalled, is identified in the tradition under consideration as one of the figures served by Harihara and Bukka before their own capture) and is related in the *Pratāparudra Caritramu* of

Ekāmranātha, an early sixteenth-century Telugu historiographic text focusing on the Kākatīyas, who ruled the Andhra country between the twelfth and fourteenth centuries. Another example is the story told in the Tamil *Kōil Oḷugu*—the chronicle of the Śrīrangam temple—of the capture of the image of Alagiyamaṇavāḷa Perumāḷ from Śrīrangam and its removal to Delhi; here, of course, the "hero" is not a mere human but an all-powerful divinity, but in any case the dividing line between these two poles of existence was not sharp, as we shall see. Both narratives resonate closely with that of Harihara and Bukka's encounter with the sultan; in particular, we will see that they similarly revolve around the motif of the hero's capture and transfer to Delhi by the forces of the sultan, and that they likewise climax in an extraordinary nocturnal encounter revealing the captive's true nature—even though the particular form of this encounter and the conclusions drawn about the heroes' natures are quite different in these two cases.

Let us begin with the *Pratāparudra Caritramu* account:

> Hearing the news from his spies that Pratāparudra had been captured and was being brought to Delhi, the sultan went out from the city to meet him. He escorted him into the capital with great pomp and bestowed various honors upon him. He sat Pratāparudra down on the Lion Throne and took his own seat on a lowly stool. As they were conversing, an eye appeared in the middle of Pratāparudra's forehead [suggesting that he was none other than Śiva himself]. When the sultan noticed this, he was astonished and jumped up, thinking, "Good heavens! What have I done!" The sultan left Pratāparudra to wait in the palace and ran off to tell his mother what had happened. That respectable woman, who happened to be devoted to the worship of Lord Mādhava of Prayāg, consoled her son and said, "You and Pratāparudra go and lie down on a big bed together. When you are asleep, I will be able to judge your relative greatness. We shall see . . ."
>
> That night, Pratāparudra and the sultan lay down together on an upper terrace of the palace. When they were sound asleep, the sultan's mother came up to have a look. There she beheld in them a great radiance consisting of the forms of Śiva and Viṣṇu themselves. Brilliant light came out of their bodies and, merging together, rose up into the sky. The sultan's mother thought for a moment and then woke the two men up. "Stop this fighting between yourselves," she admonished them. "It is not in keeping with your true greatness! Separately, you are the glory of Śiva and

Viṣṇu themselves, and together you present the composite form of Harihara!"

[The next morning] the sultan gave three crores of silver to the brahmins who had followed Pratāparudra to Delhi, and he gave all manner of gifts to Pratāparudra. With the greatest politeness, the sultan said, "Please try to forget this terrible thing I have done to you. Return now to Warangal; I shall be anxiously awaiting the good news that you have entered the city and reoccupied its Lion Throne. This is all I request."[28]

The account of the *Kōil Oḷugu* reads as follows:

The Sultan of Delhi came to Srirangam and entered the temple through the northern gateway. When the invaders approached, the local king Panjukondan did battle with them, but was easily overpowered by a number of assailants, who plunged in and plundered the treasury, carrying away the image of Alagiyamaṇavāḷa Perumāḷ and all the treasures of the temple. At this time, there was in Karambanūr a woman who observed the vow of taking her daily food only after worshipping Alagiyamaṇavāḷa Perumāḷ. When the Perumāḷ left the place, she left her family, and foodless, entered the war-camp of the Sultan of Delhi. [She follows the Muslim army back to Delhi, and enters the Sultan's house, disguised as one of the women of the palace.]

The Sultan placed the idol in the store-room of the palace. The daughter of the Sultan of Delhi, seeing the idol of Alagiyamaṇavāḷa Perumāḷ, took it to play with and placed it in her bedroom. The woman of Karambanūr decided that such a position was not quite conducive to the sacred body of Alagiyamaṇavāḷa Perumāḷ, and wanted to make this known in the temple. She returned to the sacred shrine at Srirangam and revealed the news in the Holy Presence. The great god in the temple, along with his human servants, gladly received her and gave her the name Pincenravalli, "she who followed," and honored her with many presents. [The authorities decide to go to Delhi to get the image back.]

They barred the door to the sanctum of the temple with a stone slab and suspended all worship and festivals. Thus deserting the temple, all the temple servants—sixty in number—followed the lead of Pincenravalli to Delhi. As before, Pincenravalli entered the palace disguised and, winning the confidence of the women there, saw how Alagiyamaṇavāḷan was capriciously playing with the

Sultāni, in the form of an idol during the day time and in his *vibhava* manifestation at night, in all splendor. She informed the temple servants of what she saw. They, with the temple singer before them, attracted the pleasure of the Sultan, by means of the "Jaggiṇi" dance. The Sultan of Delhi was much pleased and offered them enormous treasure, but the singer refused and instead requested the Sultan simply to give back the image of Alagiyamaṇavāḷan. The Sultan ordered his servants to allow the temple servants to take the idol they wanted from the storehouse. But on searching the storehouse they found the idol missing and felt sorely vexed. On hearing from Pincenravalli, they said to the Sultan, "Our Perumāḷ is in the possession of your daughter," to which the Sultan replied, "You can yourselves call back your God." Consequently, when the temple singer invoked Alagiyamaṇavāḷa Perumāḷ in intense and divine melody, the God brought sleep to the girl, slipped away, and hastened to rejoin the servants. When the singer informed the Sultan about this, he was amazed and allowed them to take back their God. . . . [When the Sultan's daughter awakes, she is heartbroken to find her lover absent. She sets out with her father's army to pursue the missing image. She is ready to end her life but for the desire of seeing the Perumāḷ.]

When they reached Chandragiri, near Tiruvengadam, the temple retinue learned of the Sultani's approach, and adopted the plan of fleeing dispersed lest they be found and caught and the Perumāḷ be carried away again. Three servants, who were related to each other as uncle, brother-in-law, and nephew, ascended the Tiruvengadam mountain with the Perumāḷ. The other fifty-seven took diverse routes. The Muslims, not finding the temple retinue on their way, went to Srirangam, where they heard that the Perumāḷ had not yet returned and saw the temple gateway barred by a piece of rock. Losing all hope, the Sultani breathed her last, unable to bear the separation. [Some sixty years later, after being hidden on the Tiruvengadam mountain, the image is finally returned to the temple; the Sultani undergoes an apotheosis and becomes Tulukka-Nācciyar, the "Turkic consort" of the god.][29]

Although there are significant differences between these two stories and the story of Harihara and Bukka, we cannot help but be struck by the many fundamental similarities. Indeed, I would suggest that the three stories are so alike that they can be productively analyzed in terms of a common narrative structure, which consists of a sequence of five elements (see table 12.1).

Table 12.1 NARRATIVE STRUCTURE

	Vidyāraṇyakāla jñāna	*Pratāparudra Caritramu*	*Kōil Oḷugu*
1. Sultan launches military campaign into South	Sultan attacks Warangal, "Kampili"	Sultan attacks Warangal	Sultan attacks Warangal, etc., and marches on Srirangam
II. Hero captured by sultan and taken to Delhi	Harihara and Bukka captured and taken to Delhi	Pratāparudra captured and taken to Delhi	Alagiyamaṇavāḷ a Perumāḷ image captured and taken to Delhi
III. Hero kept in captivity as sultan's prisoner	Harihara and Bukka imprisoned	Pratāparudra captive, but treated honorably	Alagiyamaṇavāḷa Perumāḷ put in storeroom, discovered by sultan's daughter, and taken to her room as a toy
IV. Extraordinary nocturnal encounter reveals captive's true nature	Another prisoner escapes during nighttime storm; Harihara and Bukka are so honest that they remain where they are	Sultan's mother watches the sultan and Pratāparudra sleeping; has vision of them as Viṣṇu and Śiva; she informs her son and chastises him for keeping such a great being in captivity	(A) The god manifests in "living," *vibhava* form to "play" at night with sultan's daughter (B) The priests call their god, who miraculously comes to them from the sultan's daughter's bedroom

continued on next page

Table 12.1—*continued*

	Vidyāraṇyakāla jñāna	*Pratāparudra Caritramu*	*Kōil Oḻugu*
V. Recognizing captive's true nature, sultan releases prisoner and allows to return to South India	Sultan is amazed at Harihara and Bukka's trustworthiness; he gives them territory to rule and sends them back to the South	Sultan is chastened, gives gifts and apologies to Pratāparudra and sends him to Warangal to reoccupy his throne	Sultan is amazed and allows the priests to take their god back to Srirangam (but not without further adventures and temporary reversals); sultan's daughter dies of a broken heart and becomes the god's consort, Tulukka-nacciyar
FINAL OUTCOME:	Former subordinates are elevated to new status as kings by accepting their subordination to an alien ruler	Order and balance restored, king returns to throne and the alien ruler is familiarized as a Hindu deity	Order and balance restored, god reestablished in his temple, and alien ruler is familiarized as father-in-law of a Hindu deity

Thus, all three stories begin with the sultan launching a military campaign into the south (I), as a result of which the South Indian hero is defeated, captured, and taken to Delhi (II). Once in Delhi, the hero is the sultan's prisoner (III). The turning point of the story in each case takes the form of an extraordinary nocturnal encounter, in which the captive's true nature is revealed (IV); as a result, the sultan releases the captive hero and allows him to return to South India (V). In view of this overall structural similarity, we may posit the existence of an established narrative type in South India—a narrative of capture, transfer, and return from Delhi—and conceive of the three stories in question as variant expressions of this single narrative pattern.

Although all three stories may thus be seen as specific actualizations of this underlying narrative formula of capture, transfer, and release, it should also be clear that the narratives of Pratāparudra and of Alagiyamaṇavāḷa Perumāḷ share more in common with each other than either does with the story of Harihara and Bukka. By viewing our narrative in contrast with these other tales of capture, transfer, and release, we may better grasp the uniqueness of several of its key elements, which provide important clues as to its actual historiographic significance.

First, there is a significant difference in terms of the nature of the hero's captivity. In the stories of both Pratāparudra and Alagiyamaṇavāḷa Perumāḷ, the hero enjoys a comfortable situation even while he is a captive. Pratāparudra is greeted and honored personally by the sultan, is given a seat on the imperial throne itself, and is invited to sleep at night with the sultan on an upper terrace of the palace. Alagiyamaṇavāḷa Perumāḷ is not treated so well at first, being confined to a storeroom. But once he is discovered by the sultan's daughter, he does better, being taken to her bedroom in the heart of the zenana where he passes the night in her company. In stark contrast, Harihara and Bukka are treated as common prisoners. Although the texts are silent on the matter of where they are incarcerated, they are clearly kept with other captives, one of whom escapes during the night. Certainly, they are shown no special consideration or respect by their captor.

Second, there is a decisive difference in the status of the captive hero as revealed through the extraordinary nocturnal encounter. Both Pratāparudra and Alagiyamaṇavāḷa Perumāḷ are revealed to be all-powerful beings, whom the sultan has affronted by removing from their proper domains. Thus, Pratāparudra is revealed to be not just an ordinary mortal ruler but a veritable incarnation of none other than Śiva, and thus he is in the same league as the sultan, who is himself an embodiment of Viṣṇu. Similarly, in the account of the *Kōil Oḷugu,* Alagiyamaṇavāḷa Perumāḷ is revealed to be not an inanimate, insensate object—an "idol"—but a living deity, who is equally capable of enticing the sultan's daughter to "play" with him and of hearing the calls of his devotees and responding by physically returning to their presence. Harihara and Bukka, on the other hand, remain in a position of unquestioned subordination to the sultan even as their true nature is revealed. The sultan is in control and they are his prisoners; even when presented with the opportunity to escape, they do not take it, but willfully remain in captivity. In their case, the nocturnal epiphany reveals them not as the sultan's equals but quite the opposite, as the very models of the honorable, trustworthy subordinate.

Finally, and perhaps most important, there is a fundamental difference in the overall dynamic aspect of the narratives. The stories of both Pratāparudra and Alagiyamaṇavāḷa Perumāḷ are ultimately static, since they conclude with the restoration of an order that has been temporarily disrupted. Pratāparudra begins as a king and ends as a king, after a brief period in which his status is called into question by outside forces. The same is true of Alagiyamaṇavāḷa Perumāḷ, who is restored to his status as a sovereign deity after having been temporarily misperceived as an inanimate idol. In striking contrast, Harihara and Bukka are at the outset merely political underlings, migrating from court to court in the service of other rulers. But through their fateful encounter with the sultan they are transformed and elevated to the status of paramount rulers themselves. In the dramatis personae of these three narratives, they are the only heroes whose identities actually change through the process of capture, transfer, and return, and who are represented as positively benefiting from their encounter with the sultan.

Ultimately, I would suggest that the stories of Pratāparudra and Alagiyamaṇavāḷa Perumāḷ may best be understood as "narratives of resistance,"[30] through which certain axiomatic beliefs relating to the established order are reaffirmed and upheld when challenged by an alien cultural formation. In the case of Pratāparudra, it is the assumption that kings in some sense embody divinity that is graphically affirmed; in the case of Alagiyamaṇavāḷa Perumāḷ, it is the belief that divine images are in some sense actually alive. But in both cases, this resistant affirmation is effected through a range of very similar means, including the conceit that the hero undergoes no hardship even while in captivity; the insistence that the sultan in both cases recognizes the error of his perception (that Pratāparudra is merely human; that Alagiyamaṇavāḷa Perumāḷ is merely an idol) and corrects his error by releasing his captive; and most amusingly, by the co-opting of the person of the sultan into the traditional Indic order, by casting him as an embodiment of Viṣṇu in the one case and, implicitly, as the "father-in-law" of the Perumāḷ in the other.[31] In contrast, the story of Harihara and Bukka is anything but a narrative of resistance. It reads instead as a willing endorsement of the alternate political-cultural order represented by the Sultanate, in that the account traces the origins of Vijayanagara to Harihara and Bukka's relationship of service to the sultan. The narrative of capture, transfer, and return has here been recast as part of what can only be read as a foundation myth for the Vijayanagara state. The sultan is no longer represented as the villain who challenges the traditional order; rather, he is seen as the ultimate source of Vijayanagara authority.

If the Sultanate was so important in the political imagination of sixteenth-century Vijayanagara elites, one might object, then why should there be no further mention of Delhi or the sultan subsequent to this episode in the texts of this historiographic tradition? Here there would appear to be a striking similarity between the political ideology expressed in this Vijayanagara tradition and that reflected in the well-known account of Viśvanātha Nāyaka's founding of the Nāyaka kingdom of Madurai, one of Vijayanagara's most important successor states.[32] Here, too, at the beginning of the narrative, there is an elaborate story of a personal interaction between the Vijayanagara Raya and the loyal subordinate Viśvanātha Nāyaka, which serves to establish Viśvanātha's "unnatural" devotion to his master. In this case, Viśvanātha volunteers to march against his own father, Nāgama Nāyaka, who has rebelled against the king; in reward for this unflinching loyalty and obedience to his master—echoing Harihara and Bukka's extreme obedience to the will of the sultan, in not fleeing even when presented with the opportunity—Viśvanātha is given the kingdom of Madurai to rule on behalf of the Raya. As Dirks has pointed out, it is highly significant that "at the very point at which the kingship of the Madurai Nayakars is firmly established under Visvanatha, we find no further references in the chronicle to the Vijayanagara Rayar."[33]

Both narratives revolve around the invoking of what Narayana Rao, Shulman, and Subrahmanyam have termed "vertical linkages," which they characterize as one of the necessary components of Nāyaka statehood: "The entire process of creating a Nāyaka state seems to depend upon establishing a linkage, articulated in terms of personal loyalty, with a higher centre of authority—here embodied in the Vijayanagara overlord. No Nāyaka king can do without this empowering source from above. On the other hand this vertical linkage is optimally activated under conditions that effectively undermine its controlling power. Viśvanātha wins the emperor's blessing even as he extricates himself from the latter's proximity and potential demands."[34] Precisely the same observations hold true for the sixteenth-century representation of Vijayangara's origins as well—if we substitute "sultan" for "Vijayanagara overlord," and "Harihara and Bukka" for "Viśvanātha." In view of this striking ideological continuity, it would appear that Nāyaka kingship does not represent quite the "exotic departure from earlier political forms" that Narayana Rao et al. have suggested.[35] Rather, it is clearly in the late Vijayanagara period itself, and particularly in the pivotal sixteenth century, that we begin to witness this intriguing ideological transition.

Once we recognize this narrative of Harihara, Bukka, and the sultan for what it is—an attempt to cast Vijayanagara as a successor state to Delhi—we can begin to make sense of a number of other seemingly anomalous references to the Sultanate that occasionally appear in Vijayanagara period texts. These references are difficult to comprehend in terms of the received communal view, which posits the Sultanate and Vijayanagara as antithetical states, politically in opposition due to their presumed dedication to opposing religions and worldviews. From such a perspective, it would seem inexplicable, for example, that the *Rāyavācakamu*, a late sixteenth-century Telugu historiographic text, should identify the Muslim ruler of Delhi as the occupant of one of the "Three Lion Thrones" along with the Hindu rulers of Vijayanagara and the Gajapati kingdom of Orissa. According to the conception presented in this text, the "Three Lion Thrones" represent the imperial centers of the three ancient, legitimate kingdoms that together account for almost the entire Indian subcontinent; each Lion Throne is occupied by a worthy "dharmic" king, who himself happens to exist as an "emanation" (*aṃśa*) of one of the great gods of Hinduism (the incumbent of Delhi's Lion Throne is identified as an *aṃśa* of Viṣṇu).[36] The sultan of Delhi is represented here not as a Muslim "Other" but, strikingly, as an "insider" who is culturally no different from his royal Vijayanagara and Gajapati cohorts. While this geopolitical schema appears strikingly anomalous from the perspective of the received communal paradigm, it is easily harmonized with the view of Delhi presented in the *Vidyāraṇya-kālajñāna* and related texts. If the Sultanate loomed large enough in the political imagination of Vijayanagara that the sultan should be represented as the source of Harihara and Bukka's sovereignty in the fourteenth century, then there certainly would have been nothing odd in representing his contemporary successor to the throne of Delhi[37] as belonging to the same imperial brotherhood as the sixteenth-century rulers of Vijayanagara and Orissa. Nor should it surprise us when the brahmin hero in a fifteenth-century Telugu poem, *Krīḍābhirāmamu*, declares to Mācaladēvi, the most illustrious courtesan in Warangal, that her fame surpasses that of the sultan of Delhi (nīku-gala prasiddhi ḍhilli suratāṇikini lēdu).[38] The very fact that the poet has chosen to use this comparison vividly suggests the power that the Sultanate continued to exercise in the elite imagination of South India, even more than a century after the last Tughluq incursions.

III

Why, in the sixteenth century, should Vijayanagara elites have thought it appropriate to establish conceptual links between Vijayanagara and Delhi and to trace the origin of their state to the sultan's gift of territory and authority? To answer this question, we must now move beyond the literary dimensions of the narrative to consider the broader cultural historical context in which it was redacted. Specifically, we must recognize the fact that by the time this pedigree was constructed, elite society at Vijayanagara had been deeply transformed through nearly two centuries of intense and creative interaction with the Islamic world—both within the Indian subcontinent and beyond. As a result of this process, many elements of Islamicate culture had been adopted by the elite members of Vijayanagara courtly society, and by the sixteenth century, it could be seen in such diverse areas as architecture, dress, titulature, and military and administrative technology. Given the synchronism between the widespread occurrence of Islamicate cultural elements and the sixteenth-century historiographic insistence on a link with Delhi, might we then hypothesize that the two phenomena are in some significant way related?

In a 1996 article on Vijayanagara court dress, I argued that the appearance of Islamic-inspired cultural forms at the Indic court was symptomatic of a larger process of fundamental cultural change, for which I proposed the term *Islamicization*. The local Indic elite publicly adopted these forms, I suggested, as a means of effecting their symbolic participation in the more universal culture of Islam, thereby enhancing their political status and credibility in the eyes of other participants in the Islamicate cultural system. Specific examples of this process may be vividly seen in the areas of court dress, courtly architectural styles, and formal titles adopted by Vijayanagara's rulers. Thus, from at least the fifteenth century, men at the Vijayanagara court renounced traditional forms of Indic dress in public, opting instead to wear the Islamic-inspired *kabāyi*, a long-sleeved, long-hemmed tunic derived from the Arab *qabāʿ*, and the *kuḷḷāyi*, a high conical cap of brocaded fabric, derived from the Perso-Turkic *kulāh*.[39] Architecturally, many of the public spaces in which these elites moved were defined by buildings constructed of plaster-coated masonry, with the forms of their plans, vaulting, and carved plaster decoration inspired by contemporary Indo-Islamic architectural practice at such nearby Bahmani sites as Gulbarga, Firuzabad, and Bidar.[40] And from the middle of the fourteenth century on through the early seventeenth, Vijayanagara's rulers described themselves with the official title "sultan among Hindu kings" (*hiṃdurāya-suratrāṇa*), or in some cases simply as "sultan" (*suratāḷu*), a usage which vividly proclaimed their willingness to adopt the political discourse of Islamicate civilization.[41] In all these cases, the cultural forms and practices borrowed have nothing to do with religion, but pertain to the sphere of secular courtly culture; even more important, we should note that all of the forms adopted were clearly embraced for their value as symbolic capital and not on account of any inherent superiority they happened to bear in terms of practical, utilitarian value. In simple terms, an Islamicate-inspired *kuḷḷāyi* is inherently no better as a head-covering than the traditional Indic turban (*śiroveṣṭhi*); what makes it more desirable is the fact that it is similar to what was worn in the contemporary Timurid courts of Central Asia and Iran and elsewhere in the expanding Islamicate world into which Vijayanagara was being drawn.

At the same time, there was another type of cultural appropriation, in which elements of Islamicate political technology were adopted by Vijayanagara elites, not so much for their symbolic value as for their practical effectiveness in enhancing the actual political power of their users. This type of borrowing is seen most notably in the areas of military technology and the techniques of revenue administration. In both cases, the appropriated Islamicate technologies were clearly far more effective than the previously available techniques had been as instruments of political control. Judging from the evidence of Hoysala sculptural friezes depicting military processions, it is clear that military technology in the regional Indic kingdoms of the Deccan had already begun to change significantly as early as the second half of the thirteenth century, some seventy-five years before the rise of Vijayanagara. Specifically, there is a new array of equipment used in cavalry warfare, including stirrups, horseshoes, horse armor, and most important, a new type of saddle provided with pommel and cantle to keep the rider more securely mounted, as Jean Deloche has demonstrated in his analysis of these friezes.[42] What Deloche stops short of stating, however, is that every one of these "innovative" features was in fact a regular part of the equipment of the Islamicate horseman at the time of the Turkic conquest of northern India.[43] The appearance of these features in the southern Deccan must thus represent the first step in the adaptation of Turkic-Islamicate military technology by local Indic military elites.

This process further intensified under the patronage of the early Vijayanagara state. Firishta credits Devarāya II (1422–46) with the policy of modernizing the Vijayanagara army along Turkic lines, by recruiting large numbers of mounted Turkic mercenaries and relying more systematically on highly trained (mounted?) bowmen. According to Firishta, Devarāya was cautioned by his nobles and brahman advisers that the military superiority of the Turks rested on two factors:

> First, that their horses were stronger and able to endure more fatigue than the weak animals of the Carnatic; secondly, that a great body of excellent archers was always maintained in pay by the kings of the house of Bahmuny, of whom the Ray had but a few in his army. . . . Accordingly, Devaraya gave orders to enlist Mussulmans in his service, allotting them estates, and erecting a mosque for their use in the city of Beejanuggur [=Vijayanagara]. He also commanded that no one should molest them in the exercise of their religion, and moreover, he ordered a Koran to be placed before his throne on a rich desk, so that the faithful might perform the ceremony of obeisance in his presence without sinning against their laws. He also made all the Hindoo soldiers learn the art of archery; to which both he and his officers so applied themselves, that he could soon muster two thousand Mahome-

> dans and sixty-thousand Hindoos, well skilled in archery, besides eighty thousand cavalry, and two hundred thousand infantry, armed in their usual manner with pikes and lances.[44]

Firishta wrote nearly two hundred years after Devarāya II's reign, but the evidence of contemporary inscriptions indeed appears to substantiate his claims; thus, an inscription of 1430, for example, states that Devarāya II had 10,000 Turuṣka horsemen in his service.[45] Another epigraph, dated 1439, records the construction in the Vijayanagara capital of a mosque for the merit of the king by one Ahmad Khan, a Turkic warrior *(kaṭigeya)* in Devarāya II's service;[46] this foundation may be the basis for Firishta's intriguing claim that the king "erected a mosque" for the use of the Muslim warriors in his service.

In the technology of revenue administration, too, much appears to have been borrowed from Islamicate sources. Indeed, an extensive body of evidence suggests that the Vijayanagara "*nāyaka* system" originated as an Indic adaptation of the Islamicate system of administration through *iqtāʿ* assignments. As formulated under the Saljuqs, the *iqtāʿ* was an assignment of the right to collect land revenue, in return for which the *iqtāʿ*-holder was obliged to provide military service for the state. The areas granted as *iqtāʿ* were expected to generate certain definite sums of revenue, which in turn enabled the *iqtāʿ*-holder to provide a military contingent of fixed size. Such arrangements depended on an elaborate system of precise record keeping and the maintenance of registers recording the details relating to each *iqtāʿ* and the number of troops its holder was required to furnish.[47] Detailed consideration of Sanskrit and Telugu inscriptions and literary sources pertaining to Vijayanagara *nāyaṃkara* tenures, as well as of Persian historical texts relating to the expansion of the *iqtāʿ* system into the Deccan, reveals that the *nāyaka* system was practically identical in its operation to the *iqtāʿ* system, and this suggests in the strongest possible terms that the Vijayanagara arrangement was developed as a direct adaptation from an Islamicate model.[48] Even the materials used in administrative record keeping and communication changed during the Vijayanagara period, as palm-leaf and stylus gave way to the superior Islamicate technology of writing with paper and pen. That paper was introduced into South India through an Islamicate source is clearly suggested by the etymology of the Telugu word for paper (*kākitam/kāgitam*, from Persian *kāghaz*); the same holds true for the pen (Telugu *kalam*, from Persian *qalam*). Doubtless, such examples could be further multiplied, but the basic point should be abundantly clear: by the sixteenth century, the secular culture of the Vijayanagara court had acquired a thick veneer of Islamicate elements, both practical and symbolic.

IV

Given the widespread adoption of Islamicate elements in the elite culture of Vijayanagara, I believe we may safely conclude that the story of Harihara, Bukka, and the sultan represents an ideological extension of this process of borrowing. Seen in this light, the significance of this historiographic construction can be understood on two interrelated levels. First, and most obviously, the narrative would have served an explanatory function, offering a historical explanation for the presence of so many Islamicate cultural forms at Vijayanagara. By presenting the state as a successor to Delhi, and casting its first kings as appointees of the sultan, the narrative suggests the existence of direct political ties with the Delhi Sultanate. Whether or not these ties ever actually existed historically, the narrative would have helped the members of sixteenth-century Vijayanagara society to make sense of the Islamicate military, administrative, and material cultural forms that had become givens in their own everyday world and yet distinguished their culture from that of neighboring Indic states. Islamicate forms and practices would have been perfectly natural in any state that had arisen—or was presumed to have arisen—as a successor state to the Delhi Sultanate, the main focus of Islamicate civilization in South Asia.

At the same time, the narrative would have functioned on a second—and, I believe, far more important—ideological level. Here, it would have gone well beyond the mere explanatory function of accounting for why Vijayanagara appeared the way it did, to contribute directly to the active construction of a unique political identity for the Vijayanagara state. At this level, the story of Harihara, Bukka, and the sultan itself articulates an ideological claim that is complementary and parallel to that articulated through Islamicizing cultural practice in such spheres as dress. In both cases, the "argument" proceeds through a dual strategy, by distinguishing the state from its Indic precursors and contemporaries in South India and, on the other hand, by proclaiming its involvement in the more universal social milieu of the broader Islamicate world. Thus, other Indic kings in South India did not cover their upper bodies, but the rulers of Vijayanagara did, and what they covered them with was a garment that was similar, both in name and in form, to the garments worn by rulers in the larger Islamicate world. And in like manner, the narrative of Harihara and Bukka's capture by the Delhi sultan serves to establish a dividing line between the founders of Vijayanagara and the last great Indic houses of the fourteenth-century Deccan. Forcibly torn from what is represented as their original political milieu—first among the Kākatīyas, then the kings of Kampili—they are taken to Delhi, the very center of the Islamicate world in South Asia. Through their direct encounter there with the source of all legitimate Islamicate power—the sultan, to whom they willfully and faithfully submit—they are transformed into something more universal. This, I believe, is the ultimate significance of this historiographic representation: it is to proclaim Vijayanagara's rulers not as "saviors of the south" as the communalist view would have it but as they chose to characterize themselves, as "sultans among Hindu kings."

Notes

1. For the relevant passages, see Mahdi Husain, ed. and trans., *'Iṣāmī's Futūḥ al-Salāṭīn*, 3 vols. (Agra, 1938), 3:864 and 902.

2. For the relevant passage, see the translation of Sir H. M. Elliot and John Dowson, *The History of India as Told by Its Own Historians*, 8 vols. (London: Trubner, 1867–77), 3:245–46.

3. The relevant passage is translated in H. A. R. Gibb, trans., *The Travels of Ibn Baṭṭūṭa, A.D. 1325–1354*, vol. 3 (1971; Millwood, N.Y.: Kraus Reprint, 1986), 711.

4. These Persian and Arabic forms represent transliterations from the vernacular "Hariyappa," the form of Harihara's name most commonly met with in Kannada inscriptions; see Vasundhara Filliozat, *L'Épigraphie de Vijayanagar du début à 1377* (Paris: École Française d'Extrême-Orient, 1973), xvi. The issue of the identity of Ibn Baṭṭūṭa's "Haryab" has been examined in detail in R. N. Saletore, "Haryab of Ibn Baṭṭūṭa and Harihara Nṛpāla," *Quarterly Journal of the Mythic Society* (Mysore) 31, no. 3 (1940): 384–406.

5. At one point in his history, 'Iṣāmī observes that "an apostate (*murtadd*) has seized the province of Kannar [i.e., Karnataka]; he has seized the territory from the Godavari to the boundary of Ma'bar" (3:902). From what is known of the circumstances under which 'Iṣāmī produced his *Futūḥ al-Salāṭīn*, this remark would have to apply to the period between 1347 and 1350, by which time inscriptions confirm that Harihara had indeed established himself as a major power in this general region (although it seems doubtful that the early Sangama domains would already have extended quite as far as 'Iṣāmī's "from the Godavari to the boundary of Ma'bar" by this early date). 'Iṣāmī does not mention the name of this "apostate" in this passage, but at another point in the text, some forty pages earlier, he does state that Ala al-Din Bahman Shah had sent a

cavalry unit from Sagar "into the territory of Harip" where they attacked the citadel of Diz-i Karri and took the citadel keeper back to Sagar (3:864). "Harip" almost certainly refers to Harihara, who frequently referred to himself in inscriptions as "Hariyappa," which would be the apparent source of the Persianized form "Harip." Diz-i Karri may refer to Anegondi, or possibly Raichur, or yet some other site that would in any case have to have been within striking distance from Sagar. Since this citadel was located within the "territory of Harip," and since any one of these locations lies within the broad expanse of the territory "from the Godavari to the boundary of Ma'bar," which is said to have been occupied by an "apostate," there does appear to be some ground for inferring that 'Iṣāmī's "apostate" would in fact have referred to Harihara.

Baranī also speaks of an unnamed apostate who rebelled from Delhi in this same general region and period. Writing in 1357 with reference to a period some twenty years earlier, Baranī states that at "about the same time, one of the relations of Kanya Naik, whom the Sultan [of Delhi] sent to Kambila, apostatized from Islam and stirred up a revolt. The land of Kambila also was thus lost, and fell into the hands of the Hindus" (Elliot and Dowson, *History of India*, 3:245–46). However, nowhere does Baranī state or even imply that this apostate was Harihara or any other member of the Sangama family. To the contrary, he identifies this personage only as "one of the relations of Kanya Naik," a figure who has in turn been plausibly identified as Kapaya Nayaka, the Musunuri chief who held Warangal from the mid-1340s to c. 1360. Since Vijayanagara's Sangama dynasty is not otherwise known to have been related to the family of the Musunuri chiefs, Barani's statement would not appear in and of itself to constitute evidence of Harihara's having been the apostate in question.

6. It must be noted that there is one further text which is sometimes appealed to as a source informing upon the circumstances of Vijayanagara's founding: the sixteenth-century Portuguese chronicle of Fernao Nuniz, written between 1535 and 1537 on the basis of an otherwise unknown Indic "chronicle" (in Kannada?), in Robert Sewell, *A Forgotten Empire (Vijayanagara): A Contribution to the History of India* (1900; reprint, Delhi: National Book Trust, 1962, 279–86). This account begins with the sultan launching an expedition against the Bisnaga kingdom (apparently a confused representation of the Kampili kingdom, seen as the precursor of Vijayanagara) and capturing six old men, including the king's minister and treasurer, and taking them to Delhi; the minister and treasurer are later deputed to the annexed kingdom to rule on behalf of the sultan, since the local people have in the meantime rebelled against the sultan's deputy, who is a "Moor." The former minister is none other than "Deorao" (=Devarāya; Sewell suggests that this is not to be taken in the sense of a proper name but as a generic title for the Vijayanagara ruler), who proceeds to build the city of Vijayanagara. Nuniz's account is thus allied in significant respects to the sixteenth-century Sanskrit texts, in that it too makes no mention of conversion and apostasy, and it traces the founding of the kingdom to an erstwhile servant of the Kampili king-

dom (or what seems to be the Kampili kingdom) who is captured and taken to Delhi.

7. Certain important aspects of the construction were anticipated by Sewell (*A Forgotten Empire,* 1900), who first characterized Vijayanagara as "a Hindu bulwark against Muhammadan conquests" (ibid., 1), but never suggested that the brothers had converted to Islam or apostatized.

8. See N. Venkataramanayya, *Kampili and Vijayanagara* (Madras: Christian Literature Society, 1929), 25ff.; N. Venkataramanayya, *Vijayanagara: Origin of the City and the Empire* (1933; reprint, New Delhi: Asian Educational Services, 1990), 91ff.; and K. A. Nilakanta Sastri and N. Venkataramanayya, eds., *Further Sources of Vijayanagara History,* 3 vols., Madras University Historical Series, no. 18 (Madras: University of Madras, 1946), 1:22–53.

9. Venkataramanayya writes that "this behaviour of the Sultan is very inexplicable. Probably, they obtained the Sultan's pardon by embracing Islam. The fact of their conversion to the religion of the Prophet, must have been one of the considerations which prompted the Sultan to send them to govern Karnāṭa as his deputies" (*Kampili and Vijayanagara,* 27).

10. Nilakanta Sastri and Venkataramanayya, *Further Sources of Vijayanagara History,* 1:22–53.

11. R. C. Majumdar, ed., *The Delhi Sultanate,* vol. 6 of *The History and Culture of the Indian People* (1960; Bombay: Bharatiya Vidya Bhavan, 1967), 271–72.

12. Percival Spear, *India: A Modern History,* rev. ed. (Ann Arbor: University of Michigan Press, 1972), 110; Romila Thapar, *A History of India,* vol. 1 (1966; Harmondsworth: Penguin Books, 1976), 323–24; Stanley Wolpert, *A New History of India,* 4th ed. (New York: Oxford University Press, 1993), 116; Joseph E. Schwartzberg, *A Historical Atlas of South Asia,* 2d ed. (New York: Oxford University Press, 1992), 198; and Vincent Smith, *Oxford History of India,* 4th ed., ed. Percival Spear (1919; Delhi: Oxford University Press, 1981), 304.

It must be noted that proponents of the so-called Hoysala theory for the origin of Vijayanagara have nothing to say about Harihara and Bukka's conversion and apostasy, and they reject the notion that the two brothers were ever captured by the sultan. Instead, according to the Hoysala theory, the Sangamas began as local, Kannada-speaking subordinates of the Hoysalas (*not* Telugu speakers) who had been charged with protecting the northern borders of the Hoysala kingdom from the attacks of the Sultanate. See, for example, S. Krishnaswami Aiyangar, "Foundation of Vijayanagar," in *Ancient India and South Indian History and Culture: Papers on Indian History and Culture,* 2 vols. (1920; Poona: Oriental Book Agency, 1941); Rev. H. Heras, *Beginnings of Vijayanagara History* (Bombay: Indian Historical Research Institute, 1929); and B. A. Saletore, "Theories Concerning the Origin of Vijayanagara," in *Vijayanagara: Sexcentenary Volume* (Dharwar: Vijayanagara Sexcentenary Association, 1936), 139–59.

13. Venkataramanayya writes: "There is, however, one point where tradition appears to differ from the contemporary records. The Muhammadan historians,

both 'Iṣāmī and Barnī, state that the person whom the Sulṭān sent to Kampila was a Hindu convert to Islām, who subsequently reverted to his original faith and asserted his independence. Tradition does not allude to the change of faith of Harihara and Bukka implying thereby that they had always remained within the fold of the Hindu religion." He continues to explain away this discrepancy in the following manner: "The silence of the *Kālajñāna*, the *Vṛttānta*, and other works of the kind must not, however, be taken as a contradiction of the statements of contemporary historians. The Hindu writers did not like to record the unpleasant fact, *viz.*, the conversion of the founders of a Hindu kingdom to Islām. Therefore, they kept a judicious silence over it" (Nilakanta Sastri and Venkataramanayya, *Further Sources of Vijayanagara History*, 1:32–33).

14. K. A. Nilakanta Sastri, *A History of South India from Prehistoric Times to the Fall of Vijayanagar*, 4th ed. (1947; Madras: Oxford University Press, 1976), 237.

15. Hermann Kulke, "Maharajas, Mahants, and Historians: Reflections on the Historiography of Early Vijayanagara and Sringeri," in *Vijayanagara—City and Empire: New Currents of Research*, ed. Anna Libera Dallapiccola and Stephanie Zingel-Avé Lallement (Stuttgart: Steiner, 1985), 1:120–43, 125; Burton Stein, *Vijayanagara: New Cambridge History of India*, vol. 1, pt. 2 (Cambridge: Cambridge University Press, 1989), 20; Hermann Kulke and Dietmar Rothermund, *A History of India* (London: Routledge, 1990), 188–90; and the critique of Kulke offered in Phillip B. Wagoner, "'Sultan among Hindu Kings': Dress, Titles, and the Islamicization of Hindu Culture at Vijayanagara," *Journal of Asian Studies* 55, no. 4 (November 1996): 851–80, 873–74.

16. Venkataramanayya, *Kampili and Vijayanagara*, 25.

17. Nilakanta Sastri and Venkataramanayya, *Further Sources of Vijayanagara History*, 1:28

18. No. A–47; the manuscript as a whole is also known as *Vidyāraṇya-kālajñāna* and is not to be confused with the manuscript just discussed, which is from the Mackenzie Collection, Government Oriental Manuscripts Library, Madras.

19. *ARMAD: Annual Report of the Mysore Archaeological Department for the Year 1932* (Bangalore: Government Press, 1935), 108.

20. At least with respect to this episode, *Rāja-kālanirṇaya* (RK), *Vidyāraṇya-kālajñāna*, and *Vidyāraṇya-śaka* (VS) show such close verbal parallelism that they would appear to be related as slightly different manuscript variants within a single textual tradition. But the *Vidyāraṇya-vṛttānta* (VV) differs significantly; it constitutes a distinct text representing a different redaction from the same body of shared historiographic tradition. Still needed is a thorough textual study and analysis of this historiographic tradition. It would almost certainly reveal the existence of still further texts and manuscript copies. An important beginning in this direction has been made by Hermann Kulke in "Maharajas, Mahants, and Historians"; see also Phillip B. Wagoner, *Tidings of the King: A Translation and Ethnohistorical Analysis of the Rāyavācakamu* (Honolulu: University of Hawaii Press, 1993), appendix B and 33–50, for a translation and analysis of another

narrative relating to Vijayanagara's founding from the Mysore University Library *Vidyāraṇya kālajñāna* series.

21. RK adds that they were born in the Kuru line and that the elder was named Harihara and the younger Bukka.

22. VV does not include the brothers' migration to Kampili, but has them captured and taken to Delhi directly from Warangal.

23. RK instead describes them as "the two famous brothers, endowed with the marks of heroism."

24. RK does not explicitly state that they were taken back to the sultan's city; it merely says that they were captured. VV states that they were taken to the sultan's camp.

25. Nilakanta Sastri and Venkataramanayya construe this key passage somewhat differently in their translation (explaining that "the words within brackets are supplied from another text which elucidates the obscure original"): "When, during their captivity there was once a thunderstorm at night [the jailguards deserted their posts] and the Sultan was asleep. [When he got up] he came out and found the two prisoners standing [inside] far from the gateway and asked them why they were standing there" (*Further Sources of Vijayanagara History*, 3:13–14). VV reads, in Nilakanta Sastri and Venkataramanayya's translation, "All the sentries that were guarding the camp fled in panic one evening owing to the outburst of a thunder-storm. Nevertheless, Harihara and Bukka sat in obedience to the orders within the prison. The Sultān saw them and, being convinced of their uprightness, took them into his service and retained them at the court" (3:11). According to the published synopsis, VS reads: "It so happened that at night it rained heavily accompanied with thunder and lightning. The brothers however did not fear and although the Sultan who was nearby was asleep they did not escape but remained near the door. The Sultan awoke after some time and finding out who the prisoners were and perceiving their honesty he ordered their release and granted them a kingdom in Karnata" (*ARMAD* 1932: 108). The equivalent passage in RK appears to be textually corrupt, and it does not easily yield a coherent sense *(rātrau sāśani-parjanya-megha-ghoṣa-nirākulau / dvāra-bhittiḥ samāpattau suratrāṇeva-nirvane // prātar-dṛṣṭvā bhaṭair nītau suratrāṅo 'tiharṣitaḥ / gṛhītau bhrātarau jñātvā satyasandho tataḥ sudhīḥ //)*. In any case, it is clear that the various texts are in fundamental agreement as to the substance of what happened during the night: the thunderstorm provided the captives Harihara and Bukka with a natural chance to escape, but they refused to do so, thus revealing their upright, trustworthy natures.

26. VV explains that the "Nava Ballāḷas" had rebelled against the sultan and that the two brothers were sent to the Karnata country by the sultan for the express purpose of subduing them.

27. According to VV, it is only at this point that the sultan entrusts the brothers with governing the Karnata country on his behalf, in recognition of their service in vanquishing the Ballāḷas.

28. C. V. Ramachandra Rao, ed., *Ekamranathuni Prataparudra Caritramu* (Hyderabad: Andhra Pradesh Sahitya Akademi, 1984), 66–67, translation mine.

29. V. N. Hari Rao, trans., *Kōil Oḷugu: The Chronicle of the Śrī-Raṅgam Temple* (Madras: Rouchouse, 1961), 24ff.

30. I owe this formulation to Aziz Ahmad's discussion of North Indian Hindu "epics of resistance," such as the Prithvī Rāj Rāsō and *Hammīr Mahākāviya*, which he sees as arising in response to the Muslim "epics of conquest" in Persian, such as Amīr Khusrau's *'Āshiqa* and *Tughluq Nāma;* see Aziz Ahmad, "Epic and Counter-Epic in Medieval India," *Journal of the American Oriental Society* 83 (1963): 470–76.

31. For a more detailed discussion of the sultani's relationship with Alagiyamaṇavāḷa Perumāḷ and her apotheosis as Tulukka-Nācciyar, see Richard Davis, *Lives of Indian Images* (Princeton: Princeton University Press, 1997), and Davis, "Muslims Worshipping in Hindu Temples," forthcoming.

32. The account is narrated in such texts as the Telugu *Tanjāvūri Āndhra Rājula Caritra*, discussed by Velcheru Narayana Rao, David Shulman, and Sanjay Subrahmanyam, *Symbols of Substance: Court and State in Nāyaka Period Tamil Nadu* (Delhi: Oxford University Press, 1992), 44–56, and a Tamil chronicle of the Madurai Nayakas in the Mackenzie Collection, discussed by Nicholas B. Dirks, *The Hollow Crown: Ethnohistory of an Indian Kingdom*, Cambridge South Asian Studies, no. 39 (Cambridge: Cambridge University Press. 1987), 97–106.

33. Dirks, *The Hollow Crown*, 104.

34. Narayana Rao, Shulman, and Subrahmanyam, *Symbols of Substance*, 55.

35. Ibid., 56.

36. See Wagoner, *Tidings of the King*, 60–63 and 122–123.

37. The text is in fact far from unequivocal with regard to the identity of the occupant of the Aśvapati Lion Throne and his capital, and in effect offers a composite representation that combines attributes of both the then-reigning Mughals and the earlier Delhi Sultanate. This suggests that the author of the *Rāyavācakamu* saw the difference between the Delhi Sultanate and the Mughal empire as representing nothing more than a dynastic change within an otherwise stable and continuous imperial polity centered on Delhi.

38. B. V. Singaracharya, ed., *Vinukoṇḍa Vallabharāyani Krīḍābhirāmamu* (Machilipatnam [A.P.]: M. Seshachalam, 1972), 42.

39. Wagoner, "'Sultan among Hindu Kings.'"

40. George Michell, *The Vijayanagara Courtly Style: Incorporation and Synthesis in the Royal Architecture of Southern India, 15th–17th Centuries*, Vijayanagara Research Project Monograph Series, vol. 3 (New Delhi: Manohar and American Institute of Indian Studies, 1992).

41. Wagoner, "'Sultan among Hindu Kings,'" 861ff.

42. Jean Deloche, "Techniques Militaires dans les Royaumes du Dekkan au Temps des Hoysala (XIIe-XIIIe Siècle), d'après l'Iconographie," *Artibus Asiae* 47 (1986): 147–232.

43. See David C. Nicolle, *Arms and Armour of the Crusading Era, 1050–1350*, 2 vols. (White Plains, N.Y.: Kraus International Publications, 1988), esp. entries 334A-334BJ for visual evidence from the late twelfth-century or early thirteenth-century illustrated manuscript *Warqa wa Gulshāh*, produced in Azerbayjan.

44. John Briggs, trans., *History of the Rise of the Mahomedan Power in India till the Year 1612*, translated from the original Persian of Mahomed Kasim Ferishta, 3 vols. (1829; reprint, Calcutta: Editions Indian, 1966), 2:266.

45. EC III, Sr. 15, cited in T. V. Mahalingam, *Administration and Social Life under Vijayanagar* (Madras: University of Madras, 1940), 319.

46. SII IX/2, no. 447, discussed in Phillip B. Wagoner, "Fortuitous Convergences and Essential Ambiguities: Transcultural Political Elites in the Medieval Deccan," forthcoming.

47. Ann Lambton, *Landlord and Peasant in Persia: A Study of Land Tenure and Land Revenue Administration* (London: I. B. Tauris, 1991), 62.

48. Cynthia Talbot, "Local Lordship in Sixteenth-Century Andhra: The Epigraphic Perspective on Amara-Nayankara"; Phillip B. Wagoner, "*Iqtāʿ* and Nāyamkara: Military Service Tenures and Political Theory from Saljuq Iran to Vijayanagara South India"; and Richard M. Eaton, "*Iqtāʿ* Tenure in the Deccan in the Age of Timur"—three papers presented at the 25th Annual Conference on South Asia, Madison, Wisconsin, October 18–20, 1996; and Richard M. Eaton, Cynthia Talbot, and Phillip B. Wagoner, "The 'Nāyaka System' Reconsidered: Vijayanagara Military Service Tenures and State Organization from a Comparative Deccan Perspective" (forthcoming).

13

Maratha Patronage of Muslim Institutions in Burhanpur and Khandesh

Stewart Gordon

At its height, in the second half of the eighteenth century, the Maratha polity, based in Pune in current-day Maharashtra, encompassed almost one-third of the South Asian subcontinent and groups who spoke many different languages and practiced a variety of cultural customs. Regions under Maratha control besides Maharashtra included Gujerat, Karnataka, portions of Rajasthan, coastal Tanjore, the Nagpur areas, Orissa, all of Madhya Pradesh, and the areas around Delhi-Agra. Although divided by faction and family, the Maratha polity was a strong rival to the expanding British colonial power. Over the nearly two centuries since the conquest of the Maratha polity by the British, writers and historians have found an extraordinary variety of "meanings" in the story of the Marathas. To the British conquerors, the Marathas were perfidious robbers with no regular administrative system beyond loot. Maharashtrian Brahmin writers of the mid-nineteenth century found the stories of Maratha resistance to invading forces under Aurangzeb thrilling. Late nineteenth-century writers found the Marathas a "proto-nationalist" force against the "foreign" Muslim. More recently, there have been attempts to portray the eighteenth-century Maratha polity on one hand as a well-administered bureaucracy and on the other as based on a principle of faction and strife. The latest in this long line of interpretation has been the portrayal of the Marathas as a profoundly "Hindu" state, motivated primarily by the traditional duties of a Hindu king, a veritable bulwark of Hinduism against invading Muslim forces of the Mughal empire.

Like every other interpretation of the Marathas, there is some truth to this view, plus many problems and ironies. Certainly, we have writings from Maharashtra in the seventeenth and eighteenth centuries that were anti-Muslim. The writings of Ram Das and the *Shiva Bharat* come to mind. Even in more pragmatic, mirror-of-princes writings, there are statements of the king's obligations that sound profoundly Brahmanical. Nevertheless, as we shall see, the evidence of practice, what the government actually did at the local level, looks quite different than any of these high-level normative documents.

Let us begin with the duties of a king in one of these mirror-of-princes documents, the *Ajnapatra,* a late seventeenth-century treatise on government written by Ramchandrapant Amatya, at that time an old and experienced government servant. It was written between the death of Aurangzeb in 1707 and the major Maratha invasion of North India in the 1720s. Amatya observes:

> To give the gift of land for the purpose of maintenance of *Dharma* is an act of eternal merit. But this gift of land should be made after seeing the place, the time, and fitness, and after inquiring, according to *Sastras* thoroughly into what is *dharma* and *adharma*. Grants of revenue-free villages or land should be made at auspicious times or in great holy places . . . to those Brahmins who are versed in sacred lore, family men, and those well versed in *Vedasastra* and possessing no income of their own, and whose leaving the house for begging for alms would lead to a loss [of] religious duties or merit. Similarly, villages or lands should be granted to great temples . . . , to hermitages of saints, to places of *Samadhi.*[1]

The Documents

For some years, I have been working on fine-grid Maratha revenue documents of the city of Burhanpur, on the Tapti River on the northern border of Maharashtra, and the *suba* of Khandesh, which runs westward along the Tapti River toward Gujerat. These documents are housed at the Pune Daftar in Pune.

The series begins in 1721, when—by military success—Marathas began "dual administration" with the Nizam of the surrounding countryside of Khandesh. The Marathas were entitled to *chauth* and *sardeshmukhi,* in effect, 35 percent of the government's share of the revenue, and they sent their own collectors into the countryside to do settlement and collection.

Initially Maratha documentation was scrappy, but it got progressively better, more detailed and predictable, through the course of the eighteenth century. By the time that the Marathas actually won Burhanpur, in the 1750s, as a result of a military victory over the Nizam, they knew perfectly well what documentation they needed to rule. As part of the treaty, the Nizam's administrators turned over a variety of tax and revenue documents, both normative and actual, which the Marathas copied into Modi and carefully preserved. To these were added the accounts—often down to daily transactions—of the income from mint and market, fines and transit duties, and the minutiae of government expenditure over the next half century.[2]

Maratha Patronage of Religious Men and Ceremonies

The detailed accounts of the city of Burhanpur during the first years of administration in the 1760s give a remarkably clear picture of Maratha patronage during this period. A category called "monthly wages" was dominated by Muslim recipients, for example, Bab Sayib Vedya, Vali ulk Mujawar Dargha, Faj al ulk Mujawar, Varas Mujawar, and Said Bakar Din. In passing, this list also included "Udasi Fakir of the Nanak sect." In the same document, the category of "Miscellaneous fakirs" included twenty-six men, all of them Muslims. The government also allotted money for the celebration of Muharram and Ramadan, including the Qur'an recitation, the expenses of *pagoti* for the celebration of Id, and the *qazi*'s fee on these occasions.

We should not, however, have the impression that the Maratha government was only supporting Muslim religious men and festivals. Quite to the contrary, listed right along with the Muslim recipients are seventy-nine Brahmins, plus cash grants for the new moon ceremonies, *sankrant*, *diwali*, *dasara*, *Shivaratra*, Ganesh festival, new year, ceremonies to ward off an inauspicious day, and small contributions for temple expenses in Burhanpur.[3]

Four years later, in 1765, we get a fuller list of grantees, in a section entitled "Miscellaneous people as per the assignment register." Of the 338 men given grants, most were Muslims and more than 100 were fakirs, shaikhs, or qazis. Salaries, of course, varied, from more than 400 rupees per year all the way down to only a few rupees per year.[4]

Dargahs and Other Muslim Sites

If we move from support of individuals to support of institutions, the evidence is equally clear. For example, the largest item under "misc. expenses" in a year-end accounting of 1761 was for the *dargah* of Hazar Shah Bhikari. The taxes to support this dargah came from various bazaars in the city.

At the same time, we get villages in Khandesh assigned for the maintenance of dargahs. Consider, for example, an account dated 1765: "The following villages are continued in *inam* for maintenance of the dargah of Shahi Safu Nula. 4 villages in Zainpur *pargana* [just outside Burhanpur], 1 in Raver, and 1 in Majrod [west into the hinterland of Burhanpur]. To these were added 3 in Zainpur and 3 in Majrod."[5] An exact parallel is found in inam villages in southern Maharashtra dedicated to shrines and dargahs. Recent research has found continuation throughout the eighteenth century of earlier grants of three inam villages for the support of the dargah of Jamal Saheb and the dargah of one Pirjade.[6]

There is also evidence that grants for mosques were continued under the Marathas. Consider the following letter from the Peshwa to his local representative in the Tapti Valley in 1754: "For the expenses of mosques, 9 villages in Raver and Zainabad [two parganas near Burhanpur] were given in *mokassa;* these are to be continued as per the former Mughal government. A *sanad* is granted and given in accordance with Salabat Jung."[7]

Aima

Perhaps the simplest definition of *aima* is a maintenance grant for persons of learning or merit. Let us look at Burhanpur's hinterland, specifically the pargana of Adilabad, located thirty miles west of Burhanpur along the Tapti Valley. Consider an account of aima from the village of Khadke from 1739 that gives all the typical details of this type of grant. "The marked ground (*zamin*) of 100 *bighas* of Haji Ibrahim is fixed (*mukrar*) at 1 3/4 less [than the standard rate of taxation]. For uncultivated land: 1 *taka* and 1 *rukha*. For cultivated land: no takas and 4 rukhas. It is given to him to cultivate. Therefore, the takas are fixed at 39." The document was signed by the representative of the Maratha collector and the patil of the village.[8]

This sort of grant had a number of notable features. First, of course, it was a development grant; taxes were much lower on the cultivated land than the uncultivated. Second, the land was still taxed, though at a much lower than standard rate. Third, the rate was fixed, so benefits of cultivation accrued much more to the grantee than to the government.

A document from 1748 gives all the aima grants in the whole pargana.[9] Aima grants are found in 17 of Adilabad's 108 cultivated villages. The register lists slightly more than 100 recipients by name, the amount of land granted to them, whether it was cultivated or not, what offices—if any—the recipient held and, incidentally, the signature of the local official involved. Of the total number of grantees, about 60 percent were Hindu names and 40 percent were Muslim names. Often the grants were only a bigha or two of land, often half or more uncultivated. Most men held no specific offices.

The land was not tax-free. Taxes were paid at a lower than prevailing rate on all aima land. About two-thirds stayed with the aima holder; the remainder consisted of taxes divided between the local officials—the *muqqadam* and the *patwari*—but the lion's share went to the Maratha government.[10]

Through the actual conquest of all of Khandesh by the Marathas, there was remarkable continuity in these aima grants. For example, in 1751, of Adilabad pargana's 124 villages, 18 were vacant. Of the remaining 106 *jama* villages, 16 were aima, compared with 17 aima villages in the documents of the late 1740s, immediately before the full Maratha conquest.[11]

Aima grants were found not only in Adilabad but throughout Khandesh Province. For example, a broad-scale document of 1759 lists thirty of Khandesh's parganas; eight of them have aima grants, and therefore aima taxation, generally from 1,000 to 3,000 rupees. If taxation rates were similar to Adilabad, this would mean 25–50 bighas of cultivated land, per pargana.[12]

There is some evidence that such eighteenth-century Maratha aima grants were found throughout much of Maharashtra. For example, K. N. Chitnis's recent book about southern Maharashtra in the eighteenth century discusses an inam grant to the *mulla* of a suburb of Dharwad. This area had long been under the rule of Bijapur, and the mulla serviced the resident Muslim population. The first extant grant is from the Aurangzeb period, when the area passed into Mughal control, and it was regularly renewed throughout Aurangzeb's reign. The family continued in possession of the inam and continued performing duties in the mosque, officiating at marriage ceremonies, and at Muharram through the whole of Maratha rule. The only change was the levying of a rent on the inam land, which had been entirely rent-free under Aurangzeb. It is interesting that the form of the grant is identical to inam land granted to the village headman and to those termed "village servants" (*ballutedars*), such as the leatherworker, the Mahar, the carpenter, and so forth.[13]

Zakat

What happened to *zakat* under the Marathas was much more problematic. To illustrate, let me give the definitions from Wilson's glossary of administrative and revenue terms: "*Zakat*. Alms, a contribution of a portion of income, obligatory on every Muslim possessed of capital. It is received by the *imam* and payable to the poor and needy . . . the term literally signifying purification, is applied to zakat; because the alms, etc., given sanctify the use of the remainder."[14] Compare this with the term *jakat*, in the nineteenth-century Marathi dictionary by Molesworth: "*Jakat*. Customs duties; land or transit duties."[15]

Throughout the eighteenth century in the areas of northern Maharashtra and Central India which I have studied, the Marathas always collected zakat. It appears as a significant tax in every area that had trade and commerce—market towns, serai towns, large cities like Burhanpur, every pargana producing for the cash market. Everywhere, the collection was just added to the general funds along with taxes on agriculture, fines, and so forth. Clearly, it was never allotted for maintenance for indigent virtuous Muslims, and the funds never reached the hands of the imam.

Private Donations

"He is not dead who leaves behind him on earth bridge and mosque, well and serai."[16] It is hard to overestimate the importance of private donations for the maintenance of many of the core features of Muslim culture in India, such as mosques, madrasas, serais, wells, tree planting, building of tombs and shrines, building of markets, irrigation systems, gardens. None of these were "government" functions. Any might be built by a king, but they were equally likely to be built by nonroyal patrons with substantial landed income. This pattern, for example, prevails at Shah Jahanabad in the seventeenth century, just as it prevails at Burhanpur in the same period.[17]

In 1751, the Marathas seized what they termed the "Muglai Amals" of the entire suba of Khandesh. They seized, by force, all the estates on which mainly Muslim military grantees of the Nizam were resident. Warfare raged up and down the hinterland of Burhanpur for four years. Villages became deserted as cultivators fled the fighting. Village headmen and pargana *deshmukhs* were imprisoned. By 1755, dozens of Muslim military leaders, large and small, had simply been displaced from their estates in the countryside around Burhanpur. Hundreds more had been displaced from the rest of the Khandesh Valley. The *jagirs* were transferred to Maratha generals.

For example, in 1754 the Peshwa wrote to his official, Manaji Nikam, in the pargana of Adilabad: "The Muglai Amals of the pargana of Adilabad and Lohari have been granted to Jayaji Shinde as jagir. All collection after the subtraction of *sardeshmukhi, babti,* and expenses goes to him."[18]

In the mid-eighteenth century, the military class capable of private support for all these crucial institutions was simply displaced from Khandesh.[19] As Sauda laments of North India in one of his *shahr ashobs:*

> The income from *jagirs* is all but cut off now
> For years the country has been at the pleasure of outlaws and renegades
> He who was once sole lord of twenty-two *subas*
> Can't even retain the *foujdari* of Kol.

In addition to the Mughal military elite, the Mughal tax collecting bureaucracy was also displaced. For thirty years before 1751, the Marathas and the Mughals had shared the revenue from Khandesh, the hinterland of Burhanpur. Each collected their share of the taxes. When the Marathas took over the province, the Mughals did not reappear as Maratha collectors. In the whole of Khandesh province, all tax collectors of the second half of the eighteenth century were Maharashtrian or Konkanastha Brahmin. Thus, a second crucial group of private Muslim patrons in Khandesh was no longer able to provide support for individuals and institutions. This process is exactly paralleled in the area of southern Maharashtra studied by K. N. Chitnis. As in the area of Khandesh, Chitnis finds that the most important change from Muslim rule to Maratha rule was the disappearance of Muslim jagir military grants and the replacement of Muslim tax collecting officials by Brahmins in the service of the Maratha government.[20]

Traders

The glory days of Burhanpur were long over by the mid-eighteenth century. For three decades in the early seventeenth century, it had been a royal Mughal capital, with all the expected wealth, pomp, glory, and patronage. Even when the Mughal capital moved to Aurangabad, Burhanpur remained an important provincial capital and a trading and manufacturing center, especially for cloth. It was also an important transshipment point for goods moving between the north and Surat.

What is unexpected is that under Maratha rule, Muslims retained certain trade advantages that they had enjoyed under the Mughal administration. Specifically, a "Musalman" paid 2.5 percent ad valorem transit duty, while a "Hindu" paid 5 percent. This differential remained in place throughout the eighteenth century. Similar differentials remained in place for those "Musalmans" bringing bullion or old coins to the mint: the duties were twice as high for a "Hindu." These tax advantages were, however, not universal. All dealers, regardless of religion, paid the same duties on vegetables, timber, services, shops, and the like.[21] Thus, the overall pattern was distinct tax advantages for Muslims engaged in long-distance, high-value trade, or bankers needing coinage. Local Muslim traders in hinter-to-city staples had no particular advantage.

Those likely to benefit from such advantages were, in fact, Burhanpur's most powerful traders under Mughal rule, the Borah Muslims; they remained dominant right through Maratha rule. Their patronage patterns, of course, would have been profoundly different than mainline Sunni Islam. They did not take over much of the patronage lost when the military elite and the bureaucratic elite were displaced.

There are two interesting points about these tax advantages. First, we find evidence of these tax advantages for Muslims continuing at other sites in the Maratha domains, such as Ahmedabad.[22] Second, these documents, describing or levying urban taxes, are the only administrative documents of the Marathas I have ever seen that use the actual terms *Musalman* and *Hindu*. Nowhere else, neither in judicial cases, nor in revenue documents, nor in letters do we find equivalent terms to *Musalman* and *Hindu*.

Conclusion

An obvious question is why the normative patronage expectations of the *Ajnapatra*, quoted at the beginning of this chapter, differ so dramatically from actual practice in the Burhanpur and Khandesh area. Maratha rulers and, later, Brahmin de facto rulers were patronizing Muslim holy men and institutions right along with Hindu saints and festivals.

We are, I believe, seeing here three competing systems of legitimacy, side by side, none decisively dominant. The first is the vision of the Dharmic king. In this concept, the foremost responsibility of a ruler was the protection of gods, cows, and Brahmins. Any ruler who failed in these duties, in this formulation, had no claim to legitimate rule. This position was laid out in the *Ajnapatra*, but much more strongly in other texts of the late seventeenth century, such as the *Shiva Bharat* or the writings of Ram Das. Indeed, the failure of Muslim rulers to fulfill these kingly duties was the basis for demonizing them in these texts.

Nevertheless, a second entire concept of legitimacy came to the Marathas as warrior families in the Deccan. As direct heirs to both the Deccan Sultans and, later, Mughal rule, Marathas' sense of honor, even their sense of differentiation from Kunbi-cultivators, was completely enmeshed with service to the Deccan Sultans. Even Shivaji, we should recall, although he disdained active Bijapuri service, became a Mughal *mansabdar* and took part in active Mughal service. Their material reward for such service, whether with Bijapur or the Mughals, consisted of a series of inams or sanads, granting government's share of tax revenue in a home area (a *watan*, or a *watan jagir*). In court cases of disputed local rights, possession of a properly signed, sealed sanad was the strongest piece of evidence a family could bring before any Maratha court. This legitimacy by sanad was, if anything, stronger in the eighteenth century. In the carefully worded treaty of 1721, for example, the Marathas took seriously their rights to Mughal authority as *naib-subadars* of the Deccan.

At the practical level, this concern with precedent and established rights lends an intensely conservative flavor to Maratha administration. In practice, the legitimacy of precedent seems far stronger than the legitimacy of fulfilling the Dharmic duties of Hindu kingship. Consider this letter from the Peshwa to Sankraji Nikam, his representative in eastern Malwa (1745–46): "From the pargana Sironj to Burhanpur elephants and camels carry goods. The cess should be taken only at Sironj and not at Burhanpur. . . . It is understood that you are not taking the cess at

Sironj but double at Burhanpur. Why so? You should act according to the old custom and no new rules should be promulgated."[23]

Both of these notions of legitimacy were competing with yet a third concept, that of universal kingship. The overall tone of the *Ajnapatra,* for example, is that a king must be pragmatic in order to rule. His legitimacy came neither strictly from dharmasastra nor from a sanad, but rather from promoting peace and prosperity among all his subjects. The *Ajnapatra* is a rather Machiavellian document that spends its time on ways to control the king's own military nobility, the construction and stocking of forts, and the delicate relation between kings and ministers. It is interesting that the only groups which the *Ajnapatra*'s author singled out for caution were those he perceived to be a direct threat to the state—the Siddis of Janjira, Aurangzeb's forces, and European merchants, the latter because they were, unlike other merchants, "representatives of kings." Nowhere in the work are Muslims treated as a group. It seems to be assumed that they will benefit from a vigilant and resourceful king.

Overall, in the Maratha kingdom of the seventeenth and eighteenth centuries, there seems to have been a constant tension between rhetoric and policy that centered on these three competing systems of legitimacy. We must envision constant dialogue within the ruling elite—both Marathas and Brahmins—on policy and strategy. The documents that remain, produced entirely by Brahmins, reflect a whole range of sentiment, from fiercely opposing Muslims to consciously aligning with them.

Where the structure of patronage radically changed was in the area of private donations. None of these three systems of legitimacy prevented the invading Marathas from displacing the Mughal military and bureaucratic elite in Burhanpur and Khandesh. The new Brahmin officials and Maratha generals shifted patronage to the channels they knew. Ram Chandra Baba, for example, was a Konkanastha Brahmin who prospered in the Peshwa's service in Malwa; he used his new wealth to build and endow a large temple in his native Goa.[24] In the wider sphere of eighteenth-century India, the Marathas—by control of the "Muglai amals"—replaced Rajputs as the largest patrons of *ghats,* rest houses, and temples at Benares and other major temple sites throughout India.

Notes

1. "The *Ajnapatra* or Royal Edict," *Journal of Indian History* 8, pt. 2 (August 1929): 218.

2. For the terms of the treaty, see *Selections from the Peshwa Daftar*, n.s., vol. 1 (Poona, 1954), document 149, also 155 (hereafter *SPD*). For the political and military events surrounding the treaty, see Dharma Banu, "The Mughal-Maratha Treaty of April, 1752," *Journal of Indian History* 29–30 (1951–52): 245–58. A perspective from the Nizam's camp is found in the letters of Shah Navaz Khan, who was the Nizam's chief minister, found in P. Setu Rao, *Eighteenth-Century Deccan* (Bombay, 1963), 179–83.

3. Pune Daftar, *Peshwa Khandesh Rumals*, document 196 (hereafter *PK*), Jhadti [yearly audit] of Burhanpur, 1761, in the name of Krishnaji Vishwanath. See also *SPD*, IV, document 102. This document details cash grants for Hindu festivals and ceremonies for Muslim saints.

4. *PK* 119, Jhadti of Burhanpur, 1765.

5. *PK* 203, account dated 1765.

6. K. N. Chitnis, *Glimpses of Maratha Social and Economic History* (New Delhi, 1994), 134.

7. *PK* 198, 1754, Yadi [account]. A similar grant has been published in *SPD*, 45, document 10128. It is an inam [grant] for the lamps of a mosque.

8. *PK* 194, Hisseb Aima [account of grants], 1739.

9. *PK* 194, Hakikat Aima, pa. Adilabad, 1748.

10. *PK* 194, accompanying documents to Hakikat Aima 1748, Adilabad.

11. *PK* 194, Jhadhti, 1751.

12. *PK* 229, Rajamandal [the king's daybook] paper, 1759.

13. Chitnis, *Glimpses*, 54–56.

14. H. H. Wilson, *A Glossary of Judicial and Revenue Terms*, 2d ed. (Delhi, 1968), 652.

15. J. T. Molesworth, George Candy, and Thomas Candy, *A Dictionary of Marathi and English*, 2d ed. (Bombay, 1857), 301.

16. Quoted in Stephen P. Blake, *Shahjahanabad: The Sovereign City in Mughal India, 1639–1739* (Cambridge, 1991), 69.

17. Jean-Baptiste Tavernier, *Travels in India*, trans. V. Ball (New Delhi, 2d ed., reprinted 1995), pt. 3, 71–72.

18. *PK* 198, Yadi, 1754. See for comparison the analysis of the distribution of the *jagirdar* estate in P. V. Kate, *Marathwada under the Nizams* (Delhi, 1987), 92–93.

19. There just weren't that many Muslims in this whole area of the Tapti River Valley, despite 250 years of Muslim rule in the area. The Muslim population seems urban and involved in trades and business, bureaucracy, and the army. They certainly did not entrench themselves as local cultivators or village officials. For example, I copied out a mid-eighteenth-century register of the whole pargana of Dhulia, in central Khandesh, which named every landholder in ev-

ery village, and I found no Muslims at all. *PK* 156, Tahsil Zdadti, Pargana Leling, 1760.

20. Chitnis, *Glimpses*, 15–20, 48–50.

21. *PK* 156, Tahsil Zdadti, Pargana Leling, 1760.

22. Rao Bahadur G. C. Wad and D. B. Parasnis, *Selections from the Satara Raja's and the Peishwa's Diaries* (Bombay, 1907), 3:321.

23. Ibid., 3:1.

24. Shantaram Suntkakhar, *Ashaihe Srishantdurga* (Belgaum, 1973).

Glossary

ʿadat (Arabic): custom, customary practice.
adharma (Sanskrit): that which falls outside of the *dharma*, or Hindu religious law.
ʿadl (Arabic): justice; equity.
aima (Persian): land grant to persons who maintain a saint's tomb, or a similar form of charity land.
akam (Tamil): inner love, deep devotion in Tamil poetry.
akhlaq (Arabic): morals; ethical norms; ethics.
al-lauh al-mahfūẓ (Arabic): the preserved or memorized tablet (in heaven, on which are written all the deeds of persons during their lifetime).
ʿāmm (Arabic): common; ordinary; masses of people.
ʿaql (Arabic): intellect; reason; wisdom.
asura (Sanskrit): demon; playful or threatening spirit.
avatāra [avatara] (Sanskrit): rebirths or incarnations of religious heroes, prophets, or gods.
Babri Masjid [Baburi Masjid]: a mosque built on the site where the Hindu God Ram(a) was alleged to have been born.
baraka (Arabic): beneficence; blessing; prosperity.
batin (Arabic): inner, interior, hidden.
bayʿat (Arabic): initiation; pledge of loyalty.
bhakti (Sanskrit): devotion.
bidʿa [bidʿat] (Arabic): innovation, especially in opposition to religious usage or law.
brāhmaṇa (Sanskrit): brahmin; or a category of Vedic scripture.
brahmin (Sanskrit): highest caste in Hindu social ranking and prestige.
but-khāna (Persian): idol house of worship.
but-parastī (Persian): idol worship.
Chishtī [Chishti] (Persian): a devotee linked to the most popular South Asia–specific order of institutional Sufism.
da'irah (Persian): circle; closed group of initiates to a religious organization.
dargāh [dargah] (Persian): Sufi hospice or dwelling.

darsan [darshan] (Sanskrit): viewing of an icon or religiously important individual or site.

dervish [darvish] (Persian): member of a religious brotherhood, or one who acts like such a member.

deśī (Hindi): belonging to the country, nation.

dharma (Sanskrit): highest category of Hindu religious law; the proper order of things.

dharmashala (Sanskrit): place of religious instruction.

dhikr (Arabic): remembrance, specifically, religious remembrance of the name of God in Sufi meditation.

dig-vijaya (Sanskrit): conqueror of the four corners of the earth.

dīn (Arabic): religion, usually, the religion of Islam but also any formal religious structure.

fakīr [faqir] / *fuqarā'* (Arabic): mendicants, those who embrace poverty in pursuit of religious ideals.

fana (Arabic): annihilation, i.e., denial of self and self-worth in submission to God.

fatwa [fatva; fatawa] (Arabic): juridical decree, binding on Muslims within the jurisdiction of a specific legal school.

fiqh (Arabic): Islamic jurisprudence.

fitna [fitnah] (Arabic): rebellion; sedition.

ghazal (Arabic/Persian): popular verse form, more often in Persian than in Arabic.

ghāzi (Arabic): warrior, soldier, combatant, especially in defense of Islamic goals and Muslim territorial claims.

hadīth [hadith] (Arabic): report or saying, but specifically statements and deeds ascribed to the Prophet Muhammad.

haveli (Persian): a residence or land attached to a residence or a district.

hayākil (Arabic): temples, temples of a god.

hijra (Arabic): the Indian community of transvestites.

hijrah (Arabic): emigration, but especially emigration of the Prophet Muhammad from Mecca to Medina in 632 C.E.

'id-gāh (Persian): place of ritual worship for the two major Muslim festivals.

ihsān (Arabic): preference of the good over all other interests and goals.

ijtihād (Arabic): independent reasoning in religious law.

ikhtilāf (Arabic): difference of opinion in religious matters.

imām (Arabic): prayer leader, or founder of one of the major schools of Islamic law.

īmān (Arabic): faith, specifically, faith in God, the Prophet, the Law in Islam.
in'ām (Arabic): gift or grant of rent-free land.
'ishq (Arabic): passion; ardor; total devotion.
jagārdār (Persian): person who holds a rent-free land grant (*jagir*) given by the ruler as a reward for services.
jahāndāri (Persian): rule, dominion, government.
jihād (Arabic): struggle but also war, in particular, war in defense of the faith or Islam.
jinn (Arabic): invisible creatures, both good and evil.
jizya (Arabic): tax imposed on non-Muslims in a Muslim polity.
kāfī (Punjabi/Sindhi): popular verse form.
kāfir/kuffār (Arabic): heretic, one who renounces Islamic faith and leaves off Islamic practice.
kalima (Arabic): profession of faith in God as One and Muhammad as His Prophet.
kāvya (Sanskrit): Sanskrit epic poems; in Tamil, known as *kappiyam*.
khalīfa/khulafā' (Arabic): successor to the Prophet Muhammad, or to the master of a Sufi order.
khānaqāh (Persian): hospice or lodge for Sufi disciples, guests and their master.
liṅga (Sanskrit): the male generative organ of the Hindu god, Śiva, iconically expressed.
madrasa (Arabic): major institution for Islamic religious education.
maḥalla (Arabic): dwelling or residence.
maḥfūẓ (Arabic): memorized.
majālis (Arabic): councils or circles of instruction, particularly for Sufi novices.
malfuzāt (Arabic): recorded statements of Sufi masters.
manṣabdār (Persian): major landowner.
mantra (Sanskrit): sacred sounds, more effective if often repeated.
marai (Tamil): synonym for Veda, meaning in Tamil, "mystery."
ma'rifa [ma'rifat] (Arabic): knowledge, often secret knowledge about the mysteries of Sufism.
masnavi (Persian): a popular verse form.
mleccha (Sanskrit): impure, unclean, outcaste; lit., one ignorant of Sanskrit.
murīd [murid] (Arabic/Persian): novice or disciple on the Sufi path.
murshid (Arabic/Persian): master, guide in directing others to the Sufi path.

musalmān (Persian): one who professes Islam; a Muslim.
namāz (Persian): Muslim ritual prayer; one of the five obligatory daily prayers.
namāz-i ma'kūs (Persian): inverted upside down performance of prayer, done only by advanced Sufi ascetics.
Naqshbandī [Naqshbandi] (Persian): one of the major Sufi brotherhoods.
naskh (Arabic): abrogation of one Qur'anic verse by another, later verse.
pargana (Persian): a measurement of space, especially designating a taxable region.
phiringī/farangī (Persian): foreigner, literally, Frank.
pīr [pir] (Persian): spiritual master, Sufi leader.
pūjā (Sanskrit): actual of ritual worship before a god or goddess, either at home or within temple confines.
purāṇa [purana] (Sanskrit): major category of Hindu scripture.
qānūn (Arabic): imperial law, not tied to religious practice.
qasīda (Arabic): a popular verse form.
qawm [qaum] (Arabic): nation or group of people.
qāzi (Arabic): qualified judge of religious law in Islam.
qiṣṣa [qissa; kissa] (Arabic): stories of prophets and other Muslim notables.
qutb (Arabic): the axis or defining spiritual authority of any age.
rāga (Sanskrit): popular musical form.
rasm (Arabic): color.
raṣṭra-devatā (Sanskrit): state deity, or god linked to a particular class and ideology.
rūh (Arabic): spirit, the highest level of connection between the human and the divine.
Śaiva (Sanskrit): "belonging to Śiva"; a follower of the Hindu god, Śiva.
sajjāda-nishīn (Persian): hereditary custodian of a Sufi shrine or tombsite.
śakti (Sanskrit): extraordinary power usually emanating from a female deity in Hindu worship.
samā' (Arabic): music, above all, music in a ritual setting devoted to a saintly forebear.
samadhi (Sanskrit): state of enlightenment, conferred by divine favor.
saṃnyāsī (Sanskrit): one pursuing the highest stage of self-denial and spiritual engagement within the Hindu tradition.
śāstra (Sanskrit): Hindu scripture.
shahīd (Arabic): martyr to the Islamic faith.
sharī'a [shari'a; sharī'at] (Arabic): the most comprehensive term for Islamic law from common daily activities to the highest religious ideals.

sharīf/ashraf (Arabic): noble person, usually due to noble birth.
shaykh [shaikh] (Arabic): Muslim spiritual master; literally, "old man."
silsila (Arabic): saintly lineage.
sīrah [sira] (Arabic): life story of the Prophet Muhammad.
śirṇi (Sanskrit): a form of *puja,* or offering to a holy man or divine figure.
śruti (Sanskrit): "scripture" in general, but in Tamil usage, restricted to the Vedas, although also applicable to the Qur'an.
stotra (Sanskrit): a genre of panegyric poetry in classical Sanskrit.
suba (Persian): a district subject to taxation; larger than a *pargana.*
tabaqāt (Arabic): generations of notables or saints, as recounted in biographies.
takhallus (Arabic): poetic name.
taqlīd (Arabic): tradition; fixed usage.
taqva (Arabic): piety.
tarīqa/turuq (Arabic): path or way, linked to a Sufi order.
tavakkul (Arabic): trust in divine favor and absence of human ego.
tazkira (Arabic): biographical account of a deceased person or lineage, often one who is famed as a poet or saint or other Muslim notable.
tīrtha (Sanskrit): a holy place in Hindu pilgrimage.
tiru (Tamil): epithet for a divine being, god or goddess; śrī in Sanskrit.
'ulamā' [ulama] (Arabic): authorized religious scholars.
'urf (Arabic): major land tax.
'urs: wedding, but especially the celebration of a saint's wedding with God, that is, his death.
Uwaysī (Arabic): someone linked to a spiritual path without having a spiritual mentor, as the Yemeni Muslim Uways al-Qarni was drawn to the prophet Muhammad without actually meeting him.
vairāgī (Sanskrit): a holy mendicant, separated from all but the divine presence; also linked to *saṃnyāsī.*
Vaiṣṇava (Sanskrit): belonging to Viṣṇu; a follower of the Hindu god Viṣṇu.
wahdat al-shuhūd (Arabic): philosophical assertion of divine transcendence.
wahdat al-wujūd (Arabic): philosophical assertion of divine immanence.
wahy (Arabic): divine revelation.
wali [vali] (Arabic): friend of God; saint or holy man.
watanjagir (Arabic/Persian): one's territory of origin (*watan*) and the income to be derived from it.
wazīr (Arabic): minister of state.
yavana (Sanskrit): foreigner, outsider.

yogī (Sanskrit): religious ascetic, spiritual devotee.
zāhir (Arabic): external, outer, formal.
zakāt (Arabic): one of the five defining pillars of Islam, incumbent on all Muslims, it is a duty to give a fixed percentage of one's own income to the poor and the needy.
zamindār (Persian): landholder.
zawābit (Arabic): rules or regulations.
zenāna (Arabic): women's quarters, separate from the rest of domestic space.
zimmi (Arabic): member of protected religious minority in a Muslim polity.

Contributors

Muzaffar Alam, professor of history at Jawaharlal Nehru University, specializes in the history of the Mughal Empire.

Catherine B. Asher, associate professor of art history at the University of Minnesota, has written extensively on Mughal art and architecture.

David W. Damrel, assistant professor of religion at Arizona State University, is an expert on Naqshbandi Sufism.

Richard M. Eaton, professor of Asian history at the University of Arizona, has written prize-winning monographs on both Deccani and Bengali history.

Carl W. Ernst, professor and chair of religious studies at the University of North Carolina, Chapel Hill, focuses on the history of Hindu-Muslim intertextuality and Deccan Sufism.

David Gilmartin, professor of history at North Carolina State University, studies the modern history of the Punjab.

Stewart Gordon, an independent scholar based in Ann Arbor, Michigan, is among the leading historical interpreters of the Maratha Empire.

Marcia K. Hermansen, associate professor of theology at Loyola University, Chicago, is an authority on late Mughal and early modern Sufism.

Bruce B. Lawrence, Nancy and Jeffrey Marcus Professor of Religion at Duke University, specializes in premodern South Asian Sufism and postmodern religious movements, both within and beyond the Muslim world.

Derryl N. MacLean, associate professor of history at Simon Fraser University, Vancouver, B.C., has written on the history of Muslims in Sind and on the Mahdavi movement in the time of the Mughal Empire.

Vasudha Narayanan, professor of Indian religions at the University of Florida, is a pioneering contributor to the study of South Indian religion.

Christopher Shackle, professor of North Indian literature in the School of Oriental and African Studies, University of London, is a leading translator and interpreter of Punjabi Muslim poetry and prose.

Tony K. Stewart, associate professor of religion at North Carolina State University, writes on the history of Bengali devotionalism.

Cynthia Talbot, assistant professor of Asian history at the University of Texas–Austin, writes on medieval and early modern Deccani history.

Philip B. Wagoner, professor of art history at Wesleyan University, has studied the history of the expressive and aesthetic traditions of the Vijayanagar Empire.

Index

Abul-Fazl (Abu al-Fazl), 165, 199, 201
Afghans, and expansion of Mughal states, 258–60, 277–78n.37
Ahmad, Aziz, 16, 177, 291
Aima, 330–32
Akbar, 108, 254, 258; and Chisti order, 252–54; court of, 181 (preserved imperial sessions of, 202–11; real and false men at, 199–211; and 'ulama', 203); and Dihlawi (Shaykh Abd al-Haqq Muhaddith), 165–67; and Gujarati (Shaykh Mustafa), 199, 203–4, 206–8; and Islam, 12; and Naqshbandī reaction; and religion, 236–37; and temples, 123, 260, 262; and Tusi's *Akhlaq*, 232
Akhlaq texts, 14, 217, 231–33, 235–41
al-Ashmawy, Judge Muhammad, 1
'Ali Jinnah, Muhammad, 3
Allāh, 39, 43
Arabic literature forms, 92
Architecture, 4–9, 121–39. *See also* Ellora; Hindu temples; Mosques; Religious structures; Temples
Aurangzeb, 125, 237, 239; and Ellora, 109–11; and land taxes, 331–32; Maratha resistance to, 327; and temples and mosques, 254, 263–67
Āzād, Muḥammad Ḥusain, 157, 169

Babur, Zahir-ud-Din Muhammed, 182–84; and Chistis, 253, 266; mosque of, 246; and Muslim iconoclasm, 115–16; and Naqshbandīs, 187; and Tusi's *Akhlaq*, 230–33
Baburi Masjid, 8, 26–27
Badauni (Badaoni or Bada'uni), Abd al-Qadir al-, 199, 205, 254; and biographies, 163–65; and *shari'a*, 237; and Sufi tazkiras, 160–61
Bahmani Revolution, 252–53
Bakhsh, Imām, 65
Bakhsh, Miyāḥ Muḥammad, 60–62, 66–68
Bāqī Billāh (Bāqībillā), Khwaja (Birangi), 166, 182, 186–89, 191, 194
Barani, Zia-ud-Din, 252, 301; and *shari'a*, 14, 216–18, 220–28, 232, 235, 239
Bengal, settling of, 38
Biographies, 151, 171n.7, 295
British colonial rule, 19, 246–47, 283–84, 327
Buddha, images of, 114–15
Buddhist viharas, conversion into Hindu temples, 114–15
Bukka, 16–17, 300–320
Bullhe Shāh, 6–7, 56–57, 60, 62, 66
Burhanpur, Maratha patronage of Muslim institutions in, 329–36

Caitanya, Kṛṣṇa, 21
Cakravartī, 25
Cāndbibi, 39
Cemetery, and Indo-Muslim identity, 167–68
Chishtis, 151–52, 165, 239, 252–54, 276n.25; Chisti Nizami order, 155, 162–64; Chisti Sabiri order, 162–63, 177–78, 181–83, 187–88, 190–94
Cirappuranam, 7–8, 74–94; Mecca in, 87–88; significance of, 92; Tamil literary conventions in, 87–90, 92, 94; uses of, 8; women in, 86–90
Class, 55–56, 59–60, 62–65, 71n.25
Colonial rule, 19, 246–47, 283–84, 327
Community, 168, 199–201, 204
Cultural geography, 58, 59, 70n.18
Cultural production, 160–61
Culture, and Mughal rule, 232

Dāsa, Kṛṣṇahari, 25, 39, 43
Dayāla, 35
Deccan, division of, 287–90, 297n.11
Delhi: conquest by Muslims, and North Indian temple architecture, 138; links with Vijayanagara, 315–19; Muslim and non-Muslim population of, 126; structures in, 129–30, 135–39
Delhi Sultanate: founding of, 290–91; and Indic hero in medieval South Indian narratives, 307–13; in political imagination of Vijayanagara, 300–320; raids on peninsular Inda, 257–58; Vijayanagara as counter polity to, 301–2
Dihlawi (Dihlavi), Shaykh Abd al-Haqq Muhaddith, 159, 161, 163, 165–67
Diversity, 216
Divine institute, as expressed in *shari'a*, 229
Donations, to maintain Muslim culture, 332–33, 337–38n.19

Eaton, Richard, 29
Ellora: construction of, 108; interpretation of, 113, 119–20n.33; reaction to, 98–117; Shīrāzī's location of account of, 100; significance of non-Islamic origin of, 110–11
Emigration, as religious duty, 200–201
Equity, protection of in Mughal tradition, 236–37
Ethics, Nasirean, 229–31, 233–36
Explorers, in Asia, 113–14

Faizi, 165
Fakīr, 25, 29, 38, 41–42, 45; defined, 32
Female sexuality, as controlled by Islamic patriarchalism, 73n.43

Gangōhi, Shaykh 'Abd al-Quddūs, 176–93
Gender: and Indo-Muslim identity, 66–67, 73n.43; and legitimate identity, 12–13; and 'ulama', 206–9
Genres, 4–9, 150–51, 168, 295
Geographic origin, and religious affiliation, 95n.4
Geography, cultural, 58, 59, 70n.18
Ghalib, 149–50, 153, 155, 170
Governance: in Indo-Islamic context, 216–41; Iranian, 223; model of, 240; Mughal appropriation of Nasirean norms of, 232–33; and Muslims, 219–20; patterns of, 223, 234; principles of, 224–27; and religion, 231–32. *See also* Kingship; Rulership
Greco-Hellenic ideas: appropriation of, by Muslims, 227–28
Group identity, formation of, 295–96
Gujarati, Shaykh Mustafa, 12–13, 164, 199–211, 212nn.7, 9
Gulātī, Rānjhā, 63

Hamid, K. P. S., 76
Harihara, 16–17, 300–320
Hasan, Mīr, 59
Heredity, principle of, 226
Hindu: category of, 18 (and narrative codes, 27–28; and Satya Pīr, 29–30; and syncretism, 22; as undermined by Indo-Muslim romance, 56–59); defined, 282–83, 296n.2; use of term, 4–5
Hindu historiography, 282–96; and identity formation, 290–95; repudiation of Muslims in, 293
Hindu identity: origin of, 282–84; and prominent temples in North India, 138; and Vijayanagara state, 16–17
Hindu/Indian body politic, and Muslims, 282–83
Hindu literature, 79–80
Hindu-Muslim identity: mapping of, through architecture, 121–39; paintings providing insight into, 122, 129, 142n.23, 142–43n.32; prior to construction of Shahjahanabad and Jaipur, 122; in sixteenth and seventeenth centuries, 123–24, 127, 139
Hindu nationalism, 92–94, 296n.2. *See also* Nationalism
Hindu political elites, historical writing by, 291–92
Hindu rituals, 91
Hindus: in dyad of real and false Muslims, 208–9; interaction with Muslims,

1; interpretation of Ellora, 114; shared landscape with Muslims, 122; Tamil, and Islamic literature in Tamil, 75
Hindu states: and construction of temples and mosques, 130–34; and Muslim polities, power distribution amongst, 294
Hindu stories, by Satya Pīr, 24
Hindu temples: conversion of Buddhist viharas into, 114–15; destruction of, 14, 269–70; Islamic monuments constructed from, 122; materials of, 98–99, 114–15; Muslim writing on, 115–17. *See also* Ellora, Temples
Historiographic genre, of Sanskrit literature, 295
Historiography: emergence of nationalist, 283; Hindu, 290–95; of non-Muslim Indians, after establishment of Muslim rule in North India, 291; pan-Indian scope of, 166; representation in, 320; rise of, 295–96; tradition of, 283–84, 291
History, construction of, 22–23, 220–27, 282
Hodgson, Marshall G. S., 2, 10
Humayun, 230–31

Iconoclasm, 115–17, 255, 269–70
Identity: civilizational, 13; cultural, and Persian poetry, 56; and cultural geography, 58; disputation of, in Indo-Muslim history, 199–211; and gender, 12–13; genealogies of, 2–4; group, formation of, 295–96; Hindu, origin of, 282–84 (and prominent temples in North India, 138; and Vijayanagara state, 16–17); Hindu-Muslim, mapping of, through architecture, 121–39 (paintings providing insight into, 122, 129, 142n.23, 142–43n.32; prior to construction of Shahjahanabad and Jaipur, 122; in sixteenth and seventeenth centuries, 123–24, 127, 139); Indic and Indo-Muslim compared, 55; and Indic state legitimacy in Islamicate context, 17; Indo-Muslim, 55 (and architectural forms, 4–9; and cemetery, 167–68; and class, 55–56; and cultural geography, 55, 68–69n.1; and foreign versus native authority, 66–67, 73n.43; and gender, 66–67, 73n.43; and Indic compared, 55; and Indo-Persian tazkiras, 149–70; interpreting, 98–99; nature of, 209–11; and Sufism, 11, 164; and tazkiras, 158–59); Islamicate, 13, 319–20 (and Islamicate state, 13–14; and literary genres, 4–9; Mahdavi, 209–11); Muslim, concept of, 99 (and heroes in Indo-Muslim romance, 62–63; origin of, 282–84; and Tamil literary conventions, 92); origin of, 6, 282–84 (and Other, 291; political, construction of, for Vijayanagara, 319–20; and power, 6; regional, 4–5, 74–97); religious, 56–57, 69n.8 (historicizing, 18–19; vocabulary of, 4–5, 74–97); and religious structures, 9 (*see also* Ellora; Hindu temples; Mosques; Religious structures; Temples); of Satya Pīr, 24, 33–34, 49–50n.5, 51n.18; and space, 168–70; and Sufi poetry, 58; supralocal, 283–84, 295–96; Tamil, and Tamil literary conventions, 92; Tamil Muslim, 75–94
Identity analysis, 3–5
Identity construction, 9–10, 294; and authority of ruler, 18; and difference, 4; and historical tradition, 283–84; and manipulation of genre, 4–5; process of, 19–20; role of context in language of, 16; for Vijayanagara, 319–20
Imagined community, 168
Independence movement, and Muslims, 94
Indian, meaning of category, 12
Indic: and Hindu, distinction obscured between, 2–3; use of term, 2
Indic identity, compared with Indo-Muslim identity, 55
Indic literary practice, and Turkic Muslims in Indian subcontinent, 291
Indic state, in Islamicate context, 17
Indo-Islamic governance, 216–41
Indo-Muslim authors, view of Ellora temples, 98–117
Indo-Muslim buildings, in North India, 251

Indo-Muslim elites, links with Sufi tazkiras, 160
Indo-Muslim history, 199–211, 291
Indo-Muslim identity: and cemetery, 167–68; and class, 55–56; and cultural geography, 55, 68–69n.1; and foreign versus native authority, 66–67, 73n.43; and gender, 66–67, 73n.43; and history, 199–211; and Indic identity compared, 55; and Indo-Persian tazkiras, 149–70; interpreting, 98–99; nature of, 209–11; and Sufism, 11, 164; and tazkiras, 158–59
Indo-Muslim political philosophers, 217–27
Indo-Muslim romance, 55–68, 71n.25
Indo-Muslim state: Chishtis and political fortunes of, 252; expansion of, 258–59; maintenance of, and temple protection, 261–63; and temple destruction, 246–60, 268, 270–71
Iranian governance, 223
Islam: and Akbar, 12; Delhi's structures associated with, 129–30, 135–37; monolithic, defined by twentieth-century discourse, 99; orthodox, and *shari'a*, 217; responsibility to uphold, 219–20; stability of symbols, 238–39; and Sufi lyrics, 57–58, 69–70n.11; Tamil literature on, 76–77
Islamic architecture, North Indian, 121–22
Islamicate, 10, 13; and Muslim, distinction obscured between, 2–3
Islamicate identity, 13, 319–20
Islamicate romances, 61–62
Islamicate state, 13–20
Islamic civilization, in tazkira genre, 150–51
Islamic culture, Mongol impact on, 229
Islamicization, 315–19
Islamic justice, 224, 232–33, 239–40. *See also shari'a*
Islamic law. *See shari'a*
Islamic literature, in Tamil, and Tamil Hindus, 75
Islamic mysticism, 176–77, 188–89, 192–94. *See also* Sufi orders
Islamic orthodox political code, 236
Islamic patriarchalism, and control of female sexuality, 73n.43
Islamic states, 226, 315–19
Islamic structures, remaining, 122. *See also* Mosques; Religious structures
Islamic tradition: link with South Asian tazkira compositions, 155; and process of creation, 153–54
Ismail, M. M., 74–75

Jahāngīr, 67–68, 182, 185; and Chistis, 253–54; and *shari'a*, 236–40; and Tusi's *Akhlaq*, 231–33
Jains, in dyad of real and false Muslims, 208–9
Jaipur, 121–39
Jakat, 332
Jāmī, 60
Justice, 224–25, 234–40. *See also shari'a*

Kampan, 74–75
Kanhadade Prabandha, compared with *Prataparudra Caritramu*, 292–93
Kāśīkānta, 44–47
Kavi, Ayodhyārāma, 25
Khandesh, Maratha patronage of Muslim institutions in, 329–36
Khusrau, 60
Kingship: duties of, 218, 327–28, 335; hereditary, 218; history of, 295–96; ideal, 228–29; and religion, 255, 267–68, 276n.27; universal, 17–18, 336. *See also* Rulership
Kṛṣṇa, 43

Lahore, 167
Lakṣmī, ṣaṣṭhī, 38, 41
Language, 4–5, 55–56, 94, 299n.32
Law, Islamic. *See shari'a*
Literary genealogy, and Punjabi lyrics, 59–62
Literary genres, 4–9, 150–51, 168, 295
Literary typologies, of Satya Pīr, 24–30
Literature: and class, 55–56; and cultural geography, 55, 68–69n.1; Hindu, 79–80; Islamic, and Tamil Hindus, 75; Persianate, status of lyric in, 57; and

public memory, 155; religious, vocabulary from Tamil, 90–91; Sanskrit, historiographic genre of, 295; and *shari'a*, 216; Tamil, landscape in, 74–75, 81–88, 97n.37; Vaishnava, 80; Vedic, 296n.2

Madurai, reconquest of, 290–91
Mahdavi community, 204
Mahdavi identity, 209–11
Mahdaviyah, secondary literature on, 209
Mahdaviyah community, 199–201
Mahdaviyah movement, 209–10
Mahdi, death of, 200–201, 211n.4
Mahmud of Ghazni, 222–25, 250–51, 257–58, 261–62, 268
Maidānava, 39
Malfuẓat, 151–52
Marathas, 17, 327–36
Mecca, 32, 167, 207–8; descriptions of, in *Cirappuranam*, 87–88
Meditation, 200–201
Memorative communication, 149–70, 171n.5
Memory, 153–55, 166
Military, and temple destruction, 257, 277n.32
Mongols, impact on Islamic culture, 229
Mosques: appearance of, 132–38, 145n.61; construction of, in Jaipur, 130–34; contrasted with temples, 266–68, 280n.62; converted from temples, 259, 278n.38; in Mughal India, destruction of, 280n.61; uniformity in, 135–36. *See also* Religious structures
Mughal emperors. *See* Akbar, Aurangzeb (Awrangzib), Babur, Humayun, Jahangir, Shah Jahan
Mughal rule, 232–33, 236–41, 254, 258–63, 277–78n.37, 279n.50, 333
Mughal Sufism, 11
Muhammad, 7–8, 39, 41, 43, 75–76, 180, 191, 219, 221, 223, 225
Musalmān, 41, 219, 334; and Muslim compared, 51n.16
Muslim: category of, 18 (and narrative codes, 27–28; and Satya Pīr, 29–30; and syncretism, 22; as undermined by Indo-Muslim romance, 56–59); and Musalmān compared, 51n.16
Muslim culture, donations to maintain, 332–33, 337–38n.19
Muslim-Hindu interaction, 1
Muslim holy spaces, for Sufi tazkira authors, 166–67
Muslim iconoclasm, 115–17
Muslim identity: concept of, 99; and heroes in Indo-Muslim romance, 62–63; origin of, 282–84; and Tamil literary conventions, 92
Muslim institutions, Maratha patronage of, 329–36
Muslim politics, conflict with shari'a theory, 222–23
Muslim rule, 222, 226–27, 246–47
Muslims: alignment of, in India, 94; appropriation of Greco-Hellenic ideas, 227–28; conquest of Delhi, and North Indian temple architecture, 138; in Delhi, 126; documentation of temple destruction by, 246; and Ellora, reaction to, 108–14, 116–17; in Hindu historiography, 293; and Hindu/Indian body politic, 282–83; and independence movement, 94; as indigenous to South Asia, 1; origin of, in Tamilnadu, 75–76; relations between Tamil and other South Asian Muslims, 92; relations with non-Muslims in India, 184–88; and rituals, 91; stories of Satya Pīr, 24; Tamil, 74–75, 92, 94; Tamil literature by, 76–77; Tamil Muslims' claim to superior status as, 92; and Tamil religion, 92; Tamil spoken by, 74; writing of Tamil songs by, 91–94; and yavana category, 31–32
Muslim South Asia, concept of memory in, 153–55
Muslim state, 14, 219–20, 289–90, 294
Muslim tales, contrasted with Vaisnava tales, 40–41, 47
Muslim Turks, and temple destruction, 256–57, 259
Muslim writers, on Hindu monuments, 115–17
Mysticism, Islamic, 166–67, 188–89, 192–94

Naqshbandīs, 160, 176–94
Nārada, defined, 30
Nārāyaṇa, 30–33, 37, 43
Narrative codes, 27–28
Nasīm, Pandit Dayā Shankar, 59
Nasirean ethics, 229–31, 233–36
Nationalism, 5, 92–94, 283, 296n.2
Niẓāmī, 60

Omar the Poet. *See* Umaru Pulavar
Orthodox Islam, 236
Other: construction of, and difference, 4; in Satya Pīr's narratives, 48–49; and self-identity, 291

Paintings, and Hindu-Muslim identity, 122, 129, 142n.23, 142–43n.32
Pakistan, founder of, 3
Parchand Rāō, 99–102
Partition, effect on South Asia, 92
Patriarchalism, Islamic, and control of female sexuality, 73n.43
Persianate literature, 56, 57, 61, 92
Perso-Islamic, conception of interrelation of religion and politics, 251–52
Pillai, K. K., 76
Power, and identity, 6
Prataparudra, 282–96, 300, 307–9, 311–13
Prataparudra Caritramu, 15–16, 284–89, 292–95, 307–8
Punjabi lyrics, 6–7, 56, 59–62, 68, 70n.18. *See also* Sufi lyrics
Purana, 79–80

Qādirī (Qādrī), 161, 165, 182
Qissa. *See* Punjabi lyrics
Qur'ān, 25, 61, 153–54

Rāḥat, Bhagvant Rā'e, 59
Rāma, Phakīr, 25
Rāmeśvara, 25, 33–34
Regional identity, and religious vocabulary, 74–97
Religion: crossing boundaries of, in Indo-Muslim romance, 62–65, 71n.25; and governance, 231–32; invoked by Muslim writers in relation to Hindu monuments, 115–17; and Islamicate world, 19–20; and justice, 235–36; and kingship, 232, 255, 267–68, 276n.27; and Mughal rule, 232; nonsectarian approach to, 236–41; Perso-Islamic conception of interrelation with politics, 251–52; public display of, 184; and Punjabi lyrics, 59–60; Tamil, Muslim participation in, 92; typologies of, and Satya Pīr, 24–30; vocabulary of, 74–97
Religious affiliation, and geographic origin, 95n.4
Religious authority, as defined by Islamicate state, 18
Religious boundaries, 62–65, 71n.25, 94
Religious categories, 22–24, 27–30, 51n.15
Religious history, South Asian, 22–23
Religious identity: conception of South Asian, 56–57, 69n.8; historicizing, 18–19; vocabulary of, 4–5
Religious structures, 8–9, 15, 246, 270. *See also* Ellora; Hindu temples; Mosques; Temples
Resistance, narratives of, 312–13
Ritual practices, 26–27, 50nn.8–10, 91, 121, 329–30
Royal biography, 295
Rulership, 222, 226–27, 231. *See also* Kingship

Saiva, 18
Sandhyāvatī, 39–40
Śaṅkarācārya, 33–34
Sanskrit literature, historiographic genre of, 295
Sastri, Nilakanta, 300–301, 303
Satya Pīr: appeal of, 21, 23–27, 30, 31; appropriation of image of, 33–34; and authority, 24; categorizing, 21–24; dual character of, 25; and frontiers, 29–30; as God, 30–39; and Hindu category, 29–30; Hindu stories of, 24; identity of, 24, 33–34, 49–50n.5, 51n.18; interpreting, 21–30; as Islamic exemplar, 39–49; literary typologies of, 24–30; and Muslim cat-

egory, 29–30; Muslim stories of, 24, 40–41; as mythical figure, 37–38, 40, 53n.29; and narrative codes, 27–28; Other in, 48–49; power of recognition, 44, 46; and religion, 24–30; scholarly attention to, 21–22, 49n.2, 53–54n.31; significance of, 23–24; as source of local power, 24, 38–39; and syncretism, 22, 23; themes of, 27; types of narratives of, 28–30; Vaisnava tales, 30–39 (contrasted with Muslim tales, 40–41; domestication and appropriation in, 30–36; Sanscritizing of, 34, 52–53n.22; and settling of Bengal, 38; teachings and morals of, 47, 54n.43); works, destruction of, 26–27, 50n.11; (range of, 25–27; ritual in, 26–27, 50nn.8–10)
Schimmel, Annemarie, 56, 64, 153, 176, 191
Sects, and types of temples, 135–37
Self-identity, and Other, 291
Sexuality, female, as controlled by Islamic patriarchalism, 73n.43
Shāh, Fażal, 66
Shah, Hāshim, 66
Shah Jahan, 109, 126, 129, 161, 233; and temples, 253–54, 262–64
Shahjahanabad, 9, 121–39
Shāh, Vāriṣ, 63–64
shari'a: administration of, 233–34; aim of, 233–34; conflict with Muslim politics, 222–23; defined, 216–18, 234, 236, 239; in early Islamic writing, 217–18; in Indo-Islamic context, 216–41; in Islamicate political order, 14; in Mughal tradition, 236–41; and orthodox Islam, 217; political meanings of, 14; and secular legislation, 216–17; in writing, 216, 227–28
Shi'a, 18
Shikoh, Dara, 161–63
Shīrāzī, Rafī' al-Dīn, 8–9, 15, 99–117
Shivaji, 17
Shrines. *See* religious structures
Sirhindī, Shaykh Ahmad, 12–13, 166, 176–94, 238–39
Spiritual authenticity, 164–65
State: construction of, 239 (and Sufism, 251–54; and temple destruction, 254–60, 268–69, 280n.63); maintenance of, and temple destruction, 263–66, 279–80n.58; objective of, 236
Stewart, Tony, 55–56
Sufi, spiritual power of, and tomb, 252
Sufi biographies, 165
Sufi lyrics, 57–58, 69–70n.11. *See also* Punjabi lyrics
Sufi orders, opposition between syncretic and purifying, 12; and tazkiras, 160. *See also* Chistis, Naqshbandī, Qādirī
Sufi poetry, and identity, 58
Sufism, 36–39; and Indo-Muslim identity, 11, 164; influence on biographical genre, 151; Mughal, 11; Persian/Indo-Persian, and Sufi tazkiras, 162–64; and state building, 251–54; structure of, 18
Sufi tazkiras, 156, 160–68
Sultan, Tippu, 76
Sunni, 18, 164, 227
Syncretism, 5–6, 12, 22, 23, 43, 176–77

Tadhkirat al-mulūk, 99–112
Tamil Hindus, and Islamic literature in Tamil, 75
Tamil identity, and Tamil literary conventions, 92
Tamil language, 74, 94
Tamil literature, 74–77, 81–92, 94, 97n.37
Tamil Muslim identity, 75–94
Tamil Muslim patriotism, 92–94
Tamil Muslims, 74–75; adapting Arabic and Persian literature forms to Tamil genres, 92; alignment with other Muslims in India, 94; claim to superior status as Muslims, 92; relations with other South Asians, 92–94
Tamil Muslim songs, strategies of, 94
Tamilnadu, origin of Muslims in, 75–76
Tamil religion, 90–92
Tamil songs, written by Muslims, 91–94
Tarain, battle of, 290–91
Taxes, and Marathas, 330–32

Tazkiras: ambiguity of, 150; cataloging, 166; categorization of, 157–58; composition of, 155, 157–58; defined, 149; early, 156–57, 169–70; genre of, 150–51, 168; historical accuracy of, 158; and Indo-Muslim identity, 149–70; Indo-Persian, 160–61 (and Indo-Muslim identity, 149–70; as memorative communications, 149–70); model for, 156; poetic, parallels with Sufi, 160 (patterns in, 156–60; role of, 11, 159–60, 168–70; urban/regional focus of, 158–60)); premodern, 168; recent, 169–70; scholarship on, 156–60; Sufi, 160–61
Telugu warriors, 289–90, 294
Temples: appearance of, 4–9, 121–39, 145n.61; contrasted with mosques, 266–68, 281n.62; conversion into mosques, 259, 278n.38; destruction of, 108 (by military or ruling authority, 257, 277n.32; claims of, in Indo-Muslim literary sources, 250; contemporary evidence on, 246–47; documentation of, 246, 256–57, 277n.34, 280n.63; early instances, of, 250–51, 275nn.11, 12; forms of, 257–60; and iconoclasm, 255, 269–70; and Indo-Muslim states, 14, 246–74; maps of, 272–74; and Muslim Turks, 256–57, 259; and political conflict, 255–60; and state building, rhetoric of, 268–69, 281n.63; and state maintenance, 263–66, 279–80n.58; and Tughluq imperialism, 258); and images, 254–57, 259; in North India, and Hindu identity, 138; North Indian, 121–26, 130–34, 138; origins of, 126–27; political relevance of, 254–60, 267–68, 277n.28; as products of imperial patronage, 138; protection of, and Indo-Muslim state maintenance, 261–63; (and Mughals, 261–63, 279n.50); and rituals, 121; royal patrons of, 254–57, 259; scholarly interest in, 121; types of, and sects, 135–37; under Akbar, 123; in Varanasi, 125; visibility of, 127–34, 138–39, 144n.53. *See also* Ellora; Hindu temples; Mosques; Religious structures
Theology, Sufi and Vaisnava, 36–39. *See also* Religion
Tomb, and spiritual power of Sufi, 252
Translation, 57
"Treatise of Wonders of Rarities," 100–108
Tughluqs, 252, 258
Tusi, Nasir-ud-din, 227–28

'Ulama': and gender, 206–9; interpretation of, 205–6; and sociopolitical contexts for court of Akbar, 203
Umaru Pulavar, 77–93
Unity, and construction of common history, 282

Vaishnava literature, 80
Vaiṣṇava, 18; alliance with yavana, 31–32
Vaiṣṇava tales, 30–39; contrasted with Muslim tales, 40–41, 47; Sanscritizing of, 34, 52–53n.22; and settling of Bengal, 38; teachings and morals of, 47, 54n.43
Vaiṣṇava theology, pragmatic implications of, 36–39
Varanasi, temples in, 125
Vedic literature, 296n.2
Venkataramanayya, N., 302–3, 305
Vijayanagara, 16–17; construction of political identity for, 319–20; as counter polity to Delhi Sultanate, 301–2; Islamicate cultural forms at, 319; links with Delhi, 315–19; origin of, 287–88, 300–320, 320–22nn.5–7, 322n.12; political imagination of, Delhi Sultanate in, 300–320
Vijayanagara court, Islamic elements in, 318–19
Vijayanagara texts, references to Delhi Sultanate in, 314–15
Vocabulary, 74–97

Wilk, Colonel, 76
Women: descriptions of, in *Cirappuranam*, 86–90

Yār, Aḥmad, 65–66
Yār, Qādir, 66
Yavana, 31–32

Zakat, 332

www.ingramcontent.com/pod-product-compliance
Lightning Source LLC
Chambersburg PA
CBHW022100150426
43195CB00008B/213